D1474046

THE LOEB CLASSICAL LIBRARY
FOUNDED BY JAMES LOEB 1911

EDITED BY
JEFFREY HENDERSON

HISTORIA AUGUSTA
I

LCL 139

THE SCRIPTORES
HISTORIAE
AUGUSTAE

WITH AN ENGLISH TRANSLATION BY

DAVID MAGIE

VOLUME I

HARVARD UNIVERSITY PRESS
CAMBRIDGE, MASSACHUSETTS
LONDON, ENGLAND

First published 1921
Reprinted 1930, 1953, 1960, 1967, 1979,
1991, 2000, 2006

LOEB CLASSICAL LIBRARY® is a registered trademark
of the President and Fellows of Harvard College

ISBN 0-674-99154-0

Printed on acid-free paper and bound by
Edwards Brothers, Ann Arbor, Michigan

CONTENTS

PREFACE

In the preparation of this book others have laboured and I have entered into the fruits of their labours. Their co-operation has been of inestimable service.

The translation of the biographies from Antoninus Pius to Pescennius Niger and from the Maximini to Maximus and Balbinus inclusive has been furnished by my friend Mr. Ainsworth O'Brien-Moore. In the translation of the other lives also his fine taste and literary discrimination have been responsible for many a happy phrase. But for the promise of his collaboration the task of preparing this edition had not been undertaken.

The Latin text of the first six biographies has been supplied by Miss Susan H. Ballou of Bryn Mawr College, who had in mind the preparation of a new text of these biographies, based on her study of the manuscripts. Unfortunately, however, other interests have claimed her time and her efforts and she has been unable to complete the work for this edition. It is to be earnestly hoped that she will yet publish a critical text of the entire series.

In the lack of Miss Ballou's text I nave been forced to base this edition, from the *Commodus*

onward, on the text of Hermann Peter, for the long-promised edition by Dr. Ernst Hohl has not yet appeared. Its aid would have been invaluable. While only too well aware of the inadequacies of Peter's text, I have not felt able to introduce many changes. The suggestions offered by various scholars since the appearance of Peter's second edition have been carefully considered, and a few have been adopted. The text, therefore, is that of the Codex Palatinus (P), with the introduction of a few emendations and whatever changes in punctuation and spelling might seem in accordance with modern usage. All the more important variations from P, as well as the most significant of the variant readings afforded by the later correctors of the manuscript, and, in addition, the divergencies from the text of Peter have been entered in the critical notes.

In the Introduction I have sought to give a brief account of the *Historia Augusta*, the authors, their method and style, and a summary of the study expended on it from the close of the classical period to the present and its use by later historians. A discussion of its authorship and sources and of the theories which have found in it a work of the late fourth or early fifth century has, for reasons of space, been reserved for the second volume.

The somewhat voluminous commentary has seemed necessary on account of the obscurity of the narrative and the abundance of technical terms. In the preparation of it I have tried to keep in mind not only the needs of the general reader but also those of the student of Roman History, and it is for the benefit of the latter that some of the more technical material has been included.

PREFACE

A list of the books and articles to which I am indebted would fill many pages. The greatest amount of aid has been furnished by Lessing's Lexicon, Mommsen's *Römisches Staatsrecht*, the *Prosopographia Imperii Romani*, and the admirable articles on the various Emperors that have appeared in the Real-Encyclopädie of Pauly-Wissowa-Kroll. In the commentary to the biography of Hadrian valuable assistance has been rendered by Wilhelm Weber's *Untersuchungen zur Geschichte des Kaisers Hadrian*. A complete bibliography will be included in the second volume.

Of the work as a whole, perhaps it can be said : " Sunt bona, sunt quaedam mediocria, sunt mala plura, quae legis hic ".

DAVID MAGIE.

PRINCETON, NEW JERSEY,
   15th June, 1921.

INTRODUCTION

I

THE SCOPE AND LITERARY CHARACTER

OF THE

HISTORIA AUGUSTA

AMONG the remnants of Roman literature preserved
by the whims of fortune is a collection of biographies
of the emperors from Hadrian to Carinus—the *Vitae
Diversorum Principum et Tyrannorum a Divo Hadriano
usque ad Numerianum Diversis compositae*, as it is entitled in the principal manuscript, the *Codex Palatinus*
of the Vatican Library. It is popularly known, apparently for convenience' sake, as the *Historia Augusta*,
a name applied to it by Casaubon, whereas the original
title was probably *de Vita Caesarum* or *Vitae Caesarum*.[1]
The collection, as extant, comprises thirty biographies,
most of which contain the life of a single emperor,
while some include a group of two or more, classed
together merely because these emperors were either
akin or contemporary. Not only the emperors who
actually reigned, the "Augusti," but also the heirs

[1] See Mommsen, *Hermes*, xiii. (1878), p. 301 = *Gesammelte
Schriften*, vii. p. 301.

presumptive, the " Caesares," and the various claim-
ants to the empire, the " Tyranni," are included in the
series.

According to the tradition of the manuscripts the
biographies are the work of six different authors;
some of them are addressed to the Emperor
Diocletian, others to Constantine, and others to important personages in Rome. The biographies of
the emperors from Hadrian to Gordian are attributed
to four various authors, apparently on no principle
whatsoever, for not only are the lives of successive,
or even contemporary, princes ascribed to different
authors and those of emperors widely separated in
time to the same writer, but in the case of two of
the authors some lives are dedicated to Diocletian
and some to Constantine.

In the traditional arrangement the biographies are
assigned to the various authors as follows:

I. Aelius Spartianus: the *vitae* of Hadrian, Aelius,
Didius Julianus, Severus, Pescennius Niger, Caracalla,
and Geta. Of these, the *Aelius*, *Julianus*, *Severus*,
and *Niger* are addressed to Diocletian, the *Geta* to
Constantine. The preface of the *Aelius*[1] contains
mention of the Caesars Galerius Maximianus and
Constantius Chlorus, and from this it may be inferred
that the *vitae* of the Diocletian group were written
between 293, the year of the nomination of these
Caesars, and 305, the year of Diocletian's retirement.
In the same preface[2] Spartianus announces that it is
his purpose to write the biographies, not only of the
emperors who preceded Hadrian, but also of all the
princes who followed, including the Caesars and the
pretenders.

[1] *Ael.*, ii. 2. [2] *Ael.*, i. 1.

INTRODUCTION

II. Julius Capitolinus: the *vitae* of Pius, Marcus
Aurelius, Verus, Pertinax, Clodius Albinus, Macrinus,
the Maximini, the Gordiani, and Maximus and
Balbinus. Of these, the *Marcus, Verus,* and *Macrinus*
are addressed to Diocletian, while the *Albinus,* the
Maximini, and the *Gordiani* are addressed to
Constantine, evidently after the fall of Licinius in
324.[1] Like Spartianus, Capitolinus announces his
purpose of composing an extended series of imperial
biographies.[2]

III. Vulcacius Gallicanus: the *vita* of Avidius
Cassius, addressed to Diocletian. He too announces
an ambitious programme[3]—the composition of biographies of all who have worn the imperial purple,
both regnant emperors and pretenders to the throne.

IV. Aelius Lampridius: the *vitae* of Commodus,
Diadumenianus, Elagabalus, and Severus Alexander.
Of these, the last two are addressed to Constantine;
according to the author, they were composed at the
Emperor's own request,[4] and they were written after
the defeat of Licinius at Adrianople in 323.[5] Lampridius claims to have written the biographies of at
least some of the predecessors of Elagabalus and to
cherish the plan of composing biographies of the
emperors who reigned subsequently, beginning with
Alexander and including in his work not only Diocletian but Licinius and Maxentius, the rivals of
Constantine.[6]

---

[1] *Gord.*, xxxiv. 5; see H. Peter, *Die Scriptores Historiae
Augustae* (Leipzig, 1892), p. 35.
[2] *Max.*, i. 1-3; *Gord.*, i. 1-5.
[3] *Av. Cass.*, iii. 3.
[4] *Heliog.*, xxxv. 1.
[5] *Heliog.*, vii. 7; see Peter, *Scriptores*, p. 32.
[6] *Heliog.*, xxxv.; *Alex.*, lxiv. 1.

INTRODUCTION

V. Trebellius Pollio: the *vitae* from Philip to Claudius; of his work, however, the earlier part, containing the biographies from Philip to Valerian, has been lost from the collection,[1] and we have only the *vitae* of the Valeriani (in part), the Gallieni, the Tyranni Triginta, and Claudius. Pollio's biographies were dedicated, not to the emperor, but to a friend, apparently an official of high degree. His name has been lost, together with the preface which must have preceded the *vita* of Philip. The only clue to his identity is a passage in which he is addressed as a kinsman of an Herennius Celsus, a candidate for the consulship.[2] The extant biographies were written after Constantius' nomination as Caesar in 293,[3] and, in the case of the *Tyranni Triginta*, after the commencement of the Baths of Diocletian in 298.[4] The collection was finished, according to his successor and continuer Vopiscus, in 303.[5]

VI. Flavius Vopiscus: the *vitae* of Aurelian, Tacitus, Probus, Firmus and his three fellow-tyrants, and Carus and his sons. These biographies, like those of Pollio, are not dedicated to any emperor, but to various friends of the author. Vopiscus wrote, he declares in his elaborate preface,[6] at the express request of his friend Junius Tiberianus, the city-prefect. Tiberianus was city-prefect for the second time in 303-4,[7] and, even granting that his conversation with the author as well as his promise of

---

[1] These biographies were included in the collection by Pollio; see *Aur.*, ii. 1.

[2] *Tyr. Trig.*, xxii. 12.

[3] *Gall.*, vii. 1 and elsewhere.

[4] *Tyr. Trig.*, xxi. 7; see Peter, *Scriptores*, p. 36 f.

[5] *Aur.*, ii. 1.   [6] *Aur.*, i.-ii.

[7] B. Borghesi, *Oeuvres Complètes* (Paris, 1862-97), ix. p. 392.

the documents from Trajan's library are merely rhetorical ornaments,[1] this date is usually regarded as marking the beginning of Vopiscus' work. It is confirmed by an allusion to Constantius as *imperator*[2] (305-306) and to Diocletian as *iam privatus* (after 305).[3] This collection was completed, according to internal evidence, before the death of Diocletian in 316,[4] perhaps even before that of Galerius in 311.[5] The series written by Vopiscus has been preserved in its entirety, for it was his intention to conclude his work with the lives of Carus and his sons, leaving to others the task of writing the biographies of Diocletian and his associates.[6]

The plan to include in the collection not only " Augusti," but also " Caesares " and " Tyranni," has resulted in a double series of biographies in that section of the *Historia Augusta* which includes the emperors between Hadrian and Alexander. To the life of a regnant emperor is attached that of an heir-presumptive, a colleague, or a rival. In each case the minor *vita* stands in a close relationship to the major, and, in many instances, passages seem to have been transcribed bodily from the biography of the " Augustus " to that of the " Caesar " or " Tyrannus ".

In the composition of these biographies the model used by the authors, according to the testimony of two of them,[7] was Suetonius. The *Lives* of Suetonius are not biographies in the modern sense of the word, but merely collections of material arranged according

[1] Peter, *Scriptores*, p. 39.
[2] *Aur.*, xliv. 5.   [3] *Aur.*, xliii. 2.
[4] *Car.*, xviii. 5; see Peter, *Scriptores*, p. 45 f.
[5] *Car.*, ix. 3.
[6] *Prob.*, i. 5; *Bonos.*, xv. 10.
[7] *Max.—Balb.*, iv. 5; *Prob.*, ii. 7; *Firm.*, i. 2.

to certain definite categories,[1] and this method of composition is, in fact, employed also by the authors of the *Historia Augusta*. An analysis of the *Pius*, the most simply constructed of the series, shows the general scheme most clearly.[2] This *vita* falls naturally into the following divisions: ancestry (i. 1-7); life previous to his accession to the throne (i. 8—v. 2); policy and events of his reign (v. 3—vii. 4); personal traits (vii. 5—xii. 3); death (xii. 4-9); personal appearance (xiii. 1-2); honours after death (xiii. 3-4).

A fundamental scheme similar to this, in which the several sections are more or less clearly marked, serves as the basis for all the biographies. The series of categories is compressed or extended according to the importance of the events to be narrated or the material that was available, and at times the principle of composition is obscured by the elaboration of a particular topic to an altogether disproportionate length. Thus the mention of the peculiar cults to which Commodus was addicted (the category *religiones*) leads to a long and detailed list of acts of cruelty,[3] while nearly one half of the life of Elagabalus is devoted to an enumeration of instances of his luxury and extravagance,[4] and in the biography of Severus Alexander the fundamental scheme is almost unrecognizable as a result of the confused combination of various narratives.[5]

---

[1] *Proposita vitae eius velut summa partes singillatim neque per tempora sed per species exsequar;* Suetonius, *Aug.*, ix.

[2] Peter, *Scriptores*, p. 106 f.; F. Leo, *Die Griechisch-Römische Biographie* (Leipzig, 1901), p. 273 f.

[3] *Com.*, ix. 6—xi. 7.

[4] *Heliog.*, xviii. 4—xxxiii. 1.

[5] Leo, p. 280 f.

INTRODUCTION

It was also characteristic of Suetonius that he amplified his biographies by means of gossip, anecdotes, and documents, but nowhere in his *Lives* are these used as freely as in certain of the *vitae* of the *Historia Augusta*. The authors take a peculiar delight in the introduction of material dealing with the personality of their subjects. Not content with including special divisions on personal characteristics, in which are enumerated the individual qualities of an emperor,[1] they devote long sections to elaborate details of their private lives, particularly before their elevation to the throne. For this more intimate detail there was much less material available than for the narration of public events. The careers of short-lived emperors and pretenders afforded little of public interest, and consequently their biographies were padded with trivial anecdotes. In fact, a comparison between a major *vita* and its corresponding minor biography shows that the latter contains little historical material that is not in the former. The rest is made up of amplifications, anecdotes, speeches, letters and verses, and at best these minor *vitae* represent little more than a working over of the material contained in the major biographies with the aid of rhetorical expedients and literary embellishments.

The model for the emphasizing of the private life of an emperor seems to have been not so much Suetonius as Marius Maximus, the author of a series of imperial biographies from Nerva to Elagabalus or Severus Alexander. Not content with the narration

---

[1] *e.g.* in the *Pius*, *liberalitas et clementia* (viii. 5—ix. 5); *auctoritas* (ix. 6-10); *pietas* (x. 1-5); *liberalitas* (x. 6-9); *civilitas* (xi.); see Peter, *Scriptores*, p. 157.

INTRODUCTION

of facts in the manner of Suetonius, Maximus sought
to add interest to his biographies by the introduction
of personal material. His lives are cited by the
authors of the earlier *vitae* of the *Historia Augusta*
as their sources for gossip, scandal, and personal
minutiae,[1] and he is probably justly referred to as
*homo omnium verbosissimus qui et mythistoricis se vol-
uminibus implicavit.*[2] In gossip and search after
detail, however, Maximus seems to have been out-
done by Aelius Junius Cordus, cited in the *vitae* of
Albinus, Maximinus, the Gordiani, and Maximus and
Balbinus. He made it a principle to describe the
emperor's appearances in public, and his food and
clothing,[3] and the citations from him include the
enumeration of the amounts of fruit, birds and oysters
consumed by Albinus.[4] Readers who desire further
information on trivial or indecent details are scorn-
fully referred to his biographies.[5]

The manner of Marius Maximus and Cordus is
most clearly reproduced in the lives attributed to
Vopiscus. The more pretentious biographies of
Aurelian and Probus especially[6] contain a wealth of
personal detail which quite obscures the scant historical material. After an elaborate preface of a
highly rhetorical nature, there follows a description
of the character of the emperor in which the
emphasis is laid on his noble deeds and his virtues.
These are illustrated by anecdotes and attested by
"documents," much to the detriment of the narration

[1] *Hadr.*, ii. 10; xxv. 3; *Ael.*, v. 4; *Avid. Cass.*, ix. 9; *Heliog.*, xi. 6.
[2] *Firm.*, i. 2.   [3] *Macr.*, i. 4.
[4] *Cl. Alb.*, xi. 2-3.
[5] *Cl. Alb.*, v. 10; *Max.*, xxix. 10; *Gord.*, xxi. 3.
[6] Leo, p. 291 f.

of facts. No rhetorical device is neglected and the whole gives the impression of an eulogy rather than a biography.

The method employed by Marius Maximus and Cordus was, however, productive of a still more detrimental element in the *Historia Augusta*—the alleged documents which are inserted in many of the *vitae*. Suetonius, as secretary to Hadrian, had had access to the imperial archives and thus obtained various letters and other documents which he inserted in his biographies for the illustration or confirmation of some statement. His practice was continued by his successors in the field of biographical literature. Thus Marius Maximus inserted documents, both speeches and letters, in the body of his text and even added them in appendices.[1] Some of these may have been authentic; but since the references to them in the *Historia Augusta* indicate that they were very numerous, and since there is no reason to suppose that Maximus had access to the official archives, considerable doubt must arise as to their genuineness. Cordus, too, inserted in his biographies letters alleged to have been written by emperors[2] and speeches and acclamations uttered in the senate-house,[3] but, to judge from the specimens preserved in the *Historia Augusta*, these "documents" deserve even less credence than those of Maximus.

The precedent thus established was followed by some of the authors of the *Historia Augusta*. The collection contains in all about 150 alleged documents, including 68 letters, 60 speeches and proposals

---

[1] *Marc.*, xxv. 8; *Com.*, xviii. 1; *Pert.*, ii. 8; xv. 8; see Peter, *Scriptores*, p. 108 f.

[2] *Cl. Alb.*, vii. 2-6; *Max.*, xii. 5.   [3] *Gord.*, xi.

to the people or the senate, and 20 senatorial decrees and acclamations.[1] The distribution of these, however, is by no means uniform. Of the major *vitae* from Hadrian to Elagabalus inclusive, only the *Commodus* and the *Macrinus* are provided with "documents," and these have but two apiece.[2] On the other hand, the group of *vitae* of the Maximini, the Gordiani, and Maximus and Balbinus contains in all 26 such pieces, and Pollio's *Valeriani*, *Tyranni Triginta* and *Claudius*[3] have together 27. It is, however, Vopiscus who heads the list, for his five biographies contain no less than 59 so-called documents of various kinds.

In a discussion of the genuineness of these documents a distinction must be drawn between the speeches, on the one hand, and the letters and senatorial decrees and acclamations on the other. Since the time of Thucydides it had been customary for an historian to insert speeches in his history, and it was an established convention that they might be more or less fictitious. Accordingly, none would question the right of the biographer to attribute to the subject of his biography any speech that he might wish to insert in his narrative. With the letters and decrees, however, the case is different. Like those cited by Suetonius, these claim to be actual documents and it is from this claim that the question of their authenticity must proceed. In spite of occasional expressions of scepticism, the genuineness of these documents was not seriously questioned until 1870, when C. Czwalina published an examination of the letters contained in

[1] C. Lécrivain, *Études sur l'Histoire Auguste* (Paris, 1904), p. 45 f.

[2] *Com.*, xviii.-xix.; xx.; *Macr.*, ii. 4-5; vi. 2-9.

[3] There are none in the *Gallienus*.

INTRODUCTION

the *vita* of Avidius Cassius.[1] He showed that various letters, professedly written by different persons, show the same style and tricks of expression, that they were all written with the purpose of praising the clemency and generosity of Marcus, and that they contain several historical errors. He thus reached the conclusion that they were forgeries, but not composed by the author of the *vita* since his comments on them are inconsistent with their content.[2]

A similar examination of the letters and documents in the other biographies, particularly in those attributed to Pollio and Vopiscus, reveals the hand of the forger even more plainly.[3] They abound not only in errors of fact that would be impossible in genuine documents, but also in the rhetorical bombast and the stylistic pecularities that are characteristic of the authors of these series. The documents cited by Pollio, moreover, show the same aim and purpose as his text—the glorification of Claudius Gothicus as the reputed ancestor of Constantius Chlorus and the vilification of his predecessor Gallienus,—while the documents of Vopiscus show the same tendency to sentimentalize over the past glories of Rome and over the greatness of the senate that is characteristic of his own work, and, like those cited by Pollio, they too have a purpose—the praise of Vopiscus' hero Probus.

An entirely different type of spurious material is represented by the frequent interpolations in the text. These consist of later additions, of passages

---

[1] *De Epistolarum Actorumque quae a Scriptoribus H. A. proferuntur Fide atque Auctoritate.* Pars I. (Bonn, 1870); see also E. Klebs, *Rhein. Mus.*, xliii. (1888), p. 328 f.

[2] *e.g.* ix. 10 and xiv. 8; see Peter, *Scriptores*, p. 197 f.

[3] Peter, *Scriptores*, p. 156 f.

introduced by editors of the whole series, and of notes added by commentators, presumably on the margins, and subsequently incorporated in the body of the work.[1] Frequently they are inserted with utter disregard to the context, so that the continuity of a passage is completely interrupted. They vary in size from passages of several pages to brief notes of a few lines. The most extensive is a long passage in the *vita* of Marcus, which is inserted between the two main portions of the biography.[2] It consists of an epitome of the events of the latter part of his reign, enumerated again and at greater length in the second main portion of the *vita*. That this epitome is an interpolation is evident not only from the double narrative of certain events, but also from the fact that it agrees closely with the narrative of Marcus' reign which is found in Eutropius.[3]

An extensive interpolation has been made also in the *Vita Severi*. Here, however, the problem is less simple. The detailed narrative of the earlier part of Severus' reign [4] is followed by a brief summary of the events of the whole period of his rule,[5] closing with a long address to Diocletian.[6] This summary is little more than a duplicate of the account of Severus' reign as given by Aurelius Victor in his *Caesares*,[7]

---

[1] Peter has attempted in his second edition of the text to distinguish the various types by different kinds of parentheses; see his *Praefatio*, p. xxxiv.

[2] c. xv. 3.—xix. 12.

[3] *Breviarium*, viii. 11-14. Eutropius' material is generally supposed to have been taken from an extensive history of the empire, now lost, which is usually termed the "Imperial Chronicle" (*Kaiserchronik*); see A. Enmann, *Eine Verlorene Geschichte der Römischen Kaiser, Philologus*, Suppl. Band iv. (1884), pp. 337-501.

[4] c. i.—xvii. 4.

[5] c. xvii. 5—xix.

[6] c. xx.-xxi.

[7] *Caes.*, xx. 1-3.

INTRODUCTION

and either it has been taken directly from Victor
or it is a parallel excerpt from his source, the
"Imperial Chronicle". It, in turn, is followed by a
section containing the narration of single incidents,
frequently repetitions of what has preceded, forming
a loosely composed and ill connected appendix to the
whole.[1]

Similar additions are to be found in the *vita* of
Caracalla;[2] they contain repetitions and elaborations
of previously narrated incidents and are evidently
not the work of the writer of the bulk of the life.
Besides these longer and more obvious interpolations
there are countless others of varying extent, consisting
of entries of new material and corrections and
comments of later writers. Many of these have been
inserted in the most inappropriate places, to the great
detriment of the narrative, and the excision of these
passages would contribute greatly to the intelligibility
of many a *vita*.

The literary, as well as the historical, value of the
Historia Augusta has suffered greatly as a result of
the method of its composition. In the arrangement
in categories of the historical material, the authors did
but follow the accepted principles of the art of biography as practised in antiquity, but their narratives,
consisting often of mere excerpts arranged without
regard to connexion or transition, lack grace and
even cohesion. The over-emphasis of personal
details and the introduction of anecdotal material
destroy the proportion of many sections, and the
insertion of forged documents interrupts the course
of the narrative, without adding anything of historical
value or even of general interest. Finally, the

[1] c. xxii.-xxiv. [2] c. vii.-viii.; x. 1—xi. 4.

later addition of lengthy passages and brief notes, frequently in paragraphs with the general content of which they have no connexion, has put the crowning touch to the awkwardness and incoherence of the whole, with the result that the oft-repeated charge seems almost justified, that these biographies are little more than literary monstrosities.

II

THE TRADITION

OF THE

HISTORIA AUGUSTA

IN spite of its defects in style, its deliberate falsifications, and the trivial character of much of its content, the *Historia Augusta* has always been a subject for scholarly research and an important source for the history of the second and third centuries. At the beginning of the sixth century it was used by Aurelius Memmius Symmachus,[1] the last member of a famous family, in his *Historia Romana*, the sole extant fragment of which [2] cites at considerable length the *vita* of the Maximini. Later, several selections from it were included in the elaborate *Collectaneum*,[3] or col-

---

[1] Consul in 485.

[2] Preserved in Jordanes, *de Rebus Geticis*, xv. 83.

[3] Preserved in a manuscript of the twelfth century in the library of the Hospital of St. Nicholas at Cues, near Trier, to which it was bequeathed by the famous collector of manuscripts, Nicholas of Cues (Nicolaus Cusanus), on his death in 1464; see L. Traube, *Abh. d. Bayer. Akad.*, xix. 2 (1891), p. 364 f., and S. Hellman, *Sedulius Scottus*, in L. Traube, *Quellen u. Unters. z. lat. Philol. d. Mittelalters*, i. (1906).

lection of excerpts, made at Liège about 850 by the Irish scholar Sedulius Scottus, and citations from the *Marcus*, the *Maximini*, and the *Aurelian* are contained in Sedulius' *Liber de Rectoribus Christianis*, written about 855.

During the period in which Sedulius was compiling his *Collectaneum* there was copied at the monastery at Fulda our chief manuscript, the *Codex Palatinus*, now in the Vatican Library (No. 899). This manuscript, written in the ninth century in the Carolingian minuscule of that period,[1] represents a recension of the text which is somewhat different from that of the excerpts preserved in the *Collectaneum*.[2] As early, then, as the ninth century there were two editions of the *Historia Augusta*, depending, of course, on a common original, but exhibiting minor differences in the text.

Such was the interest in Germany in the *Historia Augusta* that not long after this Fulda manuscript was finished a copy of it was made, now preserved in the library at Bamberg, written in Anglo-Saxon characters and dating from the ninth or tenth century. About the same period, also, another manuscript was made either from the original of the Fulda manuscript or from this codex itself. This was contained in the library of the Abbey at Murbach in the eleventh century, in the catalogue of which it is listed as *Codex Spartiani*. It was the fate of this manuscript to be sent to Erasmus to be used in the preparation of the Froben edition of the *Historia Augusta*, published at

---

[1] H. Dessau, *Hermes*, xxix. (1894), p. 397 f.

[2] Th. Mommsen, *Hermes*, xiii. (1878), p. 298 f. But for a modification of this view see S. H. Ballou, *The Manuscript Tradition of the Hist. Aug.* (Leipzig, 1914), p. 77 f.

Basel in 1518.[1] The first half of the biographies, however, had been printed before its arrival, and accordingly it could be used for this portion only as a source for variant readings, while for the later *vitae*, from the *Diadumenus* onward, it served as the basis of the text. Unfortunately, however, it then disappeared, and as early as 1738 no trace of it could be found.

At some time between the latter half of the tenth and the beginning of the fourteenth century the Fulda Codex was taken to Italy and was placed in the library of the Cathedral of Verona.[2] Here it was used by Giovanni de Matociis in the preparation of his *Historia Imperialis*, written at Verona at the beginning of the fourteenth century, and in the *de Originibus Rerum* of Guglielmo da Pastrengo of Verona.[3] Moreover, excerpts from it were included in the so-called *Flores Moralium Auctoritatum*, transcribed in 1329, and still preserved in the Cathedral library.

While in Verona the codex containing the *Historia Augusta* came to the notice of Petrarch, presumably through Pastrengo, his friend and correspondent. That it came into the actual possession of the great humanist and formed part of his library has been asserted [4] and denied [5] with equal vehemence. It is conceded by all, however, that he inscribed on its

---

[1] H. Dessau, *Hermes*, xxix. (1894), p. 415.

[2] See R. Sabbadini, *Le Scoperte dei Codici Latini e Greci ne' Secoli xiv. e xv.* (Florence, 1905), p. 2 f.; S. H. Ballou, p. 38 f.

[3] Sabbadini, p. 15 f.

[4] See P. de Nolhac, *Pétrarque et l'Humanisme*, Nouv. Sér. (Paris, 1907), ii. p. 47 f.; S. H. Ballou, p. 13 f.

[5] E. Hohl, *Hermes*, li. (1916), p. 154 f.

margins many notes and comments, and that he had a copy of it made at Verona in 1356,[1] to which he later added many a comment and correction. The results of his study of the biographies, furthermore, appear in his works. Thus in his letter *de Militia Veterum*,[2] he cites the *Hadrian*, the *Pescennius*, the *Avidius Cassius*, the *Maximini*, and the *Probus*; and in the *de Re Publica bene administranda*[3] he quotes from the *Hadrian*, the *Avidius Cassius*, the *Elagabalus*, the *Alexander*, and the *Aurelian*.

After the death of Petrarch, the Fulda Codex, it has been maintained, came into the possession of Coluccio Salutati,[4] and many of the marginal corrections which it bears are said to be his. On the other hand, it has been asserted with equal vigour that Coluccio did not even see this manuscript.[5] However this may be, the *Historia Augusta* was well known to Coluccio, and his letters written in the years 1381-93 cite the *vitae* of Hadrian, Pius, Marcus, and Alexander[6]; moreover, the fact that in one letter he names the six authors of the *Historia Augusta* in the order in which they are contained in the manuscript[7] seems to indicate that he had a first-hand acquaintance with the text.

[1] *Codex Parisinus* 5816.

[2] *Epist. de Rebus Familiaribus*, xxii. 14 (written in 1360); see also *de Reb. Fam.*, xx. 4.

[3] *Epist. Seniles*, xiv. 1 (1373); see also *Ep. Sen.*, ii. 1; xv. 3.

[4] H. Dessau, *Hermes*, xxix. (1894), p. 410, n. 2; S. H. Ballou, p. 30 f.

[5] Coluccio's use of this codex is denied by Hohl, *l.c.*, p. 158, and *Klio*, xv. (1918), p. 87 f.

[6] *Epistolario di Coluccio Salutati*, ed. by F. Novati (Rome, 1891-6), vol. ii., pp. 40 f., 55, 415.

[7] *Epistolario di Coluccio Salutati*, ed. by F. Novati (Rome, 1891-6), vol. ii., p. 299.

INTRODUCTION

In the fifteenth century the famous codex passed into the hands of the merchant and theologian Giannozzo Manetti (1396-1459). His possession is attested by the presence of his name on the first page,[1] and he too is supposed to have shown his interest in the *Historia Augusta* by inscribing many a note on the margins. Later, probably in 1587,[2] with other of Manetti's books, the codex containing the *Historia Augusta* passed to the Palatine Library at Heidelberg, there to be known as the *Codex Palatinus* and there to remain until, with the rest of that famous collection, it was sent to Rome in 1623 by Maximilian of Bavaria, and placed in the library of the Vatican.

The general interest in the *Historia Augusta* in the fifteenth century is well attested by the number of manuscripts that were made in that period.[3] Among them was the copy of the *Codex Palatinus* which was made by the famous Poggio Bracciolini with his own hand and is still preserved in Florence.[4]

The same interest in the *Historia Augusta* that led to the multiplication of the manuscripts was responsible for its early appearance in printed form. One of the recent copies of the *Codex Palatinus*[5] came into the hands of Bonus Accursius and from this was made the *Editio Princeps*, published in Milan in 1475. This was soon followed by an Aldine edition published

[1] H. Dessau, *l.c.*, p. 409.
[2] S. H. Ballou, p. 40.
[3] See Peter's text, 2nd Ed. *Praefatio*, p. xxiii. f.
[4] *The Codex Riccardianus* 551 ; see S. H. Ballou, p. 29.
[5] Usually supposed to have been the *Codex Vaticanus* 5301 ; see Dessau, *l.c.*, p. 400 f. It has been maintained by Miss S. H. Ballou (p. 82 f.), however, that Accursius used Petrarch's manuscript, the *Parisinus* 5816.

at Venice in 1516, and by the more famous text edited by Erasmus, and published by Froben in Basel in 1518.

In these early editions the emphasis had been laid on the Latin text, but in the seventeenth century the work of the editors included not only textual emendation, but comment and illustration. Of these editions the first was that of Casaubon, published in 1603. It was not unnatural that these biographies should have attracted the editor of Suetonius and Polybius and the scholar who wrote in the preface to his edition of the *Historia Augusta* that "political philosophy may be learned from history, and ethical from biography".[1]

Casaubon's edition was soon followed by that of Gruter, published at Hanover in 1611. As professor in Heidelberg, Gruter had access to the *Codex Palatinus* and based his text on this manuscript. It is therefore not unnatural that he should have concerned himself most of all with the text. Yet his notes are by no means confined to a discussion of the readings of his manuscript, but include comment on the narrative and the citation of parallels from other classical authors. Yet his commentary lacks the scope of Casaubon's, and in many a note he refers the reader to the work of his great predecessor, *amicissimus noster*, as he calls him.[2]

The work of Casaubon and Gruter was carried on by the great Salmasius (Claude de Saumaise) in his edition published in 1620. His contribution consisted, not in the text, which was merely a re-publi-

---

[1] M. Pattison, *Isaac Casaubon*, 2nd Ed. (London, 1892), p. 440.

[2] *e.g.* note to *Hadr.*, ii. 5.

cation of Casaubon's, but in his commentary. As
might be expected from one of his great learning, he
included in his edition notes of wide scope and vast
erudition, and little was left unnoticed that the
knowledge of the age afforded.[1]

So far, the *Historia Augusta* had been a subject for
textual criticism and comment rather than a source
for Roman history. The historical researches of the
humanistic period dealt almost exclusively with the
Roman Republic, or, at the latest, with Augustus,[2]
and left these imperial biographies untouched. Besides Giovanni de Matociis and Guglielmo da
Pastrengo, only Benvenuto Rambaldi da Imola[3] in
his *Romuleon,* a compendium of Roman history from
the founding of Rome to the period of Constantine,
written soon after 1360, seems to have been largely
dependent on the *Historia Augusta* for the history of
the second and third centuries. In the later Renais-
sance, when the interest of scholars concerned itself
with antiquarian,[4] rather than strictly historical,
research, the biographies would be valuable only for
incidental information[5] rather than for historical
material. In the seventeenth century, on the other
hand, they received serious attention. The *de*

---

[1] The notes of Casaubon, Gruter, and Salmasius are all
incorporated in the *variorum* edition, published at Leyden in
1671.

[2] G. Voigt, *Wiederbelebung d. Class. Alt.* (Berlin, 1893),
ii. p. 490 f.

[3] Used by Casaubon and erroneously cited by him as
Robertus a Porta Bononiensis, *e.g.,* note to *Hadr.,* i. 1 ; see
E. Hohl, *Berl. Philol. Woch.,* xxxv. (1915), 221 f.

[4] See C. Wachsmuth, *Einleitung i. d. Stud. d. Alt. Gesch.*
(Leipzig, 1895), p. 7 f.

[5] *e.g.,* the *Antiquitates Romanae* of J. Rosinus (Basel,
1585 f.), where the *vitae* are frequently cited.

INTRODUCTION

Historicis Romanis of G. J. Vossius, published in 1627, devoted considerable space not only to the six biographers themselves, their respective dates, and the problem of the distribution of the various *vitae* among them, but also to the authors cited by them, especially Marius Maximus and Junius Cordus.[1] Of much more importance, however, was their use by Lenain de Tillemont in his *Histoire des Empereurs et des autres Princes qui ont régné durant les six premiers Siècles de l'Eglise.*[2] In spite of his general denunciation of the biographers as unworthy of the name of historian,[3] and his occasional strictures on their self-contradictions,[4] the chronological inexactness of Spartianus,[5] and the crime-inspiring character of Lampridius' work,[6] the *Historia Augusta* was a main source, together with Cassius Dio, for that part of his work which dealt with the second and third centuries.

Similarly important was the place that the *Historia Augusta* occupied among the sources used by Gibbon. Although his critical acumen detected many an instance of historical inaccuracy, and although he did not hesitate to score single instances with characteristic vigour,[7] he accepted in general the information that it offered and even the point of view of the biographer.[8]

[1] See *Lib.* ii., cap. 2 f.   [2] In five volumes. Paris, 1690 f.
[3] *Ib.*, vol. iii. p. 217.
[4] *e.g.*, *ib.*, iii. p. 447 (Spartianus); iii. p. 489 f. (Capitolinus); iii. p. 526 (Pollio.)
[5] *Ib.*, ii. p. 518; iii. pp. 448 f., 459.   [6] *Ib.*, ii. p. 281.
[7] *e.g.*, his contrast between Cassius Dio who spoke "as a senator who had supped with the emperor" and Capitolinus who spoke "like a slave who had received his intelligence from one of the scullions"; Gibbon-Bury, vol. i. p. 99.
[8] *e.g.*, his erroneous judgment on Gallienus, due to the *vita*; see Gibbon-Bury, vol. i. p. 446.

INTRODUCTION

In the nineteenth century the work of the biographers was still accorded respectful, though not
uncritical, consideration. Thus Merivale held that
"we may perhaps rely upon them generally for the
account of the salient events of history and their
views of character; but we must guard against the
trifling and incredible anecdotes with which they
abound,"[1] and, true to his principle, he constantly
cites them as sources. Schiller, too, while observing
that the later biographies are inferior to the earlier
ones and that the value of their information varied
with the source employed, regarded the material that
they afford as useful for the political history of the
empire,[2] and used them as sources, considering them,
apparently, as important as Dio and Herodian. Even
Mommsen in his *Römisches Staatsrecht* does not dis-
dain these biographies, but cites them among his
authorities in his reconstruction of the public law and
administration of imperial Rome. It was left for the
last decade of the nineteenth century and the first
two decades of the twentieth to bring the charge of
utter spuriousness against the *Historia Augusta* and to
assert that it is the work of a forger[3]—a charge which,
in return, has led to a somewhat fanciful attempt to
trace through many of the biographies the purple
thread of an otherwise unknown historian of prime
importance.[4]

[1] *Hist. of the Romans under the Empire*, 4th Ed. (American
reprint, New York 1863-65), vii. p. 321, n. 1.
[2] *Gesch. d. Röm. Kaiserzeit* (Gotha, 1883), pp. 595 f. and
701.
[3] H. Dessau, *Hermes*, xxiv. (1889), pp. 337-392; xxvii. (1892),
pp. 561-605.
[4] O. Th. Schulz, *Beiträge z. Kritik uns. litt. Ueberlieferung
f. d. Zeit von Commodus' Sturze bis auf d. Tod d. M. Aurelius
Antoninus (Caracalla)*, Leipzig, 1903.

THE MANUSCRIPTS

THE manuscripts of the *Historia Augusta* are divided
into two main classes, each of which has such definite
characteristics that the distinction between them is
sharp and clear. Both classes are, indeed, derived
from a common original, made after the loss of the
vitae of the emperors from Philip to Valerian [1] and
of considerable portions of the *vitae* of the Valeriani
and the Gallieni. On the other hand, there is a conspicuous difference between the two classes in the
manner in which the text has been treated. In one
class, usually designated as Class II, the treatment
has been most conservative. The text has been preserved free from all interpolations or additions, and
especially the *lacunae* in the biographies of the Valeriani and the Gallieni have been carefully indicated
by dots marking the missing letters. This class is
also characterised by a confusion in the order of the
biographies between Verus and Alexander and by
the misplacement of two long passages from the
Alexander and the *Maximini* (*Alex.*, xliii. 7—lviii. 1,
and *Max.*, v. 3—xviii. 2), each of which corresponds
to a quire of the original which became loose and
and was then inserted in a wrong place. A similar

[1] See Intro., p. xiv.

transposition occurs in the *Carus*, where c. xiii. 1—
xv. 5 has been inserted in c. ii.

The manuscripts of the other class, designated as
Class Σ, differ from those of Class Π in that the text
has been treated with the utmost freedom. In many
places, where the original was corrupt, drastic emendations have been made, and where none seemed
possible, the corrupt parts have been omitted altogether. This is especially conspicuous in the *lacunae*
in the *vitae* of the Valeriani and the Gallieni, where
all trace of the loss has been covered up by the insertion of words and the formation of a continuous
text. In all this the aim has been to construct a
smooth and easily readable narrative. In other places,
such as the end of the *Caracalla* and of the *Maximus-
Balbinus* and the beginning of the *Valeriani*, additions
have been made to the text; and in the case of the
Marcus considerable sections have been shifted about
and then connected in their new places by arbitrary
changes in the context. It is also characteristic of
this class that the *vitae* (with the single exception of
the *Avidius Cassius*) are arranged in chronological
order and that the sections transposed in Class Π are
in their rightful places.

The manuscripts of Class Π were supposed by
Peter to consist of three main groups, all derived
from the same archetype, and represented respectively by the *Codex Palatinus* 899 (P); the *Codex
Bambergensis* (B); and the *Codex Vaticanus* 5301
with others. Peter accordingly regarded the Palatinus and the Bambergensis as equally authoritative.
More recent investigation, however, as carried on by
Mommsen[1] and Dessau,[2] has shown that the *Codex*

[1] *Herm.*, xxv. (1890), pp. 281-292 = *Ges. Schr.*, vii., pp.
352-362.
[2] *Herm.*, xxix. (1894), pp. 893-416.

Palatinus is the parent manuscript, and that all the others of Class II are only direct or indirect copies of it. All contain errors and omissions which can be due only to a transcription of the Palatinus, over faithful or unskilful, as the case may be. Accordingly, only the Palatinus can be regarded as authoritative in this class, and the others may be used only for the purpose of confirmation or supplement.

The tradition contained in the manuscripts of Class Σ, though regarded as untrustworthy by Peter, was admitted by him to be possibly independent of that of Class II. This independence is more strongly maintained by Dr. Ernst Hohl.[1] He points to the chronological order of the *vitae* and to the correct arrangement of the quires transposed in the manuscripts of Class II as evidence for his conviction that the manuscripts of this class represent a tradition different from that of Class II, although, as the various omissions show, derived from a common original. He has, furthermore, cited in proof of his theory various passages in the biographies of Alexander and Aurelian contained in the manuscripts of Class Σ but not in the *Codex Palatinus*, and argues that these were excised from the original of the latter because of allusions to pagan deities. These considerations, together with a number of readings which are better than those of the Palatinus, have convinced him that the Σ manuscripts are derived ultimately from an original at least as old as the Palatinus and retaining more correctly many of the readings of their common archetype. On the other hand,

---

[1] *Klio.*, xiii. (1913), pp. 258-288, 387-423; xv. (1918), pp. 78-98.

THE MANUSCRIPTS

Miss Susan H. Ballou,[1] following the opinion expressed by Dessau, argues that these divergencies from the tradition of Class Π are of such a character that they can be merely the work of a clever, though unscrupulous, redactor. She holds that this man made his transcription from the *Codex Palatinus*, having before him all the corrections and additions that had been introduced by all the later correctors, and taking from all of them as many as suited his purpose. This transcription, she believes, was the original of the extant Σ manuscripts, which, accordingly, represent, not an independent tradition, but merely the work of an editor, who by means of intelligent and original treatment of the material contained in the Palatinus and by the unscrupulous use of interpolation and re-arrangement, created a readable but unsound version of the text.

With only the present evidence available the problem of the value of the manuscripts of Class Σ must be regarded as still unsolved. The arguments advanced by Dr. Hohl are not altogether convincing, and it has not yet been fully demonstrated that the tradition of the Σ manuscripts is independent of those of Class Π. For the present, therefore, any constitution of the text must be based on the readings of the *Codex Palatinus*.

---

[1] *The Manuscript Tradition of the Historia Augusta*, Leipzig, 1914.

EDITIONS AND TRANSLATIONS.

EDITIONS—

Editio Princeps: edited by Bonus Accursius, Milan, 1475.

Venice Editions: printed by Bernadinus Ricius (Rizus), 1489, and J. Rubens de Vercellis, 1490.

Aldine Edition: edited by J. B. Egnatius, Venice, 1516; Florence, 1519.

Desiderius Erasmus: published by Froben, Basel, 1518.

Isaac Casaubon: Paris, 1603.

Janus Gruter: Hanover, 1611.

Claudius Salmasius; containing also Casaubon's notes: Paris, 1620; London, 1652.

C. Schrevel: Leyden, 1661.

Variorum Edition; containing the commentaries of Casaubon, Gruter, and Salmasius: published by Hack, Leyden, 1671.

Ulrich Obrecht: Strassburg, 1677.

J. P. Schmidt, with preface by J. L. E. Püttmann: Leipzig, 1774.

Bipontine Edition, 2 vols.: Zweibrücken and Strassburg, 1787 and 1789.

Panckouke, 3 vols.: Paris, 1844-1847.

Thomas Vallaurius: Turin, 1853.

H. Jordan and F. Eyssenhardt, 2 vols.: Berlin, 1864.

Hermann Peter, 2 vols. (Teubner Text): Leipzig, 1st Edition, 1865; 2nd Edition, 1884.

TRANSLATIONS—
GERMAN—

J. P. Ostertag, 2 vols.: Frankfurt a. Main, 1790, 1793.

L. Storch; Hadrian, Aelius, and Antoninus Pius: Prenzlau, 1829.

C. A. Closs, 6 vols.: Stuttgart, 1856-1857.

FRENCH—

G. de Moulines, 3 vols.: Berlin, 1783; 2nd Edition, Paris, 1806.

Th. Baudement (collection Nisard): Paris, 1845.

SPANISH—

F. Navarro y Calvo, 2 vols.: Madrid, 1889-1890.

EDITORIAL NOTE (1991)

SCHOLARLY research pursued since the first publication of this work in 1922 now requires modification of some of the editor's views. Most authorities today are persuaded that the ostensible multiple authorship of these lives is a wilful deception, that one person is responsible for the collection and the insertion into it of documents which are sheer fabrications, and that the date of this activity is about A.D. 395.

Volume III of this edition contains on pages vii-x a bibliographical appendix (1919–1967), to which the following important works (the first two with extensive bibliographies) must now be added:

SYME, SIR RONALD: *Ammianus and the* Historia Augusta, Oxford 1968.

SYME, SIR RONALD: *Emperors and Biography: Studies in the* Historia Augusta, Oxford 1971.

BARNES, T. D.: *Sources of the* Historia Augusta, Bruxelles 1978.

SYME, SIR RONALD: *Historia Augusta Papers*, Oxford 1983.

G. P. G.

SCRIPTORES
HISTORIAE AUGUSTAE

AELII SPARTIANI

DE VITA

HADRIANI

I. Origo imperatoris Hadriani vetustior a Picentibus, posterior ab Hispaniensibus manat; si quidem Hadria ortos maiores suos apud Italicam Scipionum temporibus resedisse in libris vitae suae Hadrianus ipse 2 commemorat.[1] Hadriano pater Aelius Hadrianus cognomento Afer fuit, consobrinus Traiani imperatoris; mater Domitia Paulina Gadibus orta, soror Paulina nupta Serviano, uxor Sabina, atavus Marullinus, qui primus in sua familia senator populi Romani fuit.
3   Natus est Romae VIIII kal. Feb. Vespasiano septies

---

[1] *commemorat* P corr. ; *commemoret* P[1], Petschenig.

---

[1] For the Autobiography of Hadrian, now lost, cf. c. xvi. It seems to have been written toward the close of his life, and, to judge from scanty citations from it, its purpose was to contradict current statements about himself which he considered derogatory to his reputation and to present him in a favourable light to posterity.

[2] An ancient town of Picenum, which became a Roman colony, probably about the time of Sulla.

[3] In Hispania Baetica, on the Baetis (Guadalquiver),

2

HADRIAN

BY

AELIUS SPARTIANUS

I. The original home of the family of the Emperor
Hadrian was Picenum, the later, Spain; for Hadrian
himself relates in his autobiography[1] that his fore-
fathers came from Hadria,[2] but settled at Italica[3] in
the time of the Scipios. The father of Hadrian was
Aelius Hadrianus, surnamed Afer, a cousin of the
Emperor Trajan; his mother was Domitia Paulina, a
native of Cadiz; his sister was Paulina, the wife of
Servianus,[4] his wife was Sabina,[5] and his great-grandfather's grandfather was Marullinus, the first of his
family to be a Roman senator.

Hadrian was born in Rome[6] on the ninth day be- 24 Jan., 76.
fore the Kalends of February in the seventh consul-

---

founded by Scipio Africanus about 205 B.C., received the
rights of a municipality under Julius or Augustus, and was
made a colony by Hadrian.

[4] L. Julius Ursus Servianus frequently mentioned in this
biography. He governed several provinces under Trajan, and
was made consul for a third time by Hadrian in 134. On his
death in 136, see c. xxiii. 2, 8; xxv. 8; Dio, lxix. 17.

[5] See c. ii. 10 and note.

[6] This is, of course, a fiction, and the biography contradicts
itself, for Italica is clearly the *patria* referred to in c. ii. 1
and 2, and c. xix. 1.

3

4 et Tito quinquies consulibus. ac decimo aetatis anno
patre orbatus Ulpium Traianum praetorium tunc,[1]
consobrinum suum, qui postea imperium tenuit, et
Caelium Attianum equitem Romanum tutores habuit.
5 imbutusque impensius Graecis studiis, ingenio eius
sic ad ea declinante ut a nonnullis Graeculus
II. diceretur. quintodecimo anno ad patriam rediit ac
statim militiam iniit, venandi[2] usque ad reprehen-
2 sionem studiosus. quare a Traiano abductus a patria
et pro filio habitus nec multo post decemvir litibus
iudicandis datus atque inde tribunus secundae
3 Adiutricis legionis creatus. post hoc in inferiorem
Moesiam translatus extremis iam Domitiani[3] tempori-
4 bus. ibi a mathematico quodam de futuro imperio
id dicitur comperisse quod a patruo magno Aelio
Hadriano peritia caelestium callente praedictum esse
5 compererat. Traiano a Nerva adoptato ad gratula-
tionem exercitus missus in[4] Germaniam superiorem

---

[1] *tunc* P[1]; *uirum* P corr.   [2] *uenandi* Novak; *uenando*
P, Peter.   [3] *domitianis* P[1], Petschenig.   [4] *in* omitted
by P[1], added by P corr.

---

[1] Trajan was praetor about 85, and so, until he became
consul, in 91, was a *vir praetorius*.

[2] The name Caelius is an error. His name was Acilius
Attianus, as it appears on an inscription from Elba; see *Röm.
Mitt.*, xviii. 63-67. He became prefect of the guard under
Trajan and seems to have been instrumental in securing the
throne for Hadrian. On his retirement from the prefecture,
see c. viii. 7; ix. 3-5.

[3] The *decemviri stlitibus iudicandis* had originally, in the
republican period, the duty of determining disputed claims
to freedom. Augustus removed suits for freedom from their
jurisdiction, and gave them the conduct of the court of the
Centumviri, which dealt with suits for inheritances. Appointment to this, or to one of five other minor magisterial

ship of Vespasian and the fifth of Titus. Bereft of
his father at the age of ten, he became the ward of
Ulpius Trajanus, his cousin, then of praetorian rank,[1]
but afterwards emperor, and of Caelius Attianus,[2] a
knight. He then grew rather deeply devoted to
Greek studies, to which his natural tastes inclined so
much that some called him "Greekling." II. He
returned to his native city in his fifteenth year and
at once entered military service, but was so fond of
hunting that he incurred criticism for it, and for this
reason Trajan recalled him from Italica. Thenceforth he was treated by Trajan as his own son, and not
long afterwards he was made one of the ten judges
of the inheritance-court,[3] and, later, tribune of the
Second Legion, the Adjutrix.[4] After this, when
Domitian's principate was drawing to a close, he was
transferred to the province of Lower Moesia.[5]
There, it is said, he heard from an astrologer the
same prediction of his future power which had been
made, as he already knew, by his great-uncle, Aelius
Hadrianus, a master of astrology. When Trajan was
adopted[6] by Nerva, Hadrian was sent to convey to
him the army's congratulations and was at once

boards constituting the *vigintiviri*, was the first step in a
career of public office.
  [4] So called because it had been recruited (by Vespasian)
from an auxiliary force of marines. At this time it was serving probably in the province of Pannonia Inferior.
  [5] As tribune of the Fifth Legion, the Macedonica. This
command is listed among his other offices in an inscription
set up in his honour at Athens in 112 (*C.I.L.*, iii. 550 = Dessau,
Inscr. Sel., 308), and it is known that this legion was quartered
in Moesia Inferior at this time.
  [6] Trajan was governor of the province of Germania
Superior; he seems to have been appointed by Nerva in 96.

6 translatus est. ex qua festinans ad Traianum, ut
primus nuntiaret excessum Nervae, a Serviano, sororis
viro, (qui et sumptibus et aere alieno eius prodito
Traiani odium in eum movit) diu detentus fractoque consulte vehiculo tardatus, pedibus iter faciens
7 eiusdem Serviani beneficiarium antevenit. fuitque
in amore Traiani, nec tamen ei per paedagogos
puerorum quos Traianus impensius diligebat, . . .
8 Gallo favente [1] defuit. quo quidem tempore cum
sollicitus de imperatoris erga se iudicio, Vergilianas
sortes consuleret,

> Quis procul ille autem ramis insignis olivae
> sacra ferens? nosco crines incanaque menta
> regis Romani, primam qui legibus urbem
> fundabit, Curibus parvis et paupere terra

missus in imperium magnum, cui deinde subibit . . .
sors excidit, quam alii ex Sibyllinis versibus ei prove
9 nisse dixerunt. habuit autem praesumptionem imperii mox futuri ex fano quoque Nicephorii Iovis
manante responso, quod Apollonius Syrus Platonicus
10 libris suis indidit. denique statim suffragante Sura
ad amicitiam Traiani pleniorem rediit, nepte per

---

[1] Lacuna suggested by Gemoll; *diligebat Gallo fauente defuit* P.

---

[1] As tribune of the Twenty-second Legion, the *Primigenia
Pia Fidelis*, according to the Athenian inscription (see p. 5,
n. 5).
[2] A *beneficiarius* was a soldier who had been relieved of
active service by some commandant and was attached to the
suite of this official.
[3] For similar consultations, cf. *Cl. Alb.*, v. 4; *Alex.*, iv. 6;
xiv. 5; *Claud.*, x. 4f.
[4] *Aen.*, vi. 808-812. The passage refers to Numa Pompilius.
[5] Perhaps the place of this name near Pergamon.
[6] Unknown.

transferred to Upper Germany.¹   When Nerva died, Oct., 97.
he wished to be the first to bring the news to Trajan,
but as he was hastening to meet him he was detained
by his brother-in-law, Servianus, the same man who
had revealed Hadrian's extravagance and indebted-
ness and thus stirred Trajan's anger against him.   He
was further delayed by the fact that his travelling-
carriage had been designedly broken, but he nevertheless proceeded on foot and anticipitated Servianus'
personal messenger.²   And now he became a
favourite of Trajan's, and yet, owing to the activity of
the guardians of certain boys whom Trajan loved
ardently, he was not free from . . . which Gallus
fostered.   Indeed, at this time he was even anxious
about the Emperor's attitude towards him, and consulted the Vergilian oracle.³   This was the lot given
out : ⁴

But who is yonder man, by olive wreath
Distinguished, who the sacred vessel bears ?
I see a hoary head and beard.   Behold
The Roman King whose laws shall stablish Rome
Anew, from tiny Cures' humble land
Called to a mighty realm.   Then shall arise . . .

Others, however, declare that this prophecy came to
him from the Sibylline Verses.   Moreover, he received a further intimation of his subsequent power,
in a response which issued from the temple of Jupiter
at Nicephorium ⁵ and has been quoted by Apollonius of Syria,⁶ the Platonist.   Finally, through the
good offices of Sura,⁷ he was instantly restored to a
friendship with Trajan that was closer than ever, and

---

⁷ L. Licinius Sura was consul for the third time in 107.
He commanded the army in the wars in Dacia and received
the triumphal insignia and other high honours.

HADRIAN

sororem Traiani uxore accepta favente Plotina, Traiano
leviter, ut Marius Maximus dicit, volente.

III. Quaesturam gessit Traiano quater et Articuleio
consulibus, in qua cum orationem imperatoris in
senatu agrestius pronuntians risus esset, usque ad
summam peritiam et facundiam Latinis operam dedit.
2 post quaesturam acta senatus curavit atque ad bellum
3 Dacicum Traianum familiarius prosecutus est ; quando
quidem et indulsisse vino se dicit Traiani moribus
obsequentem atque ob hoc se a Traiano locupletissime
4 muneratum. tribunus plebis factus est Candido et
5 Quadrato iterum consulibus, in quo magistratu ad
perpetuam tribuniciam potestatem omen sibi factum
adserit, quod paenulas amiserit, quibus uti tribuni
plebis pluviae tempore solebant, imperatores autem
numquam. unde hodieque imperatores sine paenulis
6 a togatis videntur. secunda expeditione Dacica
Traianus eum primae legioni Minerviae praeposuit
secumque duxit ; quando quidem multa egregia eius
7 facta claruerunt. quare adamante gemma quam Tra-

---

¹ Vibia Sabina, the daughter of L. Vibius and Matidia, who
was the daughter of Marciana, Trajan's sister. Plotina was
Trajan's wife.
² L. Marius Maximus was the author of biographies of the
emperors from Nerva to Elagabalus, frequently cited in these
Vitae; see Intro., p. xvii f. He is probably the senator of
the same name who held many important administrative
posts under Septimius Severus and his successors.
³ He is called in the Athenian inscription *quaestor imperatoris Traiani, i.e.* he was one of the quaestors detailed to
transact business for the emperor, and particularly to convey his messages to the senate and read them before the
house.
⁴ The official known as *curator actorum senatus* or *ab actis
senatus* drafted the record of the senate's transactions,

8

he took to wife the daughter of the Emperor's sister [1]
—a marriage advocated by Plotina, but, according to
Marius Maximus,[2] little desired by Trajan himself.

He held the quaestorship [3] in the fourth consulship of Trajan and the first of Articuleius, and 101.
while holding this office he read a speech of the Emperor's to the senate and provoked a laugh by his
somewhat provincial accent. He thereupon gave
attention to the study of Latin until he attained
the utmost proficiency and fluency. After his
quaestorship he served as curator of the acts of the
senate,[4] and later accompanied Trajan in the Dacian
war [5] on terms of considerable intimacy, seeing, indeed, that falling in with Trajan's habits, as he says
himself, he partook freely of wine, and for this was
very richly rewarded by the Emperor. He was made
tribune of the plebs in the second consulship of 105.
Candidus and Quadratus, and he claimed that he received an omen of continuous tribunician [6] power
during this magistracy, because he lost the heavy
cloak which is worn by the tribunes of the plebs in
rainy weather, but never by the emperors. And
down to this day the emperors do not wear cloaks
when they appear in public before civilians. In the 105-106.
second Dacian war, Trajan appointed him to the
command of the First Legion, the Minervia, and took
him with him to the war ; and in this campaign his
many remarkable deeds won great renown. Because
of this he was presented with a diamond which

[5] The first Dacian war (101-102). The inscription cited
above reads : *Comes expeditionis Dacicae, donis militaribus
ab eo* (Traiano) *donatus bis.*

[6] An allusion to the tribunician power held by the emperors,
which was regarded as the basis of their civil powers; see
note to *Marc.*, vi. 6.

9

ianus a Nerva acceperat donatus ad spem successionis
8 erectus est. praetor factus est Suburano[1] bis et Serviano iterum consulibus, cum sestertium iterum[2] vicies
9 ad ludos edendos a Traiano accepit. legatus postea
praetorius in Pannoniam inferiorem missus Sarmatas
compressit, disciplinam militarem tenuit, procuratores
10 latius evagantes coercuit. ob hoc consul est factus.
in quo magistratu ut[3] a Sura comperit adoptandum
se a Traiano esse, ab amicis Traiani contemni desiit
11 ac neglegi. et defuncto[4] quidem Sura Traiani ei
familiaritas crevit,[5] causa praecipue orationum quas
IV. pro imperatore dictaverat. usus Plotinae quoque
favore, cuius studio etiam legatus expeditionis
2 Parthicae tempore destinatus est. qua quidem
tempestate utebatur Hadrianus amicitia Sosii Papi et
Platorii[6] Nepotis ex senatorio ordine, ex equestri

---

[1] *Suburano* Mommsen; *sub surano* P, Peter. [2] *iterum*
deleted by Mommsen. [3] *ut* P corr.; *et* P[1]. [4] *defuncto*
P corr.; *definito* P[1]. [5] *creuit* P corr.; *creauit* P[1]; *crebuit*
Peter. [6] *Platori* Borghesi; *pletori* P.

---

[1] Due to a precedent established by Augustus, who, when
ill in 23 B.C., gave his ring to Agrippa, apparently intending
him to be his successor; see Dio, liii, 30.

[2] The reading of P is impossible, for no such person as
Suranus is known, but it is difficult to emend the text
satisfactorily, since Suburanus was consul for the second time
in 104, and Servianus was consul for the second time in 102.
The consuls of 107, in which year Hadrian was probably
praetor, were Sura, for the third time, and Senecio, for the
second time.

[3] This province was one of the " imperial provinces," which
were governed in theory by the emperor but in practice by a
deputy appointed by him with the title *legatus Augusti pro
praetore*. The governor of the province under the control of
the senate, on the other hand, had the title of *proconsul*.

Trajan himself had received from Nerva, and by this gift he was encouraged in his hopes of succeeding to the throne.[1] He held the praetorship in the second consulship of Suburanus and Servianus,[2] and again received from Trajan two million sesterces with which to give games. Next he was sent as praetorian legate to Lower Pannonia,[3] where he held the Sarmatians in check, maintained discipline among the soldiers, and restrained the procurators,[4] who were overstepping too freely the bounds of their power. In return for these services he was made consul. While he was holding this office he learned from Sura that he was to be adopted by Trajan, and thereupon he ceased to be an object of contempt and neglect to Trajan's friends. Indeed, after Sura's death Trajan's friendship for him increased, principally on account of the speeches which he composed for the Emperor. IV. He enjoyed, too, the favour of Plotina,[5] and it was due to her interest in him that later, at the time of the campaign against Parthia, he was appointed the legate of the Emperor.[6] At this same time he enjoyed, besides, the friendship of Sosius Papus and Platorius Nepos,[7] both of the

108.

114.

Hadrian is called here *legatus praetorius* because he held this position as a *vir praetorius*, *i.e.* one who had been praetor but not yet consul.

[4] The procurator was charged with the collection of taxes and other sources of revenue in an imperial province and their transmission to the *fiscus*, or privy purse.

[5] Cf. c. ii. 10.

[6] The appointment as legate refers to his governorship of Syria; see § 6.

[7] A. Platorius Nepos was prominent under Trajan as a magistrate at Rome and the governor of several important provinces and was consul with Hadrian in 119. He afterward incurred Hadrian's enmity; see c. xv. 2; xxiii. 4.

autem Attiani, tutoris quondam sui, et Liviani et[1]
[3] Turbonis. in adoptionis sponsionem venit Palma
et Celso, inimicis semper suis et quos postea ipse
insecutus est, in suspicionem adfectatae[2] tyrannidis
[4] lapsis. secundo consul favore Plotinae factus totam
[5] praesumptionem adoptionis emeruit. corrupisse eum
Traiani libertos, curasse delicatos eosdemque saepe
inisse[3] per ea tempora quibus in aula familiarior[4] fuit,
opinio multa firmavit.

[6]   Quintum iduum Augustarum diem legatus Syriae
litteras adoptionis accepit ; quando et natalem adop-
[7] tionis celebrari iussit. tertium iduum earundem,
quando et natalem imperii statuit celebrandum, ex-
cessus ei Traiani nuntiatus est.

[8]   Frequens sane opinio fuit Traiano id animi fuisse
ut Neratium Priscum, non Hadrianum, successorem
relinqueret, multis amicis in hoc consentientibus,
usque eo ut Prisco aliquando dixerit : "commendo
[9] tibi provincias, si quid mihi fatale contigerit". et
multi quidem dicunt Traianum in animo id habuisse,
ut exemplo Alexandri Macedonis sine certo succes-

---

[1] *et* omitted by P, added by Hirschfeld.   [2] *adfectatae*
Petschenig; *adiectae* P; *adiectae* Peter with Salm.   [3] *saepe*
inisse Ellis, von Winterfeld; *sepelisse* P; *ad se pellexisse* Peter[2].
[4] *familiarior* P; *familiariorum* B, Peter.

---

[1] T. Claudius Livianus was prefect of the guard under
Trajan and held a command in the first Dacian war; see
Dio, lxix. 9.

[2] For the career of Q Marcius Turbo under Trajan and
Hadrian see c. v-vii. He was finally appointed prefect of the
guard; see c. ix. 4.

[3] A. Cornelius Palma and L. Publilius Celsus held important offices under Trajan and statues were erected in their

senatorial order, and also of Attianus, his former guardian, of Livianus,[1] and of Turbo,[2] all of equestrian rank. And when Palma and Celsus,[3] always his enemies, on whom he later took vengeance, fell under suspicion of aspiring to the throne, his adoption seemed assured ; and it was taken wholly for granted when, through Plotina's favour, he was appointed consul for the second time. That he was bribing Trajan's freedmen and courting and corrupting his favourites all the while that he was in close attendance at court, was told and generally believed.

On the fifth day before the Ides of August, while 9 Aug.,117. he was governor of Syria, he learned of his adoption by Trajan, and he later gave orders to celebrate this day as the anniversary of his adoption. On the third day before the Ides of August he received the news 11 Aug., of Trajan's death, and this day he appointed as the 117. anniversary of his accession.

There was, to be sure, a widely prevailing belief that Trajan, with the approval of many of his friends, had planned to appoint as his successor not Hadrian but Neratius Priscus,[4] even to the extent of once saying to Priscus : " I entrust the provinces to your care in case anything happens to me ". And, indeed, many aver that Trajan had purposed to follow the example of Alexander of Macedonia and die without naming a successor. Again, many others declare that

honour. Nothing is known of the suspicion alluded to here, but the two men, together with Nigrinus and Lusius Quietus, were later accused of a conspiracy against Hadrian and put to death ; see c. vii. 1-3.

[4] L. Neratius Priscus was a famous jurist and his works were used in the compilation of Justinian's *Digest*. He was a member of Trajan's imperial council, and later was one of Hadrian's advisers in legal questions ; see c. xviii. 1.

13

sore moreretur, multi ad senatum eum orationem
voluisse mittere petiturum, ut, si quid ei evenisset,
principem Romanae rei publicae senatus daret, additis dum taxat nominibus ex quibus optimum idem
10 senatus eligeret nec desunt qui factione Plotinae
mortuo iam Traiano Hadrianum in adoptionem ad-
scitum esse prodiderint, supposito qui pro Traiano
fessa voce loquebatur.[1]

V. Adeptus imperium ad priscum se statim morem
instituit et tenendae per orbem terrarum paci operam
2 impendit.[2] nam deficientibus iis nationibus quas
Traianus subegerat, Mauri lacessebant, Sarmatae
bellum inferebant, Britanni teneri sub Romana
dicione non poterant, Aegyptus seditionibus urge-
batur, Libya[3] denique ac Palaestina rebelles animos
3 efferebant. quare omnia trans Euphraten ac Tigrim
reliquit exemplo, ut dicebat, Catonis, qui Macedones
liberos pronuntiavit, quia tueri non poterant.
4 Parthamasirin,[4] quem Traianus Parthis regem fecerat,

---

[1] *loqueretur* P corr.   [2] *impendit* P corr., Petschenig, No-
vak, and Lessing; *intendit* P[1], Peter.   [3] *Libya* Cas.; *licia*
P.   [4] *Parthamasirin*, see *Prosop.* III, p. 13; *sarmatosirin*
P; *Partomasirin* Peter[2].

---

[1] Augustus had bequeathed as a policy the *consilium coer-
cendi intra terminos imperii* (Tacitus, *Annals*, i. 11), these
natural boundaries being the Rhine, Danube, and Euphrates.
This policy had been abandoned by Trajan in his conquests
of Dacia, Armenia, Mesopotamia, and Assyria. Hadrian's
new policy is proclaimed in the legends on his coins, *Iustitia*
(Cohen, ii[2], p. 179, No. 874 f.) and *Pax* (Cohen, ii[2], p. 190, No.
1011 f.).
[2] Cf. § 8 and c. vi. 7.   [3] Cf. c. vi. 6.
[4] *i.e.* Alexandria, where the Jews were rioting, incited perhaps by the example of their fellow-countrymen in Palestine.

14

he had meant to send an address to the senate, requesting this body, in case aught befell him, to appoint a
ruler for the Roman empire, and merely appending
the names of some from among whom the senate
might choose the best.   And the statement has even
been made that it was not until after Trajan's death
that Hadrian was declared adopted, and then only
by means of a trick of Plotina's; for she smuggled in
someone who impersonated the Emperor and spoke
in a feeble voice.

V. On taking possession of the imperial power
Hadrian at once resumed the policy of the early
emperors,[1] and devoted his attention to maintaining
peace throughout the world.   For the nations which
Trajan had conquered began to revolt; the Moors,
moreover, began to make attacks,[2] and the Sarmatians
to wage war,[3] the Britons could not be kept under
Roman sway, Egypt[4] was thrown into disorder by
riots, and finally Libya[5] and Palestine[6] showed the
spirit of rebellion.   Whereupon he relinquished all
the conquests east of the Euphrates and the Tigris,
following, as he used to say, the example of Cato,
who urged that the Macedonians, because they could
not be held as subjects, should be declared free and
independent.[7]   And Parthamasiris,[8] appointed king

[5] i.e. the Cyrenaica, where at the end of Trajan's reign
the Jews had risen and massacred many Greeks and Romans;
see Dio, lxviii. 32.

[6] Cf. § 8.

[7] This measure was apparently advocated in a speech made
before the senate in 167 B.C. after the defeat of Perseus, the
last king of Macedonia, at Pydna (see Livy, xlv. 17-18).
Macedonia was divided into four independent districts, an
arrangement which proved untenable.

[8] An error for Parthamaspates. This prince had deserted
his cousin, the Parthian king, and sided with Trajan in the

15

quod eum non magni ponderis apud Parthos videret,
proximis gentibus dedit regem.

5 Tantum autem statim clementiae studium habuit
ut, cum sub primis imperii diebus ab Attiano per
epistolas esset admonitus, ut et Baebius Macer praefectus urbis, si reniteretur eius imperio, necaretur et
Laberius Maximus, qui suspectus imperio in insula
exsulabat, et Frugi Crassus, neminem laederet;
6 quamvis Crassum postea procurator egressus insula,
quasi res novas moliretur, iniusso[1] eius occiderit.
7 militibus ob auspicia imperii duplicem largitionem
8 dedit. Lusium Quietum sublatis gentibus Mauris,
quos regebat, quia suspectus imperio fuerat, exarmavit,
Marcio Turbone Iudaeis compressis ad deprimendum
tumultum Mauretaniae destinato.

9 Post haec Antiochia digressus est ad inspiciendas

---

[1] *iniusso* P, accepted by Petschenig; *iniussu* Peter[1].

Parthian war; he was rewarded by being made king after
Trajan's victory in 116-117. The Parthians deposed him,
and Hadrian accordingly assigned to him, at least for a time,
the district of Osrhoene in north-western Mesopotamia. Cf.
c. xxi. 10, and Dio, lxviii. 30 and 33.

[1] The biography is anticipating here. This letter was
doubtless written after Attianus had returned to Rome with
Trajan's ashes; see § 10.

[2] Baebius Macer was one of the friends and correspondents
of the younger Pliny; see Pliny, *Epist.*, iii. 5. The prefect
of the city was in command of the three cohorts which were
responsible for the maintenance of order in Rome.

[3] M'. Laberius Maximus seems to have held a command
in the first Dacian war, and was consul for the second time
in 103. Nothing further is known of these "designs".

[4] C. Calpurnius Crassus Frugi conspired against Nerva and
was banished to Tarentum. He was later brought to trial on
the charge of conspiring against Trajan and was condemned
(Dio, lxviii. 3 and 16).

[5] Lusius Quietus, a Moor by birth and a captain of a squad-

of the Parthians by Trajan, he assigned as ruler to the
neighbouring tribes, because he saw that the man was
held in little esteem by the Parthians.

Moreover, he showed at the outset such a wish to
be lenient, that although Attianus advised him by
letter in the first few days of his rule [1] to put to death
Baebius Macer,[2] the prefect of the city, in case he opposed his elevation to power, also Laberius Maximus,[3]
then in exile on an island under suspicion of designs
on the throne, and likewise Crassus Frugi,[4] he nevertheless refused to harm them. Later on, however,
his procurator, though without an order from Hadrian,
had Crassus killed when he tried to leave the island,
on the ground that he was planning a revolt. He
gave a double donative to the soldiers in order to ensure
a favourable beginning to his principate. He deprived
Lusius Quietus [5] of the command of the Moorish
tribesmen, who were serving under him, and then dismissed him from the army, because he had fallen
under the suspicion of having designs on the throne;
and he appointed Marcius Turbo, after his reduction
of Judaea, to quell the insurrection in Mauretania.

After taking these measures he set out from
Antioch to view the remains of Trajan,[6] which were

ron. of Moorish horse, had been a commander in Trajan's
Parthian war. He had subsequently been appointed governor
of Judaea by Trajan. The dismissal of the Moorish troops
was a preliminary to the enforced retirement of Quietus,
since he was now unable to offer any resistance to Hadrian.
He was afterwards accused of conspiring against Hadrian and
was put to death; see c. vii. 1-3.
[6] Probably to Seleucia, whither Trajan's body was brought
from Selinus in Cilicia, the place of his death. Here the body
was burned and the ashes sent to Rome; cf. Victor, *Epit.*,
xiv. 12.

reliquias Traiani, quas Attianus, Plotina et Matidia
10 deferebant. quibus exceptis et navi Romam dimissis
ipse Antiochiam regressus praepositoque Syriae Catilio
Severo per Illyricum Romam venit.

VI. Traiano divinos honores datis ad senatum et quidem accuratissimis litteris postulavit et cunctis volentibus meruit, ita ut senatus multa, quae Hadrianus non
postulaverat, in honorem Traiani sponte decerneret.
2 cum ad senatum scriberet, veniam petiit, quod de
imperio suo iudicium senatui non dedisset, salutatus
scilicet praepropere a militibus imperator, quod esse
3 res publica sine imperatore non posset. cum triumphum ei senatus, qui Traiano debitus erat, detulisset, recusavit ipse atque imaginem Traiani curru
triumphali vexit, ut optimus imperator ne post mortem
4 quidem triumphi amitteret dignitatem. patris patriae
nomen delatum sibi statim et iterum postea distulit,
5 quod hoc nomen Augustus sero meruisset. aurum

---

[1] See note to c. ii. 10.

[2] L. Catilius Severus was a friend and correspondent of
Pliny; see Pliny, *Epist.*, i. 22; iii. 12. He became consul for
the second time in 120, was proconsul of Asia, and in 138 prefect of the city; see c. xxiv. 6-8. He was the great-grandfather of Marcus Aurelius; see *Marc.*, i. 4.

[3] Used here to denote the provinces along the southern
bank of the Danube. His route lay across Asia Minor, and it
was probably in this region that he received the news of the
war threatened by the tribes north of the river; cf. c. vi. 6.
He arrived in Moesia in the spring of 118, and finally reached
Rome in July, 118; cf. c. vii. 3.

[4] Acclamation by the army constituted a strong *de facto*
claim to the imperial power, but it is now generally recognized
(in spite of Mommsen's theory to the contrary) that only the
senate could legally confer the *imperium*.

[5] This triumph was commemorated by coins bearing on the
obverse the head of Trajan with the legend *Divo Traiano Parth*

being escorted by Attianus, Plotina, and Matidia.[1] He received them formally and sent them on to Rome by ship, and at once returned to Antioch; he then appointed Catilius Severus[2] governor of Syria, and proceeded to Rome by way of Illyricum.[3]

VI. Despatching to the senate a carefully worded letter, he asked for divine honours for Trajan. This request he obtained by a unanimous vote; indeed, the senate voluntarily voted Trajan many more honours than Hadrian had requested. In this letter to the senate he apologized because he had not left it the right to decide regarding his accession,[4] explaining that the unseemly haste of the troops in acclaiming him emperor was due to the belief that the state could not be without an emperor. Later, when the senate offered him the triumph which was to have been Trajan's, he refused it for himself, and caused the effigy of the dead Emperor to be carried in a triumphal chariot, in order that the best of emperors might not lose even after death the honour of a triumph.[5] Also he refused for the present the title of Father of his Country, offered to him at the time of his accession and again later on, giving as his reason the fact that Augustus had not won it until late in life.[6] Of the crown-

(ico) *Aug(usto) Patri* and on the reverse a four-horse chariot driven by the Emperor who holds a laurel-branch and a sceptre, with the legend *triumphus Parthicus;* see Cohen, ii², p. 78, No. 585.

[6] This title was conferred on Augustus in 2 B.C., twenty-five years after he received the *imperium* and the name of Augustus. In the case of the Julio-Claudian emperors after Tiberius (who never held this title) about a year was allowed to elapse before the honour was conferred. Hadrian finally accepted it in 128; see note to c. xiii. 4. The precedent of a postponement was also followed by Pius (*Pius*, vi. 6), and Marcus (*Marc.*, ix. 3).

19

coronarium Italiae remisit, in provinciis minuit, et
quidem difficultat bus aerarii ambitiose ac diligenter
expositis.

6 Audito dein tumultu Sarmatarum et Roxolanorum
7 praemissis exercitibus Moesiam petiit. Marcium
Turbonem post Mauretaniam [1] praefecturae infulis
ornatum Pannoniae Daciaeque ad tempus praefecit.
8 cum rege Roxolanorum, qui de inminutis stipendiis
querebatur, cognito negotio pacem composuit.

VII. Nigrini insidias, quas ille sacrificanti Hadriano
conscio sibi Lusio et multis aliis paraverat, cum etiam
successorem Hadrianus sibimet destinasset, evasit.
2 quare Palma Tarracinis, Celsus Baiis, Nigrinus
Faventiae, Lusius in itinere senatu iubente, invito
3 Hadriano, ut ipse in vita sua dicit, occisi sunt. unde
statim Hadrianus ad refellendam tristissimam de se

---

[1] *Mauretaniam* Peter; *mаurataneae* P[1]; *mauritaniae*
P corr.

---

[1] A contribution for the purpose of providing gold wreaths
(in imitation of laurel) which were held over the head of the
general in his triumph. Such contributions were originally
voluntary, but soon became obligatory. Augustus had remitted them (*Mon. Anc.*, c. 21), but his example does not seem
to have been followed by his immediate successors. Partial
remission is recorded in the cases of Pius (*Pius*, iv. 10) and
Alexander (*Alex.*, xxxii. 5), and proclamations of remission
by Trajan and Marcus are preserved in a papyrus (*Fayoum
Towns and their Papyri*, No. 116).
[2] The compressed style of the narrative combines those two
tribes here, but they must be carefully distinguished. The
Roxolani lived at the mouth of the Danube; they had been
constituted a vassal-state by Trajan. On the other hand, the
term *Sarmatae* is used to denote the independent Iazyges

money [1] for his triumph he remitted Italy's contribution, and lessened that of the provinces, all the while setting forth grandiloquently and in great detail the straits of the public treasury.

Then, on hearing of the incursions of the Sarmatians and Roxolani,[2] he sent the troops ahead and set out for Moesia. He conferred the insignia of a prefect on Marcius Turbo after his Mauretanian campaign and appointed him to the temporary command of Pannonia and Dacia.[3] When the king of the Roxolani complained of the diminution of his subsidy, he investigated his case and made peace with him.

VII. A plot to murder him while sacrificing was made by Nigrinus, with Lusius and a number of others as accomplices, even though Hadrian had destined Nigrinus [4] for the succession; but Hadrian successfully evaded this plot. Because of this conspiracy Palma was put to death at Tarracina, Celsus at Baiae, Nigrinus at Faventia,[5] and Lusius on his journey homeward, all by order of the senate, but contrary to the wish of Hadrian, as he says himself in his autobiography. Whereupon Hadrian entrusted

who lived in the great plain between the Theiss and the Danube.

[3] This was an extraordinary command, for Pannonia and Dacia, like other imperial provinces, were always assigned to senatorial legates, and Turbo was a knight. The only instance of an equestrian governor was the prefect of Egypt, the viceroy of the emperor (who in theory was king of Egypt), and this appointment of a knight to govern the provinces on the Danube seemed to have a precedent in the prefecture of Egypt (cf. c. vii. 3).

[4] Probably C. Avidius Nigrinus, mentioned by Pliny in *Epist. ad Traian.*, lxv. and lxvi. On the other conspirators see notes to c. iv. 3, and v. 8.

[5] Now Faenza; in the Po valley, about thirty miles S.E. of Bologna.

opinionem, quod occidi passus esset uno tempore quattuor consulares, Romam venit, Dacia Turboni credita, titulo Aegyptiacae praefecturae, quo plus auctoritatis haberet, ornato, et ad comprimendam de se famam congiarium duplex praesens populo dedit, 4 ternis iam per singulos aureis se absente divisis. in senatu quoque excusatis quae facta erant iuravit se numquam senatorem nisi ex senatus sententia pu-5 niturum. statum[1] cursum fiscalem instituit, ne 6 magistratus hoc onere gravarentur. ad colligendam autem gratiam nihil praetermittens, infinitam pecuniam, quae fisco debebatur, privatis debitoribus in urbe atque Italia, in provinciis vero etiam ex reliquiis ingentes summas remisit, syngraphis in foro divi Traiani,[2] quo magis securitas omnibus roboraretur, 7 incensis. damnatorum bona in fiscum *privatum

---

[1] *statum* Peter; *statim* P (defended by Herzog *R. Stvf.* II, 359, 1).   [2] *hadriani* P[1]; *al' traiani* P corr.

---

[1] As he had already done for the soldiers; see c. v. 7.

[2] A gold coin of the value of 100 sesterces or 25 denarii, or (very approximately) five dollars.

[3] It had long been a moot question whether the emperor had the right to put senators to death without formal trial and condemnation by the senate. Neither the later Julio-Claudian nor the Flavian emperors had recognized the right of a senator to trial by his fellow-senators only. Nerva, on the other hand, took an oath that he would not put a senator to death (Dio, lxviii. 2), and Trajan seems to have followed his example (Dio, lxviii. 5). For the practice of later emperors see *Marc.*, x. 6; xxv. 6; xxvi. 13; xxix. 4.

[4] Also called *cursus vehicularius* (*Pius*, xii. 3), and *munus vehicularium* (*Sev.* xiv. 2). Previous to Hadrian's reform the cost of the maintenance of the post had fallen on the provincial towns, but henceforth it was borne by the *fiscus*. The department was under the direction of an official of equestrian rank, known as the *praefectus vehiculorum*.

[5] The sum remitted was 900,000,000 sesterces; see coins

the command in Dacia to Turbo, whom he dignified, in order to increase his authority, with a rank analogous to that of the prefect of Egypt. He then hastened to Rome in order to win over public opinion, which was hostile to him because of the belief that on one single occasion he had suffered four men of consular rank to be put to death. In order to check the rumours about himself, he gave in person a double largess to the people,[1] although in his absence three aurei[2] had already been given to each of the citizens. In the senate, too, he cleared himself of blame for what had happened, and pledged himself never to inflict punishment on a senator until after a vote of the senate.[3] He established a regular imperial post,[4] in order to relieve the local officials of such a burden. Moreover, he used every means of gaining popularity. He remitted to private debtors in Rome and in Italy immense sums of money owed to the privy-purse,[5] and in the provinces he remitted large amounts of arrears ; and he ordered the promissory notes to be burned in the Forum of the Deified Trajan,[6] in order that the general sense of security might thereby be increased. He gave orders that the property of condemned persons should not accrue to the privy-

of 118, Cohen, ii[2], p. 208 f., Nos. 1210-1213, and an inscription found at Rome, *C.I.L.*, vi. 967.* He also issued an order providing for a similar cancelling every fifteen years ; see Dio, lxix. 8, 1 ; cf. also *Marc.*, xxiii. 3, and note.

[6] Situated at the south-western corner of the Esquiline Hill, a part of which was cut away in order to provide sufficient space. It was surrounded by colonnades, portions of which are extant, and on its north-western side was the Basilica Ulpia ; north-west of this was the column of Trajan, flanked by two buildings containing the *Bibliotheca Ulpia*. Just beyond was the *Templum Divi Traiani et Plotinae*, erected by Hadrian (c. xix. 9).

redigi vetuit, omni summa in aerario publico recepta.
8 pueris ac puellis, quibus etiam Traianus alimenta
9 detulerat, incrementum liberalitatis adiecit. senatoribus, qui non vitio suo decoxerant, patrimonium
pro liberorum modo senatoriae professionis explevit,
ita ut plerisque in diem vitae suae dimensum sine
10 dilatione praestiterit.[1] ad honores explendos non
solum amicis, sed etiam passim aliquantis multa
11 largitus est. feminas nonnullas ad sustentandam
12 vitam sumptibus iuvit. gladiatorium munus per sex
dies continuos exhibuit et mille feras natali suo
edidit.

VIII. Optimos quosque de senatu in contubernium
2 imperatoriae maiestatis adscivit. ludos circenses prae-
3 ter natalicios decretos sibi sprevit. et in contione et
in senatu saepe dixit ita se rem publicam gesturum ut
4 scirent[2] populi rem esse, non propriam. tertio consules, cum ipse ter fuisset, plurimos fecit, infinitos
5 autem secundi consulatus honore cumulavit. ipsum
autem tertium consulatum et quattuor mensibus

---

[1] *praestiterit* Cas. ; *restiterit* P[1] ; *restituerit* P corr.   [2] *sci-rent* Ellis ; *sciret* P, Peter.

---

[1] The *alimenta* were grants of money paid by the imperial government to the children of the poor of Italy. The plan was made by Nerva but actually carried out by Trajan. For the purpose of the distribution of these grants Italy was divided into districts, often known by the name of the great roads which traversed them (see *Pert.*, ii. 2).

[2] The sum necessary for the position of senator was 1,000,000 sesterces.

[3] The custom had arisen that on important occasions in

purse, and in each case deposited the whole amount in the public treasury. He made additional appropriations for the children to whom Trajan had allotted grants of money.[1] He supplemented the property of senators impoverished through no fault of their own, making the allowance in each case proportionate to the number of children, so that it might be enough for a senatorial career[2]; to many, indeed, he paid punctually on the date the amount allotted for their living. Sums of money sufficient to enable men to hold office he bestowed, not on his friends alone, but also on many far and wide, and by his donations he helped a number of women to sustain life. He gave gladiatorial combats for six days in succession, and on his birthday he put into the arena a thousand wild beasts.

VIII. The foremost members of the senate he admitted to close intimacy with the emperor's majesty. All circus-games decreed in his honour he refused, except those held to celebrate his birthday.[3] Both in meetings of the people and in the senate he used to say that he would so administer the commonwealth that men would know that it was not his own but the people's. Having himself been consul three times, he reappointed many to the consulship for the third time and men without number to a second term; his own third consulship he held for only four months, and during his term he often administered justice.

the reign of an emperor races in the Circus should be voted by the senate as a mark of honour. From the time of Augustus the birthday of the emperor was similarly celebrated, and in the case of some emperors, *e.g.* Pertinax and Severus, also the *natalis imperii* or day of the accession to the throne; see *Pert.*, xv. 5, and Dio, lxxviii. 8. Pius followed Hadrian's example in accepting birthday-games only; see *Pius*, v. 2.

6 tantum egit et in eo saepe ius dixit. senatui legitimo,
cum in urbe vel iuxta urbem esset, semper interfuit.
7 senatus fastigium in tantum extulit, difficile faciens
senatores ut, cum Attianum ex praefecto praetorii
ornamentis consularibus praeditum faceret senatorem,
nihil se amplius habere quod in eum conferri posset
8 ostenderit. equites Romanos nec sine se de sena-
9 toribus nec secum iudicare permisit. erat enim tunc
mos ut, cum princeps causas agnosceret, et senatores
et equites Romanos in consilium vocaret et sententiam
10 ex omnium deliberatione proferret. exsecratus est
denique principes qui minus senatoribus detulissent.
11 Serviano sororis viro, cui tantum detulit ut ei venienti
de cubiculo semper occurrerit, tertium consulatum,
nec secum tamen, cum ille bis ante Hadrianum fuisset, ne esset secundae sententiae, non petenti ac sine
precatione concessit.

IX. Inter haec tamen et multas provincias a Traiano
adquisitas reliquit et theatrum, quod ille in Campo

---

¹ This did not include a seat in the senate, but consisted
of the privilege of sitting with the senators of consular rank
at the public festivals and at sacred banquets and of wearing
the *toga praetexta* on such occasions. Since the time of Nero
this honorary rank had often been bestowed on prefects of the
guard on their retirement from office; see also *Pius*, x. 6.
² See note to c. vii. 4.
³ The *consilium* of the emperor was a development from the
old principle that a magistrate, before rendering an important
decision, should ask advice from trusted friends. So Augustus

He always attended regular meetings of the senate if he was present in Rome or even in the neighbourhood. In the appointment of senators he showed the utmost caution and thereby greatly increased the dignity of the senate, and when he removed Attianus from the post of prefect of the guard and created him a senator with consular honours,[1] he made it clear that he had no greater honour which he could bestow upon him. Nor did he allow knights to try cases involving senators[2] whether he was present at the trial or not. For at that time it was customary for the emperor, when he tried cases, to call to his council[3] both senators and knights and give a verdict based on their joint decision. Finally, he denounced those emperors who had not shown this deference to the senators. On his brother-in-law Servianus, to whom he showed such respect that he would advance to meet him as he came from his chamber, he bestowed a third consulship, and that without any request or entreaty on Servianus' part; but nevertheless he did not appoint him as his own colleague, since Servianus had been consul twice before Hadrian, and the Emperor did not wish to have second place.[4]

IX. And yet, at the same time, Hadrian abandoned many provinces won by Trajan,[5] and also destroyed,

and his successors had their boards of advisers. Until the time of Hadrian this board was not official or permanent, but from his reign on its members, the *consiliarii Augusti*, had a definite position and received a salary. Jurists of distinction were included in it; see c. xviii. 1.

[4] If Servianus, who was consul for the second time in 102, were associated with Hadrian in the Emperor's second consulship in 118 or third in 119, he would by reason of his seniority outrank his imperial colleague; see Mommsen, *Röm. Staatsrecht*, iii. p. 976, n. 4.

[5] Cf. c. v, 3.

2 Martio posuerat, contra omnium vota destruxit. et
haec quidem eo tristiora videbantur, quod omnia,
quae displicere vidisset [1] Hadrianus, mandata sibi ut
3 faceret secreto [2] a Traiano esse simulabat. cum Attiani, praefecti sui et quondam tutoris, potentiam
ferre non posset, nisus est eum obtruncare, sed revocatus est, quia iam quattuor consularium occisorum,
quorum quidem necem in Attiani consilia refundebat,
4 premebatur invidia. cui cum successorem dare non
posset, quia non petebat, id egit ut peteret, atque
ubi primum petiit, in Turbonem transtulit potestatem; cum quidem etiam Simili alteri praefecto
Septicium Clarum successorem dedit.

6 Summotis his a praefectura, quibus debebat imperium, Campaniam petiit eiusque omnia oppida
beneficiis et largitionibus sublevavit, optimum quem-
7 que amicitiis suis iungens. Romae vero praetorum
et consulum officia frequentavit, conviviis amicorum
interfuit, aegros bis ac ter die et nonnullos equites
Romanos ac libertinos visitavit, solaciis refovit, con-

---

[1] *displicere uidisset* P corr. ; *displicerentur uidisse* P[1].
[2] *secreto* Mommsen ; *decreto* P[1] ; *decreta* P corr.

---

[1] Cf. c. vii. 2-3.

[2] The term of office of the prefect of the guard was unlimited, and often was for life. This passage seems to show
that at least a form of voluntary resignation from the office
was customary. Attianus, according to precedent, was advanced to senatorial rank with the *ornamenta consularia;*
see c. viii. 7.

[3] C. Sulpicius Similis was prefect of the grain-supply, of
Egypt, and, finally, of the praetorian guard. According to
Dio (lxix. 20), it was only with difficulty that he secured
Hadrian's permission to retire.

[4] From the time of Augustus the old republican principle
of colleagueship had been applied to the command of the
praetorian guard and there were ordinarily two prefects with

contrary to the entreaties of all, the theatre which
Trajan had built in the Campus Martius. These
measures, unpopular enough in themselves, were still
more displeasing to the public because of his pre-
tence that all acts which he thought would be offensive had been secretly enjoined upon him by Trajan.
Unable to endure the power of Attianus, his prefect
and formerly his guardian, he was eager to murder
him. He was restrained, however, by the knowledge
that he already laboured under the odium of murdering four men of consular rank,[1] although, as a matter
of fact, he always attributed their execution to the
designs of Attianus. And as he could not appoint a
successor for Attianus except at the latter's request,
he contrived to make him request it,[2] and at once
transferred the power to Turbo; at the same time
Similis[3] also, the other prefect,[4] received a successor,
namely Septicius Clarus.[5]

After Hadrian had removed from the prefecture
the very men to whom he owed the imperial power, 119.
he departed for Campania, where he aided all the
towns of the region by gifts and benefactions[6] and
attached all the foremost men to his train of friends.
But when at Rome, he frequently attended the official
functions of the praetors and consuls, appeared at the

equal powers. The principle, however, had been disregarded
at times, e.g. in the case of Sejanus under Tiberius (Dio, lvii.
19). Under the later emperors there were sometimes three
prefects; cf. Com., vi. 12; Did. Jul., vii. 5; Zosimus, i. 11.

[5] C. Septicius Clarus was the friend of Suetonius, who
dedicated to him his Lives of the Caesars. He also encouraged Pliny to publish his letters; see Plin., Epist., i. 1.
On his retirement from the prefecture see c. xi. 3.

[6] The following are attested by inscriptions of the years
121-122: Antium, Caiatia, Surrentum, and the road from
Naples to Nuceria; see C.I.L., x. 6652, 4574, 676, 6939, 6940.

8 siliis sublevavit, conviviis suis semper adhibuit.   omnia
9 denique ad privati hominis modum fecit.   socrui suae
honores praecipuos impendit ludis gladiatoriis ceterisque officiis.

X. Post haec profectus in Gallias omnes civitates
2 variis [1] liberalitatibus sublevavit.   inde in Germaniam
transiit.   pacisque magis quam belli cupidus militem,
quasi bellum immineret, exercuit tolerantiae docu-
mentis eum imbuens, ipse quoque inter manipula
vitam militarem magistrans, cibis etiam castrensibus
in propatulo libenter utens, hoc est larido caseo et
posca, exemplo Scipionis Aemiliani et Metelli et
auctoris sui Traiani, multos praemiis nonnullos honoribus donans, ut ferre possent ea quae asperius iube-

---

[1] *ciuitates uariis* (*libertatibus*) Rob. Bonon., supported by
Rösinger and Damsté ; *casuariis* P ; *causarios* Peter.

---

[1] By a largess of spices (see c. xix. 5), and by issuing coins
bearing the legend *Divae Matidiae Socrui* with a representation of a temple-like building in which Matidia is seated between niches holding statuettes of Victory ; see Cohen, ii[2],
p. 152, No. 550.

[2] His first journey is described in c. x. 1—xi. 2 and xii. 1—
xiii. 3.   It covered the years 121-125.   Then followed a journey
to Africa and back in 128.   This was followed by his second
journey, which included the eastern part of the empire only,
in 128-134 ; see c. xiii. 6—xiv. 6 (the portion of the journey
which fell after 130 is not included).

[3] His visit was commemorated by coins with the legends
Adventui Galliae (Cohen, ii[2], p. 109 f., Nos. 31-35) and *Re-
stitutor Galliae* (Cohen, ii[2], p. 211, Nos. 1247-1257).

[4] His journey probably lay along the road from Lugdunum

banquets of his friends, visited them twice or thrice
a day when they were sick, even those who were
merely knights and freedmen, cheered them by words
of comfort, encouraged them by words of advice, and
very often invited them to his own banquets. In
short, everything that he did was in the manner of a
private citizen. On his mother-in-law he bestowed Dec., 119.
especial honour by means of gladiatorial games and
other ceremonies.[1]

X. After this he travelled[2] to the provinces of 121.
Gaul,[3] and came to the relief of all the communities
with various acts of generosity; and from there he
went over into Germany.[4] Though more desirous
of peace than of war, he kept the soldiers in training
just as if war were imminent, inspired them by
proofs of his own powers of endurance, actually led a
soldier's life among the maniples,[5] and, after the
example of Scipio Aemilianus,[6] Metellus, and his
own adoptive father Trajan, cheerfully ate out of
doors such camp-fare as bacon, cheese and vinegar.
And that the troops might submit more willingly to
the increased harshness of his orders, he bestowed
gifts on many and honours on a few. For he reestablished the discipline of the camp,[7] which since

(Lyon) to Augusta Treverorum (Trier), which was repaired in
121; see Brambach, *Corp. Inscr. Rhen.*, 1936. His visit to the
German armies was commemorated on coins with the legend
Exercitus Germanicus; see Cohen, ii[2], p. 156, Nos. 573 and 574.
    [5] Used here merely to denote the common soldiers; the
" maniple " consisted of two *centuriae*.
    [6] *i.e.* Scipio Africanus the younger, conqueror of Carthage.
Q. Caecilius Metellus Numidicus commanded in the war
against Jugurtha in 109-107 B.C. (cf. Sall. *Jug.*, 43-80).
    [7] Hadrian's reforms are also described in Dio, lxix. 9. They
are commemorated by coins with the legend *Disciplina
Aug(usti)*; see Cohen, ii[2], p. 151 f., Nos. 540-549.

3 bat; si quidem ipse post Caesarem Octavianum
labantem disciplinam incuria superiorum principum
retinuit. ordinatis et officiis et impendiis, numquam
passus aliquem a castris iniuste abesse, cum tribunos
4 non favor militum sed iustitia commendaret. exemplo
etiam virtutis suae ceteros adhortatus, cum etiam
vicena milia pedibus armatus ambularet, triclinia de
5 castris et porticus et cryptas et topia dirueret, vestem
humillimam frequenter acciperet, sine auro balteum
sumeret, sine gemmis fibula stringeret, capulo vix
6 eburneo spatham clauderet, aegros milites in hospitiis
suis videret, locum castris caperet, nulli vitem nisi
robusto et bonae famae daret, nec tribunum nisi plena
barba faceret aut eius aetatis quae prudentia et annis
7 tribunatus robor impleret, nec pateretur quicquam tribunum a milite accipere, delicata omnia undique
summoveret, arma postremo eorum supellectilemque
8 corrigeret. de militum etiam aetatibus iudicabat, ne
quis aut minor quam virtus posceret, aut maior quam
pateretur humanitas, in castris contra morem veterem
versaretur, agebatque, ut sibi semper noti essent, et
XI. eorum numerus sciretur. laborabat praeterea, ut
condita militaria diligenter agnosceret, reditus quoque
provinciales sollerter explorans, ut, si [1] alicubi quippiam deesset, expleret. ante omnes tamen enite-
batur, ne quid otiosum vel emeret aliquando vel
pasceret.

<hr />

[1] *si* omitted by P[1], added by P corr.

the time of Octavian had been growing slack through the laxity of his predecessors. He regulated, too, both the duties and the expenses of the soldiers, and now no one could get a leave of absence from camp by unfair means, for it was not popularity with the troops but just deserts that recommended a man for appointment as tribune. He incited others by the example of his own soldiery spirit; he would walk as much as twenty miles fully armed; he cleared the camp of banqueting-rooms, porticoes, grottos, and bowers, generally wore the commonest clothing, would have no gold ornaments on his sword-belt or jewels on the clasp, would scarcely consent to have his sword furnished with an ivory hilt, visited the sick soldiers in their quarters, selected the sites for camps, conferred the centurion's wand on those only who were hardy and of good repute, appointed as tribunes only men with full beards or of an age to give to the authority of the tribuneship the full measure of prudence and maturity, permitted no tribune to accept a present from a soldier, banished luxuries on every hand, and, lastly, improved the soldiers' arms and equipment. Furthermore, with regard to length of military service he issued an order that no one should violate ancient usage by being in the service at an earlier age than his strength warranted, or at a more advanced one than common humanity permitted. He made it a point to be acquainted with the soldiers and to know their numbers. XI. Besides this, he strove to have an accurate knowledge of the military stores, and the receipts from the provinces he examined with care in order to make good any deficit that might occur in any particular instance. But more than any other emperor he made it a point not to purchase or maintain anything that was not serviceable.

2 Ergo conversis regio[1] more militibus Britanniam
petiit, in qua multa correxit murumque per octoginta
milia passuum primus duxit, qui barbaros Romanosque
divideret.
3 Septicio Claro praefecto praetorii et Suetonio
Tranquillo epistularum magistro multisque aliis, quod
apud Sabinam uxorem iniussu eius[2] familiarius se
tunc egerant quam reverentia domus aulicae postula-
bat, successores dedit, uxorem etiam ut morosam et
asperam dimissurus, ut ipse dicebat, si privatus fuisset.
4 et erat curiosus non solum domus suae sed etiam
amicorum, ita ut per frumentarios occulta omnia
exploraret, nec adverterent amici sciri ab imperatore
suam vitam, priusquam ipse hoc imperator ostenderet.
5 unde non iniucundum est rem inserere, ex qua con-
6 stet eum de amicis multa didicisse. nam cum ad
quendam scripsisset uxor sua, quod voluptatibus

---

[1] *egregio* Novak ; *rigido* Frankfurter ; *recto* Baehrens.
[2] *iniussu eius* P corr. (*uniussu* P[1]), defended by Bitschofsky
(meaning " without his consent ") ; *in usu eius* Peter[2], following Petschenig.

---

[1] From Germany he visited the provinces of Raetia and
Noricum, and then returned to the lower Rhine, where his
presence is commemorated in the name Forum Hadriani
(near Leyden). From Holland he crossed to Britain. The
legend *Adventui Aug. Britanniae* appears on coins ; see
Cohen, ii[2], p. 109, No. 28.
[2] This fortification extended from Wallsend at the mouth
of the Tyne to Bowness on the Firth of Solway, a distance
of 73½ English miles. Its remains show that it consisted of
two lines of embankment with a moat between them, and a
stone wall running parallel on the north. In the space between the embankment and the wall were small strongholds
about a mile apart with an occasional larger stronghold, all

And so, having reformed the army quite in the manner of a monarch, he set out for Britain,[1] and there he corrected many abuses and was the first to construct a wall,[2] eighty miles in length, which was to separate the barbarians from the Romans.

He removed from office Septicius Clarus,[3] the prefect of the guard, and Suetonius Tranquillus,[4] the imperial secretary, and many others besides, because without his consent they had been conducting themselves toward his wife, Sabina, in a more informal fashion than the etiquette of the court demanded. And, as he was himself wont to say, he would have sent away his wife too, on the ground of ill-temper and irritability, had he been merely a private citizen. Moreover, his vigilance was not confined to his own household but extended to those of his friends, and by means of his private agents[5] he even pried into all their secrets, and so skilfully that they were never aware that the Emperor was acquainted with their private lives until he revealed it himself. In this connection, the insertion of an incident will not be unwelcome, showing that he found out much about his friends. The wife of a certain man wrote to her husband, complaining that he was so preoccupied by

122.

connected by a military road; see inscriptions dating from Hadrian's time, *C.I.L.*, vii. 660 f., 835.

[3] See c. ix. 5.

[4] The author of the *de Vita Caesarum* and the *de Viris Illustribus*.

[5] The *frumentarii*, at first petty-officers connected with the commissary of the army, became, probably under Trajan, couriers charged with the conveyance of military dispatches; see *Max.-Balb.*, x. 3; Victor, *Caes.*, xiii. 5, 6. Many of them were then attached to the imperial service as a sort of secret police; see also *Macr.*, xii. 4 and *Claud.*, xvii. 1.

detentus et lavacris ad se redire nollet, atque hoc
Hadrianus per frumentarios cognovisset, petente illo
commeatum Hadrianus ei lavacra et voluptates ex-
probravit. cui ille : "num et tibi uxor mea, quod et
7 mihi, scripsit ? " et hoc quidem vitiosissimum putant
atque huic adiungunt quae de adultorum amore ac
nuptarum adulteriis, quibus Hadrianus laborasse
dicitur, adserunt, iungentes quod ne amicis quidem
servaverit fidem.

XII. Compositis in Britannia rebus transgressus in
Galliam Alexandrina seditione turbatus, quae nata
est ob Apidem, qui, cum repertus esset post multos
annos, turbas inter populos creavit, apud quem
2 deberet locari, omnibus studiose certantibus. per
idem tempus in honorem Plotinae basilicam apud
3 Nemausum opere mirabili exstruxit. post haec
Hispanias petiit et Tarracone hiemavit, ubi sumptu
4 suo aedem Augusti restituit. omnibus Hispanis
Tarraconem in conventum vocatis dilectumque

---

¹ The sacred bullock of the Egyptians, begotten, according
to their belief, by a ray of light from heaven (Herodotus, iii.
28). He was recognized by certain markings, including representations of the sun and the moon, and his appearance was
the occasion of great rejoicing. It was apparently customary
at this period to keep the young Apis, for a time at least, in the
locality in which he appeared (Aelian, *Nat. An.*, xi. 10). The
riot was checked by a severe letter from Hadrian (Dio, lxix.
8, 1, frag. from Petr. Patr. exc. Vat. 108).
² According to Dio, lxix. 10, 3, the building was erected in

they refused to submit to a levy, the Italian settlers [1]
jestingly, to use the very words of Marius Maximus,
and the others very vigorously, he took measures
characterized by skill and discretion.   At this same
time he incurred grave danger and won great glory ;
for while he was walking about in a garden at Tarra-
gona one of the slaves of the household rushed at him
madly with a sword.   But he merely laid hold on
the man, and when the servants ran to the rescue
handed him over to them.   Afterwards, when it was
found that the man was mad, he turned him over to
the physicians for treatment, and all this time showed
not the slightest sign of alarm.

During this period and on many other occasions
also, in many regions where the barbarians are held
back not by rivers but by artificial barriers, Hadrian
shut them off by means of high stakes planted deep
in the ground and fastened together in the manner
of a palisade.[2] He appointed a king for the Germans,
suppressed revolts among the Moors,[3] and won from
the senate the usual ceremonies of thanksgiving.
The war with the Parthians had not at that time advanced beyond the preparatory stage, and Hadrian
checked it by a personal conference.[4]

XIII. After this Hadrian travelled by way of Asia
and the islands to Greece,[5] and, following the 123-125.

[4] The process of abbreviation has obscured the narrative
by omitting the description of Hadrian's journey from Spain
to Syria in the spring of 123.   This journey was almost certainly made by sea from Spain to Antioch.   The danger of
the Parthian war seems to have been connected with the
overthrow of the Romanized pretender, Parthamaspates (see
note to c. v. 4), and the restoration of the legitimate dynasty
in the person of Osrhoes (cf. c. xiii. 8).
[5] His route lay from the Euphrates across Asia Minor to
Ancyra in Galatia (cf. *I.G.R.*, iii. 209) and thence to Bithynia,

navigavit et Eleusinia sacra exemplo Herculis Philippique suscepit, multa in Athenienses contulit et pro
2 agonotheta resedit. et in Achaia quidem etiam illud observatum ferunt quod, cum in sacris multi cultros haberent, cum Hadriano nullus armatus ingressus
3 est. post in Siciliam navigavit, in qua Aetnam montem conscendit, ut solis ortum videret arcus
4 specie, ut dicitur, varium. inde Romam venit atque ex ea in Africam transiit ac multum beneficiorum
5 provinciis Africanis adtribuit. nec quisquam fere principum tantum terrarum tam [1] celeriter peragravit.
6 Denique cum post Africam Romam redisset, statim

---

[1] *tam* Peter; *tantum* P, Petschenig.

---

where his arrival is commemorated on coins inscribed *Adventui Aug(usti) Bithyniae* (Cohen, ii², p. 109, Nos. 26 and 27) and *Restitutori Bithyniae* (*id.*, p. 210 f., Nos. 1238-1246). He then travelled through Mysia, founding the town of Hadrianotherae (see c. xx. 13), to Ilion and thence southward to Ephesus. From here he sailed to Rhodes (see an inscription from Ephesus, Dittenberger, *Sylloge²*, No. 388), northwest through the Aegean to Samothrace and Thrace (see an inscription from Callipolis of 123-124, *C.I.G.*, 2013). Thence he visited the provinces of Moesia and Dacia (see Weber, p. 150 f.), and travelled southward through Macedonia and Thessaly to Athens, where he arrived probably in September, 124.

[1] Father of Alexander the Great.

[2] Admitted to the lower grade of μύστης. On his second visit to Athens in 128-129 he was initiated into the higher grade, of ἐπόπτης; see Dio, lxix. 11. An epigram inscribed on the base of a statue erected in honour of the priestess who initiated him is extant (*I.G.*, iii. 900 = Kaibel, *Epigr. Gr.*, 864).

[3] The Dionysia, in March, 125. Previous to this he had made a journey through the Peloponnesus, visiting the principal cities; dedications to him are recorded in extant inscriptions, and various benefactions of his are mentioned by Pausanias.

example of Hercules and Philip,[1] had himself initiated into the Eleusinian mysteries.[2] He bestowed
many favours on the Athenians and sat as president
of the public games.[3] And during this stay in
Greece care was taken, they say, that when Hadrian
was present, none should come to a sacrifice armed,
whereas, as a rule, many carried knives. Afterwards
he sailed to Sicily,[4] and there he climbed Mount
Aetna to see the sunrise, which is many-hued, they
say, like the rainbow. Thence he returned to Rome,[5]
and [6] from there he crossed over to Africa,[7] where he 128.
showed many acts of kindness to the provinces.
Hardly any emperor ever travelled with such speed
over so much territory.

Finally, after his return to Rome from Africa,
he immediately set out for the East, journeying by

[4] Travelling by way of the Corinthian Gulf, he visited
Delphi (cf. *C.I.G.*, 1713), Actium, and Dyrrhachium, and
sailed thence to Sicily. His arrival was commemorated by
coins inscribed *Adventui Aug(usti) Siciliae* (Cohen, ii², p. 112,
No. 75), and *Restitutori Siciliae* (*id.*, ii², p. 214, Nos. 1292-
1295).

[5] In the summer of 125. Coins commemorating his return
bear the legend *Adventui Aug(usti) Italiae* (Cohen, ii², p. 110,
Nos. 42-50).

[6] Here a period of over three years is omitted, in which
Hadrian built many public buildings in the towns of Italy.
Early in 128 he finally accepted the title of *Pater Patriae*
(cf. note to c. vi. 4); see Eckhel, *D.N.*, vi. 515 f.

[7] See the coins inscribed *Adventui Aug(usti) Africae* and
Restitutori Africae (Cohen, ii², p. 107 f., Nos. 8-15, and p. 209 f.,
Nos. 1221-1232), and *Adventui Aug(usti) Mauretaniae* (Cohen,
ii², p. 111, Nos. 63-71). His stay in Africa lasted about four
months in the spring and early summer of 128. On the
Kalends of July was delivered his famous *allocutio* or address
to the troops at Lambaesis, fragments of which are now in
the Louvre.

ad orientem profectus per Athenas iter fecit atque
opera, quae apud Athenienses coeperat, dedicavit, ut
Iovis Olympii aedem et aram sibi, eodemque modo
per Asiam iter faciens templa sui nominis consecravit.
7 deinde a Cappadocibus servitia castris profutura sus-
8 cepit. toparchas et reges ad amicitiam invitavit,
invitato etiam Osdroe rege Parthorum remissaque illi
filia, quam Traianus ceperat, ac promissa sella, quae
9 itidem capta fuerat. cumque ad eum quidam reges
venissent, ita cum his egit ut eos paeniteret, qui
venire noluerunt, causa speciatim Pharasmanis qui
10 eius invitationem superbe neglexerit. et circumiens
quidem provincias procuratores et praesides pro factis
supplicio adfecit, ita severe ut accusatores per se
XIV. crederetur immittere. Antiochenses inter haec ita
odio habuit ut Syriam a Phoenice separare voluerit,
ne tot civitatum metropolis Antiochia diceretur.

[1] His stay in Athens was from September 128 to March 129.
[2] The Olympieion, on the southern edge of the city near
the Ilissos. After the dedication of this building in 131-132,
Hadrian accepted the title 'Ολύμπιος and received divine
honours in the temple (Dio, lxix. 16, 1) ; hence the *ara* mentioned here.
[3] They were later called simply " Hadrian's temples," and
it was asserted that he had intended to consecrate them to
Christ; see *Alex.*, xliii. 6. They were, in fact, temples dedicated to the cult of the emperors, including Hadrian himself,
who was worshipped in the cities of Asia Minor as well as in
the Olympieion at Athens. In inscriptions he has the cult-
name Olympios or Zeus Olympios.
[4] The camp of a Cappadocian legion (12th., Fulminata)
was at Melitene, near the upper Euphrates. Hadrian probably
travelled thither from Antioch. His visit to the camp was
commemorated by coins inscribed *Exercitus Cappadocicus*
(Cohen, ii², p. 153, No. 553).
[5] More correctly Osrhoes ; see also note to c. xii. 8.
[6] Antoninus Pius refused to keep this promise; see *Pius*, ix. 7.

way of Athens.[1] Here he dedicated the public works which he had begun in the city of the Athenians, such as the temple to Olympian Jupiter[2] and an altar to himself; and in the same way, while travelling through Asia, he consecrated the temples called by his name.[3] Next, he received slaves from the Cappadocians for service in the camps.[4] To petty rulers and kings he made offers of friendship, and even to Osdroes,[5] king of the Parthians. To him he also restored his daughter, who had been captured by Trajan, and promised to return the throne captured at the same time.[6] And when some of the kings came to him, he treated them in such a way that those who had refused to come regretted it. He took this course especially on account of Pharasmanes,[7] who had haughtily scorned his invitation. Furthermore, as he went about the provinces he punished procurators and governors as their actions demanded, and indeed with such severity that it was believed that he incited those who brought the accusations. XIV. In the course of these travels he conceived such a hatred for the people of Antioch that he wished to separate Syria from Phoenicia, in order that Antioch might not be called the chief city of so many communities.[8] At this time also the

---

[7] King of the Hiberi, who inhabited part of the district which is now Trans-Caucasia. On the gifts exchanged by him and Hadrian see c. xvii. 11-12 and xxi. 13.

[8] The statement that Hadrian hated Antioch seems to be contradicted by the fact that he built many public buildings there; see Malalas, p. 278 B. It may be a deduction from the fact that he did raise three other cities of Syria, Tyre, Damascus and Samosata, to the rank of μητρόπολις. The actual division of Syria into two provinces, Syria Coele and Syria Phoenice, took place under Severus in 194. The object of the division was to lessen the power of the governor of so important a province.

2 moverunt ea tempestate et Iudaei bellum, quod
3 vetabantur mutilare genitalia. sed in monte Casio,
cum videndi solis ortus gratia nocte ascendisset,
imbre orto fulmen decidens hostiam et victimarium
4 sacrificanti adflavit. peragrata Arabia Pelusium
venit et Pompeii tumulum magnificentius exstruxit.
5 Antinoum suum, dum per Nilum navigat, perdidit,
6 quem muliebriter flevit. de quo varia fama est, aliis
eum devotum pro Hadriano adserentibus, aliis quod
et forma eius ostentat et nimia voluptas Hadriani.
7 et Graeci quidem volente Hadriano eum conse-
cr.averunt, oracula per eum dari adserentes, quae
Hadrianus ipse composuisse iactatur.

---

[1] According to Dio, lxix. 12-14, probably a more correct
account, the outbreak of the war was due to the anger of the
Jews at the dedication of a temple to Jupiter Capitolinus on
the site of the Temple of Jehovah. This was done in connection with the "founding" of the new colony in 130; accordingly, this sentence is not in chronological order. The
war was actually begun after Hadrian's departure from
Egypt, and finally necessitated his return. The outbreak
was quelled, after much bloodshed, in 134.

[2] Probably the mountain of this name at the mouth of the
river Orontes. This incident is also narrated as having
happened to Hadrian at Antioch immediately after he became emperor; see Dio, lxix. 2, 1.

[3] See the coins inscribed *Adventui Aug(usti) Arabiae*
(Cohen, ii², p. 108 f., Nos. 20-23). He seems to have travelled
thither by way of Palmyra and Damascus. His visit to
Gerasa (mod. Djerash), in the north-western part of the province of Arabia, is attested by an inscription of 130 (*I.G.R.*,
iii. 1347). From here he went probably by way of Phila-
delphia (mod., 'Ammân) to Jerusalem, which he "founded"
as the *Colonia Aelia Capitolina*.

[4] According to Dio, lxix. 11, 1, Hadrian offered a sacrifice
to the *manes* of Pompey and in a line of poetry expressed his
sorrow at the meanness of the tomb.

[5] He also visited Alexandria, and his arrival was commemorated by coins of the city struck in 130; see also the

Jews began war, because they were forbidden to practise circumcision.[1]   As he was sacrificing on Mount Casius,[2] which he had ascended by night in order to see the sunrise, a storm arose, and a flash of lightning descended and struck both the victim and the attendant.   He then travelled through Arabia[3] 130. and finally came to Pelusium,[4] where he rebuilt Pompey's tomb on a more magnificent scale.[5]   During a journey on the Nile he lost Antinous,[6] his favourite, and for this youth he wept like a woman.   Concerning this incident there are varying rumours[7]; for some claim that he had devoted himself to death for Hadrian, and others—what both his beauty and Hadrian's sensuality suggest. But however this may be, the Greeks deified him at Hadrian's request, and declared that oracles were given through his agency, but these, it is commonly asserted, were composed by Hadrian himself.[8]

Roman coins with the legend *Adventui Aug(usti) Alexandriae* (Cohen, ii², p. 108, Nos. 15-18).

[6] This beautiful youth was a native of Bithynium in Bithynia; see Dio, lxix. 11.   He died near Besa, near the southern end of the Heptanomis. Here Hadrian founded a new city, called Antinoe or Antinoopolis, and consecrated a shrine to him.

[7] According to Dio, lxix. 11, Hadrian claimed in his autobiography (see note to c. i. 1) that Antinous was drowned in the Nile; he then adds that the true cause of his death was his voluntary sacrifice of himself, apparently in consequence of some prophecy, in order to save the Emperor's life.

[8] Here the narrative of Hadrian's journey breaks off abruptly.   After a visit to Thebes, where he and Sabina heard "the singing Memnon" (*I.G.R.*, i. 1186 and 1187), he returned to Alexandria, and thence travelled, apparently by ship (Cat. of Coins in the Brit. Mus., *Alex.*, p. 101, No. 871), to Syria and Asia Minor. During a stay at Athens he dedicated the Olympieion (cf. note to c. xiii. 6) in 131-132; see Dio, lxix. 16, 1.   He was then called to Judaea on account of the long duration of the Jewish revolt (see note to c. xiv. 2). He finally returned to Rome early in 134.

8 Fuit enim poematum et litterarum nimium studio-
sissimus. arithmeticae geometriae picturae peritis-
9 simus. iam psallendi et cantandi scientiam prae se
ferebat. in voluptatibus nimius; nam et de suis
dilectis multa versibus composuit. amatoria carmina
10 scripsit.[1] idem armorum peritissimus et rei militaris
11 scientissimus, gladiatoria quoque arma tractavit. idem
severus comis, gravis lascivus, cunctator festinans,[2]
tenax liberalis, simulator simplex,[3] saevus clemens, et
semper in omnibus varius.

XV. Amicos ditavit et quidem non petentes, cum
2 petentibus nihil negaret. idem tamen facile de
amicis, quidquid insusurrabatur, audivit atque ideo
prope cunctos vel amicissimos vel eos, quos summis
honoribus evexit, postea ut hostium loco habuit, ut
3 Attianum et Nepotem et Septicium Clarum. nam
Eudaemonem prius conscium imperii ad egestatem
4 perduxit, Polaenum et Marcellum ad mortem volun-
5 tariam coegit, Heliodorum famosissimis litteris laces-
6 sivit, Titianum ut conscium tyrannidis et argui passus
7 est et proscribi, Ummidium Quadratum et Catilium

---

[1] Probably merely a gloss. [2] So Novak, deleting as a
gloss for *comis laetus*, which follows *seuerus* in P, and adding
festinans to offset *cunctator* ; Peter divides: *seuerus laetus,
comis grauis, lasciuus cunctator.* [3] *simplex*, omitted in P,
is supplied by Peter[2], following Reimarus ad Dio LXIX, 5,
p. 652 ; *uerus* Peter[1], Novak.

---

[1] But see c. viii. 7, and ix. 4. [2] See c. iv. 2, and xxiii. 4.
[3] Probably C. Publicius Marcellus, governor of Syria about
132.
[4] Apparently the philosopher mentioned in c. xvi. 10, and

In poetry and in letters Hadrian was greatly
interested. In arithmetic, geometry, and painting
he was very expert. Of his knowledge of flute-play-
ing and singing he even boasted openly. He ran to
excess in the gratification of his desires, and wrote
much verse about the subjects of his passion. He
composed love-poems too. He was also a connoisseur
of arms, had a thorough knowledge of warfare, and
knew how to use gladiatorial weapons. He was, in
the same person, austere and genial, dignified and
playful, dilatory and quick to act, niggardly and
generous, deceitful and straightforward, cruel and
merciful, and always in all things changeable.

XV. His friends he enriched greatly, even though
they did not ask it, while to those who did ask, he
refused nothing. And yet he was always ready to
listen to whispers about his friends, and in the end
he treated almost all of them as enemies, even the
closest and even those whom he had raised to the
highest of honours, such as Attianus [1] and Nepos [2]
and Septicius Clarus. Eudaemon, for example, who
had been his accomplice in obtaining the imperial
power, he reduced to poverty; Polaenus and Marcellus [3] he drove to suicide; Heliodorus [4] he assailed
in a most slanderous pamphlet; Titianus [5] he allowed
to be accused as an accomplice in an attempt to seize
the empire and even to be outlawed; Ummidius Quadratus,[6] Catilius Severus, and Turbo he persecuted

probably to be identified with Avidius Heliodorus, the father
of Avidius Cassius; see *Av. Cass.*, i. 1.

[5] Probably either T. Atilius Rufus Titianus, consul in 127,
or Atilius Titianus, who was accused *affectati imperii* under
Pius and condemned; see *Pius*, vii. 3.

[6] Mentioned as a *iuvenis egregiae indolis* by Pliny the younger
(*Epist.*, vi. 11; vii. 24). He was consul with Hadrian in 118.

8 Severum et Turbonem graviter insecutus est, Servianum sororis virum nonagesimum iam annum
9 agentem, ne sibi superviveret, mori coegit; libertos
10 denique et nonnullos milites insecutus est. et quamvis esset oratione et versu promptissimus et in omnibus artibus peritissimus, tamen professores omnium artium semper ut doctior risit contempsit
11 obtrivit. cum his ipsis professoribus et philosophis libris vel carminibus invicem editis saepe certavit.
12 et Favorinus quidem, cum verbum eius quondam ab Hadriano reprehensum esset, atque ille cessisset, arguentibus amicis, quod male cederet Hadriano de verbo quod idonei auctores usurpassent, risum
13 iucundissimum movit. ait enim : "Non recte suadetis, familiares, qui non patimini me illum doctiorem omnibus credere, qui habet triginta legiones".

XVI. Famae celebris Hadrianus tam cupidus fuit ut libros vitae suae scriptos a se libertis suis litteratis dederit, iubens ut eos suis nominibus publicarent. nam et Phlegontis libri Hadriani esse dicuntur.
2 Catachannas libros obscurissimos Antimachum imi-
3 tando scripsit. Floro poetae scribenti ad se:

---

[1] A well-known rhetorician, a native of Arelate (Arles) in Gaul. He was a friend of Plutarch and of Aulus Gellius, whose *Noctes Atticae* are full of allusions to him.

[2] On the autobiography see note to c. i. 1. The ruse described in this passage was not successful, for the true authorship of the autobiography was known to the writer of the present biography (see c. i. 1; iii. 3 and 5; vii. 2), and also to Cassius Dio (lxix. 11, 2).

[3] Antimachus of Colophon about 400 B.C.; the author of

vigorously; and in order to prevent Servianus, his brother-in-law, from surviving him, he compelled him to commit suicide, although the man was then in his ninetieth year. And he even took vengeance on freedmen and sometimes on soldiers. And although he was very deft at prose and at verse and very accomplished in all the arts, yet he used to subject the teachers of these arts, as though more learned than they, to ridicule, scorn, and humiliation. With these very professors and philosophers he often debated by means of pamphlets or poems issued by both sides in turn. And once Favorinus,[1] when he had yielded to Hadrian's criticism of a word which he had used, raised a merry laugh among his friends. For when they reproached him for having done wrong in yielding to Hadrian in the matter of a word used by reputable authors, he replied: "You are urging a wrong course, my friends, when you do not suffer me to regard as the most learned of men the one who has thirty legions".

XVI. So desirous of a wide-spread reputation was Hadrian that he even wrote his own biography; this he gave to his educated freedmen, with instructions to publish it under their own names.[2] For indeed, Phlegon's writings, it is said, are Hadrian's in reality. He wrote Catachannae, a very obscure work in imitation of Antimachus.[3] And when the poet Florus [4] wrote to him:

an epic, the *Thebais*, and of an elegiac poem, on the death of his wife Lyde. In general, his style was considered obscure, and his poems were full of learned allusions. According to Dio, lxix. 4, Hadrian preferred him to Homer. Nothing is known of the *Catachannae*.

[4] Probably the poet Annius Florus, some of whose verse is preserved in the Codex Salmasianus, a collection of miscellaneous poetical selections; see Riese, *Anthologia Latina*, i., Nos. 87 and 245-252.

HADRIAN

> Ego nolo Caesar esse,
> ambulare per Britannos,
> latitare per . . .[1]
> Scythicas pati pruinas,

4 rescripsit :

> Ego nolo Florus esse,
> ambulare per tabernas,
> latitare per popinas,
> culices pati rotundos.

5 amavit praeterea genus vetustum dicendi. contro-
6 versias declamavit. Ciceroni Catonem, Vergilio
Ennium, Sallustio Caelium praetulit eademque iacta-
7 tione de Homero ac Platone iudicavit. mathesin sic
scire sibi visus est ut vero[2] kalendis Ianuariis scripserit, quid ei toto anno posset evenire, ita ut eo anno
quo periit usque ad illam horam qua est mortuus
scripserit quid acturus esset.

8 Sed quamvis esset in reprehendendis musicis
tragicis comicis grammaticis rhetoribus facilis, tamen
omnes professores et honoravit et divites fecit, licet
9 eos quaestionibus semper agitaverit. et cum ipse
auctor esset, ut multi ab eo tristes recederent,
dicebat se graviter ferre, si quem tristem videret.
10 in summa familiaritate Epictetum et Heliodorum
philosophos et, ne nominatim de omnibus dicam,
grammaticos rhetores musicos geometras pictores
astrologos habuit, prae ceteris, ut multi adserunt,

---

[1] Omitted in P, but to be supplied from § 4 (where Spengel
would delete *latitare per popinas*, Abh. d. bayer. Akad. hist.
phil. Kl. IX, p. 317).   [2] *uero* Meursius ; *sero* P.

---

[1] L. Caelius Antipater, an historian living in the second
century B.C., who wrote a history of the Second Punic War.
[2] According to *Ael.*, iii. 9, this statement is made on the
authority of Marius Maximus.

"I don't want to be a Cæsar,
　　Stroll about among the Britons,
　　Lurk about among the . . . .
　　And endure the Scythian winters,"
he wrote back
　　"I don't want to be a Florus,
　　Stroll about among the taverns,
　　Lurk about among the cook-shops,
　　And endure the round fat insects."

Furthermore, he loved the archaic style of writing, and he used to take part in debates. He preferred Cato to Cicero, Ennius to Vergil, Caelius [1] to Sallust; and with the same self-assurance he expressed opinions about Homer and Plato. In astrology he considered himself so proficient that on the Kalends of January he would actually write down all that might happen to him in the whole ensuing year, and in the year in which he died, indeed, he wrote down everything that he was going to do, down to the very hour of his death. [2]

However ready Hadrian might have been to criticize musicians, tragedians, comedians, grammarians, and rhetoricians, he nevertheless bestowed both honours and riches upon all who professed these arts, though he always tormented them with his questions. And although he was himself responsible for the fact that many of them left his presence with their feelings hurt, to see anyone with hurt feelings, he used to say, he could hardly endure. He treated with the greatest friendship the philosophers Epictetus [3] and Heliodorus, and various grammarians, rhetoricians, musicians, geometricians—not to mention all by name—painters and astrologers; and among

[3] The well-known Stoic philosopher.

11 eminente Favorino. doctores, qui professioni suae
inhabiles videbantur, ditatos honoratosque a profes-
sione dimisit.

XVII. Quos in privata vita inimicos habuit, imperator tantum neglexit, ita ut uni, quem capitalem ha-
2 buerat, factus imperator diceret "Evasisti". iis quos
ad militiam ipse per se vocavit equos mulos vestes
3 sumptus et omnem ornatum semper exhibuit. satur-
nalicia et sigillaricia frequenter amicis inopinantibus
misit et ipse ab his libenter accepit et alia invicem
4 dedit. ad deprehendendas obsonatorum fraudes,
cum plurimis sigmatibus pasceret, fercula de aliis
5 mensis etiam ultimis sibi iussit adponi.[1] omnes
reges muneribus suis vicit. publice frequenter et
6 cum omnibus lavit. ex quo ille iocus balnearis innotuit : nam cum quodam tempore veteranum
quendam notum sibi in militia dorsum et ceteram
partem corporis vidisset adterere parieti,[2] percontatus,
cur se marmoribus destringendum daret, ubi audivit
hoc idcirco fieri quod servum non haberet, et servis
7 eum donavit et sumptibus. verum alia die cum plures
senes ad provocandam liberalitatem principis parieti
se adtererent, evocari eos iussit et alium ab alio
8 invicem defricari. fuit et plebis iactantissimus
amator. peregrinationis ita cupidus ut omnia quae
legerat de locis orbis terrarum praesens vellet addis-

---

[1] *sibi iussit adponi* Mommsen ; *quibusque* (quiq P[a]) *adponi*
P[1]; *quibusque iussit adponi* P corr. ; *quibusque adponit* Peter.
[2] *parieti* inserted here by Kellerbauer and accepted by Peter[2];
omitted in P.

---

[1] The name Sigillaria was given to the last days of the
Saturnalia, in which it was customary to send as gifts little
figures (*sigilla*) of pottery or pastry.

them Favorinus, many claim, was conspicuous above all the rest. Teachers who seemed unfit for their profession he presented with riches and honours and then dismissed from the practice of their profession.

XVII. Many whom he had regarded as enemies when a private citizen, when emperor he merely ignored; for example, on becoming emperor, he said to one man whom he had regarded as a mortal foe, " You have escaped ". When he himself called any to military service, he always supplied them with horses, mules, clothing, cost of maintenance, and indeed their whole equipment. At the Saturnalia and Sigillaria [1] he often surprised his friends with presents, and he gladly received gifts from them and again gave others in return. In order to detect dishonesty in his caterers, when he gave banquets with several tables he gave orders that platters from the other tables, even the lowest, should be set before himself. He surpassed all monarchs in his gifts. He often bathed in the public baths, even with the common crowd. And a jest of his made in the bath became famous. For on a certain occasion, seeing a veteran, whom he had known in the service, rubbing his back and the rest of his body against the wall, he asked him why he had the marble rub him, and when the man replied that it was because he did not own a slave, he presented him with some slaves and the cost of their maintenance. But another time, when he saw a number of old men rubbing themselves against the wall for the purpose of arousing the generosity of the Emperor, he ordered them to be called out and then to rub one another in turn. His love for the common people he loudly expressed. So fond was he of travel, that he wished to inform himself in

9 cere.   frigora et tempestates ita patienter tulit ut
10 numquam caput tegeret.[1]   regibus multis plurimum
detulit, a plerisque vero etiam pacem redemit, a
11 nonnullis contemptus est ; multis ingentia dedit
munera, sed nulli maiora quam Hiberorum, cui et
elephantum et quinquagenariam cohortem post
12 magnifica dedit dona.   cum a Pharasmane ipse quoque ingentia dona[2] accepisset atque inter haec
auratas quoque chlamydes, trecentos noxios cum
auratis chlamydibus in arenam misit ad eius munera
deridenda.

XVIII. Cum iudicaret, in consilio habuit non amicos
suos aut comites solum sed iuris consultos et praecipue Iuventium[3] Celsum, Salvium Iulianum, Neratium Priscum aliosque, quos tamen senatus omnis
2 probasset.   constituit inter cetera, ut in nulla civitate
domus aliqua[4] transferendae ad aliam urbem ullius[5]
3 materiae causa dirueretur.   liberis proscriptorum

---

[1] *tegeret* Exc. Cus. and P corr. ; *texeret* P[1] ; *texerit* Peter.
[2] *ingentia munia dona* P ; *munia* deleted by Petrarch ;
munia dono Peter.   [3] *Iuuentium* Cas. ; *iulium* P.   [4] *aliqua . . . dirueretur* Petschenig ; *alique . . . dirueretur* P[1] ;
diruerentur P corr.   [5] *ullius* P corr. (so Peter, but conj.
illius) ; *ullis* P[1] ; *utilis* Cornelissen ; *uilis* Mommsen.

---

[1] Especially in connection with his conference with the
minor potentates of the Orient ; see c. xiii. 8.
[2] Pharasmanes ; see also c. xiii. 9 and note.
[3] See c. viii. 9 and note.
[4] His *Digesta* in thirty-nine books were used in the compilation of the *Digest* of Justinian.
[5] Famous as the compiler of the *Edictum Perpetuum*, a
systematized collection of praetors' *edicta*, or statements of

person about all that he had read concerning all parts of the world. Cold and bad weather he could bear with such endurance that he never covered his head. He showed a multitude of favours to many kings,[1] but from a number he even purchased peace, and by some he was treated with scorn; to many he gave huge gifts, but none greater than to the king of the Hiberi,[2] for to him he gave an elephant and a band of fifty men, in addition to magnificent presents. And having himself received huge gifts from Pharasmanes, including some cloaks embroidered with gold, he sent into the arena three hundred condemned criminals dressed in gold-embroidered cloaks for the purpose of ridiculing the gifts of the king.

XVIII. When he tried cases, he had in his council[3] not only his friends and the members of his staff, but also jurists, in particular Juventius Celsus,[4] Salvius Julianus,[5] Neratius Priscus,[6] and others, only those, however, whom the senate had in every instance approved. Among other decisions he ruled that in no community should any house be demolished for the purpose of transporting any building-materials to another city.[7] To the child of an outlawed person he

the principles to be used in administering justice; see Eutrop., viii. 17, and *Codex Iust.*, vi. 61, 5. His *Digesta* in ninety books are cited in Justinian's *Digest*. See also *Sev.*, xvii. 5.

[6] See note to c. iv. 8.

[7] This prohibition is an application of the general principle laid down in a *senatus consultum* of 44 (Bruns[6], No. 51), that no building in Italy shall be demolished with a view to making profit out of the demolition. The destruction of buildings for any purpose except their immediate reconstruction, unless permission has been given by the *curia*, is prohibited in the various laws of the *coloniae* and *municipia*; see *Lex Col. Genetivae*, c. 75, *Lex Mun. Malac.*, c. 62, and *Lex Mun. Tarent.*, c. 4.

4duodecimas bonorum concessit. maiestatis crimina
5non admisit. ignotorum hereditates repudiavit nec
6notorum accepit, si filios haberent. de thesauris ita
cavit ut, si¹ quis in suo repperisset, ipse potiretur,
si quis in alieno, dimidium domino daret, si quis in
7publico, cum fisco aequabiliter partiretur. servos a
dominis occidi vetuit eosque iussit damnari per
8iudices, si digni essent. lenoni et lanistae servum
9vel ancillam vendi vetuit causa non praestita. de-
coctores bonorum suorum, si suae auctoritatis essent,
catomidiari in amphitheatro et dimitti iussit. ergastula
10servorum et liberorum tulit. lavacra pro sexibus
11separavit. si dominus in domo interemptus esset,
non de omnibus servis quaestionem haberi sed de iis
qui per vicinitatem poterant sentire praecepit.

XIX. In Etruria praeturam imperator egit. per

¹ *si* lacking in P¹, added by P corr.

---

[1] It was a principle of Roman law that the property of those
executed or exiled should be confiscated; see *Digest.*, xlviii.
20, 1 pr. It had become customary, however, to allow to the
children a certain proportion. In the first century this often
amounted to a half (see Tac., *Ann.*, iii. 17; xiii. 43); in the
time of Theodosius I, the law established this amount, except
only in cases of treason, in which the children were to receive
one sixth; see *Cod. Theod.*, ix. 42, 8 and 24 = *Cod. Iust.*, ix.
49, 8 and 10. The amount prescribed by Hadrian must be
regarded as a minimum.

[2] Originally the principle seems to have been that the
finder of treasure became the owner; so Hor., *Sat.*, ii. 6, 10 f.

granted a twelfth of the property.[1] Accusations for *lèse majeste* he did not admit. Legacies from persons unknown to him he refused, and even those left to him by acquaintances he would not accept if they had any children. In regard to treasure-trove, he ruled that if anyone made a find on his own property he might keep it, if on another's land, he should turn over half to the proprietor thereof, if on the state's, he should share the find equally with the privy-purse.[2] He forbade masters to kill their slaves, and ordered that any who deserved it should be sentenced by the courts. He forbade anyone to sell a slave or a maid-servant to a procurer or trainer of gladiators without giving a reason therefor. He ordered that those who had wasted their property, if legally responsible, should be flogged in the amphitheatre and then let go. Houses of hard labour for slaves and free he abolished. He provided separate baths for the sexes. He issued an order that, if a slave-owner were murdered in his house, no slaves should be examined save those who were near enough to have had knowledge of the murder.[3]

XIX. In Etruria he held a praetorship[4] while em-

Hadrian's modification was adopted by Marcus and Verus (Just., *Digest.*, xlix. 14, 3, 10), and by Severus Alexander (*Alex.*, xlvi. 2), and was finally incorporated in Justinian's *Institutes* (ii. 1, 39).

[3] A *senatus consultum Silanianum* of A.D. 10 had ordained that on the murder of a slave-owner by a slave, all the slaves present in the house should be examined by torture; see Just., *Diges'.*, xxix. 5. This was extended by a *senatus consultum* of 57 to include all freedmen present in the house; see Tac., *Ann.*, xiii. 32. For an instance of such a murder see Tac., *Ann.*, xiv. 42-45.

[4] He held the honorary post of chief magistrate of various towns. *Praetor* was the original title of this magistrate (the Roman consuls also were originally called *praetores*), and many towns retained the old name.

HADRIAN

Latina oppida dictator et aedilis et duumvir fuit, apud
Neapolim demarchus, in patria sua quinquennalis et
item Hadriae quinquennalis, quasi in alia patria, et
Athenis archon fuit.
2   In omnibus paene urbibus et aliquid aedificavit et
3 ludos edidit.   Athenis mille ferarum venationem in
4 stadio exhibuit. ab urbe Roma numquam ullum
5 venatorem aut scaenicum avocavit.   Romae post
ceteras immensissimas voluptates in honorem socrus
suae aromatica populo donavit, in honorem Traiani
balsama et crocum per gradus theatri fluere iussit.
6 fabulas omnis generis more antiquo in theatro dedit,
7 histriones aulicos publicavit. in Circo multas feras
8 et saepe centum leones interfecit. militares pyrrichas
populo frequenter exhibuit. gladiatores frequenter
9 spectavit. cum opera ubique infinita fecisset, numquam ipse nisi in Traiani patris templo nomen suum
10 scripsit.   Romae instauravit Pantheum, Saepta, Basil-

---

¹ The *Duoviri iuri dicundo* were the chief magistrates of a
colony, analogous to the consuls at Rome, and gradually
most of the municipalities adopted this form of government.
It was customary for the emperors to hold this magistracy as
a compliment to the town.
² Naples, which was a Greek city, retained the original
title of its chief magistrate, δήμαρχος; see Strabo, v. p. 546
and many inscriptions extending down to the fourth century.
³ Italica in Hispania Baetica; see c. i. 1.
⁴ In 112, before he became emperor; see the inscription
from Athens, *C.I.L.*, iii. 550 = Dessau, *Ins. Sel.*, 308.
⁵ See c. ix. 9 and note.
⁶ Originally a war-dance, but sometimes used in pantomimes (cf. Suet., *Nero*, xii. 2).
⁷ See note to c. vii. 6.
⁸ Originally built by Agrippa in 27 B.C. The present building bears the inscription of Agrippa, *M. Agrippa L. f. consul
ter(tium) fecit*, but an examination of the bricks used in its

peror. In the Latin towns he was dictator and aedile and duumvir,[1] in Naples demarch,[2] in his native city[3] duumvir with the powers of censor. This office he held at Hadria, too, his second native city, as it were, and at Athens he was archon.[4]

In almost every city he built some building and gave public games. At Athens he exhibited in the stadium a hunt of a thousand wild beasts, but he never called away from Rome a single wild-beast-hunter or actor. In Rome, in addition to popular entertainments of unbounded extravagance, he gave spices to the people in honour of his mother-in-law,[5] and in honour of Trajan he caused essences of balsam and saffron to be poured over the seats of the theatre. And in the theatre he presented plays of all kinds in the ancient manner and had the court-players appear before the public. In the Circus he had many wild beasts killed and often a whole hundred of lions. He often gave the people exhibitions of military Pyrrhic dances,[6] and he frequently attended gladiatorial shows. He built public buildings in all places and without number, but he inscribed his own name on none of them except the temple of his father Trajan.[7] At Rome he restored the Pantheon,[8] the Voting-enclosure,[9] the Basilica of Neptune,[10] very

construction has revealed the fact that it is wholly the work of Hadrian.

[9] In the Campus Martius, where the centuries gathered for voting. The building was begun by Julius Caesar but finished by Agrippa and called *Saepta Iulia* in 27 B.C. (Dio, liii. 23). It was burned under Titus (Dio, lxvi. 24) but rebuilt under Domitian.

[10] North of the Saepta. Built by Agrippa in 25 B.C. to commemorate the victories over Sextus Pompeius and Antony (Dio, liii. 27) and burned under Titus. The north wall of Hadrian's building and eleven columns are extant, and form part of the façade of the modern stock-exchange.

icam Neptuni, sacras aedes plurimas, Forum Augusti,
Lavacrum Agrippae; eaque omnia propriis auctorum [1]
11 nominibus consecravit. fecit et sui nominis pontem
et sepulchrum iuxta Tiberim et aedem Bonae Deae.
12 transtulit et Colossum stantem atque suspensum per
Decrianum architectum de eo loco in quo nunc Templum Urbis est, ingenti molimine, ita ut operi etiam
13 elephantos viginti quattuor exhiberet. et cum hoc
simulacrum post Neronis vultum deletum, cui antea
dicatum fuerat, Soli consecrasset, aliud tale Apolo-
doro architecto auctore facere Lunae molitus est.
XX. In conloquiis etiam humillimorum civilissimus
fuit, detestans eos qui sibi hanc voluptatem humani-
tatis quasi servantes [2] fastigium principis inviderent.
2 apud Alexandriam in Museo multas quaestiones professoribus proposuit et propositas ipse dissolvit.
3 Marius Maximus dicit eum natura crudelem fuisse

[1] *auctorum* Peter, from Suet. *Domit.* 5; *ueterum* P.   [2] *ser-uantes* Roos, Mn. 41, p. 144; *seruantis* P.

---

[1] North-west of the Forum Romanum, and containing the temple of Mars Ultor.
[2] Immediately south of the Pantheon, built by Agrippa in 25 B.C. (Dio, liii. 27). These baths were burned under Titus but rebuilt under Domitian (Martial, iii. 20 and 36).
[3] The *Mausoleum Hadriani*, on the right bank of the Tiber, now the Castel S. Angelo. The bridge named after him *Pons Aelius* led to it. The Mausoleum was finally completed by Antoninus Pius in 139; see *Pius*, viii. 2, and *C.I.L.*, vi. 984 = Dessau, *Ins. Sel.*, 322.
[4] The *Aedes Bonae Deae Subsaxanae* was on the slope of the eastern peak of the Aventine Hill (the Remuria or Saxum); for its legend see Ovid, *Fast.*, v. 155.

many temples, the Forum of Augustus,[1] the Baths of Agrippa,[2] and dedicated all of them in the names of their original builders. Also he constructed the bridge named after himself, a tomb on the bank of the Tiber,[3] and the temple of the Bona Dea.[4] With the aid of the architect Decrianus he raised the Colossus [5] and, keeping it in an upright position, moved it away from the place in which the Temple of Rome [6] is now, though its weight was so vast that he had to furnish for the work as many as twenty-four elephants. This statue he then consecrated to the Sun, after removing the features of Nero, to whom it had previously been dedicated, and he also planned, with the assistance of the architect Apollodorus, to make a similar one for the Moon.

XX. Most democratic in his conversations, even with the very humble, he denounced all who, in the belief that they were thereby maintaining the imperial dignity, begrudged him the pleasure of such friendliness. In the Museum at Alexandria [7] he propounded many questions to the teachers and answered himself what he had propounded. Marius Maximus says that

---

[5] A colossal statue of Nero which stood in the vestibule of Nero's Golden House; see Suet., *Nero*, xxxi. 1. According to Suetonius it was 120 feet high, according to Pliny (*N.H.*, xxxiv. 45) 106½ feet. The statue was moved by Hadrian to a place immediately north-west of the Colosseum, where a portion of its base is still preserved.

[6] The Temple of Venus and Rome, built by Hadrian in 135 from a plan made by himself; see Dio, lxix. 4. It stood on the Velia at the highest point of the Sacra Via on a part of the site of Nero's Golden House. The western portion is built into the church of S. Francesca Romana, the eastern portion is partly extant.

[7] An academy founded by Ptolemy Philadelphus in imitation of the schools of Plato and Aristotle at Athens.

et idcirco multa pie fecisse quod timeret, ne sibi
idem quod Domitiano accidit eveniret.

4 Et cum titulos in operibus non amaret, multas
civitates Hadrianopolis appellavit, ut ipsam Cartha-
5 ginem et Athenarum partem. aquarum ductus etiam
6 infinitos hoc nomine nuncupavit. fisci advocatum
primus instituit.

7 Fuit memoriae ingentis, facultatis immensae ; nam
ipse et orationes dictavit et ad omnia respondit.
8 ioca eius plurima exstant ; nam fuit etiam dicaculus.
unde illud quoque innotuit quod, cum cuidam canes-
centi quiddam negasset, eidem iterum petenti sed
infecto capite respondit : " Iam hoc patri tuo negavi ".
9 nomina plurimis sine nomenclatore reddidit, quae
semel et congesta simul audiverat, ut nomenclatores
10 saepius errantes emendarit. dixit et veteranorum
nomina, quos aliquando dimiserat. libros statim[1]
lectos et ignotos quidem plurimis memoriter reddidit.
11 uno tempore scripsit dictavit audivit et cum amicis
fabulatus est, si potest credi.[2] omnes publicas
rationes ita complexus est ut domum privatam quivis
12 paterfamilias diligens non satis novit.[3] equos et canes

---

[1] So P ; *strictim* Peter[2] ; *raptim* Novak.   [2] *si potest*
(*potes* P[1]) *credi* removed by the edd., so Haupt, Opusc. III.
p. 421, but Vahlen (ind. lect. Ber. hib. 1880/1, p. 13) would
retain, joining to the following.   [3] *non satis nouit* P, which
Haupt would remove (loc. cit.) ; *non setius norit* Mommsen,
Peter[2].

---

[1] Domitian was assassinated by some palace-attendants.
[2] This portion of the city lay east of the Acropolis, between
the old wall of Themistocles and the Ilissus. A gate in the
old wall was replaced by a new one, bearing on its two sides
respectively the lines :—

Αἵδ' εἰσ' 'Αθῆναι Θησέως ἡ πρὶν πόλις.
Αἵδ' εἰσ' 'Αδριανοῦ καὶ οὐχὶ Θησέως πόλις.

(*I.G.*, iii. 401).

he was naturally cruel and performed so many kind-
nesses only because he feared that he might meet
the fate which had befallen Domitian.[1]

Though he cared nothing for inscriptions on his
public works, he gave the name of Hadrianopolis to
many cities, as, for example, even to Carthage and a
section of Athens;[2] and he also gave his name to
aqueducts without number. He was the first to appoint a pleader for the privy-purse.[3]

Hadrian's memory was vast and his ability was unlimited ; for instance, he personally dictated his
speeches and gave opinions on all questions. He
was also very witty, and of his jests many still survive. The following one has even become famous :
When he had refused a request to a certain gray-
haired man, and the man repeated the request but
this time with dyed hair, Hadrian replied : "I have
already refused this to your father". Even without
the aid of a nomenclator he could call by name a
great many people, whose names he had heard but
once and then all in a crowd ; indeed, he could
correct the nomenclators when they made mistakes,
as they not infrequently did, and he even knew the
names of the veterans whom he had discharged at
various times. He could repeat from memory, after
a rapid reading, books which to most men were not
known at all. He wrote, dictated, listened, and,
incredible as it seems, conversed with his friends, all
at one and the same time. He had as complete a
knowledge of the state-budget in all its details as

---

[3] The *advocatus fisci* represented the interests of the privy-
purse in law-suits in which it became involved. The office
was held by knights and constituted the first step in the
equestrian *cursus honorum.*

13 sic amavit ut iis sepulchra constitueret. oppidum
Hadrianotheras in quodam loco, quod illic et feliciter
esset venatus et ursam occidisset aliquando, constituit.

XXI. De iudicibus omnibus semper cuncta scru-
tando tamdiu requisivit quamdiu verum inveniret.
2 libertos suos nec sciri voluit in publico nec aliquid
apud se posse, dicto suo omnibus superioribus principibus vitia imputans libertorum, damnatis omnibus
3 libertis suis, quicumque se de eo iactaverant.   unde
exstat etiam illud severum [1] quidem sed prope ioculare
de servis.   nam cum quodam tempore servum suum
inter duos senatores e conspectu ambulare vidisset,
misit qui ei colaphum daret diceretque [2]: "Noli inter
4 eos ambulare quorum esse adhuc potes servus".   inter cibos unice amavit tetrapharmacum, quod erat de
phasiano sumine perna et crustulo.
5   Fuerunt eius temporibus fames pestilentia terrae
motus, quae omnia, quantum potuit, procuravit mul-
6 tisque civitatibus vastatis per ista subvenit.   fuit etiam
7 Tiberis inundatio.   Latium multis civitatibus dedit,
tributa multis remisit.

---

[1] *severum* Petschenig; *severo* P; *severe* P corr.; *seve* B²,
whence Peter *saeve*.   [2] so Mommsen; *colafum daret et
diceret* P corr. (from P¹ *colla fundar et qui*); *qui et collafum
daret; cui* "*Noli*," etc. Bitschofsky.

---

[1] Especially for his favourite hunting-horse Borysthenes,
which died at Apte in Gallia Narbonensis; in its honour he
erected a tomb with a stele and an inscription; see Dio, lxix.
10.   The inscription is preserved, *C.I.L.*, xii. 1122 = Bücheler,
Carm. Epigr., ii. 1522.

[2] In Bithynia.

[3] Also called pentapharmacum; see *Ael.*, v. 4 f.   It was also
a favourite dish of Severus Alexander's; see *Alex.*, xxx. 6.

any careful householder has of his own household. His horses and dogs he loved so much that he provided burial-places for them,[1] and in one locality he founded a town called Hadrianotherae,[2] because once he had hunted successfully there and killed a bear.

XXI. He always inquired into the actions of all his judges, and persisted in his inquiries until he satisfied himself of the truth about them. He would not allow his freedmen to be prominent in public affairs or to have any influence over himself, and he declared that all his predecessors were to blame for the faults of their freedmen; he also punished all his freedmen who boasted of their influence over him. With regard to his treatment of his slaves, the following incident, stern but almost humorous, is still related. Once when he saw one of his slaves walk away from his presence between two senators, he sent someone to give him a box on the ear and say to him: "Do not walk between those whose slave you may some day be". As an article of food he was singularly fond of tetrapharmacum,[3] which consisted of pheasant, sow's udders, ham, and pastry.

During his reign there were famines, pestilence, and earthquakes. The distress caused by all these calamities he relieved to the best of his ability, and also he aided many communities which had been devastated by them. There was also an overflow of the Tiber. To many communities he gave Latin citizenship,[4] and to many others he remitted their tribute.

[4] The *ius Latii* was a peculiar status, granted originally to certain of the cities of Latium. It conferred on their inhabitants certain private rights of a Roman citizen, especially those of holding property and trading at Rome and of intermarriage with Romans. In the time of the Empire the

8   Expeditiones sub eo graves nullae fuerunt; bella
9 etiam silentio paene transacta. a militibus propter
curam exercitus nimiam[1] multum amatus est, simul
10 quod in eos liberalissimus fuit. Parthos in amicitia
semper habuit, quod inde regem retraxit, quem
11 Traianus imposuerat. Armeniis regem habere per-
12 misit, cum sub Traiano legatum habuissent. a Mesopotamiis[2] non exegit tributum, quod Traianus im-
13 posuit. Albanos et Hiberos amicissimos habuit, quod
reges eorum largitionibus prosecutus est, cum ad
14 illum venire contempsissent. reges Bactrianorum
legatos ad eum amicitiae petendae causa supplices
miserunt.

XXII. Tutores saepissime dedit. disciplinam civi-
2 lem non aliter tenuit quam militarem. senatores et
equites Romanos semper in publico togatos esse iussit,
3 nisi si a cena reverterentur. ipse, cum in Italia esset,
4 semper togatus processit. ad convivium venientes
senatores stans excepit semperque aut pallio tectus
5 discubuit aut toga. summa diligentia in dies[3] sumptus
convivii constituit et ad antiquum modum redegit.
6 vehicula cum ingentibus sarcinis urbem ingredi pro-
7 hibuit. sederi equos in civitatibus non sivit. ante
octavam horam in publico neminem nisi aegrum lavari

[1] *nimiam* P corr., Novak; *nimiae* P[1]; *nimie* Peter[2].   [2] *a
Mesopotamiis* Novak after P corr. omitting *a; Mesopotamenos*
P[1], Peter.   [3] *toga. summa diligentia in dies* Mommsen;
toga summissa diligentia iudices P; *iudicis* Peter.

possession of this status meant chiefly local autonomy and
the bestowal of Roman citizenship on local magistrates.
  [1] Except the war in Judaea; see c. xiv. 2 and note.

There were no campaigns of importance during his
reign,[1] and the wars that he did wage were brought
to a close almost without arousing comment. The
soldiers loved him much on account of his very great
interest in the army[2] and for his great liberality to
them besides. The Parthians always regarded him
as a friend because he took away the king[3] whom
Trajan had set over them. The Armenians were
permitted to have their own king,[4] whereas under
Trajan they had had a governor, and the Mesopotam-
ians were relieved of the tribute which Trajan had
imposed. The Albanians[5] and Hiberians he made his
friends by lavishing gifts upon their kings, even
though they had scorned to come to him. The kings
of the Bactrians sent envoys to him to beg humbly
for his friendship.

XXII. He very often assigned guardians. Discipline in civil life he maintained as rigorously as he did
in military. He ordered senators and knights to wear
the toga whenever they appeared in public except
when they were returning from a banquet, and he
himself, when in Italy, always appeared thus clad.
At banquets, when senators came, he received them
standing, and he always reclined at table dressed
either in a Greek cloak or in a toga. The cost of a
banquet he determined on each occasion, all with
the utmost care, and he reduced the sums that
might be expended to the amounts prescribed by

[2] See c. x.

[3] *i.e.* Parthamaspates; see c. v. 4 and note.

[4] *i.e.* he relinquished their country together with the other
conquests of Trajan east of the Euphrates; see c. v. 1 and 3
and notes.

[5] The eastern part of Trans-Caucasia, east of the Hiberi
(for whom see c. xvii. 11).

8 passus est. ab epistulis et a libellis primus equites
9 Romanos habuit. eos quos pauperes et innocentes
vidit sponte ditavit, quos vero calliditate ditatos,
10 etiam odio habuit. sacra Romana diligentissime
curavit, peregrina contempsit. pontificis maximi
11 officium peregit. causas Romae atque in provinciis
frequenter audivit, adhibitis in consilio suo consulibus
12 atque praetoribus et optimis senatoribus. Fucinum
13 lacum emisit. quattuor consulares per omnem Italiam
14 iudices constituit. quando in Africam venit, ad ad-
ventum eius post quinquennium pluit, atque ideo ab
Africanis dilectus est.

XXIII. Peragratis sane omnibus orbis partibus
capite nudo et in summis plerumque imbribus atque
2 frigoribus in morbum incidit lectualem. factusque de
successore sollicitus primum de Serviano cogitavit,

---

[1] Beginning with the *Lex Orchia* of 181 B.C. the Roman
republic tried by a succession of sumptuary laws to restrict
the constantly increasing cost of banquets. The *Lex Fannia*
of 161 B.C. fixed a maximum of 100 *asses* for the great holidays,
of 10 *asses* for ordinary days; the latter sum was later increased to 30 *asses*. The *Lex Cornelia* of Sulla allowed three
hundred sesterces for holidays and thirty for other days ; this
latter was increased by a law of Augustus to two hundred
sesterces ; see Gellius, ii. 24 and Macrobius, *Sat.*, iii. 17. Which
sum is meant here is unfortunately not clear.

[2] One of the most important of Hadrian's reforms. The
great court-offices had previously been held chiefly by freedmen of the emperor as private posts in his household.
Hadrian, in providing that they should be held by knights,

the ancient laws.[1]   He forbade the entry into Rome
of heavily laden waggons, and did not permit
riding on horseback in cities.   None but invalids
were allowed to bathe in the public baths before
the eighth hour of the day.   He was the first to
put knights in charge of the imperial correspondence and of the petitions addressed to the emperor.[2]
Those men whom he saw to be poor and innocent he
enriched of his own accord, but those who had become
rich through sharp practice he actually regarded
with hatred.   He despised foreign cults, but native
Roman ones he observed most scrupulously; moreover, he always performed the duties of pontifex
maximus.   He tried a great number of lawsuits himself both in Rome and in the provinces, and to his
council [3] he called consuls and praetors and the foremost of the senators.   He drained the Fucine Lake.[4]
He appointed four men of consular rank as judges
for all Italy.   When he went to Africa [5] it rained on
his arrival for the first time in the space of five years,
and for this he was beloved by the Africans.

XXIII. After traversing, as he did, all parts of the
world with bare head and often in severe storms and

transformed them into official government positions.   Moreover, this opening to the equestrian order of a career of great
influence and distinction led to the result that by the end of
the third century most of the important administrative posts
were held by knights.

[3] See c. viii. 9 and note.

[4] Now Lago di Celano.   It is in the centre of Italy, due
east of Rome.   An attempt to drain it by means of a tunnel
was made by Claudius (see Tac., *Ann.*, xi. 56 and 57), but not
very successfully.   Another attempt, made by Trajan, is recorded in an inscription (*C.I.L.*, ix. 3915).

[5] See c. xiii. 4.

3 quem postea, ut diximus, mori coegit, item[1] Fuscum,
quod imperium praesagiis et ostentis agitatus speraret.
4 in summa detestatione habuit Platorium Nepotem,
quem tantopere ante dilexit ut veniens ad eum aegrotantem Hadrianus impune non admitteretur, suspic-
5 ionibus adductus, et eodem modo et Terentium
Gentianum, et hunc vehementius, quod a senatu diligi
6 tunc videbat. omnes postremo, de quorum imperio
cogitavit, quasi futuros imperatores detestatus est.
7 et omnem quidem vim crudelitatis ingenitae usque eo
repressit donec in Villa Tiburtina profluvio sanguinis
8 paene ad exitum venit. tunc libere Servianum quasi
adfectatorem imperii, quod servis regiis cenam misisset, quod in sedili regio iuxta lectum posito sedisset,
quod erectus ad stationes militum senex nonagenarius
processisset, mori coegit, multis aliis interfectis vel
9 aperte vel per insidias ; quando quidem etiam Sabina
uxor non sine fabula veneni dati ab Hadriano de-
functa est.
10 Tunc Ceionium Commodum, Nigrini generum
insidiatoris quondam, sibi forma commendatum adop-
11 tare constituit. adoptavit ergo Ceionium Commodum

---

[1] *item* om. in P, inserted by Peter.

---

[1] See c. xv. 8.

[2] Pedanius Fuscus, the grandson of Servianus, was killed
at the age of eighteen ; see Dio, lxix. 17.

[3] See c. iv. 2 and note.

[4] D. Terentius Gentianus held an important command in
Trajan's wars in Dacia and became a patron of the colony of
Sarmizegetusa, the capital of the province ; see *C.I.L.*, iii. 1463.

[5] See c. xxvi. 5.

[6] *i.e.* the guard that was regularly on duty at the Palace;
see Suetonius, *Tib.*, xxiv. 1 ; *Nero*, xxi. 1.

frosts, he contracted an illness which confined him to his bed. And becoming anxious about a successor he thought first of Servianus. Afterwards, however, as I have said,[1] he forced him to commit suicide; and Fuscus,[2] too, he put to death on the ground that, being spurred on by prophecies and omens, he was hoping for the imperial power. Carried away by suspicion, he held in the greatest abhorrence Platorius Nepos,[3] whom he had formerly so loved that, once, when he went to see him while ill and was refused admission, he nevertheless let him go unpunished. Also he hated Terentius Gentianus,[4] but even more vehemently, because he saw that he was then beloved by the senate. At last, he came to hate all those of whom he had thought in connection with the imperial power, as though they were really about to be emperors. However, he controlled all the force of his innate cruelty down to the time when in his Tiburtine Villa [5] he almost met his death through a hemorrhage. Then he threw aside all restraint and compelled Servianus to kill himself, on the ground that he aspired to the empire, merely because he gave a feast to the royal slaves, sat in a royal chair placed close to his bed, and, though an old man of ninety, used to arise and go forward to meet the guard of soldiers.[6] He put many others to death, either openly or by treachery, and indeed, when his wife Sabina died, the rumour arose that the Emperor had given her poison.

Hadrian then determined to adopt Ceionius Com- 136. modus, son-in-law of Nigrinus, the former conspirator, and this in spite of the fact that his sole recommendation was his beauty. Accordingly, despite the opposition of all, he adopted Ceionius Commodus

Verum invitis omnibus eumque Helium Verum Cae-
12 sarem appellavit. ob cuius adoptationem [1] ludos
circenses dedit et donativum populo ac militibus
13 expendit. quem praetura honoravit ac statim Pannoniis imposuit decreto consulatu cum sumptibus.[2]
eundem Commodum secundo consulem designavit.
14 quem cum minus sanum videret, saepissime dictitavit:
" In caducum parietem nos inclinavimus et perdidimus quater milies sestertium, quod populo et militi-
15 bus pro adoptione Commodi dedimus ". Commodus
autem prae valetudine nec gratias quidem in senatu
16 agere potuit Hadriano de adoptione. denique accepto largius antidoto ingravescente valetudine per
somnum periit ipsis kalendis Ianuariis. quare ab
Hadriano votorum causa lugeri est vetitus.

XXIV. Et [3] mortuo Helio Vero Caesare Hadrianus
ingruente tristissima valetudine adoptavit Arrium
Antoninum, qui postea Pius dictus est, et ea quidem [4]

---

[1] *adoptationem* P, Petschenig; *adoptionem* Peter.   [2] *consulatus consumptibus* P   [3] *et* P; *sed* Cas., Peter.   [4] *et
ea quidem* Jordan; *et eadem* P.

---

[1] More correctly, L. Ceionius Commodus; he was adopted
under the name L. Aelius Caesar. The cognomen Verus,
given to him here and in his biography (*Ael.*, ii. 1 and 6), is
not attested by inscriptions or coins, and seems to have arisen
through a confusion with his son, adopted by Antoninus Pius,
and, after his accession to the throne, called L. Aurelius
Verus. The form Helius which is used throughout the *Historia*

Verus [1] and called him Aelius Verus Caesar. On the
occasion of the adoption he gave games in the Circus
and bestowed largess upon the populace and the
soldiers.[2] He dignified Commodus with the office of
praetor [3] and immediately placed him in command of
the Pannonian provinces, and also conferred on him
the consulship together with money enough to meet
the expenses of the office. He also appointed Commodus to a second consulship. And when he saw
that the man was diseased, he used often to say:
"We have leaned against a tottering wall and have
wasted the four hundred million sesterces which we
gave to the populace and the soldiers on the adoption
of Commodus [4]". Moreover, because of his ill-health,
Commodus could not even make a speech in the senate
thanking Hadrian for his adoption. Finally, too large
a quantity of medicine was administered to him, and
thereupon his illness increased, and he died in his sleep
on the very Kalends of January.[5] Because of the date 1 Jan., 138.
Hadrian forbade public mourning for him, in order
that the vows for the state might be assumed as usual.

XXIV. After the death of Aelius Verus Caesar,
Hadrian was attacked by a very severe illness, and 25 Feb.,
thereupon he adopted Arrius Antoninus [6] (who was 138.

Augusta has no warrant whatsoever; its substitution for
Aelius is probably due to some editor.

[2] Cf. *Ael.*, iii. 3; vi. 1.

[3] This statement, as found here and in *Ael.*, iii. 2, is incorrect,
for he was praetor in 130 and consul in 136, the year in which
he was adopted. He was consul for the second time in 137
and was then placed in command of the two provinces of
Pannonia.

[4] Cf. *Ael.*, vi. 3.   [5] Cf. *Ael.*, iv. 7.

[6] More correctly, T. Aurelius Fulvus Boionius Arrius
Antoninus; see *Pius*, i. 1. After his adoption his name was
T. Aelius Caesar Antoninus.

lege ut ille sibi duos adoptaret, Annium Verum et Mar-
2 cum Antoninum. hi sunt qui postea duo pariter Augusti
3 primi rem publicam gubernaverunt. et Antoninus
quidem Pius idcirco appellatus dicitur quod socerum
4 fessum aetate manu sublevaret, quamvis alii cognomentum hoc ei dicant inditum, quod multos senatores
5 Hadriano iam saevienti abripuisset, alii, quod ipsi
Hadriano magnos honores post mortem detulisset.
6 Antonini adoptionem plurimi tunc factam esse dolue-
runt, speciatim Catilius Severus, praefectus urbi, qui
7 sibi praeparabat imperium. qua re prodita successore
accepto dignitate privatus est.
8   Hadrianus autem ultimo vitae taedio iam adfectus
9 gladio se transfigi a servo iussit. quod cum esset
proditum et in Antonini usque notitiam venisset,
ingressis ad se praefectis et filio rogantibusque ut
aequo animo necessitatem morbi ferret, dicente Antonino parricidam se futurum si Hadrianum adoptatus
10 ipse pateretur occidi,[1] iratus illis auctorem proditionis
iussit occidi, qui tamen ab Antonino servatus est.
11 statimque testamentum scripsit nec tamen actus rei

---

[1] *dicente . . . occidi* follows in P *statimque . . . praetermisit;* transposed to follow *ut . . . ferret* by Gemoll, so Peter[2].

---

[1] The names of the two adopted sons of Antoninus Pius are
entirely confused. The biographer is referring here to L.
Ceionius Commodus, the son of L. Aelius Caesar, called, after
his adoption by Antoninus, L. Aelius Aurelius Commodus.
On his succession to the throne, he took the cognomen of his
adoptive brother Annius Verus (M. Aurelius Antoninus) and
reigned as L. Aurelius Verus.
[2] His name before adoption was M. Annius Verus; after
adoption he seems to have been called M. Aelius Aurelius
Verus. On the death of Antoninus Pius he called himself
M. Aurelius Antoninus.
[3] So also *Pius,* ii. 3.   [4] See c. **xxv.** 8 and *Pius,* ii. 4.

afterwards called Pius), imposing on him the condition
that he adopt two sons, Annius Verus [1] and Marcus
Antoninus.[2]   These were the two who afterwards
ruled the empire together, the first joint Augusti.
And as for Antoninus, he was called Pius, it is said,
because he used to give his arm to his father-in-law
when weakened by old age.[3]   However, others assert
that this surname was given to him because, as
Hadrian grew more cruel, he rescued many senators
from the Emperor [4]; others, again, that it was because
he bestowed great honours upon Hadrian after his
death.[5]   The adoption of Antoninus was lamented by
many at that time, particularly by Catilius Severus,[6]
the prefect of the city, who was making plans to secure
the throne for himself.   When this fact became known,
a successor was appointed for him and he was deprived
of his office.

But Hadrian was now seized with the utmost disgust of life and ordered a servant to stab him with a
sword.   When this was disclosed and reached the
ears of Antoninus, he came to the Emperor, together
with the prefects, and begged him to endure with
fortitude the hard necessity of illness, declaring
furthermore that he himself would be no better than
a parricide, were he, an adopted son, to permit
Hadrian to be killed.   The Emperor then became
angry and ordered the betrayer of the secret to be
put to death; however, the man was saved by
Antoninus.   Then Hadrian immediately drew up his
will, though he did not lay aside the administration
of the empire.   Once more, however, after making

[5] See c. xxvii. 4 and *Pius*, ii. 5.
[6] He had been the colleague of Antoninus in the consulship
in 120; see *Pius*, ii. 9.

HADRIAN

12 publicae praetermisit. et post testamentum quidem
iterum se conatus [1] occidere subtracto pugione saevior
13 factus est. petiit et venenum a medico, qui se ipse,
ne daret, occidit.

XXV. Ea tempestate supervenit quaedam mulier,
quae diceret somnio se monitam ut insinuaret Hadriano, ne se occideret, quod esset bene valiturus; quod
cum non fecisset, esse caecatam. iussam tamen iterum
Hadriano eadem dicere atque genua eius osculare,
2 oculos [2] recepturam si id fecisset. quod cum insomnium [3] implesset, oculos recepit, cum aqua, quae in
3 fano erat, ex quo venerat, oculos abluisset. venit et
de Pannonia quidam vetus caecus ad febrientem
4 Hadrianum eumque contigit. quo facto et ipse
oculos recepit et Hadrianum febris reliquit, quamvis Marius Maximus haec per simulationem facta
commemoret.

5 Post haec Hadrianus Baias petiit Antonino Romae
6 ad imperandum relicto. ubi cum nihil proficeret,
arcessito Antonino in conspectu eius apud ipsas Baias
7 periit die VI iduum Iuliarum. invisusque omnibus
sepultus est in villa Ciceroniana Puteolis.

8 Sub ipso mortis tempore et Servianum nonaginta
annos agentem, ut [4] supra dictum est, ne sibi superviveret [5] atque, ut putabat, imperaret, mori coegit et
ob leves offensas plurimos iussit occidi, quos Anton-

---

[1] *est con.* P.   [2] *oculos* om. in P, supplied by Gleye; *uisum*
(added after *recepturam*), P corr., so Peter, but see Novak
I, p. 3.   [3] *insomnium* Cas.; *in somnio* P; *somnium* Novak.
[4] *ut* B corr., om. in P; *supra dictum est* deleted by Peter.
[5] *superuiueret* Petrarch; *suprauiueret* P, Peter.

---

[1] See c. xv. 8 and xxiii. 2 and 8.

his will, he attempted to kill himself, but the dagger
was taken from him. He then became more violent,
and he even demanded poison from his physician,
who thereupon killed himself in order that he might
not have to administer it.

XXV. About this time there came a certain woman,
who said that she had been warned in a dream to
coax Hadrian to refrain from killing himself, for he
was destined to recover entirely, but that she had
failed to do this and had become blind ; she had nevertheless been ordered a second time to give the same
message to Hadrian and to kiss his knees, and was
assured of the recovery of her sight if she did so.
The woman then carried out the command of the
dream, and received her sight after she had bathed
her eyes with the water in the temple from which
she had come. Also a blind old man from Pannonia
came to Hadrian when he was ill with fever, and
touched him ; whereupon the man received his sight,
and the fever left Hadrian. All these things, however, Marius Maximus declares were done as a hoax.

After this Hadrian departed for Baiae, leaving
Antoninus at Rome to carry on the government.
But he received no benefit there, and he thereupon
sent for Antoninus, and in his presence he died there
at Baiae on the sixth day before the Ides of July. 10 July,
Hated by all, he was buried at Puteoli on an estate 138.
that had belonged to Cicero.

Just before his death, he compelled Servianus, then
ninety years old, to kill himself, as has been said
before,[1] in order that Servianus might not outlive
him, and, as he thought, become emperor. He likewise gave orders that very many others who were
guilty of slight offences should be put to death ; these,

77

9 inus reservavit. et moriens quidem hos versus fecisse dicitur :

> Animula vagula blandula
> hospes comesque corporis,
> quae nunc abibis in loca
> pallidula rigida nudula ?
> nec ut soles dabis iocos !

10 tales autem nec multos [1] meliores fecit et Graecos.
11   Vixit annis LXII,[2] mensibus V, diebus XVII. imperavit annis XX,[3] mensibus XI.

XXVI. Statura fuit procerus, forma comptus, flexo ad pectinem capillo, promissa barba, ut vulnera, quae in facie naturalia erant, tegeret, habitudine robusta. 2 equitavit ambulavitque plurimum armisque et pilo se 3 semper exercuit. venatus frequentissime leonem manu sua occidit. venando autem iugulum et costam fregit. venationem semper cum amicis participavit. 4 in convivio tragoedias comoedias Atellanas sambucas 5 lectores poetas pro re semper exhibuit. Tiburtinam Villam mire exaedificavit, ita ut in ea et provinciarum et locorum celeberrima nomina inscriberet, velut Lyceum, Academian, Prytaneum, Canopum, Poicilen, Tempe vocaret. et, ut nihil praetermitteret, etiam inferos finxit. 6   Signa mortis haec habuit: natali suo ultimo, cum

---

[1] multos P ; multo Peter.   [2] LXII Salm. ; LXXII P.
[3] XX Cas. ; XXI P.

---

[1] Translated by A. O'Brien-Moore.
[2] The name was derived from Atella, a Campanian town, where, it was supposed, farces of this type originated.
[3] This palace was built by Hadrian during the last years of his reign; it was a characteristic expression of both his

however, were spared by Antoninus. And he is said, as he lay dying, to have composed the following lines:

> "O blithe little soul, thou, flitting away,
> Guest and comrade of this my clay,
> Whither now goest thou, to what place
> Bare and ghastly and without grace?
> Nor, as thy wont was, joke and play." [1]

Such verses as these did he compose, and not many that were better, and also some in Greek.

He lived 62 years, 5 months, 17 days. He ruled 20 years, 11 months.

XXVI. He was tall of stature and elegant in appearance; his hair was curled on a comb, and he wore a full beard to cover up the natural blemishes on his face; and he was very strongly built. He rode and walked a great deal and always kept himself in training by the use of arms and the javelin. He also hunted, and he used often to kill a lion with his own hand, but once in a hunt he broke his collar-bone and a rib; these hunts of his he always shared with his friends. At his banquets he always furnished, according to the occasion, tragedies, comedies, Atellan farces,[2] players on the sambuca, readers, or poets. His villa at Tibur [3] was marvellously constructed, and he actually gave to parts of it the names of provinces and places of the greatest renown, calling them, for instance, Lyceum, Academia, Prytaneum, Canopus, Poecile and Tempe. And in order not to omit anything, he even made a Hades.

The premonitions of his death were as follows: On

eccentricity and his magnificence. Its extensive remains, covering, together with its gardens, about 160 acres, are still to be seen on the edge of the plain about three miles south-east of Tibur (Tivoli).

HADRIAN

Antoninum commendaret, praetexta spente delapsa
7 caput ei aperuit. anulus. in quo imago ips us sculpta
8 erat, sponte de digito delapsus est. ante diem naïalis
eius nescio qui ad senatum ululans venit, contra
quem Hadrianus ita motus est quasi de sua morte
9 loqueretur, cum eius verba nullus agnosceret. idem
cum vellet in senatu dicere " post filii mei mortem,"
10 " post meam " dixit. somniavit praeterea se a patre
potionem soporiferam impetrasse. item somniavit a
leone se oppressum esse.

XXVII. In mortuum eum a multis multa sunt
2 dicta. acta eius inrita fieri senatus volebat. nec
appellatus esset[1] divus, nisi Antoninus rogasset.
3 templum denique ei pro sepulchro apud Puteolos
constituit et quinquennale certamen et flamines et
sodales et multa alia, quae ad honorem quasi numinis
4 pertinerent. qua re, ut supra dictum est, multi
putant Antoninum Pium dictum.

¹ *est* P.

---

[1] He was praying, according to the regular Roman custom,
with a part of his toga drawn over his head.

[2] For the significance of this omen see note to c. iii. 7.

[3] The Sodales were a board of priests to whom was committed the cult of a deified emperor. Under the empire there
were, in all, four such boards : the *Sodales Augustales*, created
for the cult of Augustus, and after the deification of Claudius

his last birthday, when he was commending Antoninus
to the gods, his bordered toga fell down without
apparent cause and bared his head.[1] His ring, on
which his portrait was carved, slipped of its own
accord from his finger.[2] On the day before his
birthday some one came into the senate wailing; by
his presence Hadrian was as disturbed as if he were
speaking about his own death, for no one could understand what he was saying. Again, in the senate,
when he meant to say, "after my son's death," he
said, "after mine". Besides, he dreamed that he
had asked his father for a soporific; he also dreamed
that he had been overcome by a lion.

XXVII. Much was said against him after his death,
and by many persons. The senate wished to annul
his acts, and would have refrained from naming him
"the Deified" had not Antoninus requested it.
Antoninus, moreover, finally built a temple for him
at Puteoli to take the place of a tomb, and he also
established a quinquennial contest and flamens and
sodales[3] and many other institutions which appertain
to the honour of one regarded as a god. It is for this
reason, as has been said before, that many think that
Antoninus received the surname Pius.[4]

extended to *Sodales Augustales Claudiales;* the *Sodales
Flaviales* for Vespasian, after the deification of Titus extended
to *Sodales Flaviales Titiales;* the *Sodales Hadrianales;* and
the *Sodales Antoniniani* created in 161. The theory was that
one *sodalitas* should care for the cults of the emperors of the
same house.

[4] See c. xxiv, 5 and note.

HELIUS

AELII SPARTIANI

Diocletiano Augusto Aelius Spartianus
suus sal.

I. In animo mihi est, Diocletiane Auguste, tot principum maxime, non solum eos qui principum locum
in hac statione quam temperas retentarunt, ut usque
ad divum Hadrianum feci, sed illos etiam qui vel
Caesarum nomine appellati sunt nec principes aut
Augusti fuerunt vel quolibet alio genere aut in famam
aut in spem principatus venerunt, cognitioni numinis
2 tui sternere. quorum praecipue de Helio Vero
dicendum est, qui primus tantum Caesaris nomen
accepit, adoptione Hadriani familiae principum ad-
3 scitus. et quoniam nimis pauca dicenda sunt, nec
debet prologus inormior [1] esse quam fabula, de ipso
iam loquar.

II. Ceionius Commodus, qui et Helius Verus appel-

[1] *enormior* P³; *al' morosior* P⁴.

---

[1] On his adoption by Hadrian he took the cognomen Caesar,

82

AELIUS

BY

AELIUS SPARTIANUS

To Diocletian Augustus, his devoted servant,
Aelius Spartianus, greeting:

I. It is my purpose, Diocletian Augustus, greatest
of a long line of rulers, to present to the knowledge
of your Divine Majesty, not only those who have held
as ruling emperors the high post which you maintain
—I have done this as far as the Deified Hadrian—
but also those who either have borne the name of
Caesar, though never hailed emperors or Augusti, or
have attained in some other fashion to the fame of the
imperial power or the hope of gaining it. Among
these I must tell first and foremost of Aelius Verus,
who through his adoption by Hadrian became a member of the imperial family, and was the first to receive
only the name of Caesar.[1] Since I can tell but little
of him, and the prologue should not be more extensive
than the play, I shall now proceed to tell of the man
himself.

II. The life of Ceionius Commodus, also called Aelius

but, as he did not become emperor, he never assumed any of
the imperial titles. From this time on, it was customary for
the son of the reigning emperor to bear the name Caesar.

latus est, quem sibi Hadrianus aevo ingravescente
morbis tristioribus pressus peragrato iam orbe terrarum
adoptavit, nihil habet in sua vita memorabile, nisi quod
2 primus tantum Caesar est appellatus, non testamento,
ut antea solebat, neque eo modo quo Traianus est
adoptatus, sed eo prope genere quo nostris temporibus
a vestra clementia Maximianus atque Constantius
Caesares dicti sunt quasi quidam principum filii veri
et [1] designati augustae maiestatis heredes.
3 Et quoniam de Caesarum nomine in huius praecipue
vita est aliquid disputandum, qui hoc solum nomen
indeptus [2] est, Caesarem vel ab elephanto, qui lingua
Maurorum caesai dicitur, in proelio caeso, eum qui
primus sic appellatus est doctissimi viri et eruditis-
4 simi putant dictum, vel quia mortua matre et ventre
caeso sit natus, vel quod cum magnis crinibus sit
utero parentis effusus, vel quod oculis caesiis et ultra
humanum morem viguerit. certe quaecumque illa,
5 felix necessitas fuit, unde tam clarum et duraturum
cum aeternitate mundi nomen effloruit.
6 Hic ergo, de quo sermo est, primum Lucius Aurelius Verus est dictus, sed ab Hadriano adscitus in
Heliorum familiam, hoc est in Hadriani, transcriptus

---

[1] *ueri et* Obrecht and others; *uiri et* P; *uirtute* Peter, following Bernhardy.   [2] *al' adeptus* P corr.

---

[1] On the correct form of his name see note to *Hadr.*, xxiii. 11.
[2] In 136; see *Hadr.*, xxiii. 10.
[3] The biographer seems to be thinking of the testamentary
adoption of Octavian by Julius Caesar.
[4] Trajan, on his adoption, did not assume the name Caesar;
this seems to be the only difference.
[5] The elephant appears as an emblem on a coin of Julius
Caesar; see Cohen, i[2], p. 17, No. 49.
[6] *A caeso matris utero dictus*, Plin., *Nat. Hist.*, vii. 47.
[7] *i.e.*, caesaries. This etymology is given by Festus, p. 57,

Verus,[1] adopted by Hadrian [2] after his journey through the world, when he was burdened by old age and weakened by cruel disease, contains nothing worthy of note except that he was the first to receive only the name of Caesar. This was conferred, not by last will and testament, as was previously the custom,[3] nor yet in the fashion in which Trajan was adopted,[4] but well nigh in the same manner as in our own time your Clemency conferred the name of Caesar on Maximianus and on Constantius, as on true sons of the imperial house and heirs apparent of your August Majesty.

Now whereas I must needs tell something of the name of the Caesars, particularly in a life of the man who received this name alone of the imperial titles, men of the greatest learning and scholarship aver that he who first received the name of Caesar was called by this name, either because he slew in battle an elephant,[5] which in the Moorish tongue is called *caesai*, or because he was brought into the world after his mother's death and by an incision in her abdomen,[6] or because he had a thick head of hair [7] when he came forth from his mother's womb, or, finally, because he had bright grey eyes [8] and was vigorous beyond the wont of human beings. At any rate, whatever be the truth, it was a happy fate which ordained the growth of a name so illustrious, destined to last as long as the universe endures.

This man, then, of whom I shall write, was at first called Lucius Aurelius Verus,[9] but on his adoption by Hadrian he passed into the family of the Aelii, that

and both this and the preceding derivation are listed by Isidorus (*Orig.*, ix. 3, 12).

[8] *i.e.*, *oculis caesiis*.

[9] An error; see note to *Hadr.*, xxiii. 11.

7 et appellatus est Caesar. huic pater Ceionius Commodus fuit, quem alii Verum, alii Lucium Aurelium,
8 multi Annium prodiderunt. maiores omnes nobilissimi, quorum origo pleraque ex Etruria fuit vel ex
9 Faventia. et de huius quidem familia plenius in vita Lucii Aurelii Ceionii Commodi Veri Antonini, filii huiusce, quem sibi adoptare Antoninus iussus
10 est, disseremus. is enim liber debet omnia quae ad stemma generis pertinent continere, qui habet principem de quo plura dicenda sunt.

III. Adoptatus autem Helius Verus ab Hadriano eo tempore quo iam, ut superius diximus, parum vigebat
2 et de successore necessario cogitabat. statimque praetor factus et Pannoniis dux ac rector impositus, mox consul creatus et, quia erat deputatus [1] imperio,
3 iterum consul designatus est. datum etiam populo congiarium causa eius adoptionis conlatumque militibus sestertium ter milies, circenses editi, neque quicquam praetermissum quod posset laetitiam publicam
4 frequentare. tantumque apud Hadrianum principem valuit ut praeter adoptionis adfectum, quo ei videbatur adiunctus, solus omnia, quae cuperet, etiam per
5 litteras impetraret. nec provinciae quidem, cui
6 praepositus erat, defuit ; nam bene gestis rebus vel

---

[1] *deputans* P[1]; *al' iam deputatus* P corr.

---

[1] L. Ceionius Commodus, consul in 106. None of the various names given in the following clauses was ever borne by him.
[2] For the correct form of his name and for his adoption by Antoninus Pius see *Hadr.*, xxiv. 1 and note.
[3] See *Hadr.*, xxiii. 10 f.
[4] On this error see note to *Hadr.*, xxiii. 13.

is, into Hadrian's, and received the name of Caesar.
His father was Ceionius Commodus,[1] whom some have
called Verus, others, Lucius Aurelius, and many,
Annius. His ancestors, all men of the highest rank,
had their origin for the most part in Etruria or
Faventia. Of his family, however, we will speak at
greater length in the life of his son, Lucius Aurelius
Ceionius Commodus Verus Antoninus,[2] whom Antoninus was ordered to adopt. For all that pertains
to the family-tree should be included in the work
which deals with a prince of whom there is more to
be told.

III. Aelius Verus was adopted by Hadrian at the
time when, as we have previously said,[3] the Emperor's
health was beginning to fail and he was forced to take
thought for the succession. He was at once made
praetor [4] and appointed military and civil governor of
the provinces of Pannonia ; afterwards he was created 136.
consul, and then, because he had been chosen to
succeed to the imperial power, he was named for a 137.
second consulship. On the occasion of his adoption
largess was given to the populace,[5] three hundred
million sesterces were distributed among the soldiers,
and races were held in the Circus ; in short, nothing
was omitted which could signalize the public rejoicing.
He had, moreover, such influence with Hadrian, even
apart from the affection resulting from his adoption,
which seemed a firm enough tie between them, that
he was the only one who obtained his every desire,
even when expressed in a letter. Besides, in the
province to which he had been appointed he was by
no means a failure ; for he carried on a campaign with
success, or rather, with good fortune, and achieved

[5] Cf. c. vi. 1 and *Hadr.*, xxiii. 12.

potius feliciter etiamsi non summi, medii tamen obtinuit ducis famam.

7   Hic tamen vaietudinis adeo miserae fuit ut Hadrianum statim adoptionis paenituerit potueritque[1] eum
amovere a familia imperatoria, cum saepe de aliis
8 cogitaret, si forte vixisset.[2]   fertur denique ab iis
qui Hadriani vitam diligentius in litteras rettulerunt
Hadrianum Veri scisse genituram et eum, quem non
multum ad rem publicam regendam probarat, ob hoc
tantum adoptasse ut suae satisfaceret voluptati et,
ut quidam dicunt, iuri iurando, quod intercessisse
inter ipsum ac Verum secretis condicionibus fere-
9 batur.   fuisse enim Hadrianum peritum matheseos
Marius Maximus usque adeo demonstrat ut eum dicat
cuncta de se scisse, sic ut omnium dierum usque ad
IV. horam mortis futuros actus ante perscripserit.   satis
praeterea constat eum de[3] Vero saepe dixisse :

"Ostendent terris hunc tantum fata neque ultra
    esse sinent."

2 quos versus cum aliquando in hortulo spatians canti-
taret atque adesset unus ex litteratis, quorum Hadrianus speciosa societate gaudebat, velletque addere
    "nimium vobis Romana propago
visa potens, superi, propria haec si dona fuissent,"
3 Hadrianus dixisse fertur "hos versus vita non capit
Veri," illud addens :

---

[1] So P[1]; *al' petiuerit* P corr. ; *uolueritque* Oberdick and
others.   [2] *uolueritque eum amouere . . . et amouisset si
forte vixisset* Novak.   [3] So P ; *eundem de* Peter, following
B, *endem.*

---

[1] Cf. *Hadr.*, xvi. 7.
[2] This and the two following quotations from the *Aeneid*
are taken from the famous passage, vi. 869-886, commemorat-

the reputation, if not of a pre-eminent, at least of an average, commander.

Verus had, however, such wretched health that Hadrian immediately regretted the adoption, and since he often considered others as possible successors, he might have removed him altogether from the imperial family had Verus chanced to live longer. In fact, it is reported by those who have set down in writing all the details of Hadrian's life, that the Emperor was acquainted with Verus' horoscope, and that he adopted a man whom he did not really deem suitable to govern the empire merely for the purpose of gratifying his own desires, and, some even say, of complying with a sworn agreement said to have been contracted on secret terms between himself and Verus. For Marius Maximus represents Hadrian as so expert in astrology, as even to assert that he knew all about his own future, and that he actually wrote down beforehand what he was destined to do on every day down to the hour of his death.[1] IV. Furthermore, it is generally known that he often said about Verus:

"This hero Fate will but display to earth
   Nor suffer him to stay."[2]

And once when Hadrian was reciting these verses while strolling about in his garden, one of the literary men, in whose brilliant company he delighted,[3] happened to be present and proceeded to add,

"The race of Rome,
   Would seem to You, O Gods, to be too great,
   Were such gifts to endure."

Thereupon the Emperor remarked, it is said, "The life of Verus will not admit of these lines," and added,

ing Marcellus, the nephew and heir presumptive of Augustus, who died in 23 B.C. at the age of twenty years.
   [3] Cf. *Hadr.*, xvi. 8 f.

AELIUS

" Manibus date lilia plenis ;
purpureos spargam flores animamque nepotis
his saltem accumulem donis et fungar inani
munere,"

4 cum quidem etiam illud dicitur cum [1] risione dixisse :
5 " Ego mihi divum adoptavi non filium ".   hunc [2]
tamen cum consolaretur unus de litteratis qui aderat
ac diceret: " Quid [3] ? si non recte constellatio eius col-
lecta est quem credimus esse victurum ? " Hadrianus
dixisse fertur : " Facile ista dicis tu, qui patrimonii
6 tui non rei publicae quaeris heredem ".   unde apparet
eum habuisse in animo alium deligere atque hunc
ultimo vitae suae tempore a re publica summovere.
7 sed eius consiliis iuvit eventus.   nam cum de provincia Helius redisset atque orationem pulcherrimam,
quae hodieque legitur, sive per se seu per scriniorum
aut dicendi magistros parasset, qua kalendis Ianuariis
Hadriano patri gratias ageret, accepta potione, qua
se aestimaret iuvari, kalendis ipsis Ianuariis periit.
8 iussusque ab Hadriano, quia vota interveniebant, non
lugeri.

V. Fuit hic vitae laetissimae, eruditus in litteris,
Hadriano, ut malevoli loquuntur, acceptior forma
2 quam moribus.   in aula diu non fuit, in vita privata
etsi minus probabilis, minus tamen reprehendendus

---

[1] *al' eum* P corr.   [2] *nunc tamen cum eum* P and Peter ;
tunc Petschenig.   [3] So P ; *quod* Peter[1] with B.

---

[1] An allusion to the practice of deifying deceased members
of the imperial family.   As a matter of fact, however, Aelius
was not deified.

"Bring lilies with a bounteous hand;
And I the while will scatter rosy blooms,
Thus doing honour to our kinsman's soul

With these poor gifts—though useless be the task."
At the same time, too, Hadrian, it is reported, remarked with a laugh : " I seem to have adopted, not a
son, but a god ".[1] Yet when one of these same literary
men who was present tried to console him, saying :
"What if a mistake has been made in casting the
horoscope of this man who, as we believe, is destined
to live " ? Hadrian is said to have answered : " It is
easy for you to say that, when you are looking for an
heir to your property, not to the Empire ". This
makes it clear that he intended to choose another
heir, and at the end of his life to remove Verus from
the government of the state. However, fortune aided
his purpose. For after Verus had returned from his
province, and had finished composing, either by his
own efforts or with the help of imperial secretaries
or the rhetoricians, a very pretty speech, still read
nowadays, wherein he intended to convey his thanks
to his father Hadrian on the Kalends of January, he 1 Jan., 138.
swallowed a potion which he believed would benefit
him and died on that very day of January.[2] All public
lamentation for him was forbidden by Hadrian because
it was the time for assuming the vows for the state.

V. Verus was a man of joyous life and well versed
in letters, and he was endeared to Hadrian, as the
malicious say, rather by his beauty[3] than by his
character. In the palace his stay was but a short
one ; in his private life, though there was little to be
commended, yet there was little to be blamed.

[2] Cf. *Hadr.*, xxiii. 16 f.   [3] Cf. *Hadr.*, xxiii. 10.

AELIUS

ac memor familiae suae, comptus, decorus, pulchritu-
dinis regiae, oris venerandi, eloquentiae celsioris,
3 versu facilis, in re publica etiam non inutilis. huius
voluptates ab iis qui vitam eius scripserunt multae
feruntur, et quidem [1] non infames sed aliquatenus
4 diffluentes. nam tetrapharmacum, seu potius pentapharmacum, quo postea semper Hadrianus est usus,
ipse dicitur repperisse, hoc est sumen phasianum
5 pavonem pernam crustulatam et aprunam. de quo
genere cibi aliter refert Marius Maximus, non pentapharmacum sed tetrapharmacum appellans, ut et nos
6 ipsi in eius vita persecuti sumus. fertur etiam aliud
7 genus voluptatis, quod Verus invenerat. nam lectum
eminentibus quattuor anacliteriis fecerat minuto re-
ticulo undique inclusum eumque foliis rosae, quibus
demptum esset album,[2] replebat iacensque cum concubinis velamine de liliis facto se tegebat unctus
8 odoribus Persicis. iam illa frequentantur a nonnullis
quod et accubitationes ac mensas de rosis ac liliis
fecerit et quidem purgatis, quae etsi non decora, non
9 tamen ad perniciem publicam prompta sunt. atque
idem Apicii Caelii relata, idem Ovidii libros Amorum [3]
in lecto semper habuisse, idem Martialem, epigram-
10 maticum poetam, Vergilium suum dixisse. iam illa

---

[1] *et quidem* Lessing ; *equidem* P, Peter.   [2] *udum* Oberdick ; *tabum* Novak.   [3] So Peter ; *atque idem ouidii ab
aliis relata idem apicii libros amorum* P, which Salm. arranged : *idem Apicii relata idem Ouidii libros am.*

---

[1] *Hadr.*, xxi. 4.
[2] Apparently the extant *Apicii Caelii de re coquinaria
libri* X, a collection of culinary recipes. which, however. in
its present form is to be dated in the third century. The
name of the compiler was probably taken from that of M.
Gavius Apicius, a noted gourmet of the time of Tiberius.

Furthermore, he was considerate of his family, well-dressed, elegant in appearance, a man of regal beauty, with a countenance that commanded respect, a speaker of unusual eloquence, deft at writing verse, and, moreover, not altogether a failure in public life. His pleasures, many of which are recorded by his biographers, were not indeed discreditable but somewhat luxurious. For it is Verus who is said to have been the inventor of the tetrapharmacum, or rather pentapharmacum, of which Hadrian was thereafter always fond, namely, a mixture of sows' udders, pheasant, peacock, ham in pastry and wild boar. Of this article of food Marius Maximus gives a different account, for he calls it, not pentapharmacum, but tetrapharmacum, as we have ourselves described it in our biography of Hadrian.[1] There was also another kind of pleasure, it is said, of which Verus was the inventor. He constructed, namely, a bed provided with four high cushions and all inclosed with a fine net; this he filled with rose-leaves, from which the white parts had been removed, and then reclined on it with his mistresses, burying himself under a coverlet made of lilies, himself anointed with perfumes from Persia. Some even relate that he made couches and tables of roses and lilies, these flowers all carefully cleansed, a practice, which, if not creditable, at least did not make for the destruction of the state. Furthermore, he always kept the *Recipes* of Caelius Apicius [2] and also Ovid's *Amores* at his bedside, and declared that Martial,[3] the writer of Epigrams, was his Vergil. Still more trivial was his custom of fastening wings on many of his messengers after the

---

[3] M. Valerius Martialis, born about 40, died about 102.

AELIUS

leviora quod cursoribus suis exemplo Cupidinum alas
frequenter adposuit eosque ventorum nominibus saepe
vocitavit, Boream alium, alium Notum et item Aqui-
11 lonem aut Circium ceterisque nominibus appellans et
indefesse atque inhumaniter faciens cursitare. idem
uxori conquerenti de extraneis voluptatibus dixisse
fertur : " Patere me per alias exercere cupiditates
meas ; uxor enim dignitatis nomen est, non volup-
12 tatis ".

Eius est filius Antoninus Verus, qui adoptatus est
13 a Marco, vel certe cum Marco, et cum eodem aequale
gessit imperium. nam ipsi sunt qui primi duo Augusti
appellati sunt, et quorum fastis consularibus sic nomina
14 praescribuntur ut dicantur non [1] duo Antonini sed [2]
duo Augusti. tantumque huius rei et novitas et
dignitas valuit ut fasti consulares nonnulli ab his
sumerent ordinem consulum.

2 VI. Pro eius adoptione infinitam pecuniam populo
et militibus Hadrianus dedit. sed cum eum videret
homo paulo argutior miserrimae valetudinis, ita ut
3 scutum solidius iactare non posset, dixisse fertur :
" Ter milies perdidimus, quod exercitui populoque
dependimus ; si quidem satis in caducum parietem
4 incubuimus [3] et qui non ipsam rem publicam, sed nos
5 ipsos sustentare vix possit ". et haec quidem Hadrianus cum praefecto suo locutus est. quae cum prodidisset praefectus, ac per hoc Helius Caesar in dies
magis magisque sollicitudine, utpote desperati hominis,

[1] *non tantum* P corr.   [2] *set* P corr. ; *et* P[1].   [3] So P corr.
and Peter[2] ; *incuibimus* P[1].

---

[1] On this error see *Marc.*, v. 1 and note.
[2] *i.e.* by Antoninus Pius ; see c. ii. 9 and note.

94

fashion of Cupids, and often giving them the names of the winds, calling one Boreas, another Notus, others Aquilo, or Circius, or some other like name, and forcing them to bear messages without respite or mercy. And when his wife complained about his amours with others, he said to her, it is reported: "Let me indulge my desires with others; for wife is a term of honour, not of pleasure".

His son was Antoninus Verus, who was adopted by Marcus,[1] or rather, with Marcus,[2] and received an equal share with him in the imperial power. For these are the men who first received the name of Augustus conjointly, and whose names are inscribed in the lists of the consuls, not as two Antonini but as two Augusti. And such was the impression created by the novelty and the dignity of this fact that in some of the lists the order of the consuls begins with the names of these emperors.

VI. On the occasion of the adoption of Verus, Hadrian bestowed a vast sum of money on the populace and the soldiery.[3] But, being a rather sagacious man, when he saw that Verus was in such utterly wretched health that he could not brandish a shield of any considerable weight, he remarked, it is said:[4] "We have lost the three hundred million sesterces which we paid out to the army and to the people, for we have indeed leaned against a tottering wall, and one which can hardly bear even our weight, much less that of the Empire". This remark, indeed, Hadrian made to his prefect, but the man repeated it, and as a result Aelius Cæsar grew worse every day from anxiety, as a man does who has

---

[3] Cf. c. iii. 8 and *Hadr.*, xxiii. 12.
[4] Cf. *Hadr.*, xxiii. 14.

AELIUS

adgravaretur, praefecto suo Hadrianus, qui rem pro-
diderat, successorem dedit, volens videri quod verba
6 tristia temperasset.   sed nihil profuit ; nam, ut
diximus, Lucius Ceionius Commodus Verus Helius
Caesar (nam his omnibus nominibus appellatus est)
periit sepultusque est imperatorio funere, neque quic-
7 quam de regia ni mortis habuit dignitatem.   doluit
ergo illius mortem ut bonus pater, non ut bonus
princeps.   nam cum amici solliciti quaererent, qui
adoptari posset, Hadrianus dixisse fertur iis : " Etiam
8 vivente adhuc Vero decreveram ".   ex quo ostendit
9 aut iudicium suum aut scientiam futurorum.   post
hunc denique Hadrianus diu anceps quid faceret,
Antoninum adoptavit Pium cognomine appellatum.
cui condicionem addidit, ut ipse sibi Marcum et Verum
Antoninus adoptaret filiamque suam Vero, non Marco
10 daret.   nec diutius vixit gravatus languore ac diverso
genere morborum, saepe dicens sanum principem mori
debere non debilem.

VII. Statuas sane Helio Vero per totum orbem
colossas poni iussit, templa etiam in nonnullis urbibus
2 fieri.   denique illius merito filium eius Verum, nepotem
utpote suum, qui pereunte Helio in familia ipsius
Hadriani remanserat, adoptandum Antonino Pio cum
Marco, ut iam diximus, dedit, saepe dicens : " Habeat

---

[1] On the resignation of the prefect, see note to *Hadr.*, ix. 4.
[2] See note to c. ii. 1.
[3] Annia Galeria Faustina the younger ; see *Pius*, x. 2.

lost hope.   Thereupon Hadrian appointed a successor[1]
for the prefect who had divulged the remark, wishing
to give the impression that he had qualifi.d his harsh
words.   But it profited him nothing, for Lucius
Ceionius Commodus Verus Aelius Cæsar (for he was
called by all these names[2]) died and was accorded an
emperor's funeral, nor did he derive any benefit from
his imperial position save honour at his death.
Hadrian, then, mourned his death as might a good
father, not a good emperor.   For when his friends
anxiously asked who could now be adopted, Hadrian
is said to have replied to them : " I decided that even
when Verus was still alive," thereby showing either
his good judgment or his knowledge of the future.
After Verus' death Hadrian was in doubt for a time
as to what he should do, but finally he adopted
Antoninus, who had received the surname Pius.   And
he imposed on Antoninus the condition that he in
turn should adopt Marcus and Verus, and should give
his daughter[3] in marriage to Verus, rather than to
Marcus.   Nor did Hadrian live long thereafter, but
succumbed to weakness and illnesses of various kinds,
all the while declaring that a prince ought to die,
not in an enfeebled condition, but in full vigour.
   VII. Hadrian gave orders that colossal statues of
Verus should be set up all over the world, and in some
cities he even had temples built.   Finally, out of regard for him, Hadrian gave his son Verus (who had
remained in the imperial household after his father's
death) to Antoninus Pius, as I have already said,[4] to
be adopted as his son along with Marcus, treating the
boy as if he were his own grandson ; and he often
remarked : " Let the Empire retain something of

[4] c. ii. 9 ; v. 12 ; vi. 9 ; *Hadr.*, xxiv. 1.

AELIUS

3 res publica quodcumque de Vero ". quod quidem
contrarium iis quae de adoptionis paenitentia per
auctores plurimos intimata sunt, cum Verus posterior
nihil dignum praeter clementiam in moribus habuerit,
quod imperatoriae familiae lumen adferret.

4 Haec sunt quae de Vero Caesare mandanda litteris
5 fuerunt. de quo idcirco non tacui, quia mihi propositum
fuit omnes, qui post Caesarem dictatorem, hoc est
divum Iulium, vel Caesares vel Augusti vel principes
appellati sunt, quique in adoptionem venerunt, vel
imperatorum filii aut parentes Caesarum nomine con-
secrati sunt, singulis libris exponere, meae satisfaciens
conscientiae, etiamsi multis nulla sit necessitas talia
requirendi.

Verus". This indeed contradicts all that very many authors have written with regard to Hadrian's regret for his adoption of Verus, since, save for a kindly character, there was nothing in the character of the younger Verus capable of shedding lustre on the imperial family.

These are the facts about Verus Cæsar which have seemed worthy of being consigned to letters. I was unwilling to leave him unmentioned for the reason that it is my purpose to set forth in single books the lives of all the successors of Cæsar the Dictator, that is, the Deified Julius, whether they were called Cæsars or Augusti or princes, and of all those who came into the family by adoption, whether it was as sons or as relatives of emperors that they were immortalized by the name of Cæsar, and thereby to satisfy my own sense of justice, even if there be many who will feel no compelling need of seeking such information.

ANTONINUS PIUS

IULII CAPITOLINI

I. Tito Aurelio Fulvo Boionio Antonino Pio paternum genus e Gallia Transalpina, Nemausense scilicet,
2 avus Titus Aurelius Fulvus, qui per honores diversos
ad secundum consulatum et praefecturam urbis
3 pervenit, pater Aurelius Fulvus, qui et ipse fuit con-
4 sul, homo tristis et integer, avia materna Boionia
Procilla, mater Arria Fadilla, avus maternus Arrius
Antoninus, bis consul, homo sanctus et qui Nervam
5 miseratus esset, quod imperare coepisset, soror
6 uterina Iulia Fadilla, vitricus Iulius Lupus consularis,
7 socer Annius Verus, uxor Annia Faustina, filii mares
duo, duae feminae, gener per maiorem filiam Lamia
Silanus, per minorem Marcus Antoninus fuere.

---

[1] The correct form of his name prior to his adoption was
T. Aurelius Fulvus Boionius Arrius Antoninus; see *C.I.L.*,
viii. 8239.

[2] The year is unknown; his first consulship was in 85.
He had previously commanded the Third Legion, the *Gallica*,
and had been honoured by Otho for successes against the
Sarmatians.

[3] His first consulship was in 69; the year of the second is
not known. He was one of the correspondents of the
younger Pliny.

[4] See *Marc.*, i. 2.

[5] Her full name was Annia Galeria Faustina.

[6] Their names are given in their sepulchral inscriptions
from the Mausoleum of Hadrian as M. Aurelius Fulvus

ANTONINUS PIUS

BY

JULIUS CAPITOLINUS

I. Titus Aurelius Fulvus Boionius Anton:nus Pius [1]
was descended, on his father's side, from a family which
came from the country of Transalpine Gaul, more
specifically, from the town of Nîmes. His grandfather
was Titus Aurelius Fulvus, who after various offices
of honour attained to a second consulship [2] and the
prefecture of the city ; his father was Aurelius Fulvus,
also consul, and a stern and upright man. His
mother was Arria Fadilla ; her mother was Boionia
Procilla and her father Arrius Anton:nus, twice consul [3] and a righteous man, who pitied Nerva that he
assumed the imperial power. Julia Fadilla was his
mother's daughter, his stepfather being Julius Lupus,
a man of consular rank. His father-in-law was
Annius Verus [4] and his wife Annia Faustina,[5] who
bore him two sons [6] and two daughters, of whom the
elder [7] was married to Lamia Silanus and the younger [8]
to Marcus Antoninus.

Antoninus and M. Galerius Aurelius Antoninus; see *C.I.L.*,
vi. 988 and 989. Both died before their father was adopted
by Hadrian.

[7] Aurelia Fadilla. She died before her father's adoption
(cf. c. iii. 6). Her sepulchral inscription is preserved (*C.I.L.*,
vi. 990).

[8] Annia Galeria Faustina the younger. On her marriage
to Marcus see c. x. 2 and note.

ANTONINUS PIUS

8 Ipse Antoninus Pius natus est XIII. kal. Oct.
Flavio Domitiano XII. et Cornelio Dolabella consulibus in villa Lanuvina. educatus Lorii in Aurelia,
ubi postea palatium exstruxit, cuius hodieque re-
9 liquiae manent. pueritiam egit cum avo paterno, mox
cum materno, omnes suos religiose colens, atque adeo
et consobrinorum et vitrici et multorum adfinium
hereditate ditatus est.

II. Fuit vir forma conspicuus, ingenio [1] clarus, moribus clemens, nobilis vultu, placidus ingenio, singularis [2] eloquentiae, nitidae litteraturae, praecipue
sobrius, diligens agri cultor, mitis, largus, alieni abstinens, et omnia haec cum mensura et sine iactantia,
2 in cunctis postremo laudabilis et qui merito Numae
3 Pompilio ex bonorum sententia comparatur.[3] Pius
cognominatus est a senatu, vel quod soceri fessi iam
aetatem manu praesente senatu levaret (quod quidem
non satis magnae pietatis est argumentum, cum impius
sit magis qui ista non faciat, quam pius qui debitum
4 reddat[4]), vel quod eos quos Hadrianus per malam
5 valetudinem occidi iusserat, reservavit, vel quod
Hadriano contra omnium studia post mortem infinitos
6 atque immensos honores decrevit, vel quod, cum se

---

[1] *ingenio* deleted by Peter, following Salm., who divides:
*forma conspicuus, clarus moribus, clemens, nobilis, uultu
placidus, ingenio singulari, eloquentiae nitidae, littcraturae
praecipuae, sobrius, diligens agri cultor* ; P punctuates:
*forma conspicuus ingenio clarus . moribus clemens . nobilis
uultu placidus ingenio . singulari eloquentiae . nitidae litteraturae . praecipue sobrius . diligens . agri cultor.*, etc.
[2] *singularis* P corr.   [3] *conparatus* P; *conparetur* Kellerbauer.   [4] *quod quidem . . . reddat* suspected as a marginal
comment by Kellerbauer, probably rightly.

---

[1] In southern Etruria, about ten miles W. of Rome. The
Via Aurelia ran N.W. from Rome along the coast of Etruria.

Antoninus himself was born at an estate at Lanu- 19 Sept.
vium on the thirteenth day before the Kalends of[86].
October in the twelfth consulship of Domitian and first
of Cornelius Dolabella. He was reared at Lorium[1] on
the Aurelian Way, where he afterwards built the
palace whose ruins stand there to-day. He passed
his childhood first with his paternal grandfather, then
later with his maternal; and he showed such a dutiful affection toward all his family, that he was enriched by legacies from even his cousins, his
stepfather, and many still more distant kin.

II. In personal appearance he was strikingly handsome, in natural talent brilliant, in temperament
kindly; he was aristocratic in countenance and calm
in nature, a singularly gifted speaker and an elegant
scholar, conspicuously thrifty, a conscientious land-
holder, gentle, generous, and mindful of others' rights.
He possessed all these qualities, moreover, in the
proper mean and without ostentation, and, in fine,
was praiseworthy in every way and, in the minds of
all good men, well deserving of comparison with
Numa Pompilius. He was given the name of Pius
by the senate,[2] either because, when his father-in-law
was old and weak, he lent him a supporting hand in
his attendance at the senate (which act, indeed, is
not sufficient as a token of great dutifulness, since a
man were rather undutiful who did not perform this
service than dutiful if he did), or because he spared
those men whom Hadrian in his ill-health had con-

---

[2] The first three of the following reasons for the bestowal
of the surname Pius on Antoninus are also given in *Hadr.*,
xxiv. 3-5. The third is also given in Dio, lxx. 2, 1, and
the last in Eutrop., viii. 8; Suidas, *s. v. Antoninus;* and
Orosius, vii. 14, 1.

Hadrianus interimere vellet, ingenti custodia et
7 diligentia fecit, ne id posset admittere, vel quod
vere natura clementissimus et nihil temporibus suis
8 asperum fecit. idem faenus trientarium, hoc est
minimis usuris, exercuit, ut patrimonio suo plurimos
adiuvaret.

9 Fuit quaestor liberalis, praetor splendidus, con-
10 sul cum Catilio Severo. hic in omni privata vita [1] in
agris frequentissime vixit, sed clarus in locis omnibus
11 fuit. ab Hadriano inter quattuor consulares, quibus
Italia committebatur, electus est ad eam partem Italiae
regendam in qua plurimum possidebat, ut Hadrianus
viri talis et honori consuleret et quieti.

III. Huic, cum Italiam regeret, imperii omen est
factum. nam cum tribunal ascendisset, inter alias
adclamationes dictum est 'Auguste, dii te servent'.
2 proconsulatum Asiae sic egit ut solus avum vinceret.
3 in proconsulatu etiam sic imperii omen accepit: nam
cum sacerdos femina Trallibus [2] ex more proconsules

[1] *uita* om. in P, supplied (before *priuata*) by P corr.
[2] *trallis* P.

---

[1] Cf. *Hadr.*, xxiv. 9.
[2] The early rate of interest, said to have been fixed by the
Twelve Tables, seems to have been 10 per cent. In the later
republican period 12 per cent. was frequently exacted, but in
54 B.C. money could be had for 4 per cent. and the rise of the

demned to death, or because after Hadrian's death he
had unbounded and extraordinary honours decreed
for him in spite of opposition from all, or because,
when Hadrian wished to make away with himself,
by great care and watchfulness he prevented him
from so doing,[1] or because he was in fact very kindly
by nature and did no harsh deed in his own time.
He also loaned money at four per cent, the lowest
rate ever exacted,[2] in order that he might use his
fortune to aid many.

As quaestor[3] he was generous, as praetor illustrious,
and in the consulship he had as colleague Catilius 120.
Severus. His life as a private citizen he passed
mostly on his estates but he was well-known everywhere. He was chosen by Hadrian from among the
four men of consular rank under whose jurisdiction
Italy was placed,[4] to administer that particular part
of Italy in which the greater part of his own holdings
lay ; from this it was evident that Hadrian had regard
for both the fame and the tranquillity of such a man.

III. An omen of his future rule occurred while he
was administering Italy ; for when he mounted the
tribunal, among other greetings some one cried,
" God save thee, Augustus ". His proconsulship in
Asia[5] he conducted in such a fashion that he alone
excelled his grandfather ; and in this proconsulship,
too, he received another omen foretelling his rule ;
for at Tralles a priestess, being about to greet him
after the custom of the place (for it was their custom

rate to 8 per cent. was a matter for comment; see Cicero,
ad Att., iv. 15, 7 ; *ad Quint. Fr.*, ii. 14, 4.

[3] About 111.

[4] See *Hadr.*, xxii. 13.

[5] About 135. An inscription set up at Ephesus during his
proconsulship is extant; see *C.I.L.*, iii. 2965.

semper hoc nomine salutaret, non dixit 'Ave pro
4 consule,' sed 'Ave imperator'. Cyzici[1] etiam de
simulacro dei ad statuam eius corona translata est.
5 et post consulatum in viridiario taurus marmoreus
cornibus ramis arboris adcrescentibus adpensus est,
et fulgur caelo sereno sine noxa in eius domum venit,
et in Etruria dolia, quae defossa fuerant, supra terram
reperta sunt, et statuas eius in omni Etruria examen
apium replevit, et somnio saepe monitus est dis
penatibus eius[2] Hadriani simulacrum inserere.
6 Proficiscens ad proconsulatum filiam maiorem
7 amisit. de huius uxore multa dicta sunt ob nimiam
libertatem et vivendi facilitatem, quae iste cum
8 animi dolore compressit. post proconsulatum in
consiliis Hadriani Romae frequens vixit, de omnibus,
de[3] quibus Hadrianus consulebat, mitiorem sententiam
semper ostendens.

IV. Genus sane adoptionis tale fertur: mortuo Helio
Vero, quem sibi Hadrianus adoptaverat et Caesarem
2 nuncupaverat, dies senatus habebatur; eo Arrius
Antoninus soceri vestigia levans[4] venit atque idcirco
3 ab Hadriano dicitur adoptatus. quae causa sola esse
adoptionis nec potuit omnino nec debuit, maxime
cum et semper rem publicam bene egisset Antoninus

---

[1] *cilici* P[1] (for *cidici*; Salm.) ; *cilicie* (i.e. *ae*) P corr.　　[2] So
Peter ; *monitus sed penitus eius* P ; *monitus est penatibus eius*
Cas. ; *monitus se dis penatibus eius* Salm.　　　[3] *de* om. in P,
supplied by Jordan.　　　[4] *uel lauans* P corr.

---

[1] Aurelia Fadilla ; see note to c. i. 7.

to greet the proconsuls by their title), instead of saying "Hail, proconsul," said "Hail, imperator"; at Cyzicus, moreover, a crown was transferred from an image of a god to a statue of him. After his consulship, again, a marble bull was found hanging in his garden with its horns attached to the boughs of a tree, and lightning from a clear sky struck his home without inflicting damage, and in Etruria certain large jars that had been buried were found above the ground again, and swarms of bees settled on his statues throughout all Etruria, and frequently he was warned in dreams to include an image of Hadrian among his household gods.

While setting out to assume his proconsular office he lost his elder daughter.[1] About the licence and loose living of his wife a number of things were said, which he heard with great sorrow and suppressed. On returning from his proconsulship he lived for the most part at Rome, being a member of the councils of Hadrian,[2] and in all matters concerning which Hadrian sought his advice, ever urging the more merciful course.

IV. The manner of his adoption, they say, was somewhat thus: After the death of Aelius Verus, whom Hadrian had adopted and named Caesar, a day was set for the meeting of the senate, and to this Arrius Antoninus came, supporting the steps of his father-in-law. For this act, it is said, Hadrian adopted him.[3] But this could not have been the only reason for the adoption, nor ought it to have been, especially since Antoninus had always done well in his administration of public office, and in his pro-

[2] See note to *Hadr.*, viii. 9.
[3] But see c. ii. 3; *Hadr.*, xxiv. 3.

et in proconsulatu se sanctum gravemque praebuisset.
4 ergo cum eum Hadrianus adoptare se velle publicasset,
acceptum est spatium deliberandi, utrum adrogari ab
5 Hadriano vellet. adoptionis lex huiusmodi data est,
ut quemadmodum Antoninus ab Hadriano adopta-
batur ita sibi ille adoptaret M. Antoninum, fratris
uxoris suae filium, et L. Verum, Helii Veri, qui ab
Hadriano adoptatus fuerat, filium, qui postea Verus
6 Antoninus est dictus. adoptatus est V. kal. Mart.
die, in senatu gratias agens quod de se ita sensisset
7 Hadrianus, factusque est patri et in imperio pro-
8 consulari et in tribunicia potestate collega. huius
primum hoc fertur quod, cum ab uxore[1] argueretur
quasi parum nescio quid suis largiens, dixerit:
"Stulta, posteaquam ad imperium transivimus, et
9 illud quod habuimus ante perdidimus". congiarium
10 populo[2] de proprio dedit et ea quae pater promiserat. et ad opera Hadriani plurimum contulit et
aurum coronarium, quod adoptionis suae causa
oblatum fuerat, Italicis totum, medium provincialibus reddidit.

[1] *ab uxore* P corr. (P¹ omits *ab*); *uxor* Mommsen; *cum ab
uxore argueretur quasi carum* (or *rarum*) *nescio quid suis
largiens* Salm.   [2] *militibus*, before *populo* in P, deleted by
Jordan; *militibus ac populo* vulg.

---

[1] Cf. *Hadr.*, xxiv. 1; *Ael.*, vi. 9; Dio, lxix. 21, 1. On the
names of his two adopted sons see notes to *Hadr.*, xxiv. 1.

[2] According to the Calendar of Philocalus of 354 the date
was afterwards commemorated by races in the circus at
Lorium; see *C.I.L.*, i², pp. 258 and 310.

[3] By the bestowal of these two powers, the basis of the
civil and of the military power of the emperor respectively,
he became *consors imperii*, or partner in the imperial power.
Such a position had often been bestowed on the heir apparent
of the emperor. With regard to the proconsular power,

consulship had shown himself a man of worth and dignity. At any rate, when Hadrian announced a desire to adopt him, he was given time for deciding whether he wished to be adopted. This condition was attached to his adoption,[1] that as Hadrian took Antoninus as his son, so he in turn should take Marcus Antoninus, his wife's nephew, and Lucius Verus, thenceforth called Verus Antoninus, the son of that Aelius Verus whom Hadrian had previously adopted. He was adopted on the fifth day before the Kalends of March,[2] while returning thanks in the senate for Hadrian's opinion concerning him, and he was made colleague to his father in both the proconsular and the tribunician power.[3]   It is related as his first remark, that when he was reproved by his wife because he was not sufficiently generous to his household in some trifling matter, he said: "Foolish woman, now that we have gained an empire, we have lost even what we had before". To the people he gave largess on his own account[4] and also paid the moneys that his father had promised. He contributed a large amount of money, too, to Hadrian's public works,[5] and of the crown-gold[6] which had been presented to him on the occasion of his adoption, he returned all of Italy's share, and half of their share to the provinces.

25 Feb., 138.

the convention was always observed that it was valid only in the provinces, and the title of proconsul was not borne by the emperor within the confines of Italy.

[4] Commemorated by coins of 139 with the legend *Liberalitas*; see Cohen, ii², p. 316 f., Nos. 480-482.

[5] Attested by inscriptions from various towns of Italy; see E. E. Bryant, *Reign of Ant. Pius* (Cambridge, 1896), p. 38.

[6] See *Hadr.*, vi. 5 and note.

V. Et patri, cum advixit,[1] religiosissime paruit. sed
Hadriano apud Baias mortuo reliquias eius Romam
pervexit sancte ac reverenter atque in hortis Domitiae
conlocavit, etiam repugnantibus cunctis inter divos
2 eum rettulit. uxorem Faustinam Augustam appellari
a senatu permisit. Pii appellationem recepit. patri et
matri atque avis et fratribus iam mortuis statuas decre-
tas libenter accepit. circenses natali suo dicatos non
respuit aliis honoribus refutatis. clipeum Hadriano
magnificentissimum posuit et sacerdotes instituit.
3 Factus imperator nulli eorum quos Hadrianus
provexerat successorem dedit fuitque ea constantia
ut septenis et novenis annis in provinciis bonos
4 praesides detineret. per legatos suos plurima bella
gessit. nam et Britannos per Lollium Urbicum vicit
legatum alio muro caespiticio summotis barbaris
ducto, et Mauros ad pacem postulandam coegit, et

---

[1] *cum aduixit* P¹; *quoad uixit* P corr.; *dum aduixit* Salm;
cum aduixerit Peter.

---

[1] See *Hadr.*, xxv. 6. [2] See *Hadr.*, xxvii. 2.
[3] On the coins issued in her honour during her life-time she
is regularly called *Faustina Aug. Antonini Aug. P. P.*; see
Cohen, ii². p. 424 f.
[4] The name appears on coins of the latter part of 138; see
Cohen, ii². p. 277, No. 66 f.
[5] On such games see *Hadr.*, viii. 2 and note. Races in
honour of Antoninus are listed for the 19 September (his birthday) in the Calendar of Philocalus.
[6] The clipeus was a shield-shaped plate of metal, in this
case doubtless of gold. It contained, sometimes an honorary inscription, sometimes a bust in high relief.
[7] See *Hadr.*, xxvii. 3 and note.
[8] Q. Lollius Urbicus had held a command in the war in
Judæa under Hadrian, and later had been governor of
Germania Inferior.
[9] Probably in 142, for in an inscription of this year he is
designated as Imp. II. ; see *C.I.L.*, x. 515 = Dessau, *Ins. Sel.*,

V. His father, as long as he lived, he obeyed most scrupulously, and when Hadrian passed away at Baiae [1] he bore his remains to Rome with all piety and reverence, and buried him in the gardens of Domitia ; moreover, though all opposed the measure, he had him placed among the deified.[2] On his wife Faustina he permitted the senate to bestow the name of Augusta,[3] and for himself accepted the surname Pius.[4] The statues decreed for his father, mother, grandparents and brothers, then dead, he accepted readily ; nor did he refuse the circus-games ordered for his birthday,[5] though he did refuse other honours. In honour of Hadrian he set up a superb shield [6] and established a college of priests.[7]

After his accession to the throne he removed none of the men whom Hadrian had appointed to office, and, indeed, was so steadfast and loyal that he retained good men in the government of provinces for terms of seven and even nine years. He waged a number of wars, but all of them through his legates. For Lollius Urbicus,[8] his legate, overcame the Britons [9] and built a second wall, one of turf,[10] after driving back the barbarians. Through other legates or governors, he forced the Moors to sue for peace,[11] and

340. The victory is commemorated on coins with the legend *Britannia* and designs signifying a victory ; see Cohen. ii². p. 281 f., Nos. 113-116, 119. The revolt was begun by the Brigantes, who lived just south of Hadrian's wall ; see Paus., viii. 43, 4.

[10] It ran from the Firth of Forth to the Firth of Clyde, a distance of 40 miles. It was constructed by the soldiers of three legions, the II. *Augusta*, the VI. *Victrix*, and the XX. *Valeria Victrix*; see *C.I.L.*, vii. p. 191-194.

[11] The rebellion seems to have been in western Mauretania, the province of Mauretania Tingitana; see Paus., viii. 43,

Germanos et Dacos et multas gentes atque Iudaeos
5 rebellantes contudit per praesides ac legatos. in
Achaia etiam atque Aegypto rebelliones repressit.
VI. Alanos molientis saepe refrenavit. procuratores suos
et modeste suscipere tributa iussit et excedentes [1]
modum rationem factorum suorum reddere praecepit,
nec umquam ullo laetatus est lucro, quo provincialis
2 oppressus est. contra procuratores suos conquerentes
libenter audivit.
3   Iis quos Hadrianus damnaverat in senatu indulgentias petiit, dicens etiam ipsum Hadrianum hoc
4 fuisse facturum. imperatorium fastigium ad summam
civilitatem deduxit, unde plus crevit, recusantibus
aulicis ministris, qui illo nihil per internuntios agente
nec terrere poterant homines aliquando nec ea
5 quae occulta non erant vendere. senatui tantum
detulit imperator quantum, cum privatus esset, deferri
6 sibi ab alio principe optavit. patris patriae nomen
delatum a senatu, quod primo distulerat, cum ingenti

---

[1] So P corr.; *terdecentes* P[1].

3, and *C.I.L.*, iii. 5211-5215. It probably took place about
145, although it is argued by Bryant (*op. cit.* p. 71 f.) that it is
to be placed in 152. The victory is commemorated in an inscription in Rome, *C I.L.*, vi. 1208.
    [1] This victory is also commemorated in the inscription
C.I.L., vi. 1208. The time of this campaign is set by Bryant
(p. 52) as between 140 and 145.
    [2] About 157. See Aristid., *Or.*, xiv, vol. i. 351 Dind., and
C.I.L., iii. 1416.
    [3] It is described by Aristides (*Or.*, xiv. i. 351 Dind.) as an
outbreak of those who lived on the shore of the Red Sea.
According to Joannes Malalas (p. 280 f. Bonn) Antoninus went
in person to Alexandria at the time of the revolt, but this is
almost certainly an error (cf. c. vii. 11).
    [4] This people lived in south-eastern Russia, between the Don
and the Caspian Sea, and had made raids into Armenia and

crushed the Germans[1] and the Dacians[2] and many other tribes, and also the Jews, who were in revolt. In Achaea also and in Egypt[3] he put down rebellions and many a time sharply checked the Alani[4] in their raiding. VI. His procurators were ordered to levy only a reasonable tribute, and those who exceeded a proper limit were commanded to render an account of their acts, nor was he ever pleased with any revenues that were onerous to the provinces. Moreover, he was always willing to hear complaints against his procurators.

He besought the senate to pardon those men whom Hadrian had condemned,[5] saying that Hadrian himself had been about to do so. The imperial pomp he reduced to the utmost simplicity and thereby gained the greater esteem, though the palace-attendants opposed this course, for they found that since he made no use of go-betweens, they could in no wise terrorize men or take money for decisions about which there was no concealment.[6] In his dealings with the senate, he rendered it, as emperor, the same respect that he had wished another emperor to render him when he was a private man. When the senate offered him the title of Father of his Country, he

Cappadocia in the time of Hadrian. They afterwards spread toward the west, and invaded the Empire by way of Moesia.

[5] See *Hadr.*, xxv. 8.

[6] Under those emperors who were careless in the announcement of decisions or in answers to petitions it was not unusual for a dishonest favourite or official to demand money from petitioners for securing a favourable answer; he would then either actually influence the emperor in his decision, or, more often, merely claim that a favourable decision had been secured by his own efforts, and demand the payment of the bribe. This practice was known as *fumos vendere;* see c. xi. 1; *Alex.*, xxiii. 8; xxxvi. 2.

7 gratiarum actione suscepit. tertio anno imperii sui
Faustinam uxorem perdidit, quae a senatu consecrata
est delatis circensibus atque templo et flaminicis et
statuis aureis atque argenteis; cum etiam ipse hoc
concesserit, ut imago eius cunctis circensibus ponere-
8 tur. statuam auream delatam a senatu positam
9 suscepit. M. Antoninum quaestorem consulem
10 petente senatu creavit. Annium Verum, qui postea
dictus est Antoninus, ante tempus quaestorem desig-
11 navit. neque de provinciis neque de ullis actibus
quicquam constituit, nisi quod prius ad amicos rettulit,
12 atque ex eorum sententia formas composuit. visus
est sane ab amicis et cum privatis vestibus et domes-
tica quaedam gerens.

VII. Tanta sane diligentia subiectos sibi populos
rexit ut omnia et omnes, quasi sua essent, curaret.
2 provinciae sub eo cunctae floruerunt. quadruplatores
3 exstincti sunt. publicatio bonorum rarior quam
umquam fuit, ita ut unus tantum proscriberetur

---

[1] See *Hadr.*, vi. 4 and note. Pius accepted the title in
139, for it appears for the first time on coins of this year; *e.g.*,
Cohen, ii[2]. p. 279, No. 98 f.

[2] Many coins were struck in her honour with the title
Diva Faustina. The actual apotheosis is represented by her
ascension to heaven on an eagle with the legend *Consecratio ;*
see Cohen, ii[2]. p. 427, Nos. 182-185.

[3] On the Sacra Via, near the eastern end of the Forum. It
is still standing and is used as the church of S. Lorenzo in
Miranda. It was also dedicated to Antoninus after his death

at first refused it,[1] but later accepted it with an
elaborate expression of thanks. On the death of
his wife Faustina, in the third year of his reign, the 141.
senate deified her,[2] and voted her games and a
temple[3] and priestesses and statues of silver and of
gold. These the Emperor accepted, and furthermore granted permission that her statue be erected
in all the circuses; and when the senate voted
her a golden statue, he undertook to erect it himself.
At the instance of the senate, Marcus Antoninus, 140.
now quaestor, was made consul; also Annius Verus,[4]
he who was afterwards entitled Antoninus, was appointed quaestor before the legal age.[5] Never did
he resolve on measures about the provinces or render
a decision on any question without previously consulting his friends,[6] and in accordance with their
opinions he drew up his final statement. And indeed
he often received his friends without the robes of
state and even in the performance of domestic duties.

VII. With such care did he govern all peoples
under him that he looked after all things and all men
as if they were his own. As a result, the provinces
all prospered in his reign, informers were abolished,
the confiscation of goods was less frequent than
ever before, and only one man was condemned as
guilty of aspiring to the throne. This was Atilius

(c. xiii. 4), and the names of both Antoninus and Faustina
appear in the inscription on the architrave (*C.I.L.*, vi. 1005).
    [4] *i.e.*, Lucius Verus.
    [5] In the time of the empire the minimum age was twenty-
five. Exceptions to this, however, were common in the case
of members of the imperial family; see also the case of
Marcus (*Marc.*, v. 6). Verus was made quaestor at the age
of twenty-three; see *Verus*, ii. 11.
    [6] Apparently, the members of his *consilium*; see *Hadr.*,
viii. 9.

115

ANTONINUS PIUS

4 adfectatae tyrannidis reus, hoc est Atilius Titianus,
senatu puniente, a quo conscios requiri vetuit, filio
eius ad omnia semper adiuto. periit et Priscianus
reus adfectatae tyrannidis, sed morte voluntaria. de
qua coniuratione quaeri vetuit.

5 Victus Antonini Pii talis fuit ut esset opulentia
sine reprehensione, parsimonia sine sordibus, et mensa
eius per proprios servos, per proprios aucupes pis-
6 catores ac venatores instrueretur. balneum, quo
usus fuisset, sine mercede populo exhibuit nec omnino
7 quicquam de vitae privatae qualitate mutavit. salaria
multis subtraxit, quos otiosos videbat accipere, dicens
nihil esse sordidius, immo crudelius, quam si rem
publicam is adroderet qui nihil in eam suo labore
8 conferret. unde etiam Mesomedi lyrico salarium
inminuit. rationes omnium provinciarum adprime
9 scivit et vectigalium. patrimonium privatum in
filiam contulit, sed fructus rei publicae donavit.
10 species imperatorias superfluas et praedia vendidit et
in suis propriis fundis vixit varie ac pro temporibus.
11 nec ullas expeditiones obiit, nisi quod ad agros suos
profectus est et ad Campaniam, dicens gravem esse
provincialibus comitatum principis, etiam nimis parci.
12 et tamen ingenti auctoritate apud omnes gentes fuit,
cum in urbe propterea sederet, ut undique nuntios,
medius utpote, citius posset accipere.[1]

---

[1] *al' anticipare* P corr.

---

[1] See note to *Hadr.*, xv. 6.　　　[2] *Hadr.*, vii. 4.
[3] In view of this statement, it seems necessary to refuse
credence to the assertion of Aristides (*Or.*, xxiii. i. 453 f. Dind.)
and Malalas (p. 280 Bonn) that Antoninus went in person to
Egypt and Syria; see note to c. v. 5.

Titianus,[1] and it was the senate itself that conducted his prosecution,[2] while the Emperor forbade any investigation about the fellow-conspirators of Atilius and always aided his son to attain all his desires. Priscianus did indeed die for aspiring to the throne, but by his own hand, and about his conspiracy also the Emperor forbade any investigation.

The board of Antoninus Pius was rich yet never open to criticism, frugal yet not stingy ; his table was furnished by his own slaves, his own fowlers and fishers and hunters. A bath, which he had previously used himself, he opened to the people without charge, nor did he himself depart in any way from the manner of life to which he had been accustomed when a private man. He took away salaries from a number of men who held obvious sinecures, saying there was nothing meaner, nay more unfeeling, than the man who nibbled at the revenues of the state without giving any service in return ; for the same reason, also, he reduced the salary of Mesomedes, the lyric poet. The budgets of all the provinces and the sources of revenue he knew exceedingly well. He settled his private fortune on his daughter, but presented the income of it to the state. Indeed, the superfluous trappings of royal state and even the crown-lands he sold, living on his own private estates and varying his residence according to the season. Nor did he undertake any expedition [3] other than the visiting of his lands in Campania, averring that the equipage of an emperor, even of one over frugal, was a burdensome thing to the provinces. And yet he was regarded with immense respect by all nations, for, making his residence in the city, as he did, for the purpose of being in a central location, he was able to receive messages from every quarter with equal speed.

ANTONINUS PIUS

VIII. Congiarium populo dedit, militibus donativum addidit. puellas alimentarias in honorem Faustinae
2 Faustinianas constituit. opera eius haec exstant: Romae templum Hadriani, honori patris dicatum, Graecostadium post incendium restitutum, instauratum Amphitheatrum, sepulchrum Hadriani, templum
3 Agrippae, Pons Sublicius, Phari restitutio, Caietae portus, Tarracinensis portus restitutio, lavacrum Ostiense, Antiatum aquae ductus, templa Lanuviana.
4 multas etiam civitates adiuvit pecunia, ut opera vel nova facerent vel vetera restituerent, ita ut et magistratus adiuvaret et senatores urbis ad functiones suas.
5   Hereditates eorum qui filios habebant repudiavit. primus constituit, ne poenae causa legatum relictum
6 maneret. successorem viventi bono iudici nulli dedit

---

[1] On nine different occasions, according to coins with the legend *Liberalitas;* see Cohen, ii². p. 316-322, Nos. 480-532.

[2] In 145, on the occasion of the marriage of his daughter Faustina to Marcus; see c. x. 2.

[3] Similar endowments for destitute children had been made by Nerva (Aur. Vict., *Epit.,* xii. 4) and by Trajan (Dio, lxviii. 5, and *C.I.L.,* xi. 1146). This memorial to Faustina was commemorated on coins with the legend *Puellae Faustinianae;* see Cohen, ii². p. 433, Nos. 261-263. A similar endowment in memory of the younger Faustina was established by Marcus; see *Marc.,* xxvi. 6.

[4] Situated in the Campus Martius, probably not far from the Pantheon. It is represented as an octastyle temple on a coin of 151; see Cohen, ii². p. 330, No. 618. The temple was probably dedicated in 145; see *Verus,* iii. 1.

[5] Probably the Graecostasis. It was a sort of platform, between the Senate-house and the Rostra, used by envoys from foreign nations; see Varro, *Ling. Lat.,* v. 155.

[6] See c. ix. i.   [7] *i.e.* the Colosseum.

[8] See *Hadr.,* xix. 11 and note.

[9] If this reading is correct the Pantheon must be meant; see note to *Hadr.,* xix. 10. However, perhaps it is an error

118

VIII. He gave largess to the people,[1] and, in addition, a donation to the soldiers,[2] and founded an order of destitute girls, called Faustinianae [3] in honour of Faustina. Of the public works that were constructed by him the following remain to-day: the temple of Hadrian [4] at Rome, so called in honour of his father, the Graecostadium,[5] restored by him after its burning,[6] the Amphitheatre,[7] repaired by him, the tomb of Hadrian,[8] the temple of Agrippa,[9] and the Pons Sublicius,[10] also the Pharus, the port at Caieta, and the port at Tarracina, all of which he restored, the bath at Ostia,[11] the aqueduct at Antium, and the temples at Lanuvium. Besides all this, he helped many communities[12] to erect new buildings and to restore the old; and he even gave pecuniary aid to Roman magistrates and senators to assist them in the performance of their duties.

He declined legacies from those who had children of their own and was the first to establish the rule that bequests made under fear of penalty [13] should not be valid. Never did he appoint a successor to a worthy magistrate while yet alive, except in the case

for *Templum Augusti*, the restoration of which is commemorated on coins of Pius; see Cohen, ii², p. 270, Nos. 1-12.

[10] The earliest, and for a long time the only, bridge across the Tiber. It was built of piles, and after the construction of other bridges was preserved for religious and sentimental reasons. Its site was near the Forum Boarium, now the Piazza della Bocca di Verità.

[11] This had been promised by Hadrian; see the dedicatory inscription, *C.I.L.*, xiv. 98 = Dessau, *Ins. Sel.*, 334.

[12] For a list see Bryant, p, 116 f.

[13] Apparently an allusion to the law which provided that a senator must leave a specified sum to the public treasury (or to the emperor). This was rescinded by Pius; see Zonaras, xii. 1, p. 593 D., and Malalas, xi. p. 281 Dind.

7 nisi Orfito praefecto urbi, sed petenti. nam Gavius
Maximus praefectus praetorii usque ad vicensimum
annum sub eo pervenit, vir severissimus, cui Tattius
8 Maximus successit. in cuius demortui locum duos
praefectos substituit Fabium Cornelium Repentinum
9 et Furium Victorinum.[1] sed Pepentinus fabula
famosa[2] percussus est, quod per concubinam principis
10 ad praefecturam venisset. usque adeo sub eo nullus
percussus est senator, ut etiam parricida confessus in
insula deserta poneretur, quia vivere illi naturae
11 legibus non licebat. vini olei et tritici penuriam
per aerarii sui damnum[3] emendo et gratis populo
dando sedavit.

IX. Adversa eius temporibus haec provenerunt:
fames, de qua diximus, Circi ruina, terrae motus, quo
Rhodiorum et Asiae oppida conciderunt, quae omnia
mirifice instauravit, et Romae incendium, quod tre-
2 centas quadraginta insulas vel domos absumpsit. et

[1] So Borghesi and Hirschfeld ; *Fabium Repentinum et Cor-nelium Victorinum* P.   [2] *fabula famosa* Novak ; *famosa* P ; *famosa voce* P corr. ; *famosis* Peter.   [3] So Peter ; *damno* P.

[1] Several inscriptions set up in his honour are extant ; ac-cording to these he was granted consular honours on his re-tirement ; see *Hadr.*, viii. 7 and note, and c. x. 6.
[2] Commemorated in several inscriptions. He was prefect of the *vigiles*, the watchmen and firemen, in 156, and was advanced to the prefecture of the guard about 158.
[3] See note to *Hadr.*, ix. 5.
[4] For his death see *Marc.*, xiv. 5.
[5] See note to *Hadr.*, vii. 4.
[6] It is said that 1112 persons were killed ; see Mommsen, *Chron. Min.*, i. 146.

of Orfitus, the prefect of the city, and then only at
his own request.   For under him Gavius Maximus,[1]
a very stern man, reached his twentieth year of
service as prefect of the guard ; he was succeeded by
Tattius Maximus,[2] and at his death Antoninus appointed two men [3] in his place, Fabius Cornelius
Repentinus and Furius Victorinus,[4] the former of
whom, however, was ruined by the scandalous tale
that he had gained his office by the favour of the
Emperor's mistress.   So rigidly did he adhere to his
resolve that no senator should be executed in his
reign,[5] that a confessed parricide was merely
marooned on a desert island, and that only because
it was against the laws of nature to let such a one
live.   He relieved a scarcity of wine and oil and
wheat with loss to his own private treasury, by buy-
ing these and distributing them to the people free.

IX. The following misfortunes and prodigies occurred in his reign : the famine, which we have just
mentioned, the collapse of the Circus,[6] an earthquake [7] whereby towns of Rhodes and of Asia were
destroyed—all of which, however, the Emperor restored in splendid fashion,—and a fire at Rome which
consumed three hundred and forty tenements and
dwellings.[8]   The town of Narbonne,[9] the city of

---

[7] The earthquake which destroyed Rhodes occurred about
140 ; a description of it is given in an oration of Aristides
(804 Dind.).   The neighbouring island of Cos and the city of
Stratonicea in Caria were also devastated.   There seems to
have been a second earthquake about 151, which devastated
Bithynia, Lesbos, Smyrna and Ephesus.

[8] Mentioned also by Gellius, xv. 1, 2.

[9] See C.I.L., xii. 4342 and p. 521.   Narbo Martius, which
had received the status of a colony in 45 B.C., was the capital
of the province of Gallia Narbonensis.

ANTONINUS PIUS

Narbonensis civitas et Antiochense oppidum et Car-
3 thaginiense forum arsit. fuit et inundatio Tiberis,
apparuit et stella crinita, natus est et biceps puer, et
4 uno partu mulieris quinque pueri editi sunt. visus
est in Arabia iubatus anguis maior solitis, qui se a
cauda medium comedit. lues etiam in Arabia fuit.
hordeum in Moesia in culminibus arborum natum
5 est. quattuor praeterea leones mansueti sponte se
capiendos in Arabia praebuerunt.
6   Pharasmanes rex ad eum Romam venit plusque illi
quam Hadriano detulit. Pacorum regem Laziis dedit.
Parthorum regem ab Armeniorum expugnatione solis
litteris reppulit. Abgarum regem ex orientis parti-
7 bus sola auctoritate deduxit. causas regales termina-
vit. sellam regiam Parthorum regi repetenti, quam
8 Traianus ceperat, pernegavit. Rhoemetalcen[1] in
regnum Bosphoranum audito inter ipsum et cura-
9 torem[2] negotio remisit. Olbiopolitis contra Tauroscythas in Pontum auxilia misit et Tauroscythas usque
10 ad dandos Olbiopolitis obsides vicit. tantum sane

---

[1] *rimethalcen* P.   [2] *Eupatorem* Cary, Hist. des Rois du
Bosphore, p. 64 (ed. Berol.).

---

[1] Also included among his benefactions in Paus., viii.
43, 4.
[2] King of the Hiberi; see *Hadr.*, xiii. 9 and note. He had
refused to come to meet Hadrian (*Hadr.*, xxi. 13), but now
came to Rome with his wife; see Dio, lxix. 15, 3 = lxx. 2, 1
(Boissevain).
[3] The Lazi lived on the south-eastern shore of the Black
Sea, south of the river Phasis (Rion).
[4] Vologases III. He seems to have made preparations for
a war against the Romans (*Marc.*, viii. 6), and troops were
despatched to Syria *ob bellum Parthicum;* see *C.I.L.*, ix.
2457 = Dessau, *Ins. Sel.*, 1076.
[5] Of Osrhoene.

122

Antioch, and the forum of Carthage [1] also burned.
Besides, the Tiber flooded its banks, a comet was seen,
a two-headed child was born, and a woman gave
birth to quintuplets.   There was seen, moreover, in
Arabia, a crested serpent larger than the usual size,
which ate itself from the tail to the middle; and
also in Arabia there was a pestilence, while in Moesia
barley sprouted from the tops of trees.   And besides
all this, in Arabia four lions grew tame and of their
own accord yielded themselves to capture.

Pharasmenes,[2] the king, visited him at Rome and
showed him more respect than he had shown Hadrian.
He appointed Pacorus king of the Lazi,[3] induced the
king of the Parthians [4] to forego a campaign against
the Armenians merely by writing him a letter, and
solely by his personal influence brought Abgarus the
king [5] back from the regions of the East.   He settled
the pleas of several kings.[6]   The royal throne of the
Parthians, which Trajan had captured, he refused to
return when their king asked for it,[7] and after hearing the dispute between Rhoemetalces [8] and the imperial commissioner, sent the former back his kingdom
of the Bosphorus.   He sent troops to the Black Sea
to bring aid to Olbiopolis [9] against the Tauroscythians
and forced the latter to give hostages to Olbiopolis.

[6] See the coins of 140-144 with the legends *Rex Armeniis
datus* and *Rex Quadis datus*, Cohen, ii², p. 338 f., Nos. 686-
689.

[7] It had been promised by Hadrian to Osrhoes, the predecessor of Vologases; see *Hadr.*, xiii. 8.

[8] T. Julius Rhoemetalces, king of the Cimmerian Bosphorus (the Crimea and the district east of the Strait of
Kertch) from 131 to 153.   Several inscriptions and coins of
his are extant.

[9] Olbia or Olbiopolis was a Greek city on the river Hypanis
(Bug) in south-western Russia.

ANTONINUS PIUS

auctoritatis apud exteras gentes nemo habuit, cum
semper amaverit pacem, eo usque ut Scipionis sententiam frequentarit, qua ille dicebat malle se unum
civem servare quam mille hostes occidere.

X. Mensem Septembrem atque Octobrem Antoninum atque Faustinum appellandos decrevit senatus,
2 sed id Antoninus respuit. nuptias filiae suae Faustinae, cum Marco Antonino eam coniungeret, usque
3 ad donativum militum celeberrimas fecit. Verum
4 Antoninum post quaesturam consulem fecit. cum
Apollonium, quem e Chalcide acciverat, ad Tiberianam domum, in qua habitabat, vocasset, ut ei Marcum
Antoninum traderet, atque ille dixisset "non magister
ad discipulum debet venire, sed discipulus ad magis-
trum," risit eum, dicens, "facilius fuit Apollonio a
Chalcide [1] Romam venire quam a domo sua in
Palatium". cuius avaritiam etiam in [2] mercedibus
5 notavit. inter argumenta pietatis eius et hoc habetur
quod, cum Marcus mortuum educatorem suum fleret
vocareturque [3] ab aulicis ministris ab ostentatione
pietatis, ipse dixerit: "Permittite, inquit, illi, ut
homo sit; neque enim vel philosophia vel imperium
tollit adfectus".

---

[1] *calchida* P.   [2] *in* omitted in P.   [3] *uetareturque* P
corr.; *reuocareturque* Cas.

---

[1] Cf. Eutrop., viii. 8. According to Aur. Victor, *Epit.*, xv.
4, ambassadors from the Indi, Bactri, and Hyrcani came to
him.
[2] She had been betrothed by Hadrian to Lucius Verus; see
Ael., vi. 9; *Marc.*, vi. 2; *Verus*, ii. 3.
[3] A Stoic philosopher, the teacher of both Marcus and
Verus; see *Marc.*, ii. 7; iii. 1; *Verus*, ii. 5. He is mentioned
with gratitude by Marcus in εἰς ἑαυτόν i. 8. His home

124

No one has ever had such prestige among foreign nations as he,[1] for he was ever a lover of peace, even to such a degree that he was continually quoting the saying of Scipio in which he declared that he would rather save a single citizen than slay a thousand foes.

X. When the senate declared that the months of September and October should be called respectively Antoninus and Faustinus, Antoninus refused. The wedding of his daughter Faustina, whom he espoused 145. to Marcus Antoninus,[2] he made most noteworthy, even to the extent of giving a donative to the soldiers. He made Verus Antoninus consul after his quaestor-154. ship. On one occasion, he sent word to Apollonius,[3] whom he had summoned from Chalcis, to come to the House of Tiberius [4] (where at the time he was staying) in order that he might put Marcus Antoninus in his charge, but Apollonius replied "The master ought not come to the pupil, but the pupil to the master". Whereupon the Emperor ridiculed him, saying "It was easier, then, for Apollonius to come to Rome from Chalcis than from his house to my palace". The greed of this man he had noticed even in the matter of his salary. It is related of him, too, as an instance of his regard for his family, that when Marcus was mourning the death of his tutor and was restrained by the palace servants from this display of affection, the Emperor said: "Let him be only a man for once; for neither philosophy nor empire takes away natural feeling".

was Chalcedon, according to *Marc.*, ii. 7, Nicomedia, according to Dio, lxxi. 35. 1; Chalcis is evidently an error.
[4] The Domus Tiberiana was at the northern end of the Palatine Hill; very extensive ruins are extant. It seems to have been the usual residence of Pius when at Rome; see *Marc.*, vi. 3; *Verus*, ii. 4.

ANTONINUS PIUS

6 Praefectos suos et locupletavit et ornamentis con-
7 sularibus donavit. si quos repetundarum damnavit,
eorum liberis bona paterna restituit, ea tamen lege
ut illi provincialibus redderent quod parentes ac-
8.9 ceperant. ad indulgentias pronissimus fuit. edita
munera, in quibus elephantos et corocottas et tigrides
et rhinocerotes, crocodillos etiam atque hippopotamos
et omnia ex toto orbe terrarum exhibuit. centum
etiam leones cum tigridibus[1] una missione edidit.

XI. Amicis suis in imperio suo non aliter usus est
quam privatus, quia et ipsi numquam de eo cum
libertis per fumum aliquid vendiderunt; si quidem
2 libertis suis severissime usus est. amavit histrionum
artes. piscando se et venando multum oblectavit et
deambulatione cum amicis atque sermone. vindemias
3 privati modo cum amicis agebat. rhetoribus et
philosophis per omnes provincias et honores et salaria
detulit. orationes plerique alienas esse dixerunt,
quae sub eius nomine feruntur; Marius Maximus eius
4 proprias fuisse dicit. convivia cum amicis et privata
5 communicavit et publica nec ullum sacrificium per
6 vicarium fecit, nisi cum aeger fuit. cum sibi et filiis
7 honores peteret, omnia quasi privatus fecit. fre-
8 quentavit et ipse amicorum suorum convivia. inter

---

[1] *cum tigridibus*, in P before *exhibuit*, placed after *leones*
by Peter, deieted by Salm. and Novak.

---

[1] See note to *Hadr.*, viii. 7.
[2] Probably in 148, in commemoration of the tenth anniversary of his accession to power. Coins, evidently referring
to these spectacles, were issued in 149 bearing the legend
Munificentia and representations of a lion and an elephant;
see Cohen, ii[2], p. 325, Nos. 562-566.

126

On his prefects he bestowed both riches and consular honours.[1] If he convicted any of extortion he
nevertheless delivered up the estates to their children,
providing only that the children should restore to the
provinces what their fathers had taken. He was very
prone to acts of forgiveness. He held games [2] at which
he displayed elephants and the animals called corocot-
tae and tigers and rhinoceroses, even crocodiles and
hippopotami, in short, all the animals of the whole
earth; and he presented at a single performance as
many as a hundred lions together with tigers.

XI. His friends he always treated, while on the
throne, just as though he were a private citizen, for
they never combined with his freedmen to sell false
hopes of favours,[3] and indeed he treated his freedmen with the greatest strictness. He was very fond
of the stage, found great delight in fishing and hunting and in walks and conversation with his friends,
and was wont to pass vintage-time in company with
his friends in the manner of an ordinary citizen.
Rhetoricians and philosophers throughout all the
provinces he rewarded with honours and money.
The orations which have come down in his name,
some say, are really the work of others, according to
Marcus Maximus, however, they were his own. He
always shared his banquets, both public and private,
with his friends; and never did he perform sacrifices
by proxy except when he was ill. When he sought
offices [4] for himself or for his sons all was done as by
a private individual. He himself was often present
at the banquets of his intimates, and among other

[3] See note to c. vi. 4.
[4] *i.e.* went through the formality of asking the senate to
confer them.

alia etiam hoc civilitatis eius praecipuum argumentum
est quod, cum domum Homulli visens miransque
columnas porphyreticas requisisset, unde eas haberet,
atque Homullus ei dixisset, "cum in domum alienam
veneris, et mutus et surdus esto," patienter tulit.
cuius Homulli multa ioca semper patienter accepit.

XII. Multa de iure sanxit ususque est iuris peritis
Vindio Vero, Salvio Valente, Volusio Maeciano, Ulpio
2 Marcello et Diavoleno. seditiones ubicumque factas
non crudelitate sed modestia et gravitate compressit.
3 intra urbes sepeliri mortuos vetuit. sumptum muneribus gladiatoriis instituit. vehicularium cursum summa
diligentia sublevavit. omnium quae gessit et in
senatu et per edicta rationem reddidit.
4 Periit anno septuagensimo, sed quasi adulescens
desideratus est. mors autem eius talis fuisse narratur :
cum Alpinum caseum in cena edisset avidius, nocte
5 reiectavit atque alia die febre commotus est. tertia
die, cum se gravari videret, Marco Antonino rem
publicam et filiam praesentibus praefectis commendavit Fortunamque auream, quae in cubiculo

---

[1] M. Valerius Homullus, cos. in 152. He tried to arouse
the suspicion of Pius against Lucilla, Marcus' mother; see
Marc., vi. 9.

[2] As incorporated in the *Digesta* and the *Codex* of Justinian,
these deal with the questions of inheritances, adoption and
guardianship, manumission, and the treatment of slaves by
their masters.

[3] Verus, Maecianus and Marcellus are frequently cited in
the *Digesta*. Maecianus was Marcus' instructor in law; see
Marc., iii. 6.

[4] Apparently an error for Iavolenus (Priscus), the celebrated
jurist. He, however, was an older contemporary of Pliny,

things it is a particular evidence of his graciousness that when, on a visit at the house of Homullus,[1] he admired certain porphyry columns and asked where they came from, Homullus replied "When you come to another's house, be deaf and dumb," and he took it in good part. In fact, the jibes of this same Homullus, which were many, he always took in good part.

XII. A number of legal principles [2] were established by Antoninus with the aid of certain men, experts in jurisprudence, namely, Vindius Verus,[3] Salvius Valens, Volusius Maecianus, Ulpius Marcellus, and Diavolenus.[4] Rebellions, wherever they occurred, he suppressed [5] not by means of cruelty, but with moderation and dignity. He forbade the burial of bodies within the limits of any city ; he established a maximum cost for gladiatorial games ; and he very carefully maintained the imperial post.[6] Of everything that he did he rendered an account, both in the senate and by proclamation.

He died in the seventieth [7] year of his age, but his loss was felt as though he had been but a youth. They say his death was somewhat as follows : after he had eaten too freely some Alpine cheese at dinner he vomited during the night, and was taken with a fever the next day. On the second day, as he saw that his condition was becoming worse, in the presence of his prefects he committed the state and his daughter to Marcus Antoninus, and gave orders that the golden statue of Fortune, which was wont to stand

7 Mar., 161.

and it can hardly be supposed that he was actually consulted by Pius.

[5] See c. v. 4-5.   [6] See note to *Hadr.*, vii. 5.
[7] Really in his seventy-fifth year; cf. c. i. 8.

principum poni solebat, transferri ad eum iussit,
6 signum [1] tribuno aequanimitatis dedit atque ita conversus quasi dormiret, spiritum reddidit apud Lorium.
7 alienatus in febri nihil aliud quam de re publica et de
8 iis regibus quibus irascebatur locutus est. privatum
patrimonium filiae reliquit. testamento autem omnes
suos legatis idoneis prosecutus est.

XIII. Fuit statura elevata decorus. sed cum esset
longus et senex incurvareturque, tiliaciis tabulis in
2 pectore positis fasciabatur, ut rectus incederet. senex
etiam, antequam salutatores venirent, panem siccum
comedit ad sustentandas vires. fuit voce rauca et
sonora cum iucundidate.
3   A senatu divus est appellatus cunctis certatim
adnitentibus, cum omnes eius pietatem clementiam
ingenium sanctimoniam laudarent. decreti etiam
sunt omnes honores qui optimis principibus ante
4 delati sunt. meruit et flaminem et circenses et
templum et sodales Antoninianos solusque omnium
prope principum prorsus sine [2] civili sanguine et
hostili, quantum ad se ipsum pertinet, vixit et qui
rite comparetur Numae, cuius felicitatem pietatemque
et securitatem caerimoniasque semper obtinuit.

---

[1] *signum* Novak (so Peter[1]); *signatum* P; *signum tum*
Peter[2] with Petschenig.   [2] *sine* omitted in P.

---

[1] Cf. *Marc.*, vii. 3; see also *Sev.*, xxiii. 5.
[2] Cf. c. vii. 9.   [3] See note to c. vi. 7.
[4] See note to *Hadr.*, xxvii. 3.

in the bed-chamber of the emperor,[1] be given to him.
Then he gave the watchword to the officer of the day
as "Equanimity," and so, turning as if to sleep, gave
up the ghost at Lorium.   While he was delirious with
fever, he spoke of nothing save the state and certain
kings with whom he was angry.   To his daughter he
left his private fortune,[2] and in his will he remem-
bered all his household with suitable legacies.

XIII. He was a handsome man, and tall in stature ;
but being a tall man, when he was bent by old age
he had himself swathed with splints of linden-wood
bound on his chest in order that he might walk erect.
Moreover, when he was old, he ate dry bread before
the courtiers came to greet him, in order that he
might sustain his strength.   His voice was hoarse
and resonant, yet agreeable.

He was deified by the senate, while all men vied
with one another to give him honour, and all extolled
his devoutness, his mercy, his intelligence, and his
righteousness.   All honours were decreed for him
which were ever before bestowed on the very best of
emperors.   He well deserved the flamen and games
and temple [3] and the Antoninine priesthood.[4] Almost
alone of all emperors he lived entirely unstained by
the blood of either citizen or foe so far as was in his
power, and he was justly compared to Numa, whose
good fortune and piety and tranquillity and religious
rites he ever maintained.

MARCUS ANTONINUS

IULII CAPITOLINI

I. Marco Antonino, in omni vita philosophanti viro
et qui sanctitate vitae omnibus principibus antecellit,
2 pater Annius Verus, qui in praetura decessit, avus
Annius . Verus, iterum [1] consul et praefectus urbi,
adscitus in patricios [2] a Vespasiano et Tito censoribus,
3 patruus Annius Libo consul, amita Galeria Faustina
Augusta, mater Domitia Lucilla,[3] Calvisii Tulli bis
4 consulis filia, proavus paternus Annius Verus praetorius
ex Succubitano municipio ex Hispania [4] factus senator,
proavus maternus Catilius Severus bis consul et praefectus urbi, avia paterna Rupilia Faustina, Rupilii
Boni consularis filia, fuere.

---

[1] *iterum* P ; *tertium* Petschenig.　　[2] *a principibus*, following *patricios* in P, removed by Salm.　　[3] *Lucilla* Borghesi ;
Caluilla P, Peter.　　[4] *spania* P[1], Peter ; *yspania* P corr.

---

[1] M. Annius Verus was consul three times, first under
Domitian, again in 121 and 126.
[2] See *Pius*, i. 6.

MARCUS ANTONINUS

THE PHILOSOPHER

BY

JULIUS CAPITOLINUS

I. Marcus Antoninus, devoted to philosophy as long as he lived and pre-eminent among emperors in purity of life, was the son of Annius Verus, who died while praetor. His grandfather, named Annius Verus also, attained to a second consulship,[1] was prefect of the city, and was enrolled among the patricians by Vespasian and Titus while they were censors. Annius Libo, a consul, was his uncle, Galeria Faustina Augusta,[2] his aunt. His mother was Domitia Lucilla, the daughter of Calvisius Tullus, who served as consul twice.[3] Annius Verus, from the town of Succuba in Spain, who was made a senator and attained to the dignity of praetor, was his father's grandfather; his great-grandfather on his mother's side was Catilius Severus,[4] who twice held the consulship and was prefect of the city. His father's mother was Rupilia Faustina, the daughter of Rupilius Bonus, a man of consular rank.

[3] First in 109; the second date is unknown.
[4] See note to *Hadr.*, v. 10.

5 Natus est Marcus Romae VI. kal. Maias in Monte Caelio in hortis avo suo iterum et Augure consulibus. 6 cuius familia in originem recurrens a Numa probatur sanguinem trahere, ut Marius Maximus docet; item a rege Sallentino Malemnio, Dasummi filio, qui Lupias 7 condidit. educatus est in eo loco in quo natus est et 8 in domo avi sui Veri iuxta aedes Laterani. habuit et sororem natu minorem Anniam Cornificiam, uxorem 9 Anniam Faustinam, consobrinam suam. Marcus Antoninus principio aevi sui nomen habuit[1] Catilii 10 Severi, materni proavi. post excessum vero patris ab Hadriano Annius Verissimus vocatus est, post virilem autem togam Annius Verus. patre mortuo ab avo paterno adoptatus et educatus est.

II. Fuit a prima infantia gravis. at ubi egressus est annos qui nutricum foventur auxilio, magnis prae-ceptoribus traditus ad philosophiae scita pervenit. 2 usus est magistris ad prima elementa Euphorione litteratore et Gemino comoedo, musico Androne eodemque geometra. quibus omnibus ut discip-3 linarum auctoribus plurimum detulit. usus praeterea grammaticis, Graeco Alexandro Cotiaeensi,[2] Latinis

---

[1] *et*, after *habuit* in P, deleted by Petrarch.   [2] *cotidianis* P; *Cotiaensi* Uhlig, Peter.

---

[1] In Calabria, about 20 miles S. of Brundisium.
[2] Annia Cornificia Faustina. She was married to Um-midius Quadratus.
[3] See *Pius*, i. 7.
[4] Probably M. Annius Catilius Severus.
[5] So also Dio, lxix. 21, 2. This name appears on Greek

Marcus himself was born at Rome on the sixth day 26 Apr., before the Kalends of May in the second consulship 121. of his grandfather and the first of Augur, in a villa on the Caelian Hill. His family, in tracing its origin back to the beginning, established its descent from Numa, or so Marius Maximus tells, and likewise from the Sallentine king Malemnius, the son of Dasummus, who founded Lupiae.[1] He was reared in the villa where he was born, and also in the home of his grandfather Verus close to the dwelling of Lateranus. He had a sister younger than himself, named Annia Cornificia ;[2] his wife, who was also his cousin, was Annia Faustina.[3] At the beginning of his life Marcus Antoninus was named Catilius Severus[4] after his mother's grandfather. After the death of his real father, however, Hadrian called him Annius Verissimus,[5] and, after he assumed the toga virilis, Annius Verus. When his father died he was adopted and reared by his father's father.

II. He was a solemn child from the very beginning ; and as soon as he passed beyond the age when children are brought up under the care of nurses, he was handed over to advanced instructors and attained to a knowledge of philosophy. In his more elementary education, he received instruction from Euphorion in literature and from Geminus in drama, in music and likewise in geometry from Andron ; on all of whom, as being spokesman of the sciences, he afterwards conferred great honours. Besides these, his teachers in grammar were the Greek Alexander of Cotiaeum,[6] and

coins, Eckhel, *D.N.*, vii. 69. It is perhaps an allusion to his love of frankness ; see Fronto, *Epist.*, pp. 29, 34, 49.

[6] See εἰς ἑαυτ, i. 10. His funeral oration was delivered by Aristides, *Or.*, xii.

135

MARCUS ANTONINUS

Trosio Apro et Pollione[1] et Eutychio Proculo Sic-
4 censi. oratoribus usus est Graecis[2] Aninio[3] Macro,
Caninio Celere et Herode Attico, Latino Frontone
5 Cornelio. sed multum ex his Frontoni detulit, cui
et statuam in senatu petiit. Proculum vero usque ad
proconsulatum provexit oneribus[4] in se receptis.
6 Philosophiae operam vehementer dedit et quidem
adhuc puer. nam duodecimum annum ingressus
habitum philosophi sumpsit et deinceps tolerantiam,
cum studeret in pallio et humi cubaret, vix autem
matre agente instrato pellibus lectulo accubaret.
7 usus est etiam Commodi[5] magistro, cuius ei adfinitas
fuerat destinata,[6] Apollonio Chalcedonio Stoico philo-
III. sopho. tantum autem studium in eo philosophiae
fuit ut adscitus iam in[7] imperatoriam tamen ad
2 domum Apollonii discendi causa veniret. audivit et
Sextum Chaeronensem Plutarchi nepotem, Iunium
Rusticum, Claudium Maximum et Cinnam Catulum,

[1] *polono* P ; *Pollione* Peter. [2] *graeco* P. [3] So P corr. ;
animo P[1]. [4] *oneribus* Turnebus ; *honoribus* P. [5] So
Obrecht ; *commodo* P. [6] *usus est et*, repeated before *Apoll.
Chal.* in P, removed by Obrecht. [7] *in* om. in P[1] ; *in imperatoriam dignitatem* P corr.

[1] Ti. Claudius Atticus Herodes, consul in 143. The foremost
orator of his time, he had a school at Athens attended by a
great number of students. He presented public buildings to
very many of the cities of Greece, but particularly to his
native city, Athens, where he built the Odeum on the S.E.
slope of the Acropolis and rebuilt the Stadium, using Pentelic
marble. His life by Philostratus is extant (*Vit. Soph.*, ii. 1).
[2] M. Cornelius Fronto, famous as an orator and man of

the Latins Trosius Aper, Pollio, and Eutychius Proculus of Sicca; his masters in oratory were the Greeks Aninius Macer, Caninius Celer and Herodes Atticus,[1] and the Latin Cornelius Fronto.[2] Of these he conferred high honours on Fronto, even asking the senate to vote him a statue; but indeed he advanced Proculus also—even to a proconsulship, and assumed the burdens[3] of the office himself.

He studied philosophy with ardour, even as a youth. For when he was twelve years old he adopted the dress and, a little later, the hardiness of a philosopher, pursuing his studies clad in a rough Greek cloak and sleeping on the ground;[4] at his mother's solicitation, however, he reluctantly consented to sleep on a couch strewn with skins. He received instruction, furthermore, from the teacher of that Commodus[5] who was destined later to be a kinsman of his, namely Apollonius of Chalcedon,[6] the Stoic; III. and such was his ardour for this school of philosophy, that even after he became a member of the imperial family, he still went to Apollonius' residence for instruction. In addition, he attended the lectures of Sextus of Chaeronea,[7] the nephew of Plutarch, and of Junius Rusticus,[8] Claudius Maximus,[9] and Cinna Catulus,[10] all Stoics. He also attended

letters, and for his correspondence with Pius, Marcus, and Verus.

[3] *i.e.* the giving of circus-games, the expense of which caused many to resign from the consulship; see Dio, lx. 27, 2. The cost of the games given by Fronto was borne by Pius; see Fronto, *Epist.*, p. 25.

[4] At the advice of his teacher Diognetus; see εἰς ἑαυτόν, i. 6.

[5] *i.e.* Lucius Verus; see note to *Hadr.*, xxiv. 1.

[6] See *Pius*, x. 4 and note.   [7] See εἰς ἑαυτ, i. 9.

[8] See εἰς ἑαυτ, i. 7.   [9] See εἰς ἑαυτ, i. 15.   [10] See εἰς ἑαυτ, i. 13.

3 Stoicos. Peripateticae vero studiosum [1] audivit Claudium Severum et praecipue Iunium Rusticum, quem
et reveritus est et sectatus, qui domi militiaeque
4 pollebat, Stoicae disciplinae peritissimum ; cum quo
omnia communicavit publica privataque consilia, cui
etiam ante praefectos praetorio semper osculum dedit,
5 quem et consulem iterum designavit, cui post obitum
a senatu statuas postulavit. tantum autem honoris
magistris suis detulit ut imagines eorum aureas in
lario haberet ac sepulchra eorum aditu hostiis flori-
6 bus semper honoraret. studuit et iuri, audiens Lu-
7 cium Volusium Maecianum. tantumque operis et
laboris studiis impendit ut corpus adficeret atque in
8 hoc solo pueritia eius reprehenderetur. frequentavit
et declamatorum scholas publicas amavitque e [2] con-
discipulis praecipuos senatorii ordinis Seium Fuscianum et Aufidium Victorinum, ex equestri Bae-
9 bium Longum et Calenum. in quos maxime liberalis
fuit, et ita quidem ut quos non posset ob qualitatem
vitae rei publicae praeponere, locupletatos teneret.

---

[1] So Peter ; *studiosos* P ; *studiosus* Cas., Jordan.   [2] om.
by P¹ ; *ex* P corr.

---

[1] Perhaps the " ἀδελφός " Severus mentioned in εἰς ἑαυτ,
i. 14.

[2] The custom had arisen that the emperor should bestow
a ceremonial kiss of greeting upon the senators and the foremost of the equestrian order ; see Suet., *Otho*, vi ; Plin., *Pan.*,
23 ; Tac., *Agr.*, 40.

[3] For the first time in 133, for the second in 162 ; he was
also prefect of the city.

the lectures of Claudius Severus,[1] an adherent of the
Peripatetic school, but he received most· instruction
from Junius Rusticus, whom he ever revered and
whose disciple he became, a man esteemed in both
private and public life, and exceedingly well acquainted with the Stoic system, with whom Marcus
shared all his counsels both public and private,
whom he greeted with a kiss prior to the· prefects of the guard,[2] whom he even appointed consul
for a second term,[3] and whom after his death he
asked the senate to honour with statues. On his
teachers in general, moreover, he conferred great
honours, for he even kept golden statues of them in
his chapel,[4] and made it a custom to show respect for
their tombs by personal visits and by offerings of
sacrifices and flowers. He studied jurisprudence as
well, in which he heard Lucius Volusius Maecianus,
and so much work and labour did he devote to his
studies that he impaired his health—the only fault to
be found with his entire childhood. He attended
also the public schools of rhetoricians. Of his fellow-
pupils he was particularly fond of Seius Fuscianus [5]
and Aufidius Victorinus,[6] of the senatorial order, and
Baebius Longus and Calenus, of the equestrian. He
was very generous to these men, so generous, in fact,
that on those whom he could not advance to public
office on account of their station in life, he bestowed
riches.

[4] See the similar practice of Severus Alexander, *Alex.*,
xxix. 2.
[5] Prefect of the city under Commodus (see *Pert.*, iv. 3), and
consul for the second time in 188.
[6] C. Aufidius Victorinus held a command in Germany (see
c. viii. 8), was proconsul of Africa, and consul for the second
time in 183. He married Fronto's daughter.

MARCUS ANTONINUS

IV. Educatus est[1] in Hadriani gremio, qui illum, ut supra diximus, Verissimum nominabat et qui ei 2 honorem equi publici sexenni[2] detulit, octavo aetatis 3 anno in Saliorum collegium rettulit. in saliatu omen accepit imperii : coronas omnibus in pulvinar ex more iacientibus aliae aliis locis haeserunt, huius velut manu 4 capiti Martis aptata est. fuit in eo sacerdotio et praesul et vates et magister et multos inauguravit atque exauguravit nemine praeeunte, quod ipse carmina cuncta didicisset.

5   Virilem togam sumpsit quinto decimo aetatis anno, statimque ei Lucii Ceionii Commodi filia desponsata 6 est ex Hadriani voluntate. nec multo post praefectus Feriarum Latinarum fuit. in quo honore praeclarissime se pro magistratibus agentem et in 7 conviviis Hadriani principis ostendit. post hoc patrimonium paternum sorori totum concessit, cum eum ad divisionem mater vocaret, responditque avi bonis se esse contentum, addens, ut et mater, si vellet, in sororem suum patrimonium conferret, ne inferior 8 esset soror marito. fuit autem tanta indulgentia[3]

---

[1] *est* P corr. ; *esset* P[1].   [2] *equi publici sexenni* Salm. ; *et qui publicis exenni (exenniis)* P.   [3] *fuit autem uitae indulgentia*, P, Peter ; *tanta uitae indulgentia* Novak.

---

[1] c. i. 10.
[2] At the official banquet held by the Salii in some temple on their feast-day.
[3] *i.e.*, L. Aelius Caesar, the adopted son of Hadrian ; see also c. vi. 2. The daughter was probably the Fabia mentioned in c. xxix. 10 and *Ver.*, x. 3-4.
[4] Under the republic, this official was charged with the administration of Rome when both consuls were absent from the city conducting the Feriae Latinae on Mons Albanus. In the empire the office was continued, although only as a formality, and was given to young men of high rank and

140

IV. He was reared under the eye of Hadrian, who called him Verissimus, as we have already related,[1] and did him the honour of enrolling him in the equestrian order when he was six years old and appointing him in his eighth year to the college of the Salii. While in this college, moreover, he received an omen of his future rule; for when they were all casting their crowns on the banqueting-couch [2] of the god, according to the usual custom, and the crowns fell into various places, his crown, as if placed there by his hand, fell on the brow of Mars. In this priesthood he was leader of the dance, seer, and master, and consequently both initiated and dismissed a great number of people; and in these ceremonies no one dictated the formulas to him, for all of them he had learned by himself.

In the fifteenth year of his life he assumed the 135-136 toga virilis, and straightway, at the wish of Hadrian, was betrothed to the daughter of Lucius Ceionius Commodus.[3] Not long after this he was made prefect of the city during the Latin Festival,[4] and in this position he conducted himself very brilliantly both in the presence of the magistrates and at the banquets of the Emperor Hadrian. Later, when his mother asked him to give his sister [5] part of the fortune left him by his father, he replied that he was content with the fortune of his grandfather and relinquished all of it, further declaring that if she wished, his mother might leave her own estate to his sister in its entirety, in order that she might not be poorer than her husband. So complaisant was he, moreover, that

often to princes of the imperial family; see Tac., *Ann.*, iv. 36, and Suet., *Nero*, vii.

[5] See c. i. 8 and note.

141

ut cogeretur nonnumquam vel in venationes pergere vel in theatrum descendere vel spectaculis interesse. 9 operam praeterea pingendo sub magistro Diogneto[1] dedit.   amavit pugilatum luctamina et cursum et 10 aucupatus et pila lusit adprime et venatus est.   sed ab omnibus his intentionibus studium eum philosophiae abduxit seriumque et gravem reddidit, non tamen prorsus abolita in eo comitate, quam praecipue suis, mox amicis atque etiam minus notis exhibebat, cum frugi esset sine contumacia, verecundus sine ignavia, sine tristitia gravis.

V. His ita se habentibus cum post obitum Lucii Caesaris Hadrianus successorem imperii quaereret, nec idoneus, utpote decem et octo annos agens, Marcus haberetur, amitae Marci virum Antoninum Pium Hadrianus ea lege in adoptationem legit ut sibi Marcum Pius adoptaret, ita tamen ut et Marcus 2 sibi Lucium Commodum adoptaret. sane ea die qua adoptatus est Verus in somnis se umeros eburneos habere vidit sciscitatusque, an apti essent oneri 3 ferundo, solito repperit fortiores. ubi autem comperit se ab Hadriano adoptatum, magis est deterritus quam laetatus iussusque in Hadriani privatam domum migrare invitus de maternis hortis recessit. 4 cumque ab eo domestici quaererent, cur tristis in adoptionem regiam transiret, disputavit quae mala in se contineret imperium.

[1] *Diogeneto* P, Peter.

---

[1] See *Hadr.*, xxiv. 1; *Ael.*, vi. 9; *Pius*, iv. 5. The statement that Lucius Verus was adopted by Marcus (so also *Ael.*, v. 12) is erroneous.

142

at times, when urged, he let himself be taken to hunts or the theatre or the spectacles. Besides, he gave some attention to painting, under the teacher Diognetus. He was also fond of boxing and wrestling and running and fowling, played ball very skilfully, and hunted well. But his ardour for philosophy distracted him from all these pursuits and made him serious and dignified, not ruining, however, a certain geniality in him, which he still manifested toward his household, his friends, and even to those less intimate, but making him, rather, austere, though not unreasonable, modest, though not inactive, and serious without gloom.

V. Such was his character, then, when, after the death of Lucius Cæsar, Hadrian looked about for a successor to the throne. Marcus did not seem suitable, being at the time but eighteen years of age; and Hadrian chose for adoption Antoninus Pius, the uncle-in-law of Marcus, with the provision that Pius should in turn adopt Marcus and that Marcus should adopt Lucius Commodus.[1] And it was on the day that Verus[2] was adopted that he dreamed that he had shoulders of ivory, and when he asked if they were capable of bearing a burden, he found them much stronger than before. When he discovered, moreover, that Hadrian had adopted him, he was appalled rather than overjoyed, and when told to move to the private home of Hadrian, reluctantly departed from his mother's villa. And when the members of his household asked him why he was sorry to receive royal adoption, he enumerated to them the evil things that sovereignty involved.

1 Jan., 138

[2] *i.e.*, Marcus. The story of the dream is told also by Dio (lxxi. 36, 1).

MARCUS ANTONINUS

5 Tunc primum pro Annio Aurelius coepit vocari,
quod in Aureliam, hoc est Antonini, adoptionis iure
6 transisset. octavo decimo ergo aetatis anno adoptatus
in secundo consulatu Antonini, iam patris sui, Hadriano ferente gratia aetatis facta quaestor est designatus.
7 adoptatus in aulicam domum omnibus parentibus suis
8 tantam reverentiam quantam privatus exhibuit. erat-
que haud secus rei suae quam in privata domo parcus
ac diligens, pro instituto patris volens agere dicere
cogitare.

VI. Hadriano Baiis absumpto cum Pius ad advehen-
das eius reliquias esset profectus, relictus Romae avo
iusta implevit et gladiatorium quasi privatus quaestor
2 edidit munus. post excessum Hadriani statim Pius
per uxorem suam Marcum sciscitatus est et eum [1]
dissolutis sponsalibus, quae cum Lucii Ceionii Commodi . . . [2] desponderi voluerat impari adhuc aetati,
3 habita deliberatione velle se dixit. his ita gestis
adhuc quaestorem et consulem secum Pius Marcum
designavit et Caesaris appellatione donavit et sevirum

---

[1] *et eum* P; *utrum* A. Jaekel, Klio xii, p. 124, n. 1.
[2] Cas. saw a lacuna after *Commodi* (cf. *Marc.*, iv. 5, and *Ver.*,
ii. 3), and supplied: *filia contrahere illum Hadrianus voluerat,
Faustina illi offeretur, quod Verus, cui eam Hadrianus*
(reading *et quum*, and *esset* after *aetate*); Mommsen supplied:
*sorore fecerat filiam Faustinam cum hortata esset ut duceret,
quam Hadrianus eidem Commodo*; Ellis i, p. 400, *et eum,
diss. spons. L. Ceionii Commodi* (i.e. *Veri*) *quae cum filia
fecerat, quam ei desponderi uol.*, etc.; see also Jaekel, *loc. cit.*

---

[1] On his name after his adoption see note to *Hadr.*, xxiv. 2.

At this time he first began to be called Aurelius instead of Annius,[1] since, according to the law of adoption, he had passed into the Aurelian family, that is, into the family of Antoninus. And so he was adopted in his eighteenth year, and at the instance of Hadrian exception was made for his age[2] and he was appointed quaestor for the year of the second 139 consulship of Antoninus, now his father. Even after his adoption into the imperial house, he still showed the same respect to his own relatives that he had borne them as a commoner, was as frugal and careful of his means as he had been when he lived in a private home, and was willing to act, speak, and think according to his father's principles.

VI. When Hadrian died at Baiae[3] and Pius de- 10 Jul., parted to bring back his remains, Marcus was left at 138 Rome and discharged his grandfather's funeral rites, and, though quaestor, presented a gladiatorial spectacle as a private citizen. Immediately after Hadrian's death Pius, through his wife, approached Marcus, and, breaking his betrothal with the daughter of Lucius Ceionius Commodus,[4] . . . he was willing to espouse one so much his junior in years, he replied, after deliberating the question, that he was. And when this was done, Pius designated him as his colleague in the consulship, though he was still only 140 quaestor, gave him the title of Cæsar,[5] appointed him while 'consul-elect one of the six commanders of the

---

[2] See *Pius*, vi. 9-10 and note.
[3] See *Hadr.*, xxv. 6; *Pius*, v. 1.
[4] See c. iv. 5 and note.
[5] See note to *Ael.*, i. 2. On coins of 139-140 he is called Aurelius Cæs(ar) Aug(usti) Pii f(ilius); see Cohen, ii². p. 409 f., Nos. 1-40.

MARCUS ANTONINUS

turmis equitum Romanorum iam consulem designatum creavit et edenti cum collegis ludos sevirales adsedit et in Tiberianam domum transgredi iussit et aulico fastigio renitentem ornavit et in collegia sacer-
4 dotum iubente senatu recepit. secundum etiam consulem designavit, cum ipse quartum pariter inierit.
5 per eadem tempora, cum tantis honoribus occuparetur et cum formandus ad regendum statum rei publicae patris actibus interesset, studia cupidissime frequentavit.
6 Post haec Faustinam duxit uxorem et suscepta filia tribunicia potestate donatus est atque imperio extra urbem proconsulari addito iure quintae
7 relationis. tantumque apud Pium valuit ut [1] num-
8 quam quemquam sine eo facile promoverit. erat autem in summis obsequiis patris Marcus, quamvis non
9 deessent qui aliqua adversum eum insusurrarent, et prae ceteris Valerius Homollus, qui, cum Lucillam

[1] *ut* P corr., om. by P¹.

---

[1] The *seviri equitum Romanorum* were the six commanders of the equestrian order. They received their appointment from the emperor, and were usually young men of senatorial families who had not as yet been admitted to the senate and sometimes princes of the imperial house, as Marcus, and Gaius, grandson of Augustus (Zonaras, x. 35). Marcus had also the title of *princeps iuventutis* or honorary chief of the equestrian order (Dio, lxxi. 35, 5), a title bestowed by the acclamation of the order, with the consent or at the command of the emperor, upon the heir apparent.

[2] See note to *Pius*, x. 4.

[3] Especially the four great colleges of which the emperor was always a member, *i.e.*, the *pontifices*, the *augures*, the *quindecimviri sacris faciendis* or keepers of the Sibylline Books, and the *septemviri epulonum*, and probably also the *fratres arvales* and the *sodales* of the various deified emperors (see note to *Hadr.*, xxvii. 3). The son of the emperor usually

146

equestrian order [1] and sat by him when he and his
five colleagues were producing their official games,
bade him take up his abode in the House of Tiberius [2]
and there provided him with all the pomp of a court,
though Marcus objected to this, and finally took him
into the priesthoods [3] at the bidding of the senate.
Later, he appointed him consul for a second term at 145
the same time that he began his fourth. And all
this time, when busied with so many public duties of
his own, and while sharing his father's activities that
he might be fitted for ruling the state, Marcus worked
at his studies [4] eagerly.

At this time he took Faustina to wife [5] and, after 145
begetting a daughter,[6] received the tribunician power
and the proconsular power outside the city,[7] with the
added right of making five proposals in the senate.[8]
Such was his influence with Pius that the Emperor
was never quick to promote anyone without his advice.
Moreover, he showed great deference to his father,
though there were not lacking those who whispered
things against him, especially Valerius Homullus,[9]

became a member of these colleges when he received the
name Caesar.

[4] Especially in rhetoric and literature; see Fronto, p. 36.
[5] See *Pius*, x. 2. Coins struck in honour of the occasion
bear the heads of Marcus and Faustina on the obverse and
reverse respectively; see Cohen, ii². p. 127, Nos. 3-4.
[6] Annia Galeria Aurelia Faustina, born in 146, was the
eldest of Marcus' children.
[7] See note to *Pius*, iv. 7.
[8] The newly-elected emperor was regularly empowered by
senatus consultum to propose a definite number of measures
in each meeting of the senate, these proposals to take pre-
cedence over any others. The number varied but never seems
to have exceeded five; see *Pert.*, v. 6; *Alex.*, i. 3; *Prob.*, xii. 8.
[9] Cf. *Pius*, xi. 8.

matrem Marci in viridiario venerantem simulacrum
Apollinis vidisset, insusurravit, "illa nunc rogat, ut
diem tuum claudas et filius imperet". quod omnino
10 apud Pium nihil valuit; tanta erat Marci probitas et
VII. tanta in imperatorio participatu[1] modestia. existi-
mationis autem tantam curam habuit ut et procuratores suos puer semper moneret, ne quid arrogantius
facerent, et heredidates delatas reddens proximis
2 aliquando respuerit. denique per viginti et tres
annos in domo patris ita versatus ut eius cotidie amor
3 cresceret, nec praeter duas noctes per tot annos ab eo
mansit diversis vicibus.

Ob hoc Antoninus Pius, cum sibi adesse finem
vitae videret, vocatis amicis et praefectis ut successorem eum imperii omnibus commendavit atque
firmavit statimque signo aequanimitatis tribuno dato
Fortunam auream, quae in cubiculo solebat esse, ad
4 Marci cubiculum transire iussit. bonorum mater-
norum partem Ummidio[2] Quadrato, sororis filio, quia
illa iam mortua erat, tradidit.

5 Post excessum divi Pii a senatu coactus regimen
publicum capere fratrem sibi participem in imperio
designavit, quem Lucium Aurelium Verum Commodum appellavit Caesaremque atque Augustum

[1] *participatum* P; *principatu* Peter, following B *principatum.*   [2] *Ummidio* Borghesi; *Mummio* P, Peter.

---

[1] Cf. *Pius*, xii. 5-6.
[2] M. Ummidius Quadratus, consul 167, was the son of
Annia Cornificia Faustina (c. i. 8, and iv. 7).

who, when he saw Marcus' mother Lucilla worshipping in her garden before a shrine of Apollo, whispered, "Yonder woman is now praying that you may come to your end, and her son rule". All of which influenced Pius not in the least, such was Marcus' sense of honour and such his modesty while heir to the throne. VII. He had such regard for his reputation, moreover, that even as a youth he admonished his procurators to do nothing high-handed and often refused sundry legacies that were left him, returning them to the nearest kin of the deceased. Finally, for three and twenty years he conducted himself in his father's home in such a manner that Pius felt more affection for him day by day, and never in all these years, save for two nights on different occasions, remained away from him.

For these reasons, then, when Antoninus Pius saw that the end of his life was drawing near, having summoned his friends and prefects, he commended Marcus to them all and formally named him as his successor in the empire. He then straightway gave the watch-word to the officer of the day as "Equanimity," and ordered that the golden statue of Fortune, customarily kept in his own bed-chamber, be transferred to the bed-chamber of Marcus.[1] Part of his mother's fortune Marcus then gave to Ummidius Quadratus,[2] the son of his sister, because the latter was now dead.

Being forced by the senate to assume the government of the state after the death of the Deified Pius, Marcus made his brother his colleague in the empire, giving him the name Lucius Aurelius Verus Commodus and bestowing on him the titles Cæsar and Augustus. Then they began to rule the state on 7 Mar., 16

149

6 dixit. atque ex eo pariter coeperunt rem publicam regere tuncque primum Romanum imperium duos Augustos habere coepit, cum imperium sibi relictum [1] cum alio participasset. Antonini mox ipse nomen 7 recepit. et quasi pater Lucii Commodi esset, et Verum eum appellavit addito Antonini nomine filiam- 8 que suam Lucillam fratri despondit. ob hanc con- iunctionem pueros et puellas novorum nominum 9 frumentariae perceptioni adscribi praeceperunt. actis igitur quae agenda fuerant in senatu pariter castra praetoria petiverunt et vicena milia nummum singulis ob participatum imperium militibus promiserunt et 10 ceteris pro rata. Hadriani autem sepulchro corpus patris intulerunt magnifico exsequiarum officio. mox iustitio secuto publice quoque funeris expeditus est 11 ordo. et laudavere uterque pro rostris patrem flaminemque ei ex adfinibus et sodales ex amicissimis Aurelianos creavere.

VIII. Adepti imperium ita civiliter se ambo egerunt ut lenitatem Pii nemo desideraret, cum eos Marullus, sui temporis mimographus, cavillando impune per- 2.3 stringeret. funebre munus patri dederunt.[2] dabat

---

[1] So Mommsen ; *habere coepit lictum* P ; *habere coepit . . . lictum* (*lictum cum alio participasset* perhaps a fragment of a marginal comment) Peter.   [2] This sentence Peter removed, as introduced from the margin of vii. 10.

---

[1] Coins of 161 and 162 show Marcus and Lucius standing with clasped hands and bear the legend Concord(ia) Augustor(um) ; see Cohen, iii², p. 8, Nos. 45-59.

[2] Annia Lucilla, his third child, born about 148.

[3] Like the *puellae alimentariae Faustinianae*, founded by Pius ; *see Pius*, viii. 1.

[4] *i.e.*, the centurions and other officers. Largess was also given to the populace ; see coins of 161 with legend *Lib(eralitas)*

equal terms,[1] and then it was that the Roman Empire
first had two emperors, when Marcus shared with
another the empire he had inherited.   Next, he himself took the name Antoninus, and just as though he
were the father of Lucius Commodus, he gave him the
name Verus, adding also the name Antoninus ; he also
betrothed him to his daughter Lucilla,[2] though legally
he was his brother.   In honour of this union they
gave orders that girls and boys of newly-named orders[3]
should be assigned a share in the distribution of grain.

And so, when they had done those things which
had to be done in the presence of the senate, they
set out together for the praetorian camp, and in
honour of their joint rule promised twenty thousand
sesterces apiece to the common soldiers and to the
others[4] money in proportion.   The body of their
father they laid in the Tomb of Hadrian[5] with elaborate funeral rites, and on a holiday which came
thereafter an official funeral train marched in parade.
Both emperors pronounced panegyrics for their father
from the Rostra, and they appointed a flamen for him
chosen from their own kinsmen and a college of
Aurelian priests[6] from their closest friends.

VIII. And now, after they had assumed the imperial power, the two emperors acted in so democratic
a manner that no one missed the lenient ways of Pius ;
for though Marullus, a writer of farces of the time,
irritated them by his jests, he yet went unpunished.
They gave funeral games for their father.   And

Augustor(um) and representation of the two emperors standing in front of a recipient (Cohen, iii², p. 41, Nos. 401-406).
    [5] See *Hadr.*, xix. 11.
    [6] *i.e.*, the Sodales Antoniniani ; see *Pius*, xiii. 4, and note
to *Hadr.*, xxvii. 3.

se Marcus totum et philosophiae, amorem civium ad-
4 fectans. sed interpellavit istam felicitatem securita-
temque imperatoris prima Tiberis inundatio, quae sub
illis gravissima fuit. quae res et multa urbis aedificia
vexavit et plurimum animalium interemit et famem
5 gravissimam peperit. quae omnia mala Marcus et
6 Verus sua cura et praesentia temperarunt. fuit eo
tempore etiam Parthicum bellum, quod Vologaesus
paratum sub Pio Marci et Veri tempore indixit, fugato
Attidio Corneliano, qui Syriam tunc administrabat.
7 imminebat etiam Britannicum bellum, et Chatti in
8 Germaniam ac Raetiam inruperant. et adversus Britannos quidem Calpurnius Agricola missus est, contra
9 Chattos Aufidius Victorinus. ad Parthicum vero
bellum senatu consentiente Verus frater est missus ;
ipse Romae remansit, quod res urbanae imperatoris
10 praesentiam postularent. et Verum quidem Marcus
Capuam usque prosecutus amicis comitantibus a senatu
11 ornavit additis officiorum omnium principibus. sed
cum Romam redisset Marcus cognovissetque Verum
apud Canusium aegrotare, ad eum videndum contendit susceptis in senatu votis ; quae, posteaquam

---

[1] Cf. the coins of 161 with the legend *Fel(icitas) Temp(orum)*
(Cohen, iii², p. 21, Nos. 196-198).

[2] See *Pius*, ix. 6 and note.

[3] This war, called officially *bellum Armeniacum et Parthicum*, arose, as was usually the case with wars between the
Romans and the Parthians, in a struggle for the control of
the buffer-state Armenia. After defeating Aelius Severianus,
the governor of Cappadocia, at Elegeia, on the upper Euphrates, and annihilating his legion (Dio, lxxi. 2 ; Fronto,
Prin. Hist., p. 209), the Parthians established their candidate
on the Armenian throne. Then followed the defeat of Cornelianus in 161.

[4] E. of the Rhine, N. and E. of the Taunus Mountains.

Marcus abandoned himself to philosophy, at the same
time cultivating the good-will of the citizens. But
now to interrupt the emperor's happiness [1] and repose,
there came the first flood of the Tiber—the severest
of their time—which ruined many houses in the city,
drowned a great number of animals, and caused a
most severe famine ; all these disasters Marcus and
Verus relieved by their own personal care and aid.
At this time, moreover, came the Parthian war, which 161
Vologaesus planned under Pius [2] and declared under
Marcus and Verus, after the rout of Attidius Cornelianus, then governor of Syria.[3] And besides this, 162
war was threatening in Britain, and the Chatti [4] had
burst into Germany and Raetia. Against the Britons
Calpurnius Agricola [5] was sent ; against the Chatti,
Aufidius Victorinus.[6] But to the Parthian war, with
the consent of the senate, Marcus despatched his
brother Verus, while he himself remained at Rome,
where conditions demanded the presence of an emperor. Nevertheless, he accompanied Verus as far as
Capua,[7] honouring him with a retinue of friends from
the senate and appointing also all his chiefs-of-staff.
And when, after returning to Rome, he learned that
Verus was ill at Canusium,[8] he hastened to see him,
after assuming vows in the senate, which, on his re-

---

[5] Mentioned in British inscriptions as governor (*legatus
Augusti pro praetore*) of the province of Britain. He afterwards held a command in the Marcomannic War.

[6] See c. iii. 8.

[7] Verus' departure took place in the spring of 162. It was
commemorated by coins of Verus with the legends *Profectio
Aug(usti)* and *Fort(una) Red(ux)* ; see Cohen, iii², p. 183 f.,
Nos. 132-141, and p. 180 f., Nos. 86-102.

[8] In Apulia, modern Canosa. On Verus' illness see *Ver.*,
vi. 7.

Romam rediit audita Veri transmissione, statim red-
12 didit. et Verus quidem, posteaquam in Syriam venit,
in deliciis apud Antiochiam et Daphnen vixit armisque
se gladiatoriis et venatibus exercuit, cum per legatos
bellum Parthicum gerens imperator appellatus esset,
13 cum Marcus horis omnibus rei publicae actibus in-
cubaret patienterque delicias fratris sed perinvitus ac
14 nolens[1] ferret. denique omnia quae ad bellum erant
necessaria Romae positus et disposuit Marcus et
ordinavit.

IX. Gestae sunt res in Armenia prospere per Sta-
tium Priscum Artaxatis captis, delatumque Armeniacum nomen utrique principum. quod Marcus per vere-
2 cundiam primo recusavit, postea tamen recepit. pro-
fligato autem bello uterque Parthicus appellatus est.
sed hoc[2] quoque Marcus delatum nomen repudiavit,
3 quod postea recepit. patris patriae autem nomen
delatum fratre absente in eiusdem praesentiam

---

[1] Suggested by Peter in note; *et prope inuitus ac uolens*
(*nolens* P corr.) P, Peter; *et prope non inuitus ac uolens*
Novak.   [2] *hoc* P corr., om. by P[1].

---

[1] See also *Ver.*, vi. 8–vii. 1.
[2] After the capture of Artaxata by Statius Priscus; see c.
ix. 1.
[3] The title *Armeniacus* appears on Verus' coins of 163, together with the representation of conquered Armenia; see
Cohen, iii[2], p. 172, Nos. 4–6, and p. 203, Nos. 330–331.
Marcus' coins, on the other hand, do not show it until 164;
see Cohen, iii[2], p. 5, Nos. 5–8; p. 48, Nos. 466–471, etc. The
capture of Artaxata enabled Rome to make her candidate,
Soaemus (Fronto, p. 127), king of Armenia; this event was
commemorated by coins of 164 with the legend *Rex Armeniis
Datus*; see *Ver.*, vii. 8, and Cohen, iii[2], p. 185 f., Nos. 157–165.
[4] By the capture of Seleucia and Ctesiphon in 165; see
Ver., viii. 3, and Dio, lxxi. 2, 3. The title *Parthicus Maxi-*

turn to Rome after learning that Verus had set sail, he immediately fulfilled. Verus, however, after he had come to Syria, lingered amid the debaucheries of Antioch and Daphne and busied himself with gladiatorial bouts and hunting.[1] And yet, for waging the Parthian war through his legates, he was acclaimed Imperator,[2] while meantime Marcus was at all hours keeping watch over the workings of the state, and, though reluctantly and sorely against his will, but nevertheless with patience, was enduring the debauchery of his brother. In a word, Marcus, though residing at Rome, planned and executed everything necessary to the prosecution of the war.

IX. In Armenia the campaign was successfully 163 prosecuted under Statius Priscus, Artaxata being taken, and the honorary name Armeniacus was given to each of the emperors.[3] This name Marcus refused at first, by reason of his modesty, but afterwards accepted. When the Parthian war was finished,[4] moreover, each emperor was called Parthicus; but this name also Marcus refused when first offered, though afterwards he accepted it. And further, when the title "Father of his Country" was offered him in his brother's absence, he deferred action upon it until the latter should be present.[5] In the midst of this 164 war he entrusted his daughter,[6] who was about to be married and had already received her dowry, to the care of his sister, and, accompanying them himself as far as Brundisium, sent them to Verus together with

mus appears on Verus' coins of 165 (Cohen, iii², p. 188 f., Nos. 190-196), and on Marcus' coins of 166 (Cohen, iii², p. 86 f., Nos. 877-880).

[5] It was finally taken by both Marcus and Lucius after the return of the latter in the summer of 166; see c. xii. 7.

[6] Lucilla; see c. vii. 7, and *Ver.*, vii. 7.

4 distulit. medio belli tempore et Civicam, patruum
Veri, et filiam suam nupturam commissam sorori suae
eandemque locupletatam Brundisium usque deduxit,
5 ad eum misit Romamque statim rediit, revocatus eorum
sermonibus qui dicebant Marcum velle finiti belli
gloriam sibimet vindicare atque idcirco in Syriam
6 proficisci. ad proconsulem scribit, ne quis filiae suae
iter facienti occurreret.

7 Inter haec liberales causas ita munivit ut primus iuberet apud praefectos aerarii Saturni unumquemque
civium natos liberos profiteri intra tricensimum diem
8 nomine imposito. per provincias tabulariorum publi-
corum usum instituit, apud quos idem de originibus
fieret quod Romae apud praefectos aerarii, ut, si forte
aliquis in provincia natus causam liberalem diceret,
9 testationes inde ferret. atque hanc totam legem de
adsertionibus firmavit aliasque de mensariis et auctioni-
bus tulit.

X. Senatum multis cognitionibus et maxime ad se
pertinentibus iudicem dedit. de statu etiam de-
2 functorum intra quinquennium quaeri iussit.[1] neque
quisquam principum amplius senatui detulit. in
senatus autem honorificentiam multis praetoriis et
consularibus privatis decidenda negotia delegavit,

[1] This sentence Peter[1], following Dirksen, transposed to
precede *senatum . . . dedit.*

---

[1] M. Ceionius Civica Barbarus, consul 157. a brother of L.
Aelius Cæsar.
[2] *i.e.*, of Asia. Verus met her at Ephesus ; *Ver.*, vii. 7.
[3] The officials in charge of the public treasury, kept in the
Temple of Saturn.

the latter's uncle, Civica.[1] Immediately thereafter
he returned to Rome, recalled by the talk of those
who said that he wished to appropriate to himself the
glory of finishing the war and had therefore set out
for Syria. He wrote to the proconsul,[2] furthermore,
that no one should meet his daughter as she made
her journey.

In the meantime, he put such safeguards about
suits for personal freedom—and he was the first to
do so—as to order that every citizen should bestow
names upon his free-born children within thirty
days after birth and declare them to the prefects of
the treasury of Saturn.[3] In the provinces, too, he
established the use of public records, in which entries
concerning births were to be made in the same
manner as at Rome in the office of the prefects of the
treasury, the purpose being that if any one born in
the provinces should plead a case to prove freedom,
he might submit evidence from these records. Indeed, he strengthened this entire law dealing with
declarations of freedom,[4] and he enacted other laws
dealing with money-lenders and public sales.

X. He made the senate the judge in many inquiries and even in those which belonged to his own
jurisdiction. With regard to the status of deceased
persons, he ordered that any investigations must be
made within five years.[5] Nor did any of the emperors
show more respect to the senate than he. To do the
senate honour, moreover, he entrusted the settling of

---

[4] *e.g.*, see. c. x. 1.
[5] This principle was already in existence; Marcus limited
it by the order that in case any person had been formally declared free-born, any investigation leading to a revision of
this declaration could be made only during his life-time; see
Dig., xl. 15, 1.

MARCUS ANTONINUS

quo magis eorum cum exercitio iuris auctoritas cres-
3 ceret. multos ex amicis in senatum adlegit cum
4 aediliciis aut praetoriis dignitatibus. multis senatoribus verum [1] pauperibus sine crimine dignitates tri-
5 bunicias aediliciasque concessit. nec quemquam in
6 ordinem legit, nisi quem ipse bene scisset. hoc
quoque senatoribus detulit ut, quotiens de quorum
capite esset iudicandum, secreto pertractaret atque ita
in publicum proderet [2] nec pateretur equites Romanos
7 talibus interesse causis. semper autem, cum potuit,
interfuit senatui, etiamsi nihil esset referendum, si
Romae fuit; si vero aliquid referre voluit, etiam de
8 Campania ipse venit. comitiis praeterea etiam usque
ad noctem frequenter interfuit neque umquam recessit
9 de curia nisi consul dixisset "nihil vos moramur
patres conscripti". senatum appellationibus a consule factis iudicem dedit.
10 Iudiciariae rei singularem diligentiam adhibuit.
fastis dies iudiciarios addidit, ita ut ducentos triginta
dies annuos rebus agendis litibusque disceptandis con-
11 stitueret. praetorem tutelarem primus fecit, cum
ante tutores a consulibus poscerentur, ut diligentius
12 de tutoribus tractaretur. de curatoribus vero, cum
ante non nisi ex lege Plaetoria [3] vel propter lasciviam

---

[1] So Novak; *senatibus uel pauperibus s. c. senatoribus* P;
equitibus uel pauperibus . . . senatoribus Peter[2], incorrectly (cf.
Mommsen, RSt. II³, p. 941, 2). [2] *prodiret* P. [3] *Plaetoria*
Jordan (cf. Savigny, *Opp. Misc.* II, 330); *Laetoria* P, Peter.

---

[1] See *Hadr.*, vii. 4 and note.
[2] This office was instituted before Verus' death in 169.
The first holder was Arrius Antoninus, who is described in an
inscription as *praetor cui primo iurisdictio pupillaris a sanc-
tissimis imp(eratoribus) mandata est (C.I.L.*, v. 1874 = Dessau,
Ins. Sel., 1118).

158

disputes to many men of praetorian and consular rank who then held no magistracy, in order that their prestige might be enhanced through their administration of law. He enrolled in the senate many of his friends, giving them the rank of aedile or praetor; and on a number of poor but honest senators he bestowed the rank of tribune or aedile. Nor did he ever appoint anyone to senatorial rank whom he did not know well personally. He granted senators the further privilege [1] that whenever any of them was to be tried on a capital charge, he would examine the evidence behind closed doors and only after so doing would bring the case to public trial; nor would he allow members of the equestrian order to attend such investigations. He always attended the meetings of the senate if he was in Rome, even though no measure was to be proposed, and if he wished to propose anything himself, he came in person even from Campania. More than this, when elections were held he often remained even until night, never leaving the senate-chamber until the consul announced, "We detain you no longer, Conscript Fathers". Further, he appointed the senate judge in appeals made from the consul.

To the administration of justice he gave singular care. He added court-days to the calendar until he had set 230 days for the pleading of cases and judging of suits, and he was the first to appoint a special praetor in charge of the property of wards,[2] in order that greater care might be exercised in dealing with trustees; for previously the appointment of trustees had been in the hands of the consuls. As regards guardians, indeed, he decided that all youths might have them appointed without being obliged to show cause therefor, whereas previously they were ap-

vel propter dementiam darentur, ita statuit ut omnes
adulti curatores acciperent non redditis causis.

XI. Cavit et sumptibus publicis et calumniis quad-
ruplatorum intercessit adposita falsis delatoribus nota.
2 delationes, quibus fiscus augeretur, contempsit. de
alimentis publicis multa prudenter invenit. curatores
multis civitatibus, quo latius senatorias tenderet dig-
3 nitates, a senatu dedit. Italicis civitatibus famis
tempore frumentum ex urbe donavit omnique frum-
4 entariae rei consuluit. gladiatoria spectacula omni-
fariam temperavit. temperavit etiam scaenicas dona-
tiones iubens ut quinos aureos scaenici acciperent,
ita tamen ut nullus editor decem aureos egrederetur.
5 vias [1] etiam urbis atque itinera [2] diligentissime curavit.
rei frumentariae graviter providit.
6   Datis iuridicis Italiae consuluit ad id exemplum
quo Hadrianus consulares viros reddere iura praecep-
7 erat.   Hispanis exhaustis [3] Italica adlectione contra
8 Traiani quoque [4] praecepta verecunde consuluit.   leges

---

[1] *uineas* P[1]; *al' uias* P corr.   [2] *itinera* Jordan, Novak;
itinerum P, Peter.   [3] *exhausit* P.   [4] Thus Ellis; *contra
tranique p.* P[1]; *Traianique* P corr.; *contra iniqua p.* Petschenig; Peter assumes a lacuna after *contra.*

---

[1] The *Lex Plaetoria de circumscriptione minorum annis
XXV* was passed prior to 191 B.C.; it is mentioned in Plautus,
Pseud., 303.   It aimed to protect persons under 25 from fraud,
and it accordingly directed that such persons should apply to
the praetor for guardians.
[2] The Twelve Tables provided that the *prodigus* and the
furiosus should not administer their own property but be
under guardians; see *Dig.*, xxvii. 10, 1, and Cic., *de Inv.*, ii.
50, 148.
[3] See note to *Hadr.*, vii. 8.
[4] These officials were appointed by the emperor to admini-

pointed only under the Plaetorian Law,[1] or in cases of prodigality or madness.[2]

XI. In the matter of public expenditures he was exceedingly careful, and he forbade all libels on the part of false informers, putting the mark of infamy on such as made false accusations. He scorned such accusations as would swell the privy-purse. He devised many wise measures for the support of the state-poor,[3] and, that he might give a wider range to the senatorial functions, he appointed supervisors for many communities[4] from the senate. In times of famine he furnished the Italian communities with food from the city; indeed, he made careful provision for the whole matter of the grain-supply. He limited gladiatorial shows in every way, and lessened the cost of free theatrical performances also, decreeing that though an actor might receive five aurei, nevertheless no one who gave a performance should expend more than ten. The streets of the city and the highways he maintained with the greatest care. As for the grain-supply, for that he provided laboriously. He appointed judges for Italy and thereby provided for its welfare, after the plan of Hadrian,[5] who had appointed men of consular rank to administer the law; and he made scrupulous provision, furthermore, for the welfare of the provinces of Spain, which, in defiance of the policy of Trajan, had been exhausted by

ster the finances of communities in cases where mismanagement of the public funds had made such a measure necessary.

[b] See *Hadr.*, xxii. 13; *Pius*, ii. 11. The arrangement seems to have been given up by Pius; see Appian, *Bell. Civ.*, i. 38. Under Marcus ex-praetors were appointed to this office; see *C.I.L.*, v. 1874 = Dessau, *Ins. Sel.*, 1118.

etiam addidit de vicensima hereditatum, de tutelis
libertorum, de bonis maternis et item de filiorum suc-
cessionibus pro parte materna, utque senatores pere-
9 grini quartam partem in Italia possiderent. dedit
praeterea curatoribus regionum ac viarum potestatem,
ut vel punirent vel ad praefectum urbi puniendos re-
mitterent eos qui ultra vectigalia quicquam ab aliquo
10 exegissent. ius autem magis vetus restituit quam
novum fecit. habuit secum praefectos, quorum et
auctoritate et periculo semper iura dictavit. usus
autem est Scaevola praecipue iuris perito.

XII. Cum populo autem non aliter egit quam est
2 actum sub civitate libera. fuitque per omnia moder-
antissimus in hominibus deterrendis a malo, invitandis
ad bona, remunerandis copia, indulgentia liberandis
fecitque ex malis bonos, ex bonis optimos, moderate
3 etiam cavillationes nonnullorum ferens. nam cum
quendam Vetrasinum famae detestandae honorem
petentem moneret, ut se ab opinionibus populi vindicaret, et ille contra respondisset multos, qui secum
in arena pugnassent, se praetores videre, patienter
4 tulit. ac ne in quemquam facile vindicaret, praetorem,

---

[1] Cf. *Hadr.*, xii. 4.

[2] The 5 % tax on inheritances had been instituted by
Augustus. Under Caracalla it was temporarily raised to 10 %.

[3] This was the *Senatus Consultum Orfitianum* of 178 ; see
Dig., xxxviii. 17.

[4] Trajan had already ordered that candidates for public
office must invest a third of their capital in Italian land ; see
Plin., *Epist.*, vi. 19.

[5] This marks the beginning of the change in the functions
of the prefect of the guard from purely military to pre-
eminently judicial. Under Severus and Alexander the office

levies from the Italian settlers.[1] Also he enacted
laws about inheritance-taxes,[2] about the property of
freedmen held in trust, about property inherited from
the mother,[3] about the succession of the sons to the
mother's share, and likewise that senators of foreign
birth should invest a fourth part of their capital in
Italy.[4] And besides this, he gave the commissioners
of districts and streets power either themselves to
punish those who fleeced anyone of money beyond
his due assessment, or to bring them to the prefect of
the city for punishment. He engaged rather in the
restoration of old laws than in the making of new, and
ever kept near him prefects with whose authority and
responsibility he framed his laws.[5] He made use of
Scaevola also,[6] a man particularly learned in jurisprudence.

XII. Toward the people he acted just as one
acts in a free state. He was at all times exceedingly reasonable both in restraining men from evil
and in urging them to good, generous in reward-
ing and quick to forgive, thus making bad men good,
and good men very good, and he even bore with
unruffled temper the insolence of not a few. For
example, when he advised a man of abominable
reputation, who was running for office, a certain
Vetrasinus, to stop the town-talk about himself, and
Vetrasinus replied that many who had fought with
him in the arena were now prætors, the Emperor took
it with good grace. Again, in order to avoid taking
an easy revenge on any one, instead of ordering a

was held by the foremost jurists of Rome, Papinian, Ulpian,
and Paullus.
    [6] As a member of his consilium (see *Hadr.*, viii. 9); Q.
Cervidius Scaevola is often cited in the *Digesta*.

qui quaedam pessime egerat, non abdicare se praetura
5 iussit, sed collegae iuris dictionem mandavit. fisco
6 in causis compendii numquam iudicans favit. sane,
quamvis esset constans, erat etiam verecundus.
7 Posteaquam autem e Syria victor rediit frater, patris
patriae nomen ambobus decretum est, cum se Marcus
absente Vero erga omnes senatores atque homines
8 moderatissime gessisset. corona praeterea civica ob-
lata est ambobus ; petiitque Lucius ut secum Marcus
triumpharet. petiit praeterea Lucius ut filii Marci
9 Caesares appellarentur. sed Marcus tanta fuit
moderatione ut, cum[1] simul triumphasset, tamen
post mortem Lucii tantum Germanicum se vocaret,
10 quod sibi bello proprio pepererat. in triumpho autem
liberos Marci utriusque sexus secum vexerunt, ita
11 tamen ut et puellas virgines veherent. ludos etiam
ob triumphum decretos spectaverunt habitu trium-
12 phali. inter cetera pietatis eius haec quoque moderatio
praedicanda est : funambulis post puerum lapsum
culcitas subici iussit. unde hodieque rete[2] praeten-
ditur.
13 Dum Parthicum bellum geritur, natum est Marcomannicum, quod diu eorum qui aderant arte
suspensum est, ut finito iam Orientali bello Marco-

---

[1] *cum* om. in P.   [2] *recte* P[1] ; *al' rete* P corr.

---

[1] See c. ix. 3 and note.
[2] Of oak leaves, presented to a man who had saved the life
of a fellow-citizen in battle.
[3] M. Aurelius Commodus (b. 161), and M. Annius Verus
(b. 162-3). The ceremony took place on 12 October, 166 ; see
Com., i. 10 ; xi. 13. Their effigies appear on coins (Cohen,
iii[2], p. 169 f.).
[4] This title appears for the first time in inscriptions of 172 ;

prætor who had acted very badly in certain matters
to resign his office, he merely entrusted the administration of the law to the man's colleague.
The privy-purse never influenced his judgment in
law-suits involving money. Finally, if he was firm,
he was also reasonable.

After his brother had returned victorious from 166
Syria, the title " Father of his Country " was decreed to both,[1] inasmuch as Marcus in the absence of
Verus had conducted himself with great consideration
toward both senators and commons. Furthermore,
the civic crown[2] was offered to both; and Lucius
demanded that Marcus triumph with him, and demanded also that the name Caesar should be given to
Marcus' sons.[3] But Marcus was so free from love of
display that though he triumphed with Lucius,
nevertheless after Lucius' death he called himself
only Germanicus,[4] the title he had won in his own
war. In the triumphal procession, moreover, they 166
carried with them Marcus' children of both sexes,
even his unmarried daughters; and they viewed the
games held in honour of the triumph clad in the
triumphal robe. Among other illustrations of his
unfailing consideration towards others this act of
kindness is to be told: After one lad, a rope-dancer,
had fallen, he ordered mattresses spread under all
rope-dancers. This is the reason why a net is
stretched under them to-day.

While the Parthian war was still in progress, the 166
Marcomannic war broke out, after having been postponed for a long time by the diplomacy of the men
who were in charge there, in order that the Marco-

the probable date of its assumption was 15 October; see *Com.*,
xi. 13, and cf. Dio, lxxi. 3, 5.

14 mannicum agi posset. et cum famis tempore populo
insinuasset de bello, fratre post quinquennium reverso
in senatu egit, ambos necessarios dicens bello
XIII. Germanico imperatores. tantus autem terror belli
Marcomannici fuit [1] ut undique sacerdotes Antoninus
acciverit, peregrinos ritus impleverit, Romam omni
genere lustraverit retardatusque a [2] bellica profectione
2 sit. celebravit et Romano ritu lectisternia per septem
3 dies. tanta autem pestilentia fuit ut vehiculis cadavera
4 sint exportata sarracisque. tunc autem Antonini
leges sepeliendi sepulchrorumque asperrimas sanxe-
runt, quando quidem caverunt ne quis villae ad-
fabricaretur [3] sepulchrum, quod hodieque servatur.
5 et multa quidem milia pestilentia consumpsit multos-
que ex proceribus, quorum amplissimis Antoninus
6 statuas conlocavit. tantaque clementia fuit ut et
sumptu publico vulgaria funera iuberet efferri [4] et vano
cuidam, qui diripiendae urbis occasionem cum quibusdam consciis requirens de caprifici arbore in Campo
Martio contionabundus ignem de caelo lapsurum

[1] *fuit* P corr., om. by P[1].   [2] *a* om. in P.   [3] Thus Madvig and Petschenig; *uelle abfricaretur* P; *ne quis ubi uellet
fabricaretur* s. Novak.   [4] *efferi* Jordan; *et eo ferri* P[1]; *ferri
et eo ferri* P[1] corr.

---

[1] Called officially *bellum Germanicum;* see *C.I.L.*, vi.
1549 = Dessau, *Ins. Sel.*, 1100.

[2] The Marcomanni and Quadi actually invaded Italy and
laid siege to Aquileia; see Amm. Marc., xxix. 6, 1. Furius
Victorinus, the prefect of the guard, who was sent to resist
them, was killed and a portion of his army annihilated; see
c. xiv. 5.

[3] A very ancient purificatory ceremony, in which statues of
the gods were placed on banqueting-couches in some public
place and served with an offering on a table. According to
tradition it was first celebrated in 399 B.C. in order to stay a
plague; see Livy, v. 13, 5-6.

mannic war [1] might not be waged until Rome was done with the war in the East. Even at the time of the famine the Emperor had hinted at this war to the people, and when his brother returned after five years' service, he brought the matter up in the senate, saying that both emperors were needed for the German war. XIII. So great was the dread of this Marcomannic war,[2] that Antoninus summoned priests from all sides, performed foreign religious ceremonies, and purified the city in every way, and he was delayed thereby from setting out to the seat of war. The Roman ceremony of the feast of the gods [3] was celebrated for seven days. And there was such a pestilence,[4] besides, that the dead were removed in carts and waggons. About this time, also, the two emperors ratified certain very stringent laws on burial and tombs, in which they even forbade any one to build a tomb at his country-place, a law still in force. Thousands were carried off by the pestilence, including many nobles, for the most prominent of whom Antoninus erected statues. Such, too, was his kindliness of heart that he had funeral ceremonies performed for the lower classes even at the public expense; and in the case of one foolish fellow, who, in a search with divers confederates for an opportunity to plunder the city, continually made speeches from the wild fig-tree on the Campus Martius, to the effect that fire would fall

[4] It was supposed to have been brought from the East by the returning army of Verus (see *Ver.*, viii. 1-2), and it ravaged Europe as far as the Rhine; see Amm. Marc., xxiii. 6, 24. It was still raging in 180 (see c. xxviii. 4, and *C.I.L.*, iii. 5567 of 182), and it seems to have broken out again with great violence under Commodus; see Dio, lxxii. 14, 3; Herodian, i. 12, 1-2.

finemque mundi affore diceret, si ipse lapsus ex
arbore in ciconiam verteretur, cum statuto tempore
decidisset atque ex sinu ciconiam emisisset, perducto
ad se atque confesso veniam daret.

XIV. Profecti tamen sunt paludati ambo imperatores et Victualis et Marcomannis cuncta turbantibus,
aliis etiam gentibus, quae pulsae a superioribus barbaris fugerant, nisi reciperentur, bellum inferentibus.
2 nec parum profuit ista profectio, cum Aquileiam usque
venissent. nam plerique reges et cum populis suis
se retraxerunt et tumultus auctores interemerunt.
3 Quadi autem amisso rege suo non prius se confirma-
turos eum qui erat creatus dicebant, quam id nostris
4 placuisset imperatoribus. Lucius tamen invitus profectus est, cum plerique ad legatos imperatorum
5 mitterent defectionis veniam postulantes. et Lucius
quidem, quod amissus esset praefectus praetorio
Furius Victorinus, atque [1] pars exercitus interisset,
redeundum esse censebat; Marcus autem fingere
barbaros aestimans et fugam et cetera quae securitatem
bellicam ostenderent, ob hoc ne tanti apparatus mole
6 premerentur, instandum esse ducebat. denique
transcensis Alpibus longius processerunt composue-
runtque omnia, quae ad munimen Italiae atque Illyrici
pertinebant. placuit autem urgente Lucio, ut prae-

[1] *utque* P.

---

[1] See note to c. xiii. 1.
[2] The war in Pannonia was prosecuted successfully, and
after a victory the emperors were acclaimed *Imperatores* for
the fifth time and gave honourable discharge to some soldiers;
see *C.I.L.*, iii. p. 888 (dated 5 May, 167).

down from heaven and the end of the world
would come should he fall from the tree and be
turned into a stork, and finally at the appointed
time did fall down and free a stork from his robe,
the Emperor, when the wretch was hailed before
him and confessed all, pardoned him.

XIV. Clad in the military cloak the two emperors 166
finally set forth, for now not only were the Victuali and
Marcomanni throwing everything into confusion, but
other tribes, who had been driven on by the more
distant barbarians and had retreated before them, were
ready to attack Italy if not peaceably received. And
not a little good resulted from that expedition, even
by the time they had advanced as far as Aquileia, for
several kings retreated, together with their peoples,
and put to death the authors of the trouble. And
the Quadi, after they had lost their king, said that
they would not confirm the successor who had been
elected until such a course was approved by our emperors. Nevertheless, Lucius went on, though reluctantly, after a number of peoples had sent
ambassadors to the legates of the emperors asking
pardon for the rebellion. Lucius, it is true, thought
they should return, because Furius Victorinus, the
prefect of the guard, had been lost, and part of his
army had perished;[1] Marcus, however, held that
they should press on, thinking that the barbarians, in
order that they might not be crushed by the size of so
great a force, were feigning a retreat and using other
ruses which afford safety in war, held that they
should persist in order that they might not be over-
whelmed by the mere burden of their vast preparations. Finally, they crossed the Alps, and pressing
further on, completed all measures necessary for the
defence of Italy and Illyricum.[2] They then decided,
at Lucius' insistence, that letters should first be sent

169

missis ad senatum litteris Lucius Romam rediret.
8 via quoque [1], postquam iter ingressi sunt, sedens cum
fratre in vehiculo Lucius apoplexi arreptus periit.

XV. Fuit autem consuetudo Marco ut in circensium
spectaculo legeret audiretque ac subscriberet, ex quo
quidem saepe iocis popularibus dicitur lacessitus.
2   Multum sane potuerunt liberti sub Marco et Vero
Geminas et Agaclytus.
3.   Tantae autem sanctitatis fuit Marcus ut Veri vitia
et celaverit et defenderit, cum ei vehementissime dis-
plicerent,[2] mortuumque eum divum appellaverit
amitasque eius et sorores honoribus et salariis decretis
sublevaverit atque provexerit sacrisque eum [3] plurimis
4 honoraverit. flaminem et Antoninianos sodales et
omnes honores qui divis habentur eidem dedicavit.
5 nemo est principum, quem non gravis fama perstrin-
gat, usque adeo ut etiam Marcus in sermonem venerit,
quod Verum vel veneno ita tulerit ut parte cultri
veneno lita vulvam inciderit, venenatam partem fratri
6 edendam propinans et sibi innoxiam reservans, vel
certe per medicum Posidippum, qui ei sanguinem in-
tempestive dicitur emisisse. Cassius post mortem
Veri a Marco descivit.[4]

---

[1] Thus Bitschofsky; *bia quoque* P; *uiaque* Salm., Peter.
[2] *displiceret* P, but cf. c. xvi. 4.   [3] *cum* P[1]; *uel eum* P corr.
[4] *Cassius . . . desciuit* probably from margin of c. xxiv. 5.

---

[1] In 169 at Altinum in Venetia; see *Ver.*, ix. 10-11.
[2] Cf *Ver.*, ix. 3.
[3] The section of the *vita* from this point through c. xix. is
a later interpolation; see Intro., p. xxii.
[4] Cf. c. xx. 1-2, and the coins of *Divus Verus* with the
legend *Consecratio;* see Cohen, iii[2], p. 176 f., Nos. 53-59.
[5] Cf. c. xx. 5.
[6] See note to *Hadr.*, xxvii. 3, and *Pius*, xiii. 4. ˙This
priesthood was now called *sodales Antoniniani Veriani,* after

ahead to the senate and that Lucius should then return to Rome. But on the way, after they had set out upon their journey, Lucius died from a stroke of apoplexy [1] while riding in the carriage with his brother.

XV. It was customary with Marcus to read, listen to, and sign documents at the circus-games; because of this habit he was openly ridiculed, it is said, by the people.

The freedmen Geminas and Agaclytus [2] were very powerful in the reign of Marcus and Verus.

Such was Marcus' sense of honour,[3] moreover, that although Verus' vices mightily offended him, he concealed and defended them; he also deified him after his death,[4] aided and advanced his aunts and sisters by means of honours and pensions,[5] honoured Verus himself with many sacrifices, consecrated a flamen for him and a college of Antonine priests,[6] and gave him all honours that are appointed for the deified. There is no emperor who is not the victim of some evil tale, and Marcus is no exception. For it was bruited about, in truth, that he put Verus out of the way, either with poison—by cutting a sow's womb with a knife smeared on one side with poison, and then offering the poisoned portion to his brother to eat, while keeping the harmless portion for himself [7]—or, at least, by employing the physician Posidippus, who bled Verus, it is said, unseasonably. After Verus' death Cassius revolted from Marcus.[8]

Marcus' deification *Marciani* was added, after Pertinax' death *Helviani* (*Pert.*, xv. 4), after Severus' *Severiani* (*C.I.L.*, vi. 1365), after Alexander's *Alexandriani* (*Alex.*, lxiii. 4).

[7] Cf. *Ver.*, xi. 2; Dio, lxxi. 3, 1. According to another story, he was poisoned by Faustina; see *Ver.*, x. 1-5.

[8] In 175; see c. xxiv. 6 f.; *Av. Cass.*, vii. f.

XVI. Iam in suos tanta fuit benignitate Marcus ut
cum in omnes propinquos cuncta honorum ornamenta
contulerit, tum in filium et quidem [1] scelestum atque
impurum cito nomen Caesaris et mox sacerdotium
statimque nomen imperatoris ac triumphi partici-
2 pationem et consulatum. quo quidem' tempore
sedente imperator filio [2] ad triumphalem currum in
Circo pedes cucurrit.
3 Post Veri obitum Marcus Antoninus solus rem
publicam tenuit, multo melior et feracior ad virtutes,
4 quippe qui nullis Veri iam impediretur aut simplicitatis
calidaeque veritatis,[3] qua ille ingenito vitio laborabat,
erroribus aut iis qui praecipue displicebant Marco
Antonino iam inde a primo aetatis suae tempore vel
5 institutis mentis pravae vel moribus. erat enim ipse
tantae tranquillitatis ut vultum numquam mutaverit
maerore vel gaudio, philosophiae deditus Stoicae,
quam et per optimos quosque magistros acceperat et
6 undique ipse collegerat. nam et Hadrianus hunc
eundem successorem paraverat, nisi ei aetas puerilis
7 obstitisset. quod quidem apparet ex eo quod generum
Pio hunc eundem delegit, ut ad eum, dignum utpote
virum, quandocumque Romanum perveniret imperium.

---

[1] et Commodum quidem P, Bitschofsky; Commodum removed by Jordan.   [2] So Peter; sine imperator filio P.
[3] So Peter; simulatis callidae seueritatis P.

---

[1] i.e., Commodus.   [2] See c. xii. 8 and note.
[3] On 20 January, 175; see Com., i. 10; xii. 1.   On the
priesthood held by sons of emperors see note to c. vi. 3.
[4] On 27 November, 176; see Com., ii. 4; xii. 4.
[5] On 23 December, 176; see Com., ii. 4; xii. 5.   This,
however, seems not to have been the triumph held by Marcus
in celebration of his victory in Pannonia; see c. xvii. 3 and
note.

XVI. Such was Marcus' kindness toward his own family that he bestowed the insignia of every office on all his kin, while on his son,[1] and an accursed and foul one he was, he hastened to bestow the name of Caesar,[2] then afterward the priesthood,[3] and, a little later, the title of imperator[4] and a share in a triumph[5] and the consulship. It was at this time 177 that Marcus, though acclaimed imperator, ran on foot in the Circus by the side of the triumphal car in which his son was seated.

After the death of Verus, Marcus Antoninus held the empire alone, a nobler man by far and more abounding in virtues, especially as he was no longer hampered by Verus' faults, neither by those of excessive candour and hot-headed plain speaking, from which Verus suffered through natural folly, nor by those others which had particularly irked Marcus Antoninus even from his earliest years, the principles and habits of a depraved mind. Such was Marcus' own repose of spirit that neither in grief nor in joy did he ever change countenance, being wholly given over to the Stoic philosophy, which he had not only learned from all the best masters,[6] but also acquired for himself from every source. For this reason Hadrian would have taken him for his own successor to the throne had not his youth prevented. This intention, indeed, seems obvious from the fact that he chose Marcus to be the son-in-law of Pius,[7] in order that the direction of the Roman state might some time at least come into his hands, as to those of one well worthy.

[6] Cf. c. ii. 6—iii. 3.
[7] This is an error, for Hadrian betrothed him to the daughter of Aelius Caesar; see c. iv. 5 and vi. 2.

XVII. Ergo provincias post haec ingenti moderatione ac benignitate tractavit. contra Germanos res
2 feliciter gessit. speciale ipse bellum Marcomannicum,
sed quantum [1] nulla umquam memoria fuit, cum virtute
tum etiam felicitate transegit, et eo quidem tempore
quo pestilentia gravis multa milia et popularium et
3 militum interemerat. Pannonias ergo, Marcomannis
Sarmatis Vandalis simul etiam Quadis exstinctis,
servitio liberavit et Romae cum Commodo, quem iam
Caesarem fecerat, filio, ut diximus, suo triumphavit.
4 cum autem ad hoc bellum omne aerarium exhausisset
suum neque in animum induceret, ut extra ordinem
provincialibus aliquid imperaret, in foro divi Traiani
auctionem ornamentorum imperialium fecit vendidit-
que aurea pocula et crystallina et murrina, vasa etiam
regia et vestem uxoriam sericam et auratam, gemmas
quin etiam, quas multas in repositorio sanctiore
5 Hadriani reppererat. et per duos quidem menses
haec venditio celebrata est, tantumque auri redactum
ut reliquias belli Marcomannici ex sententia per-
secutus postea dederit potestatem emptoribus, ut, si
qui vellet empta reddere atque aurum recipere, sciret
licere. nec molestus ulli fuit qui vel non reddidit

[1] *quanto* P.

---

[1] See c. xiii. 3.

[2] This sentence sums up the war from Marcus' departure
from Rome in October, 169 (cf. coins with *Profectio Augusti*,
Cohen, iii², p. 51, No. 500) to the victory over the Sarmatians
in 175, after which Marcus was acclaimed Imperator for the
eighth time and assumed the title *Sarmaticus ;* see c. xxiv. 5
and Cohen, iii², p. 91 f., Nos. 916-925.

[3] See c. xvi. 2. His triumph over the Germans and the
Sarmatians was held in 176 after his return from the East ;
see c. xxvii. 3 ; Cohen, iii², p. 17, No. 154, and p. 18, No. 164 ;
C I.L. vi. 1014 = Dessau, *Ins. Sel.*, 374. Since the coins and
the inscriptions date this triumph in the 30th year of the tri-

XVII. Toward the provinces from then on he acted with extreme restraint and consideration. He carried on a successful campaign against the Germans. He himself singled out the Marcomannic war—a war which surpassed any in the memory of man—and waged it with both valour and success, and that at a time when a grievous pestilence had carried away thousands of civilians and soldiers.[1] And so, by crushing the Marcomanni, the Sarmatians, the Vandals, and even the Quadi, he freed the Pannonias from bondage,[2] and with Commodus his son, whom he had previously named Caesar, triumphed at Rome, as we told above.[3] When he had drained the treasury for this war, moreover, and could not bring himself to impose any extraordinary tax on the provincials, he held a public sale in the Forum of the [169] Deified Trajan[4] of the imperial furnishings, and sold goblets of gold and crystal and murra,[5] even flagons made for kings, his wife's silken gold-embroidered robes, and, indeed, even certain jewels which he had found in considerable numbers in a particularly holy cabinet of Hadrian's. This sale lasted for two months, and such a store of gold was realised thereby, that after he had conducted the remainder of the Marcomannic war in full accordance with his plans, he gave the buyers to understand that if any of them wished to return his purchases and recover his money, he could do so. Nor did he make it unpleasant for anyone who did or did not return what he had bought.

bunician power of Marcus (10 December, 175—9 December, 176), and since the triumph of Commodus was held on 23 December, 176, the statement that Commodus triumphed with his father, as made here and in *Com.*, ii. 4, must be erroneous.

[4] See note to *Hadr.*, vii. 6.

[5] Probably a variety of agate; see J. Marquardt, *Privatleben d. Römer²*, ii., p. 765 f.

6 empta vel reddidit. tunc viris clarioribus permisit
ut eodem cultu quo et ipse vel ministris similibus
7 convivia exhiberent. in munere autem publico tam
magnanimus fuit ut centum leones una missione[1]
simul exhiberet et sagittis interfectos.[2]

XVIII. Cum igitur in amore omnium imperasset
atque ab aliis modo frater, modo pater, modo filius, ut
cuiusque aetas sinebat, et diceretur et amaretur, octavo
decimo anno imperii sui, sexagensimo et primo vitae,
2 diem ultimum clausit. tantusque illius amor eo die
regii funeris[3] claruit ut nemo illum plangendum cen-
suerit, certis omnibus quod ab diis commodatus ad
3 deos redisset. denique, priusquam funus conderetur,
ut plerique dicunt, quod numquam antea factum fuerat
neque postea, senatus populusque non divisis locis sed
in una sede propitium deum dixit.
4 Hic sane vir tantus et talis ac diis vita et morte
coniunctus filium Commodum dereliquit ; qui, si felix
5 fuisset, filium non reliquisset. et parum sane fuit
quod illi honores divinos omnis aetas omnis sexus
omnis condicio ac dignitas dedit, nisi quod etiam
sacrilegus iudicatus est qui eius imaginem in sua
domo non habuit, qui per fortunam vel potuit habere
6 vel debuit. denique hodieque in multis domibus
Marci Antonini statuae consistunt inter deos penates.
7 nec defuerunt homines qui somniis eum multa prae-

---

[1] *unam missionem* P; *una in missione* Peter.   [2] So P;
Peter, foll. Mommsen, *interfecit eos*.   [3] So P; *regii funeris*
removed by Peter, *eo* by Jordan.

---

[1] See c. xxviii.

At this time, also, he granted permission to the more prominent men to hold banquets with the same pomp that he used himself and with servants similar to his own. In the matter of public games, furthermore, he was so liberal as to present a hundred lions together in one performance and have them all killed with arrows.

XVIII. After he had ruled, then, with the good-will of all, and had been named and beloved variously as brother, father, or son by various men according to their several ages, in the eighteenth year of his reign and the sixty-first of his life he closed his last 17 Mar., day.[1] Such love for him was manifested on the day 180 of the imperial funeral that none thought that men should lament him, since all were sure that he had been lent by the gods and had now returned to them. Finally, before his funeral was held, so many say, the senate and people, not in separate places but sitting together, as was never done before or after, hailed him as a gracious god.

This man, so great, so good, and an associate of the gods both in life and in death, left one son Commodus ; and had he been truly fortunate he would not have left a son. It was not enough, indeed, that people of every age, sex, degree and rank in life, gave him all honours given to the gods, but also whosoever failed to keep the Emperor's image in his home, if his fortune were such that he could or should have done so, was deemed guilty of sacrilege. Even to-day, in fine, statues of Marcus Antoninus stand in many a home among the household gods. Nor were there lacking men who observed that he foretold many things by dreams and were thereby themselves enabled to predict events that did come to pass.

8 dixisse augurantes futura et vera concinuerunt. unde etiam templum ei constitutum, dati sacerdotes Antoniniani et sodales et flamines et omnia quae aede sacrata [1] decrevit antiquitas.

XIX. Aiunt quidam, quod et veri simile videtur, Commodum Antoninum, successorem illius ac filium, non 2 esse de eo natum sed de adulterio, ac talem fabellam vulgari sermone contexunt : Faustinam quondam, Pii filiam, Marci uxorem, cum gladiatores transire vidisset, unius ex his amore succensam, cum longa aegritudine 3 laboraret, viro de amore confessam. quod cum ad Chaldaeos Marcus rettulisset, illorum fuisse consilium, ut occiso gladiatore sanguine illius sese Faustina sub-4 lavaret atque ita cum viro concumberet. quod cum esset factum, solutum quidem amorem, natum vero 5 Commodum gladiatorem esse, non principem, qui mille prope pugnas publice populo inspectante gladiatorias imperator exhibuit, ut in vita eius docebitur. 6 quod quidem veri simile ex eo habetur quod tam sancti principis filius iis moribus fuit quibus nullus lanista, nullus scaenicus, nullus arenarius, nullus postremo ex omnium dedecorum [2] ac scelerum conluvione con-7 cretus. multi autem ferunt Commodum omnino ex adulterio [3] natum, si quidem Faustinam satis constet apud Caietam condiciones sibi et nauticas et gladia-8 torias elegisse. de qua cum diceretur Antonino Marco,

[1] So Peter with Madvig ; *desacrata* P ; *de sacratis* P corr.
[2] *decorum* P.   [3] *adultero* P, but cf. c. xix. 1 (see Lessing *Lex.*).

---

[1] See note to *Hadr.*, xxvii. 3, and c. xv. 4.
[2] See *Com.*, xi. 12 ; xii. 11.
[3] For similar stories see c. xxiii. 7 and xxix. 1-3 ; Victor, *Caes.*, xvi. 2. Evidence to the contrary seems to be afforded

Therefore a temple was built for him and priests were appointed, dedicated to the service of the Antonines, both Sodales [1] and flamens, and all else that the usage of old time decreed for a consecrated temple.

XIX. Some say, and it seems plausible, that Commodus Antoninus, his son and successor, was not begotten by him, but in adultery; they embroider this assertion, moreover, with a story current among the people. On a certain occasion, it was said, Faustina, the daughter of Pius and wife of Marcus, saw some gladiators pass by, and was inflamed with love for one of them; and afterwards, when suffering from a long illness, she confessed the passion to her husband. And when Marcus reported this to the Chaldeans, it was their advice that the gladiator should be killed and that Faustina should bathe in his blood and thus couch with her husband. When this was done, the passion was indeed allayed, but their son Commodus was born a gladiator, not really a prince; for afterwards as emperor he fought almost a thousand gladiatorial bouts before the eyes of the people, as shall be related in his life.[2] This story is considered plausible, as a matter of fact, for the reason that the son of so virtuous a prince had habits worse than any trainer of gladiators, any play-actor, any fighter in the arena, or, in fine, anything brought into existence from the offscourings of all dishonour and crime. Many writers, however, state that Commodus was really begotten in adultery, since it is generally known that Faustina, while at Caieta, used to choose out lovers from among the sailors and gladiators.[3] When Marcus Antoninus was told about

by Marcus' own affection and respect for her; see εἰς ἑαυτ., i. 17, 7.

ut eam repudiaret, si non occideret, dixisse fertur
9 "si uxorem dimittimus, reddamus et dotem". dos
autem quid habebatur?[1] imperium, quod ille ab
socero volente Hadriano adoptatus acceperat.
10 Tantum sane valet boni principis vita sanctitas
tranquillitas pietas ut eius famam nullius proximi
11 decoloret invidia. denique Antonino, cum suos mores
semper teneret neque alicuius insusurratione mu-
taretur, non obfuit gladiator filius, uxor infamis;
12 deusque etiam nunc habetur, ut vobis ipsis, sacratissime
imperator Diocletiane, et semper visum est et videtur,
qui eum inter numina vestra non ut ceteros sed
specialiter veneramini ac saepe dicitis, vos vita et
clementia tales esse cupere qualis fuit Marcus, etiamsi
philosophia nec Plato esse possit, si revertatur in
vitam.[2] et quidem haec breviter et congeste.

XX. Sed Marco Antonino haec sunt gesta post
fratrem: primum corpus eius Romam devectum est
2 et inlatum maiorum sepulchris. divini[3] inde honores
decreti. dein cum gratias ageret senatui quod fratrem
consecrasset, occulte ostendit omnia bellica consilia sua
3 fuisse, quibus superati sunt Parthi. addidit praeterea
quaedam, quibus ostendit nunc demum se quasi a
principio acturum esse rem publicam amoto eo qui

[1] So Petschenig with P; *dos autem quid habebatur nisi
imperium* edd. with P corr. [2] *reueratori uita* P. [3] *in*,
following *diuini*, deleted by P corr.; *inde* Peter.

[1] See c. xiv. 8. The interpolated section ends with c. xix.;
see note to c. xv. 3.
[2] *i.e.*, the Tomb of Hadrian; see *Ver.*, xi. 1. His sepulchral
inscription is *C.I.L.*, vi. 991 = Dessau, *Ins. Sel.*, 369.
[3] Cf. c. xv. 3-4.

this, that he might divorce, if not kill her, he is
reported to have said "If we send our wife away,
we must also return her dowry". And what was her
dowry ? the Empire, which, after he had been adopted
at the wish of Hadrian, he had inherited from his
father-in-law Pius.

But truly such is the power of the life, the holiness,
the serenity, and the righteousness of a good emperor
that not even the scorn felt for his kin can sully his
own good name. For since Antoninus held ever to
his moral code and was moved by no man's whispered
machinations, men thought no less of him because his
son was a gladiator, his wife infamous. Even now
he is called a god, which ever has seemed and even
now seems right to you, most venerable Emperor
Diocletian, who worship him among your divinities,
not as you worship the others, but as one apart, and
who often say that you desire, in life and gentleness,
to be such a one as Marcus, even though, as far as
philosophy is concerned, Plato himself, were he to
return to life, could not be such a philosopher. So
much, then, for these matters, told briefly and con-
cisely.

XX. But as for the acts of Marcus Antoninus after
the death of his brother,[1] they are as follows : First
of all, he conveyed his body to Rome and laid it in
the tomb of his fathers.[2] Then divine honours were
ordered for Verus.[3] Later, while rendering thanks
to the senate for his brother's deification, he darkly
hinted that all the strategic plans whereby the Parthians had been overcome were his own. He added,
besides, certain statements in which he indicated
that now at length he would make a fresh beginning
in the management of the state, now that Verus, who

4 remissior videbatur. nec aliter senatus accepit quam
Marcus dixerat, ut videretur gratias agere quod
5 Verus excessisset vita. omnibus deinde sororibus et
adfinibus et libertis iuris et honoris et pecuniae
plurimum detulit. erat enim famae suae curiosissi-
mus, requirens ad verum, quid quisque de se diceret,
emendans quae bene reprehensa viderentur.

6 Proficiscens ad bellum Germanicum filiam suam non
decurso luctus tempore grandaevo equitis Romani
filio Claudio Pompeiano dedit genere Antiochensi
7 nec satis nobili (quem postea bis consulem fecit), cum
filia eius Augusta esset et Augustae filia. sed has nuptias et Faustina et ipsa quae dabatur invitae habuerunt.

XXI. Cum Mauri Hispanias prope omnes vastarent,
2 res per legatos bene gestae sunt. et cum per Aegyptum
Bucolici milites gravia multa fecissent, per Avidium
Cassium retunsi sunt, qui postea tyrannidem arripuit.
3 sub ipsis profectionis diebus in secessu Praenestino
agens filium, nomine Verum Caesarem, exsecto sub
4 aure tubere septennem amisit. quem non plus quinque diebus luxit consultusque etiam medios[1] actibus

---

[1] Thus Peter with Lipsius ; *consolatusque etiam medicos* P.

---

[1] Cf. c. xv. 3.
[2] After his return to Rome with the body of Verus. He
set out in October, 169 ; see note to c. xvii. 3.
[3] Lucilla, the widow of Verus.
[4] Cf. c. xxii. 11. The date is probably 172-173, see *Sev.*,
ii. 4.
[5] According to *Av. Cass.*, vi. 7, this statement is taken
from Marius Maximus' Life of Marcus. The rebellion is
somewhat more fully described in Dio, lxxi. 4. The Boukoloi,
a tribe of herdsmen and brigands, lived in the N.W. of the
Delta, not far from Alexandria. According to Dio's chron-
ology, the rebellion happened after Marcus' assumption of
the name *Germanicus, i.e.* in 172-173.

had seemed somewhat negligent, was removed. And the senate took this precisely as it was said, so that Marcus seemed to be giving thanks that Verus had departed this life. Afterwards he bestowed many privileges and much honour and money on all Verus' sisters, kin, and freedmen.[1] For he was exceedingly solicitous about his good reputation, indeed he was wont to ask what men really said of him, and to correct whatever seemed justly blamed.

Just before setting out for the German war,[2] and before the period of mourning had yet expired, he married his daughter[3] to Claudius Pompeianus, the son of a Roman knight, and now advanced in years, a native of Antioch, whose birth was not sufficiently noble (though Marcus later made him consul twice), since Marcus' daughter was an Augusta and the daughter of an Augusta. Indeed, Faustina and the girl who was given in marriage were both opposed to this match.

XXI. Against the Mauri, when they wasted almost the whole of Spain,[4] matters were brought to a successful conclusion by his legates; and when the warriors of the Bucolici did many grievous things in Egypt,[5] they were checked by Avidius Cassius, who later attempted to seize the throne.[6] Just before his departure,[7] while he was living in retreat at Praeneste, Marcus lost his seven-year-old son, by name Verus Caesar,[8] from an operation on a tumour under his ear. For no more than five days did he mourn him; and even during this period, when consulted on public affairs he gave some time to them.

[6] See c. xxiv. 6 f; *Av. Cass.* vii. f.
[7] *i.e.*, for the German war; see c. xx. 6.
[8] M. Annius Verus; see note to c. xii. 8.

MARCUS ANTONINUS

publicis reddidit. et quia ludi Iovis Optimi Maximi
5 erant, interpellari eos publico luctu noluit iussitque,
ut statuae tantummodo filio mortuo decernerentur et
imago aurea circensibus per pompam ferenda et ut
saliari carmini nomen eius insereretur.

6 Instante sane adhuc pestilentia et deorum cultum
diligentissime restituit et servos, quemadmodum bello
Punico factum fuerat, ad militiam paravit, quos volun-
7 tarios exemplo volonum appellavit. armavit etiam
gladiatores, quos obsequentes appellavit. latrones
etiam Dalmatiae atque Dardaniae milites fecit.
armavit et Diogmitas. emit et Germanorum auxilia
8 contra Germanos. omni praeterea diligentia paravit
legiones ad Germanicum et Marcomannicum bellum.
9 et, ne provincialibus esset molestus, auctionem rerum
aulicarum, ut diximus, fecit in foro divi Traiani, in qua
praeter vestes et pocula et vasa aurea etiam signa
10 cum tabulis magnorum artificum vendidit. Marcomannos in ipso transitu Danuvii delevit et praedam

---

1 Probably the Ludi Capitolini, held on 15 October.

2 Germanicus' name had been similarly inserted in this
song after his death ; see Tac., *Ann.*, ii. 82.

3 See c. xiii. 3.

4 The name given to the slaves who volunteered for military service after the defeat at Cannae in the Second Punic
War ; see Livy, xxii. 57, 11, and Festus, p. 370.

5 The district east of southern Dalmatia ; it is now the
southern portion of the kingdom of Serbia.

6 The Diogmitai were the military police maintained by
the Greek cities. They were also called upon to perform
military service—the suppression of brigands—in 368 ; see
Amm. Marc., xxvii. 9, 6.

7 These new legions were named *Legio II Pia* and *Legio*

184

And because the games of Jupiter Optimus Maximus [1]
were then in progress and he did not wish to have
them interrupted by public mourning, he merely
ordered that statues should be decreed for his dead
son, that a golden image of him should be carried
in procession at the Circus, and that his name should
be inserted in the song of the Salii.[2]

And since the pestilence [3] was still raging at this
time, he both zealously revived the worship of the
gods and trained slaves for military service—just as
had been done in the Punic war—whom he called
Volunteers, after the example of the Volones.[4] He
armed gladiators also, calling them the Compliant,
and turned even the bandits of Dalmatia and Dar-
dania [5] into soldiers. He armed the Diogmitae,[6]
besides, and even hired auxiliaries from among the
Germans for service against Germans. And besides
all this, he proceeded with all care to enrol legions [7]
for the Marcomannic and German wars. And lest
all this prove burdensome to the provinces, he held
an auction of the palace furnishings in the Forum of
the Deified Trajan, as we have related,[8] and sold
there, besides robes and goblets and golden flagons,
even statues and paintings by great artists. He over-
whelmed the Marcomanni while they were crossing
the Danube,[9] and restored the plunder to the pro-

III *Concordia* : see *C.I.L.*, iii. 1980. They were afterwards
called *Legio II* and *III Italica ;* see Dio, lv. 24, 4.

[8] See c. xvii. 4-5.

[9] This is probably the victory commemorated by coins of
172 with a representation of Marcus and his soldiers crossing
a bridge, presumably over the Danube; see Cohen, iii², *v.* 99 f.,
Nos. 999-1001. Other coins of this year bear the legend
Germania Subacta ; see Cohen, iii², p. 23, Nos. 215-216. It
was in this year too that Marcus took the name Germanicus ;
see *C.I.L.*, iii. 1450.

XXII. provincialibus reddidit. gentes omnes ab Illyrici limite usque in Galliam conspiraverant, ut Marcomanni Varistae Hermunduri et Quadi Suebi Sarmatae Lacringes et Buri hi aliique [1] cum Victualis Osi Bessi Cobotes Roxolani Bastarnae Alani Peucini Costoboci. imminebat et Parthicum bellum et Britannicum. 2 magno igitur labore etiam suo gentes asperrimas vicit militibus sese imitantibus, ducentibus etiam exercitum legatis et praefectis praetorio, accepitque in deditionem Marcomannos plurimis in Italiam traductis.

3 Semper sane cum optimatibus non solum bellicas res sed etiam civiles, priusquam faceret aliquid, con-4 tulit. denique sententia illius praecipua semper haec fuit : " Aequius est ut ego tot talium amicorum consilium sequar, quam ut tot tales amici meam unius 5 voluntatem sequantur". sane quia durus videbatur ex philosophiae institutione Marcus ad militiae labores 6 atque ad omnem vitam graviter carpebatur, sed male loquentibus [2] vel sermone vel litteris respondebat. 7 et multi nobiles bello Germanico sive Marcomannico immo plurimarum gentium interierunt. quibus omni-8 bus statuas in foro Ulpio conlocavit. quare frequenter amici suaserunt, ut a bellis discederet et [3] Romam veniret, sed ille contempsit ac perstitit nec prius reces-9 sit quam omnia bella finiret. provincias ex procon-

[1] Some name is lost in these words : Petschenig suggests *Hariique.*   [2] *loquentum* P (P corr. adds *dictis*) ; *loquentibus* (or *loquentum uel sermoni*) Peter.   [3] *et* omitted in P.

---

[1] Cf. c. xxiv. 3.
[2] *i.e.*, his *consilium ;* see *Hadr.*, viii. 9 and note.
[3] See note to *Hadr.*, vii. 6.
[4] But see c. xxiv. 5 and xxv. 1.

vincials. XXII. Then, from the borders of Illyricum
even into Gaul, all the nations banded together
against us—the Marcomanni, Varistae, Hermunduri
and Quadi, the Suebians, Sarmatians, Lacringes and
Buri, these and certain others together with the
Victuali, namely, Osi, Bessi, Cobotes, Roxolani,
Bastarnae, Alani, Peucini, and finally, the Costoboci.
Furthermore, war threatened in Parthia and Britain.
Thereupon, by immense labour on his own part, while
his soldiers reflected his energy, and both legates and
prefects of the guard led the host, he conquered
these exceedingly fierce peoples, accepted the sur-
render of the Marcomanni, and brought a great
number of them to Italy.[1]

Always before making any move, he conferred with
the foremost men[2] concerning matters not only of
war but also of civil life. This saying particularly
was ever on his lips : " It is juster that I should yield
to the counsel of such a number of such friends than
that such a number of such friends should yield to
my wishes, who am but one ". But because Marcus,
as a result of his system of philosophy, seemed harsh
in his military discipline and indeed in his life in
general, he was bitterly assailed ; to all who spoke
ill of him, however, he made reply either in speeches
or in pamphlets. And because in this German, or
Marcomannic, war, or rather I should say in this
"War of Many Nations," many nobles perished, for
all of whom he erected statues in the Forum of
Trajan,[3] his friends often urged him to abandon
the war and return to Rome. He, however, disregarded this advice and stood his ground, nor did
he withdraw before he had brought all the wars
to a conclusion.[4] Several proconsular provinces he

MARCUS ANTONINUS

sularibus consulares aut ex consularibus proconsulares
10 aut [1] praetorias pro belli necessitate fecit. res etiam in
Sequanis turbatas censura et auctoritate repressit.
11 compositae res et in [2] Hispania, quae per Lusitaniam
12 turbatae erant. filio Commodo accersito ad limitem
togam virilem dedit, quare congiarium populo divisit
et eum ante tempus consulem designavit.

XXIII. Si quis umquam proscriptus est a praefecto
2 urbi, non libenter accepit. ipse in largitionibus
pecuniae publicae parcissimus fuit, quod laudi potius
3 datur quam reprehensioni, sed tamen et bonis viris
pecunias dedit et oppidis labentibus auxilium tulit et
tributa vel vectigalia, ubi necessitas cogebat, remisit.

---

[1] Hirschfeld (*Wien. Stud.*, III, p. 116) would insert *ex
procuratoriis* before *praetorias*.   [2] *in* omitted in P.

---

[1] *i.e.*, he took them from under the control of the senate
and made them imperial provinces governed by legates of
consular rank ; see note to *Hadr.*, iii. 9.

[2] *i.e.*, transferred from the control of the emperor to that
of the senate.

[3] Either the author fails to understand what he is trying
to say here, or an omission in the text must be assumed, such
as Hirschfeld's proposed insertion *ex procuratoriis*. He seems
to mean that certain provinces now received as governors
legates of praetorian rank (see note to *Hadr.*, iii. 9). As
there is no evidence for the supposition that any provinces
were transferred from the "consular" class to the "praetorian," it must be assumed that the provinces in question
were previously governed by equestrian *procurators*. Such a
transfer from "procuratory" to "praetorian" provinces was
actually made under Marcus in the cases of Raetia and Noricum, to which were sent the two new legions mentioned in
c. xxi. 8.

[4] Cf. c. xxi. 1.

changed into consular,[1] and several consular provinces into proconsular[2] or praetorian,[3] according to the exigencies of war. He checked disturbances among the Sequani by a rebuke and by his personal influence ; and in Spain,[4] likewise, he quieted the disturbances which had arisen in Lusitania. And having summoned his son Commodus to the border of the empire, he gave him the toga virilis,[5] in honour 9 Jul., 175 of which he distributed largess among the people,[6] and appointed him consul before the legal age.[7] 177.

XXIII. He was always displeased at hearing that anyone had been outlawed by the prefect of the city. He himself was very sparing of the public money in giving largess[8]—a fact which we mention rather in praise than in disparagement—but nevertheless he gave financial assistance to the deserving, furnished aid to towns on the brink of ruin,[9] and, when necessity demanded, cancelled tribute or taxes.[10] And

[5] See *Com.*, ii. 2 ; xii. 3 ; Dio, lxxi. 22, 2. The ceremony took place on the Danube frontier immediately prior to Marcus' departure for Syria.

[6] Commemorated on coins of 175 with the legend *Liberalitas Aug(usti) VI ;* see Cohen, iii², p. 43, Nos. 416-420.

[7] Under the empire the minimum age for the consulship seems to have been 33. See also note to *Pius*, vi. 10.

[8] Yet his coins record seven different largesses to the populace ; see Cohen, iii², p. 41 f., Nos. 401-427. See also c. xxvii. 5 and note. His donation to the soldiers on his accession was unusually large (see c. vii. 9), but on another occasion he is said to have refused the army's request for a donation ; see Dio, lxxi. 3, 3.

[9] See also c. xi. 3. He also came to the relief of Smyrna when destroyed by an earthquake in 178 ; see Dio, lxxi. 32, 2.

[10] In 178 all arrears due the treasury or the privy-purse were cancelled ; see Dio, lxxi. 32, 2. This was merely an application of the principle established by Hadrian ; see note to *Hadr.*, vii. 6.

MARCUS ANTONINUS

4 absens populi Romani voluptates curari vehementer
5 praecepit per ditissimos editores. fuit enim populo
hic sermo, cum sustulisset ad bellum gladiatores, quod
populum sublatis voluptatibus vellet cogere ad philo-
6 sophiam.   iusserat enim ne mercimonia impedirentur,
7 tardius pantomimos exhibere nonis [1] diebus.   de
amatis pantomimis ab uxore fuit sermo, ut superius
diximus.   sed haec omnia per epistolas suas purgavit.
8 idem Marcus sederi in civitatibus vetuit in equis sive
vehiculis. lavacra mixta summovit. mores matronarum composuit diffluentes et iuvenum nobilium.
sacra Serapidis a vulgaritate Pelusiae [2] summovit.
9 fama fuit sane, quod sub philosophorum specie quidam
rem publicam vexarent et privatos, quod ille purgavit.

XXIV. Erat mos iste Antonino ut omnia crimina
minore supplicio quam legibus plecti solent puniret,
quamvis nonnumquam contra manifestos et gravium
2 criminum reos inexorabilis permaneret. capitales
causas hominum honestorum ipse cognovit, et quidem
summa aequitate, ita ut praetorem reprehenderet, qui

---

[1] *nonis* Salm. ; *non uotis* P.   [2] *pelosiae* P ; *Pelusiaca*
Novak.

---

[1] See c. xix.   [2] Cf. *Hadr.*, xviii. 10.
[3] The Serapia, the annual festival of the Egyptian deity
Serapis, was celebrated on 25 April; see Calendar of Philocalus (*C.I.L.*, i², p. 262). A festival called *Pelusia*, celebrating
the annual overflow of the Nile, was held on 20 March ; see
Lydus, *de Mens.*, iv. 40. The statement of the biographer
has been explained by Mommsen (*C.I.L.*, i². p. 313) as meaning that the customary licence of the Pelusia was limited in
order to save the festival of Serapis from desecration. But
in view of the interval between the dates this explanation is
not altogether convincing ; furthermore, licence is an unnatural meaning for *vulgaritas* and *sacra Serapidis* does not
necessarily refer to the Serapia. The sentence seems rather

190

while absent from Rome he left forceful instructions
that the amusements of the Roman people should be
provided for by the richest givers of public spectacles,
because, when he took the gladiators away to the
war, there was talk among the people that he intended
to deprive them of their amusements and thereby
drive them to the study of philosophy. Indeed, he
had ordered that the actors of pantomimes should
begin their performances nine days later than usual
in order that business might not be interfered with.
There was talk, as we mentioned above,[1] about his
wife's intrigues with pantomimists; however, he
cleared her of all these charges in his letters. He
forbade riding and driving within the limits of any
city. He abolished common baths for both sexes.[2]
He reformed the morals of the matrons and young
nobles which were growing lax. He separated the
sacred rites of Serapis from the miscellaneous ceremonies of the Pelusia.[3] There was a report, furthermore, that certain men masquerading as philosophers
had been making trouble both for the state and for
private citizens; but this charge he refuted.

XXIV. It was customary with Antoninus to punish
all crimes with lighter penalties than were usually
inflicted by the laws; although at times, toward
those who were clearly guilty of serious crimes he
remained implacable. He himself held those trials
of distinguished men which involved the death-
penalty, and always with the greatest justice. Once,
indeed, he rebuked a praetor who heard the pleas of
accused men in too summary a fashion, and ordered

to mean that the rites of Serapis were isolated from the mass
of Egyptian cults celebrated at the Pelusia; so also Wilcken,
Klio, ix. p. 131 f.

cito reorum causas audierat, iuberetque illum iterum
cognoscere, dignitatis eorum interesse dicens ut ab
3 eo audirentur qui pro populo iudicaret. aequitatem
autem etiam circa captos hostes custodivit. infinitos
4 ex gentibus in Romano solo conlocavit. fulmen de
caelo precibus suis contra hostium machinamentum
extorsit, suis pluvia impetrata cum siti laborarent.
5   Voluit Marcomanniam provinciam, voluit etiam
6 Sarmatiam facere et fecisset, nisi Avidius Cassius
rebellasset sub eodem in Oriente ; atque imperatorem
se appellavit,[1] ut quidam dicunt, Faustina volente,
7 quae de mariti valetudine desperaret. alii dicunt
ementita morte Antonini Cassium imperatorem se
8 appellasse, cum divum Marcum appellasset. et
Antoninus quidem non est satis motus defectione
9 Cassii nec in eius affectus saevit.[2] sed per senatum
hostis est iudicatus bonaque eius proscripta per
XXV. aerarium publicum. relicto[3] ergo Sarmatico Mar-
comannicoque bello contra Cassium profectus est.
2 Romae etiam turbae fuerunt, quasi Cassius absente
Antonino adventaret. sed Cassius statim interfectus
3 est caputque eius adlatum est ad Antoninum. Marcus tamen non exultavit interfectione Cassii caputque

---

[1] So P, which Lessing restores; *rebellasset sub eodem in
oriente atque . . . appellasset* Peter.   [2] *nec eius affectus
seui* P ; restored by Peter from *Av. Cass.* vii. 5.   [3] *relecto* P.

---

[1] Cf. c. xxii. 2.
[2] In the war against the Quadi in 174; see Dio, lxxi. 8-10.
According to Dio, the thunder-storm was sent by Hermes at
the prayer of an Egyptian magician. The Christian legend,
on the other hand, declared that the storm was an answer to
the prayers of the Twelfth Legion, the Fulminata, entirely
composed of Christians; see Xiphilinus in Dio, lxxi. 9.

him to hold the trials again, saying that it was a matter of concern to the honour of the accused that they should be heard by a judge who really represented the people. He scrupulously observed justice, moreover, even in his dealings with captive enemies. He settled innumerable foreigners on Roman soil.[1] By his prayers he summoned a thunderbolt from heaven against a war-engine of the enemy, and successfully besought rain for his men when they were suffering from thirst.[2]

He wished to make a province of Marcomannia and likewise of Sarmatia,[3] and he would have done so had not Avidius Cassius just then raised a rebellion in the East.[4] This man proclaimed himself emperor, some say, at the wish of Faustina, who was now in despair over her husband's health; others, however, say that Cassius proclaimed himself emperor after spreading false rumours of Antoninus' death, and indeed he had called him the Deified. Antoninus was not much disturbed by this revolt, nor did he adopt harsh measures against Cassius' dear ones. The senate, however, declared Cassius a public enemy and confiscated his property to the public treasury. XXV. The Emperor, then, abandoning the Sarmatian and Marcomannic wars, set out against him. At Rome there was a panic for fear that Cassius would arrive during Antoninus' absence; but he was speedily slain and his head was brought to Antoninus. Even then, Marcus did not rejoice at Cassius' death, and gave

Jul., 175

---

[3] In 175, after a victory so decisive that Marcus was acclaimed Imperator for the eighth time, and took the title Sarmaticus; see Cohen, iii², p. 91 f., Nos. 916-925; *C.I.L.*, viii. 2276.

[4] Cf. *Av. Cass.*, vii f.

MARCUS ANTONINUS

4 eius humari iussit. Maecianum etiam, socium [1] Cassii,
cui Alexandria erat commissa, exercitus occidit. nam
et praefectum praetorio sibi fecerat, qui et ipse oc-
5 cisus est. in conscios defectionis vetuit senatum
6 graviter vindicare. simul petiit, ne qui senator tempore principatus sui occideretur, ne eius [2] pollueretur
7 imperium. eos etiam qui deportati fuerant revocari
iussit, cum paucissimi centuriones capite essent puniti.
8 ignovit et civitatibus quae Cassio consenserant, ignovit
et Antiochensibus, qui multa in Marcum pro Cassio
9 dixerant. quibus et spectacula et conventus publicos
tulerat et omne [3] contionum genus, contra quos
10 edictum gravissimum misit. seditiosos autem eos et
oratio Marci indicat, indita Mario Maximo, qua ille
11 usus est apud amicos. denique noluit Antiochiam
12 videre cum Syriam peteret. nam nec Cyrrhum voluit
videre, ex qua erat Cassius. postea tamen Antiochiam
vidit. fuit Alexandriae clementer cum his agens.[4]

XXVI. Multa egit cum regibus et pacem confirmavit,
sibi occurrentibus cunctis regibus et legatis Persarum.
2 omnibus orientalibus provinciis carissimus fuit. apud
3 multas etiam philosophiae vestigia reliquit. apud
Aegyptios civem se egit et philosophum in omnibus

---

[1] *socium* suggested by Peter for *filium* of P, which is certainly wrong; see c. xxvi. 11; *Av. Cass.*, vii. 4. [2] *ne nece
eius* Peter, following Madvig. [3] *omne* Peter [1]; *omnium* P,
Peter.[2] [4] This sentence, which precedes *postea . . . vidit*
in P, was transposed by Cas.

---

[1] Possibly, though not probably, the jurist L. Volusius
Maecianus (see *Pius*, xii. 1).
[2] For his general policy in the punishment of senators,
see c. x. 6.
[3] Faustina and Commodus seem to have accompanied him

194

orders that his head should be buried. Maecianus,[1] Cassius' ally, in whose charge Alexandria had been placed, was killed by the army; likewise his prefect of the guard—for he had appointed one—was also slain. Marcus then forbade the senate to impose any heavy punishment upon those who had conspired in this revolt; and at the same time, in order that his reign might escape such a stain, he requested that during his rule no senator should be executed.[2] Those who had been exiled, moreover, he ordered to be recalled ; and there were only a very few of the centurions who suffered the death-penalty. He pardoned the communities which had sided with Cassius, and even went so far as to pardon the citizens of Antioch, who had said many things in support of Cassius and in opposition to himself. But he did abolish their games and public meetings, including assemblies of every kind, and issued a very severe edict against the people themselves. And yet a speech which Marcus delivered to his friends, reported by Marius Maximus, brands them as rebels. And finally, he refused to visit Antioch when he journeyed to Syria,[3] nor would he visit Cyrrhus, the home of Cassius. Later on, however, he did visit Antioch. Alexandria, when he stayed there, he treated with clemency.

XXVI. He conducted many negotiations with kings, and ratified peace with all the kings and satraps of Persia when they came to meet him. He was exceedingly beloved by all the eastern provinces, and on many, indeed, he left the imprint of philosophy. While in Egypt he conducted himself like a

on this journey through Syria and Egypt; see c. xxvi. 4 and *Com.*, ii. 3.

MARCUS ANTONINUS

stadiis [1] templis locis.[2] et cum multa Alexandrini in
Cassium dixissent fausta, tamen omnibus ignovit et
4 filiam suam apud eos reliquit. Faustinam ·suam in
radicibus montis Tauri in vico Halalae exanimatam vi
5 subiti morbi amisit. petiit a senatu ut honores
Faustinae aedemque decernerent, laudata eadem cum
impudicitiae fama graviter laborasset. quae Anto-
6 ninus vel nesciit vel dissimulavit. novas puellas Faus-
7 tinianas instituit in honorem uxoris mortuae. divam
etiam Faustinam a senatu appellatam gratulatus est.
8 quam secum et in aestivis habuerat, ut matrem cas-
9 trorum appellaret. fecit et coloniam vicum in quo
obiit Faustina et aedem illi exstruxit. sed haec postea
aedis Heliogabalo dedicata est.

10   Ipsum Cassium pro clementia occidi passus est, non
11 occidi iussit. deportatus est Heliodorus, filius Cassii,
et alii liberum exsilium acceperunt cum bonorum parte.
12 filii autem Cassii et amplius media parte acceperunt
paterni patrimonii et auro atque argento adiuti,
mulieres autem etiam ornamentis ; ita ut Alexandria,
filia Cassii, et Druncianus gener liberam vagandi

---

[1] *stadiis* Peter with Salm. ; *studiis* P, which Mommsen
defends.   [2] *locis* P (by error *ocis* Peter[2], from which Mommsen conj. *oecis*, and Novak, *odeis*).

---

[1] According to Dio, lxxi. 29, 1, her death was by some
attributed to suicide.
[2] Cf. c. xix.
[3] Cf. *Pius*, viii. 1. See also *C.I.L.*, vi. 10222.
[4] Commemorated by coins of *Diva Faustina*, with the
legend *Consecratio ;* see Cohen, iii[2], p. 141 f., Nos. 65-83. She
also received the name Pia ; see the coins and *C.I.L.*, vi.
1019 = Dessau, *Ins. Sel.*, 382.
[5] After his victory over the Quadi in 174 ; see Dio, lxxi.
10, 5. The title appears on her coins issued both before and
after her deification ; see Cohen, iii[2], p. 149 f., Nos. 159-167.

private citizen and a philosopher at all the stadia, temples, and in fact everywhere. And although the citizens of Alexandria had been outspoken in wishing Cassius success, he forgave everything and left his daughter among them. And now, in the village of Halala, in the foothills of Mount Taurus, he lost his wife Faustina, who succumbed to a sudden ill- 176 ness.[1] He asked the senate to decree her divine honours and a temple, and likewise delivered a eulogy of her, although she had suffered grievously from the reputation of lewdness.[2] Of this, however, Antoninus was either ignorant or affected ignorance. He established a new order of Faustinian girls[3] in honour of his dead wife, expressed his pleasure at her deification by the senate,[4] and because she had accompanied him on his summer campaign, called her " Mother of the Camp ".[5] And besides this, he made the village where Faustina died a colony, and there built a temple in her honour. This, however, was afterwards consecrated to Elagabalus.[6]

With characteristic clemency, he suffered rather than ordered the execution of Cassius, while Heliodorus, the son of Cassius, was merely banished, and others of his children exiled but allowed part of their father's property.[7] Cassius' sons, moreover, were granted over half of their father's estate and were enriched besides with sums of gold and silver, while the women of the family were presented with jewels. Indeed, Alexandria, Cassius' daughter, and Druncianus, his son-in-law, were allowed to travel wherever

[6] The sun-god of Emesa in Syria, whose worship was introduced into Rome by the Emperor Elagabalus ; see *Carac.*, xi. 7 ; *Hel.*, i. 5 f.

[7] Cf. *Av. Cass.*, ix. 2-4.

potestatem haberent commendati amitae marito.
13 doluit denique Cassium exstinctum, dicens voluisse se
sine senatorio sanguine imperium transigere.

XXVII. Orientalibus rebus ordinatis Athenis fuit et
initia [1] Cereris [2] adiit, ut se innocentem probaret, et
2 sacrarium solus [3] ingressus est. revertens ad Italiam
3 navigio tempestatem gravissimam passus est. per
Brundisium veniens in Italiam togam et ipse sumpsit et
milites togatos esse iussit, nec umquam sagati fuerunt
4 sub eo milites. Romam ut venit triumphavit. et inde [4]
5 Lavinium profectus est. Commodum deinde sibi
collegam in tribuniciam potestatem iunxit, congiarium
populo dedit et spectacula mirifica; dein civilia multa
6 correxit. gladiatorii muneris sumptus modum fecit.
7 sententia Platonis semper in ore illius fuit, florere
civitates si aut philosophi imperarent aut imperantes
8 philospharentur. filio suo Bruttii Praesentis filiam
iunxit nuptiis celebratis exemplo privatorum, quare
etiam congiarium dedit populo.

---

[1] So Novak; *initalia* P; edd. *initialia*, . with Salm.
[2] *ceteris* P.   [3] *solus* Lessing with Cas.; *solum* P, Peter.
[4] *et inde* P; *inde* Lessing; *exinde* edd.

---

[1] Cf. c. xxv. 6.
[2] As Hadrian had done; see *Hadr.*, xiii. 1.
[3] See *Hadr.*, xxii. 2-3. His return was commemorated by coins with the legend *Fort(una) Red(ux)*; see Cohen, iii², p. 22, No. 210.
[4] *i.e.*, while they were in Italy.
[5] See note to c. xvii. 3.
[6] On the significance of this appointment see *Pius*, iv. 8 and note. It is commemorated on coins of Commodus of 177; see Cohen, iii², p. 326 f., Nos. 733-738.
[7] According to Dio, lxxi. 32, 1, each citizen received eight

they wished, and were even put under the protection of the Emperor's uncle by marriage. And further than this, he grieved at Cassius' death, saying that he had wished to complete his reign without shedding the blood of a single senator.[1]

XXVII. After he had settled affairs in the East he Sept., 176 came to Athens, and had himself initiated into the Eleusinian mysteries[2] in order to prove that he was innocent of any wrong-doing, and he entered the sanctuary unattended. Afterwards, when returning to Italy, he encountered a violent storm on the way. Then, reaching Italy by way of Brundisium, he donned the toga[3] and bade his troops do likewise, nor indeed during his reign were the soldiers ever clad in the military cloak.[4] When he reached Nov., 176 Rome he triumphed,[5] then hastened to Lavinium. Presently he appointed Commodus his colleague in 177 the tribunician power,[6] bestowed largess upon the people,[7] and gave marvellous games; shortly thereafter he remedied many civil abuses, and set a limit to the expense of gladiatorial shows. Ever on his lips was a saying of Plato's, that those states prospered where the philosophers were kings or the kings philosophers. He united his son in marriage with the daughter of Bruttius Præsens,[8] performing the ceremony in the manner of ordinary citizens; and in celebration of the marriage he gave largess to the people.

aurei (one for each year of Marcus' absence from Rome), a largess greater than had ever been given before.

[8] Her name was Bruttia Crispina; see Dio, lxxi. 31, 1, and *C.I.L.*, x. 408 = Dessau, *Ins. Sel.*, 1117. The marriage was commemorated by coins, Cohen, iii², p. 388 f. She was afterwards banished on a charge of adultery and put to death in exile; see Dio, lxxii. 4, 6.

MARCUS ANTONINUS

9 Dein ad conficiendum bellum conversus in adminis-
tratione eius belli obiit, labentibus iam filii moribus ab
10 instituto suo. triennio bellum postea cum Marcomannis Hermunduris Sarmatis Quadis etiam egit[1] et,
si anno uno superfuisset, provincias ex his fecisset.
11 ante biduum quam exspiraret, admissis amicis dicitur
ostendisse sententiam de filio eandem quam Philippus
de Alexandro, cum de hoc male sentiret, addens
nimium[2] se aegre ferre filium superstitem relinquen-
12 tem.[3] nam iam Commodus turpem se et cruentum
ostentabat.

XXVIII. Mors autem talis fuit: cum aegrotare
coepisset, filium advocavit atque ab eo primum petiit ut
belli reliquias non contemneret, ne videretur rem pub-
2 licam prodere. et, cum filius ei respondisset cupere
se primum sanitatem, ut vellet permisit, petens tamen
ut exspectasset paucos dies, haud[4] simul proficiscere-
3 tur. deinde abstinuit victu[5] potuque mori cupiens
4 auxitque morbum. sexta die vocatis amicis et ridens
res humanas, mortem autem contemnens ad amicos

---

[1] *triennio bellum . . . egit* Klein would transpose to precede *Dein . . . ab instituto suo.* [2] *nimium* Peter with
Sa'm.; *minime* P. [3] So Cas.; *relinquens* P, whence Novak:
se aegre ferre quod discederet f. s. relinquens. [4] *aut* P.
[5] *uictu* Jordan; *ui* P.

---

[1] He and Commodus left Rome for Pannonia on 3 August,
178; see *Com.*, xii. 6. This war seems to have been called
the *Expeditio Germanica Secunda* (*C.I.L.*, ii. 4114, and vi.
8541 = Dessau, *Ins. Sel.*, 1140 and 1573) or the *Expeditio
Sarmatica* (*C.I.L.*, x. 408 = Dessau, 1117).
[2] Probably uttered during the period of estrangement
when Alexander was living in Illyricum; see Plut., *Alex.*, ix.
[3] Cf. *Com.*, i. 7-9.

He then turned his attention to completing the war,[1] in the conduct of which he died. During this time the behaviour of his son steadily fell away from the standard the Emperor had set for himself. For three years thereafter he waged war with the Mar- 178-180 comanni, the Hermunduri, the Sarmatians, and the Quadi, and had he lived a year longer he would have made these regions provinces. Two days before his death, it is said, he summoned his friends and expressed the same opinion about his son that Philip expressed about Alexander when he too thought poorly of his son,[2] and added that it grieved him exceedingly to leave a son behind him. For already Commodus had made it clear that he was base and cruel.[3]

XXVIII. He died in the following manner:[4] When he began to grow ill, he summoned his son and besought him first of all not to think lightly of what remained of the war, lest he seem a traitor to the state. And when his son replied that his first desire was good health, he allowed him to do as he wished,[5] only asking him to wait a few days and not leave at once. Then, being eager to die, he refrained from eating or drinking, and so aggravated the disease. On the sixth day he summoned his friends, and with derision for all human affairs and scorn for death, said to them: "Why do you weep

[4] His death occurred at Sirmium (Mitrowitz on the Save) according to Tertullian, *Apologet.*, 25, at Vindobona (Vienna) according to Victor, *Caes.*, xvi. 12, *Epit.*, xvi. 12. According to a story preserved by Dio (lxxi. 33, 4), his physicians poisoned him in order to please Commodus. It has been supposed that he died of the plague (cf. §§ 4 and 8), but without very good reason.

[5] Apparently, to abandon the campaign; cf. *Com.*, iii. 5.

dixit, "quid de me [1] fletis et non magis de pestilentia
5 et communi morte cogitatis?" et cum illi vellent
recedere, ingemescens ait, "si iam me dimittitis,
6 vale vobis dico vos praecedens". et cum ab eo quaereretur, cui filium commendaret, ille respondit "vo-
7 bis, si dignus fuerit, et dis immortalibus". exercitus
cognita mala valetudine vehementissime dolebant,
8 quia illum unice amarunt. septimo die gravatus est
et solum filium admisit. quem statim dimisit, ne in
9 eum morbus transiret. dimisso filio caput operuit
10 quasi volens dormire, sed nocte animam efflavit. fertur filium mori voluisse, cum eum talem videret
futurum qualis exstitit post eius mortem, ne, ut ipse
dicebat, similis Neroni Caligulae et Domitiano esset.

XXIX. Crimini ei datum est quod adulteros uxoris
promoverit, Tertullum et Tutilium [2] et Orfitum et
Moderatum, ad varios honores, cum Tertullum et
2 prandentem cum uxore deprehenderit. de quo mimus
in scaena praesente Antonino dixit, cum stupidus
nomen adulteri uxoris a servo quaereret, et ille diceret
ter "Tullus," et adhuc stupidus quaereret, respondit
3 ille "iam tibi dixi ter, Tullus dicitur". et de hoc
quidem multa populus, multa etiam alii dixerunt
patientiam Antonini incusantes.

[1] So Peter, following Jordan; *quideme* P[1]; *quid me* P corr.
[2] *Tutilium* Scaliger; *utilium* P.

---

[1] See note to c. xiii. 3.
[2] Cf. Dio, lxxi. 34, 1, and Herodian, i. 4.
[3] Cf. Dio, lxxi. 33, 4. [4] See note to *Com.*, viii. 1.

for me, instead of thinking about the pestilence[1]
and about death which is the common lot of us all?"
And when they were about to retire he groaned and
said: "If you now grant me leave to go, I bid you
farewell and pass on before". And when he was
asked to whom he commended his son he replied:
"To you,[2] if he prove worthy, and to the immortal
gods". The army, when they learned of his sickness, lamented loudly, for they loved him singularly.
On the seventh day he was weary and admitted
only his son, and even him he at once sent away in
fear that he would catch the disease. And when his
son had gone, he covered his head as though he
wished to sleep and during the night he breathed
his last.[3] It is said that he foresaw that after his 17 Mar.,
death Commodus would turn out as he actually did, 180
and expressed the wish that his son might die, lest,
as he himself said, he should become another Nero,
Caligula, or Domitian.

XXIX. It is held to Marcus' discredit that he
advanced his wife's lovers, Tertullus and Tutilius[4]
and Orfitus and Moderatus, to various offices of
honour, although he had caught Tertullus in the very
act of breakfasting with his wife. In regard to this
man the following dialogue was spoken on the stage
in the presence of Antoninus himself. The Fool
asked the Slave the name of his wife's lover and
the Slave answered "Tullus" three times; and
when the Fool kept on asking, the Slave replied,
"I have already told you thrice Tullus is his name".[5]
But the city-populace and others besides talked a
great deal about this incident and found fault with
Antoninus for his forbearance.

[5] Ter-tullus means "Thrice-Tullus".

MARCUS ANTONINUS

4 Ante tempus sane mortis, priusquam ad bellum
Marcomannicum rediret, in Capitolio iuravit nullum
senatorem se sciente occisum, cum etiam rebelliones
5 dixerit se servaturum fuisse si scisset. nihil enim
magis et timuit et deprecatus est quam avaritiae
6 famam, de qua se multis epistulis purgat. dederunt
et vitio quod fictus [1] fuisset nec tam simplex quam
7 videretur, aut quam vel Pius vel Verus fuisset. dederunt etiam crimini quod aulicam adrogantiam
confirmaverit summovendo amicos a societate communi et a conviviis.

8 Parentibus consecrationem decrevit. amicos parentum etiam mortuos statuis ornavit.

9 Suffragatoribus non cito credidit. sed semper diu
quaesivit quod erat verum.

10 Enisa est Fabia ut Faustina mortua in eius matri-
monium coiret. sed ille concubinam sibi adscivit
procuratoris uxoris suae filiam, ne tot liberis super-
duceret novercam.

---

[1] *fictus* Novak; *ei uictus* P ; *effictus* Peter with Erasmus.

---

[1] See c. x. 6; xxv. 5-6; xxvi. 13.
[2] He had been betrothed to her in his youth; see c. iv. 5.

Previous to his death, and before he returned to the Marcomannic war, he swore in the Capitol that no senator had been executed with his knowledge and consent, and said that had he known he would have spared even the insurgents.[1] Nothing did he fear and deprecate more than a reputation for covetousness, a charge of which he tried to clear himself in many letters. Some maintain—and held it a fault—that he was insincere and not as guileless as he seemed, indeed not as guileless as either Pius or Verus had been. Others accused him of encouraging the arrogance of the court by keeping his friends from general social intercourse and from banquets.

His parents were deified at his command, and even his parents' friends, after their death, he honoured with statues.

He did not readily accept the version of those who were partisans in any matter, but always searched long and carefully for the truth.

After the death of Faustina, Fabia[2] tried to manœuvre a marriage with him. But he took a concubine instead, the daughter of a steward of his wife's, rather than put a stepmother over so many children.

VERUS

IULII CAPITOLINI

I. Scio plerosque ita vitam Marci ac Veri litteris atque historiae dedicasse ut priorem Verum intimandum legentibus darent, non imperandi secutos[1] or-2 dinem sed vivendi; ego vero, quod prior Marcus imperare coepit, dein Verus, qui superstite periit Marco, priorem Marcum dehinc Verum credidi celebrandum.

Igitur Lucius Ceionius Aelius[2] Commodus Verus Antoninus, qui ex Hadriani voluntate Aelius appellatus est, ex Antonini coniunctione Verus et Antoninus, neque inter bonos neque inter malos principes ponitur. 4 quem constat non inhorruisse vitiis, non abundasse virtutibus, vixisse deinde non in suo libero principatu sed sub Marco in simili ac paris[3] maiestatis imperio, a cuius secta lascivia morum et vitae licentioris nimie-

---

[1] *secutus* P[1]; *secuti sunt* P corr.   [2] *caelius* P.   [3] *pari* P.

---

[1] *i.e.* Marcus succeeded to the throne, and then associated Verus with himself as partner in the imperial power; see *Marc.*, vii. 5.

[2] He never bore all these names at the same time. For his names before and after his adoption by Pius see note to *Hadr.* xxiv. 1.

[3] Cf. *Ael.*, vii. 2. It would be more accurate to say that he

VERUS

BY

JULIUS CAPITOLINUS

I. Most men, I well know, who have enshrined in
literature and history the lives of Marcus and Verus,
have made Verus known to their readers first, following the order, not of their reigns, but of their lives.
I, however, have thought, since Marcus began to rule
first and Verus only afterwards [1] and Verus died while
Marcus still lived on, that Marcus' life should be
related first, and then that of Verus.

Now, Lucius Ceionius Aelius Commodus Verus
Antoninus [2]—called Aelius by the wish of Hadrian, [3]
Verus and Antoninus because of his relationship to
Antoninus [4]—is not to be classed with either the
good or the bad emperors. For, in the first place, it
is agreed that if he did not bristle with vices, no
more did he abound in virtues; and, in the second
place, he enjoyed, not unrestricted power, but a
sovereignty on like terms and equal dignity with
Marcus, from whom he differed, however, as far as
morals went, both in the laxity of his principles and

received the name Aelius when he was adopted by Pius, who
had received it on his adoption by Hadrian.
 [4] Cf. *Marc.*, vii. 7.

5 tate dissensit. erat enim morum simplicium et qui
adumbrare nihil posset.

6   Huic naturalis pater fuit Lucius Helius Verus, qui
ab Hadriano adoptatus primus Caesar est dictus et in
7 eadem statione constitutus periit. avi ac proavi et
8 item maiores plurimi consulares. natus est Lucius
Romae in praetura patris sui XVIII kal. Ianuariarum
9 die quo et Nero, qui rerum potitus est. origo eius
paterna pleraque ex Etruria fuit, materna ex Faventia.

II. Hac prosapia genitus patre ab Hadriano adoptato
in familiam Aeliam devenit mortuoque patre Caesare
2 in Hadriani familia remansit. a quo Aurelio datus
est adoptandus, cum sibi ille Pium filium Marcum
3 nepotem esse voluisset posteritati satis providens, et
ea quidem lege ut filiam Pii Verus acciperet, quae
data est Marco idcirco quia hic adhuc impar videbatur
4 aetate, ut in Marci vita exposuimus. duxit autem
uxorem Marci filiam Lucillam. educatus est in domo
5 Tiberiana. audivit Scaurinum grammaticum Latinum,
Scauri filium, qui grammaticus Hadriani fuit, Graecos
Telephum [1] atque Hephaestionem,[2] Harpocrationem,[3]

---

[1] *talephum* P.   [2] *Hefaestionem* Peter; *fertionem* P.
[3] *arpocrationem* P[b]; *acprocrationem* P[a].

---

[1] See *Marc.*, xvi. 4; xxix. 6; c. iii. 7.
[2] See *Ael.*, i. 2 and note.
[3] Cf. *Hadr.*, xxiii. 16; *Ael.*, iv. 7.
[4] His grandfather was L. Ceionius Commodus, consul in
106 (cf. *Ael.*, ii. 7); his great-grandfather was probably L.
Ceionius Commodus, consul in 78.
[5] The year is established by c. ii. 10, for he was adopted
by Pius in Jan., 138; the day is confirmed by the Calendar of
Philocalus; see *C.I.L.*, i², p. 278.
[6] Cf. Suet., *Nero*, vi. 1.   [7] Cf. *Ael.*, ii. 8.
[8] See note to c. i. 3.

the excessive licence of his life.   For in character he
was utterly ingenuous and unable to conceal a thing.[1]

His real father, Lucius Aelius Verus (who was
adopted by Hadrian), was the first man to receive the
name of Caesar [2] and die without reaching a higher
rank.[3]   His grandfathers and great-grandfathers [4] and
likewise many other of his ancestors were men of
consular rank.   Lucius himself was born at Rome
while his father was praetor, on the eighteenth day 15 Dec.,
before the Kalends of January,[5] the birthday of 130
Nero as well [6]—who also held the throne.   His
father's family came mostly from Etruria, his mother's
from Faventia.[7]

II. Such, then, was his real ancestry ; but when his
father was adopted by Hadrian he passed into the
Aelian family,[8] and when his father Caesar died, he
still stayed in the family of Hadrian.   By Hadrian
he was given in adoption to Aurelius,[9] when Hadrian,
making abundant provision for the succession, wished
to make Pius his son and Marcus his grandson ; and
he was given on the condition that he should espouse
the daughter of Pius.[10]   She was later given to Marcus, however, as we have related in his life,[11] because
Verus seemed too much her junior in years, while
Verus took to wife Marcus' daughter Lucilla.[12]   He
was reared in the House of Tiberius,[13] and received
instruction from the Latin grammarian Scaurinus (the
son of the Scaurus [14] who had been Hadrian's teacher
in grammar), the Greeks Telephus, Hephaestio,
Harpocratio, the rhetoricians Apollonius, Caninius

[9] *i.e.* Pius; see *Marc.*, v. 1 and note.
[10] See *Ael.*, vi. 9.   [11] Cf. *Marc.*, vi. 2.
[12] See *Marc.*, vii. 7 ; ix. 4.   [13] See note to *Pius*, x. 4.
[14] A famous *grammaticus ;* see Plin., *Epist.*, v. 11 ; Gellius,
xi. 15, 3.

rhetores Apollonium, Celerem Caninium et Herodem
Atticum, Latinum Cornelium Frontonem; philo-
6 sophos Apollonium et Sextum. hos omnes amavit
unice, atque ab his invicem dilectus est, nec tamen
7 ingeniosus ad litteras. amavit autem in pueritia
versus facere, post orationes. et melior quidem
orator fuisse dicitur quam poeta, immo, ut verius
8 dicam, peior poeta quam rhetor. nec desunt qui dicant eum adiutum ingenio amicorum, atque ab aliis
ei illa ipsa, qualiacumque sunt, scripta; si quidem
multos disertos et eruditos semper secum habuisse
9 dicitur. educatorem habuit Nicomedem. fuit volup-
tarius [1] et nimis laetus et omnibus deliciis ludis iocis
10 decenter aptissimus. post septimum annum in familiam Aureliam traductus Marci moribus et auctoritate
formatus est. amavit venatus palaestras et omnia
11 exercitia iuventutis. fuitque privatus in domo imperatoria viginti et tribus annis.

III. Qua die togam virilem Verus accepit, Antoninus Pius ea occasione qua patris templum dedi-
2 cabat populo liberalis fuit. mediusque inter Pium et
Marcum idem resedit,[2] cum quaestor populo munus
3 daret. post quaesturam statim consul est factus cum

---

[1] So P; *uoluptuarius* Peter.   [2] *se resedit* P.

---

[1] See *Marc.*, ii. 4.   [2] See *Pius*, x. 4; *Marc.*, ii. 7.
[3] See *Marc.*, iii. 2.   [4] *i.e.* was adopted by Pius.
[5] *i.e.* he did not hold any public office, although it was
usual to bestow such on young members of the imperial house-
210

Celer,[1] Herodes Atticus, and the Latin Cornelius Fronto, his teachers in philosophy being Apollonius[2] and Sextus.[3] For all of these he cherished a deep affection, and in return he was beloved by them, and this despite his lack of natural gifts in literary studies. In his youth he loved to compose verses, and later on in life, orations. And, in truth, he is said to have been a better orator than poet, or rather, to be strictly truthful, a worse poet than speaker. Nor are there lacking those who say that he was aided by the wit of his friends, and that the things credited to him, such as they are, were written by others; and in fact it is said that he did keep in his employ a number of eloquent and learned men. Nicomedes was his tutor. He was devoted to pleasure, too care-free, and very clever, within proper bounds, at every kind of frolic, sport, and raillery. At the age of seven he passed 138 into the Aurelian family,[4] and was moulded by the manners and influence of Marcus. He loved hunting and wrestling, and indeed all the sports of youth. And at the age of three and twenty he was still a private citizen [5] in the imperial household.

III. On the day when Verus assumed the toga virilis Antoninus Pius, who on that same occasion dedicated a temple to his father, gave largess to the people ; [6] and Verus himself, when quaestor,[7] gave the people a gladiatorial spectacle, at which he sat between Pius and Marcus. Immediately after his quaestorship he 154

hold ; see *Pius*, vi. 9-10 and note. Verus was evidently quaestor in 153.

  [6] This was probably in 145, for the toga virilis was assumed by Marcus in his fifteenth year ; see *Marc.* iv. 5. Antoninus' coins of 145 bear the legend *Liberalitas IV*; see Cohen, ii[2], p. 318 f., Nos. 490-501.

  [7] See *Pius*, vi. 10.

VERUS

Sextio [1] Laterano. interiectis annis cum Marco fratre
4 iterum factus est consul. diu autem et [2] privatus
fuit et ea honorificentia caruit qua Marcus ornabatur.
5 nam neque [3] in senatu ante quaesturam sedit neque
in itinere cum patre sed cum praefecto praetorii
vectus est nec aliud ei honorificentiae adnomen ad-
iunctum est quam quod Augusti filius appellatus est.
6 fuit studiosus etiam circensium haud aliter quam
gladiatorii muneris. hic cum tantis deliciarum et
luxuriae quateretur erroribus, ab Antonino videtur ob
hoc retentus quod eum pàter ita in adoptionem Pii
transire iusserat ut nepotem appellaret. cui, quan-
7 tum videtur, ñdem exhibuit, non amorem. amavit
tamen Antoninus Pius simplicitatem ingenii puritatemque [4] vivendi hortatusque est ut imitaretur et
8 fratrem. defuncto Pio Marcus in eum omnia contulit,
participatu etiam imperatoriae potestatis indulto,
sibique consortem fecit, cum illi soli senatus detulisset
imperium.

IV. Dato igitur imperio et indulta tribunicia potestate, post consulatus [5] etiam honorem delatum Verum
vocari praecepit, suum in eum transferens nomen,
2 cum ante Commodus vocaretur. Lucius quidem

---

[1] *Sextio* Peter with Clinton; *sestilio* P.   [2] *ei* P.   [3] *nam
neque* Jordan; *namque* P.   [4] *puritatemque* P, perhaps a
corruption; Peter suggests *hilaritatemque*.   [5] *post consulatus* Petrarch; *proconsulatos* P¹; *proconsulatus* P corr.

---

[1] See *Marc.*, vi. 3-6.
[2] This is confirmed by inscriptions, *e.g.*, *C.I.L.*, iii. 3843 =
Dessau, *Ins. Sel.*, 358.

was made consul, with Sextius Lateranus as his
colleague, and a number of years later he was created
consul for a second term together with his brother 161
Marcus. For a long time, however, he was merely
a private citizen and lacked the marks of honour with
which Marcus was continually being decorated.[1]
For he did not have a seat in the senate until he was
quaestor, and while travelling, he rode, not with his
father, but with the prefect of the guard, nor was any
title added to his name as a mark of honour save only
that he was called the son of Augustus.[2] He was
fond of circus-games no less than of gladiatorial
spectacles. And although he was weakened by such
follies of debauchery and extravagance, nevertheless
Pius retained him as a son, for the reason, it seems,
that Hadrian, wishing to call the youth his grandson,
had ordered Pius to adopt him. Towards Pius, so
far as it appears, Verus showed loyalty rather than
affection. Pius, however, loved the frankness of his
nature[3] and his unspoiled way of living, and encouraged Marcus to imitate him in these. When
Pius died, Marcus bestowed all honours upon Verus,
even granting him a share in the imperial power ;
he made him his colleague, moreover, when the
senate had presented the sovereignty to him alone.[4]

IV. After investing him with the sovereignty, then,
and installing him in the tribunician power,[5] and after
rendering him the further honour of the consulship, 161
Marcus gave instructions that he be named Verus,
transferring his own name to him, whereas previously
he had been called Commodus.[6] In return for this,

---

[3] See note to c. i. 5.   [4] Cf. *Marc.*, vii. 5.
[5] See note to *Pius*, iv. 7.
[6] On his name see note to *Hadr.*, xxiv. 1.

VERUS

Marco vicem reddens si quid susciperet[1] obsecutus
3 ut legatus proconsuli vel praeses imperatori. iam
primum enim pro ambobus[2] ad milites est locutus et
pro consensu imperii[3] graviter se et ad Marci mores
egit.

4   Ubi vero in Syriam[4] profectus est, non solum
licentia vitae liberioris sed etiam adulteriis et iu-
5 venum[5] amoribus infamatus est; si quidem tantae
luxuriae fuisse dicitur ut etiam, posteaquam[6] de
Syria rediit, popinam domi instituerit, ad quam post
convivium Marci devertebat,[7] ministrantibus sibi
6 omni genere turpium personarum. fertur et nocte
perpeti alea lusisse, cum in Syria concepisset id vitium,
atque in tantum vitiorum Gaianorum et Neronianorum
ac Vitellianorum fuisse aemulum, ut vagaretur nocte
per tabernas ac lupanaria obtecto capite cucullione
vulgari viatorio et comissaretur cum triconibus, com-
mitteret rixas, dissimulans quis esset, saepeque efflic-
tum livida facie redisse et in tabernis agnitum, cum
7 sese absconderet. iaciebat et nummos in popinas
8 maximos, quibus calices frangeret. amavit et aurigas,

---

[1] Thus Lenze; *si susciperet obsecutus* P; † *si susciperet
obsecutus* Peter.   [2] So Damsté; *Marcus pro ambobus* P.
[3] *pro consensu imperii* Jordan; *pro consensus imperio* P.
[4] *Syria* P, Peter.   [5] So Winterfeld; *iuuentis* P[1]; *iuuentutis*
P corr.; *incestis* Peter.   [6] *posteaquam* Petrarch; *quam
postea* P, Peter.   [7] *deuertebat* P, which Lessing restores;
diuertebat edd.

---

[1] *i.e.* the praetorian guard; see *Marc.*, vii. 9.
[2] See note to *Marc.*, viii. 10.   [3] Cf. *Marc.*, viii. 12.
[4] This is told about Nero (Tac., *Ann.*, xiii. 25; Suet., *Nero*,
xxvi.; Dio, lxi. 8), but not, at least by extant authors, about

214

Verus obeyed Marcus, whenever he entered upon any undertaking, as a lieutenant obeys a proconsul or a governor obeys the emperor. For, at the beginning, he addressed the soldiers[1] in his brother's behalf as well as his own, and in consideration of the joint rule he conducted himself with dignity and observed the moral standard that Marcus had set up.

When he set out for Syria,[2] however, his name was smirched not only by the licence of an unbridled life,[3] but also by adulteries and by love-affairs with young men. Besides, he is said to have been so depraved as to install a cook-shop in his home after he returned from Syria, and to repair thither after Marcus' banquets and have all manner of foul persons serve him. It is said, moreover, that he used to dice the whole night through, after he had taken up that vice in Syria, and that he so rivalled Caligula, Nero, and Vitellius in their vices as to wander about at night through taverns and brothels with only a common travelling-cap for a head-covering, revel with various rowdies, and engage in brawls, concealing his identity the while[4]; and often, they say, when he returned, his face was beaten black and blue, and once he was recognised in a tavern even though he had hidden himself. It was his wont also to hurl large coins into the cook-shops and therewith smash the cups. He was very fond also of charioteers, favouring the " Greens ".[5] He held gladiatorial

162

Caligula or Vitellius. The same thing is also told about Otho (Suet., *Otho*, ii. 1) and Commodus (*Com.*, iii. 7).

[5] The teams and drivers competing in the races were supplied by four racing syndicates, named, after the colours which they adopted, the " Greens," the " Blues," the "Reds," and the " Whites". Caligula and Nero were also partisans of the " Greens "; see Suet., *Cal.*, lv. 2, and *Nero*, xxii.

9 Prasino favens. gladiatorum etiam frequentius pugnas in convivio habuit, trahens cenas in noctem et in
toro convivali condormiens, ita ut levatus cum stro-
10 matibus in cubiculum perferretur. somni fuit permo-
dici, digestionis facillimae.

11   Sed Marcus haec omnia bene sciens [1] dissimulabat
V. pudore [2] illo ne reprehenderet fratrem. et notissi-
mum eius quidem fertur tale convivium, in quo primum
duodecim accubuisse dicitur, cum sit not ssimum
dictum de numero convivarum " septem convivium,
2 novem vero convicium ". donatos autem pueros de-
coros qui ministrabant singulis, donatos etiam struc-
tores et lances singulis quibusque, donata et viva ani-
malia vel cicurum vel ferarum avium vel quadripedum,[3]
3 quorum cibi adpositi erant, donatos etiam calices
singulis per singulas potiones, murrinos et crystallinos
Alexandrinos, quotiens bibitum est ; data etiam aurea
atque argentea pocula et gemmata, coronas quin etiam
datas lemniscis aureis interpositis et alieni temporis [4]
floribus, data et vasa aurea cum unguentis ad speciem
4 alabastrorum, data et vehicula cum mulabus ac muli-
onibus cum iuncturis argenteis, ut ita de convivio
5 redirent. omne autem convivium ꞓes imatum dicitur
6 sexagies centenis milibus sestertiorum. hoc convivium
posteaquam Marcus audivit, ingemuisse dicitur et
7 doluisse publicum fatum. post convivium lusum

---

[1] So Oberdick ; *omnia nesciens* P ; *omnia non nesciens* Peter.
[2] So Novak ; *prae* (· ℞ · *in* P) before *pudore* Peter.   [3] So P ;
quadrupedium B, Peter.   [4] So Pᵇ ; *alienis temporibus* P corr.

---

[1] This saying is not found elsewhere ; all the evidence,
both literary and monumental, shows that nine was the
normal number. There was an old principle that the number

216

bouts rather frequently at his banquets, and after
continuing the meal far into the night he would fall
asleep on the banqueting-couch, so that he had to be
lifted up along with the covers and carried to his
bedroom. He never needed much sleep, however ;
and his digestion was excellent.

But Marcus, though he was not without knowledge
of these happenings, with characteristic modesty
pretended ignorance for fear of censuring his brother.
V. One such banquet, indeed, became very notorious. This was the first banquet, it is said, at which
couches were placed for twelve, although there is a
very well-known saying about the proper number of
those present at a banquet that "seven make a dinner,
nine make a din ".[1] Furthermore, the comely lads
who did the serving were given as presents, one to
each guest ; carvers and platters, too, were presented to
each, and also live animals either tame or wild, winged
or quadruped, of whatever kind were the meats
that were served, and even goblets of murra[2] or of
Alexandrine crystal were presented to each man for
each drink, as often as they drank. Besides this, he
gave golden and silver and even jewelled cups, and
garlands, too, entwined with golden ribbons and
flowers out of season, golden vases with ointments
made in the shape of perfume-boxes, and even
carriages, together with mules and muleteers, and
trappings of silver, wherewith they might return
home from the banquet. The estimated cost of the
whole banquet, it is reported, was six million sesterces.
And when Marcus heard of this dinner, they say, he
groaned and bewailed the fate of the empire. After

at a banquet should not be less than the Graces or greater
than the Muses ; see Gellius, xiii. 11, 2.

[2] See note to *Marc.* xvii. 4.

8 est tesseris usque ad lucem. et haec quidem post
Parthicum bellum, ad quod eum misisse dicitur Marcus, ne vel in urbe ante oculos omnium peccaret, vel
ut parsimoniam peregrinatione addisceret, vel ut
timore bellico emendatior rediret, vel ut se imper-
9 atorem esse cognosceret. sed quantum profecerit,
cum alia vita tum haec quam narravimus cena mon-
stravit.

VI. Circensium tantam curam habuit ut frequenter
e provincia[1] litteras causa circensium et miserit et
2 acceperit. denique etiam praesens et cum Marco
sedens multas a Venetianis est passus iniurias, quod
3 turpissime contra eos faveret. nam et Volucri equo
Prasino aureum simulacrum fecerat, quod secum por-
4 tabat. cui quidem passas uvas et nucleos in vicem
hordei in praesepe ponebat, quem sagis fuco tinctis
coopertum in Tiberianam ad se adduci iubebat, cui
5 mortuo sepulchrum in Vaticano fecit. in huius equi
gratiam primum coeperunt equis aurei vel brabia
6 postulari. in tanto autem equus ille honore fuit, ut
ei a populo Prasinianorum saepe modius aureorum
postularetur.

7 Profectum eum ad Parthicum bellum Marcus
Capuam prosecutus est; cumque inde per omnium
villas se ingurgitaret, morbo implicitus apud Canusium

[1] *e* added by Salm.; *prouincialibus* P corr.

[1] See note to c. iv. 8.   [2] *i.e.* " Flyer ".
[3] See note to *Pius*, x. 4.   [4] See *Marc.*, viii. 9 f. and note.

218

the banquet, moreover, they diced until dawn. And all this was done after the Parthian war, whither Marcus had sent him, it is said, either that he might commit his debaucheries away from the city and the eyes of all citizens, or that he might learn economy by his travels, or that he might return reformed through the fear inspired by war, or, finally, that he might come to realize that he was an emperor. But how much good all this did is shown not only by the rest of his life, but also by this banquet of which we have just told.

VI. Such interest did Verus take in the circus-games that frequently even in his province he despatched and received letters pertaining to them. And finally, even at Rome, when he was present and seated with Marcus, he suffered many insults from the "Blues," [1] because he had outrageously, as they maintained, taken sides against them. For he had a golden statue made of the "Green" horse Volucer,[2] and this he always carried around with him; indeed, he was wont to put raisins and nuts instead of barley in this horse's manger and to order him brought to him, in the House of Tiberius,[3] covered with a blanket dyed with purple, and he built him a tomb, when he died, on the Vatican Hill. It was because of this horse that gold pieces and prizes first began to be demanded for horses, and in such honour was this horse held, that frequently a whole peck of gold pieces was demanded for him by the faction of the "Greens".

When Verus set out for the Parthian war, Marcus 162 accompanied him as far as Capua [4]; from there on he gorged himself in everyone's villa, and in consequence he was taken sick at Canusium, becoming very ill, so that his brother hastened thither to see him. And

VERUS

aegrotavit.   quo ad eum [1] visendum frater contendit.
8 multa in eius vita ignava et sordida etiam belli tem-
9 pore deteguntur.   nam cum interfecto legato, caesis
legionibus, Syris defectionem cogitantibus, oriens
vastaretur, ille in Apulia venabatur et apud Corinthum
et Athenas inter symphonias et cantica navigabat et
per singulas maritimas civitates Asiae Pamphyliae
VII. Ciliciaeque clariores voluptatibus immorabatur.   Antiochiam posteaquam venit, ipse quidem se luxuriae
dedidit, duces autem confecerunt Parthicum bellum,
Statius Priscus et Avidius Cassius et Martius Verus
per quadriennium, ita ut Babylonem et Mediam per-
2 venirent et Armeniam vindicarent   partumque ipsi
nomen est Armeniaci, Parthici, Medici, quod etiam
3 Marco Romae agenti delatum est.   egit autem per
quadriennium Verus hiemem Laodiceae, aestatem
4 apud Daphnen, reliquam partem Antiochiae.   risui
fuit omnibus Syris, quorum multa ioca in theatro in
5 eum dicta exstant.   vernas in triclinium Saturnalibus
6 et diebus festis semper admisit.   ad Euphraten tamen
impulsum comitum suorum sequendo [2] profectus est.
7 Ephesum etiam rediit, ut Lucillam uxorem, missam a
patre Marco, susciperet, et idcirco maxime ne Marcus
cum ea in Syriam veniret ac flagitia eius adnosceret.

---

[1] So Peter ; *quod eum* P[1] (*m* later erased).   [2] So Peter[2];
inpulsum ... secunde P[1] ; *inpulsu ... secum* P corr.

---

[1] Aelius Severianus, governor of Cappadocia ; see note to
Marc., viii. 6.
[2] Governor of Cappadocia ; he carried on a successful campaign in Armenia in 164.   Later, he informed Marcus of the
revolt of Avidius Cassius (see Dio, lxxi. 23), and afterwards
became Cassius' successor in the governorship of Syria.
[3] See *Marc.*, ix. 1-2 and notes.   The Armenian campaign

220

now in the course of this war there were revealed
many features of Verus' life that were weak and base.
For while a legate was being slain,[1] while legions
were being slaughtered, while Syria meditated revolt,
and the East was being devastated, Verus was hunting in Apulia, travelling about through Athens and
Corinth accompanied by orchestras and singers, and
dallying through all the cities of Asia that bordered
on the sea, and those cities of Pamphylia and Cilicia
that were particularly notorious for their pleasure-
resorts. VII. And when he came to Antioch, there
he gave himself wholly to riotous living. His generals,
meanwhile, Statius Priscus, Avidius Cassius, and
Martius Verus [2] for four years conducted the war until they advanced to Babylon and Media, and recovered Armenia.[3] He, however, gained the names
Armeniacus, Parthicus, and Medicus; and these were
proffered to Marcus also, who was then living at
Rome. For four years, moreover Verus passed his 163-166
winters at Laodicea, his summers at Daphne, and the
rest of the time at Antioch.[4] As far as the Syrians
were concerned, he was an object for ridicule, and
many of the jibes which they uttered against him on
the stage are still preserved. Always, during the
Saturnalia and on holidays he admitted his more
pampered slaves to his dining-room. Finally, however, at the insistence of his staff he set out for the
Euphrates, but soon, in order to receive his wife
Lucilla, who had been sent thither by her father
Marcus,[5] he returned to Ephesus, going there chiefly
in order that Marcus might not come to Syria with

was the first one, then followed the campaigns in Parthia and
Media.
[4] Cf. *Marc.*, viii. 12.   [5] Cf. *Marc.*, ix. 4.

VERUS

nam senatui Marcus dixerat se filiam in Syriam de-
8 ducturum.   confecto sane bello regna regibus, pro-
9 vincias vero comitibus suis regendas dedit.   Romam
inde ad triumphum invitus, quod Syriam quasi regnum
suum relinqueret, rediit et pariter cum fratre triumphavit, susceptis a senatu nominibus quae in exercitu
10 acceperat.   fertur praeterea ad amicae vulgaris arbitrium in Syria posuisse barbam ; unde in eum a Syris
multa sunt dicta.

VIII. Fuit eius fati ut in eas provincias per quas
rediit Romam usque luem secum deferre videretur.
2 et nata fertur pestilentia in Babylonia, ubi de templo
Apollinis ex arcula aurea, quam miles forte inciderat,
spiritus pestilens evasit, atque inde Parthos orbemque [1]
3 complesse.   sed hoc non Lucii Veri vitio sed Cassii,
a quo contra fidem Seleucia, quae ut amicos milites
4 nostros receperat, expugnata est.   quod quidem inter
ceteros etiam Quadratus, belli Parthici scriptor, in-
cusatis Seleucenis, qui fidem primi ruperant, purgat.
5   Habuit hanc reverentiam Marci Verus, ut nomina

[1] *urbemque* P.

---

[1] Verus' coins of 166 bear the legends *Pax* and *Pax Aug(usti)*.
[2] Armenia, Osroëne, and probably other client-kingdoms. For the coins see note to *Marc.*, ix. 1.
[3] Cf. *Marc.*, xii. 8 f.
[4] Armeniacus, Parthicus Maximus, and Medicus; see notes to *Marc.*, ix. 1-2.
[5] Probably the famous Panthea; see Marcus, εἰσέαυτ viii. 37 ; Lucian, *Imag.*, x. ; xx.
[6] Cf. *Marc.*, xiii. 3 f.

222

her and discover his evil deeds. For Marcus had told the senate that he himself would conduct his daughter to Syria. Then, after the war was finished,[1] he assigned kingdoms[2] to certain kings, and provinces to certain members of his staff, to be ruled, and returned to Rome for a triumph,[3] reluctantly, however, since he was leaving in Syria what almost seemed his own kingdom. His triumph he shared with his brother, and from the senate he accepted the names which he had received in the army.[4] It is said, furthermore, that he shaved off his beard while in Syria to humour the whim of a low-born mistress;[5] and because of this many things were said against him by the Syrians. 166

VIII. It was his fate to seem to bring a pestilence with him to whatever provinces he traversed on his return, and finally even to Rome.[6] It is believed that this pestilence originated in Babylonia, where a pestilential vapour arose in a temple of Apollo from a golden casket which a soldier had accidentally cut open, and that it spread thence over Parthia and the whole world. Lucius Verus, however, is not to blame for this so much as Cassius, who stormed Seleucia in violation of an agreement, after it had received our soldiers as friends. This act, indeed, many excuse, and among them Quadratus,[7] the historian of the Parthian war, who blames the Seleucians as the first to break the agreement.

Such respect did Verus have for Marcus, that on

[7] Asinius Quadratus, author of a history of Rome from the foundation of the city to the reign of Severus Alexander; see Suidas, *s.v.* Κοδρᾶτος. His history of the Parthian wars is cited by Stephanus of Byzantium, frag. 12 f.; see also *Av. Cass.*, i. 1.

quae sibi delata fuerant cum fratre communicaret die
[6] triumphi, quem pariter celebrarunt. reversus e
Parthico bello minore circa fratrem cultu fuit Verus ;
nam et libertis inhonestius indulsit et multa sine fratre
[7] disposuit. his accessit, quod, quasi reges aliquos ad
triumphum adduceret, sic histriones eduxit e Syria,
quorum praecipuus fuit Maximinus, quem Paridis
[8] nomine nuncupavit. villam praeterea exstruxit in Via
Clodia famosissimam, in qua per multos dies et ipse
ingenti luxuria debacchatus est cum libertis suis et
amicis imparibus,[1] quorum praesentiae[2] nulla inerat
[9] reverentia. et Marcum rogavit, qui venit, ut fratri
venerabilem morum suorum et imitandam, ostenderet
sanctitudinem, et quinque diebus in eadem villa residens cognitionibus continuis operam dedit, aut con-
[10] vivante fratre aut convivia comparante. habuit et
Agrippum histrionem, cui cognomentum erat Mem-
phii, quem et ipsum e Syria veluti tropaeum Parthicum
[11] adduxerat, quem Apolaustum nominavit. adduxerat
secum et fidicinas et tibicines et histriones scurrasque
mimarios et praestigiatores et omnia mancipiorum
genera, quorum Syria et Alexandria pascitur voluptate,
prorsus ut videretur bellum non Parthicum sed hist-
rionicum confecisse.

---

[1] So Richter ; *paribus* P, Peter.   [2] *praesentiae nulla*
Novak ; *praesentia ulla* P ; *in praesentia nulla* Peter.

---

[1] See note to c. vii. 9.   [2] Cf. c. ix. 3-5.
[3] Also mentioned by Fronto, *Prin. Hist.*, p. 209 N.
[4] Running N.W. from Rome through central Etruria,
branching off from the Via Cassia near Veii. The villa of
Verus was probably on the Via Cassia, near the modern Acqua
Traversa, north of the Pons Mulvius.
[5] *i.e.* " Enjoyable ". After his manumission he took the
name L. Aelius Aurelius Apolaustus Memphius. He is

the day of the triumph, which they celebrated together, he shared with his brother the names which
had been granted to himself.[1]   After he had returned
from the Parthian war, however, Verus exhibited less
regard for his brother; for he pampered his freedmen[2]
shamefully, and settled many things without his
brother's counsel.   Besides all this, he brought actors
out of Syria[3] as proudly as though he were leading
kings to a triumph.   The chief of these was Maximinus, on whom he bestowed the name Paris.   Furthermore, he built an exceedingly notorious villa on the
Clodian Way,[4] and here he not only revelled himself
for many days at a time in boundless extravagance
together with his freedmen and friends of inferior
rank in whose presence he felt no shame, but he even
invited Marcus.   Marcus came, in order to display to
his brother the purity of his own moral code as
worthy of respect and imitation, and for five days, staying in the same villa, he busied himself continuously
with the examination of law-cases, while his brother,
in the meantime, was either banqueting or preparing
banquets.   Verus maintained also the actor Agrippus,
surnamed Memphius, whom he had brought with him
from Syria, almost as a trophy of the Parthian war,
and named Apolaustus.[5]   He had brought with him,
too, players of the harp and the flute, actors and
jesters from the mimes, jugglers, and all kinds of
slaves in whose entertainment Syria and Alexandria
find pleasure, and in such numbers, indeed, that he
seemed to have concluded a war, not against Parthians,
but against actors.

commemorated in numerous inscriptions, and he received
many local honours in the cities of Italy.   He was put to
death in 189; see *Com.*, vii. 1.

IX. Et hanc vitae diversitatem [1] atque alia multa
inter Marcum et Verum simultates fecisse, non
aperta veritas indicabat, sed occultus rumor inseverat.
2 verum illud praecipuum quod, cum Libonem quendam
patruelem suum Marcus legatum in Syriam misisset,
atque ille se insolentius quam verecundus senator
efferret, dicens ad fratrem suum se [2] scripturum esse
si quid [3] forte dubitaret, nec Verus praesens pati posset, subitoque morbo notis prope veneni exsistentibus
interisset, visum est nonnullis, non tamen Marco, quod
eius fraude putaretur occisus. quae res simultatum
auxit rumorem.
3   Liberti multum potuerunt apud Verum, ut in vita
Marci diximus, Geminas et Agaclytus, cui dedit invito
4 Marco Libonis uxorem. denique nuptiis a Vero [4]
5 celebratis Marcus convivio non interfuit. habuit et
alios libertos Verus improbos, Coeden et Eclectum
6 ceterosque. quos omnes Marcus post mortem Veri
specie honoris abiecit [5] Eclecto retento, qui postea
Commodum filium eius occidit.
7   Ad bellum Germanicum, Marcus quod nollet
Lucium sine se vel ad bellum mittere vel in urbe
dimittere causa luxuriae, simul profecti sunt atque
Aquileiam venerunt invitoque Lucio Alpes transgressi,

[1] haec . . . diuersitas P.   [2] fratrem suum se Peter; fratres suos P.   [3] qui P.   [4] ab Vero Peter; habero P.
[5] adiecit P.

---

[1] Probably the M. Annius Libo named in a senatus consultum of the time of Pius; see C.I.L., iii. p. 7060.

[2] Marc., xv. 2.

[3] Cf. Com., xv. 2. The identification, however, of Verus'
freedman with Eclectus, the murderer of Commodus, has
been doubted.

[4] Cf. Marc., xiv. and notes.

IX. This diversity in their manner of life, as well as many other causes, bred dissensions between Marcus and Verus—or so it was bruited about by obscure rumours although never established on the basis of manifest truth. But, in particular, this incident was mentioned : Marcus sent a certain Libo,[1] a cousin of his, as his legate to Syria, and there Libo acted more insolently than a respectful senator should, saying that he would write to his cousin if he happened to need any advice. But Verus, who was there in Syria, could not suffer this, and when, a little later, Libo died after a sudden illness accompanied by all the symptoms of poisoning, it seemed probable to some people, though not to Marcus, that Verus was responsible for his death ; and this suspicion strengthened the rumours of dissensions between the Emperors.

Verus' freedmen, furthermore, had great influence with him, as we related in the Life of Marcus,[2] namely Geminas and Agaclytus. To the latter of these he gave the widow of Libo in marriage against the wishes of Marcus ; indeed, when Verus celebrated the marriage ceremony Marcus did not attend the banquet. Verus had other unscrupulous freedmen as well, Coedes and Eclectus and others. All of these Marcus dismissed after Verus' death, under pretext of doing them honour, with the exception of Eclectus, and he afterwards slew Marcus' son, Commodus.[3]

When the German war broke out, the two Em- 166 perors went to the front together, for Marcus wished neither to send Lucius to the war alone, nor yet, because of his debauchery, to leave him in the city. When they had come to Aquileia,[4] they proceeded to cross the Alps, though this was contrary to Lucius'

227

8 cum Verus apud Aquileiam tantum venatus[1] con-
vivatusque esset, Marcus autem omnia prospexisset.
9 de quo bello quid[2] per legatos barbarorum pacem
petentium, quid[3] per duces nostros gestum est, in
10 Marci vita plenissime disputatum est. composito
autem bello in Pannonia urguente Lucio Aquileiam
redierunt,[4] quodque[5] urbanas desiderabat Lucius
11 voluptates in urbem festinatum[6] est. sed non longe
ab Altino subito in vehiculo morbo, quem apoplexin
vocant, correptus Lucius depositus e vehiculo detracto
sanguine Altinum perductus, cum triduo mutus
vixisset, apud Altinum periit.

X. Fuit sermo quod et socrum Faustinam incestas-
set. et dicitur Faustinae socrus dolo aspersis ostreis
veneno exstinctus esse, idcirco quod consuetudinem
2 quam cum matre habuerat filiae prodidisset. quamvis
et illa fabula quae in Marci vita posita est abhorrens
3 a talis viri vita sit exorta, cum multi etiam uxori eius
flagitium mortis adsignent, et idcirco quod Fabiae
nimium indulserat Verus, cuius potentiam uxor
4 Lucilla[7] ferre non posset. tanta sane familiaritas
inter Lucium et Fabiam sororem fuit, ut[8] hoc quoque
usurpaverit rumor quod inierint consilium ad Marcum
5 e vita tollendum, idque cum esset per Agaclytum

[1] *uectatus* P.   [2] *quid* Novak; *quidem* P; *quidem quid*
Peter.   [3] *quidem* P.   [4] *redieret* P[b]; *rediret* P[a].   [5] *quoque* P.
[6] *festinatum* Peter; *destinatum* P.   [7] *Lucilla* Mommsen;
lucii P; *uel Marci* P corr.   [8] *ut* Novak; *ut si* P; *uti* Peter.

[1] *Marc.*, xiv. 3-4.
[2] In Venetia, at the mouth of the Plavis (Piave); its modern
name is Altino.

desire ; for as long as they remained in Aquileia he did
nothing but hunt and banquet while Marcus made
all the plans. As far as this war was concerned, we
have very fully discussed in the Life of Marcus[1] what
was accomplished by the envoys of the barbarians
when they sued for peace and what was accomplished
by our generals. When the war in Pannonia was
settled, they returned to Aquileia at Lucius' insistence,
and then, because he yearned for the pleasures of
the city, they hastened cityward. But not far from
Altinum, Lucius, while in his carriage, was suddenly
stricken with the sickness which they call apoplexy,
and after he had been set down from his carriage
and bled, he was taken to Altinum,[2] and here he 169
died, after living for three days unable to speak.

X. There was gossip to the effect that he had
violated his mother-in-law Faustina. And it is said
that his mother-in-law killed him treacherously by
having poison sprinkled on his oysters, because he
had betrayed to the daughter[3] the amour he had
had with the mother. However, there arose also
that other story related in the Life of Marcus,[4] one
utterly inconsistent with the character of such a man.
Many, again, fastened the crime of his death upon
his wife, since Verus had been too complaisant to
Fabia, and her power his wife Lucilla could not endure. Indeed, Lucius and his sister Fabia did become so intimate that gossip went so far as to claim
that they had entered into a conspiracy to make
away with Marcus, and that when this was betrayed
to Marcus by the freedman Agaclytus, Faustina cir-

[3] Lucilla.
[4] Apparently the one contained in *Marc.*, xv. 5, and repeated in the appendix to this biography, c. xi. 2.

libertum proditum Marco, anteventum[1] Lucium a Faustina,[2] ne praeveniret.

6 Fuit decorus corpore, vultu geniatus, barba prope barbarice demissa, procerus et fronte in supercilia ad-7 ductiore venerabilis. dicitur sane tantam habuisse curam flaventium capillorum, ut capiti auri ramenta respergeret, quo magis coma inluminata flavesceret. 8 lingua impeditior fuit, aleae cupidissimus, vitae semper luxuriosae atque in pluribus Nero praeter 9 crudelitatem et ludibria. habuit inter alium luxuriae apparatum calicem crystallinum nomine Volucrem ex eius equi nomine quem dilexit, humanae potionis[3] modum supergressum.

XI. Vixit annis quadraginta duobus, imperavit cum fratre annis undecim. inlatumque eius corpus est Hadriani sepulchro, in quo et Caesar pater eius naturalis sepultus est.

2 Nota est fabula, quam Marci non capit vita, quod partem vulvae veneno inlitam, cum eam exsecuisset cultro una parte venenato, Marcus Vero porrexerit. 3 sed hoc[4] nefas est de Marco putari, quamvis Veri et 4 cogitata et facta mereantur. quod nos non in medio relinquemus sed totum purgatum confutatumque respuimus, cum adhuc post Marcum praeter vestram clementiam, Diocletiane Auguste, imperatorem talem nec adulatio videatur potuisse confingere.

---

[1] *ante aduentum* P.   [2] *a Faustina* Mommsen; *a* omitted in P.   [3] *positionis* P.   [4] *se ad hoc* P.

---

[1] Cf. Dio, lxxi. 3, 1 = Zonaras, xii. 2.   [2] See c. vi. 3.
[3] Evidently an error, for he was born 15 Dec., 130 (c. i. 8), and died in Jan., 169.
[4] An error; his reign was 161-169.
[5] Cf. *Marc.*, xx. 1 and note.   [6] See note to c. x. 2.

cumvented Lucius in fear that he might circumvent her.[1]

Verus was well-proportioned in person and genial of expression. His beard was allowed to grow long, almost in the style of the barbarians; he was tall, and stately in appearance, for his forehead projected somewhat over his eyebrows. He took such pride in his yellow hair, it is said, that he used to sift gold-dust on his head in order that his hair, thus brightened, might seem yellower. He was somewhat halting in speech, a reckless gambler, ever of an extravagant mode of life, and in many respects, save only that he was not cruel or given to acting, a second Nero. Among other articles of extravagance he had a crystal goblet, named Volucer after that horse of which he had been very fond,[2] that surpassed the capacity of any human draught.

XI. He lived forty-two years,[3] and, in company with his brother, reigned eleven.[4] His body was laid in the Tomb of Hadrian,[5] where Caesar, his real father, was also buried.

There is a well-known story,[6] which Marcus' manner of life will not warrant, that Marcus handed Verus part of a sow's womb which he had poisoned by cutting it with a knife smeared on one side with poison. But it is wrong even to think of such a deed in connection with Marcus, although the plans and deeds of Verus may have well deserved it; nor shall we leave the matter undecided, but rather reject it discarded and disproved, since from the time of Marcus onward, with the exception of your Clemency, Diocletian Augustus, not even flattery, it seems, has been able to fashion such an emperor.

AVIDIUS CASSIUS[1]

VULCACII GALLICANI V.C.

I. Avidius Cassius, ut quidam volunt, ex familia
Cassiorum fuisse dicitur, per matrem tamen ; homine
novo[2] genitus Avidio Severo, qui ordines duxerat et
2 post ad summas dignitates pervenerat. cuius Quadratus in historiis meminit, et quidem graviter, cum
illum summum virum et necessarium rei publicae
3 adserit et apud ipsum Marcum praevalidum. nam
iam eo imperante perisse fatali sorte perhibetur.

4 Hic ergo Cassius ex familia, ut diximus, Cassiorum,
qui in curia in C. Iulium[3] conspiraverant, oderat
tacite principatum nec ferre poterat imperatorium
nomen dicebatque esse eo gravius nomen[4] imperii,
quod non posset e re publica tolli nisi per alterum

---

[1] In P the 9th Vita, *i.e.* following Pertinax.   [2] *homine
nouo genitus* Klebs, Prosop. i. p. 188 ; *homine* omitted in P ;
auo genitus Peter (vulg.).   [3] So P corr. ; *in ciuilium* P[1].
[4] Thus Peter with Mommsen ; *esse grauius nomine* P.

---

[1] The honorary title of *Vir Clarissimus* was regularly
borne by senators during the later empire.
[2] In reality his name was C. Avidius Heliodorus. A native
of Cyrrhus in Syria (see Dio, lxxi. 22, 2), he was made imperial secretary by Hadrian, and was prefect of Egypt under
Antoninus ; see *C.I.L.*, iii. 6025 = Dessau, *Ins. Sel.*, 2615.
He is probably to be identified with the *philosophus Heliodorus*,
mentioned in *Hadr.*, xvi. 10.   The expression *novus homo*

AVIDIUS CASSIUS.

BY

VULCACIUS GALLICANUS.

Of the Senatorial Order.[1]

I. Avidius Cassius is said, according to the statements of some, to have belonged to the family of the
Cassii, but only on his mother's side.   His father was
Avidius Severus,[2] the first of the family to hold public
office, who at first commanded in the ranks,[3] but later
attained to the highest honours of the state.   Quadratus[4] mentions him in his history, and certainly with
all respect, for he declares that he was a very distinguished man, both indispensable to the state and influential with Marcus himself; for he succumbed to
the decrees of fate, it is said, when Marcus had
already begun to rule.

Now Cassius, sprung, as we have said, from the
family of the Cassii who conspired against Gaius
Julius,[5] secretly hated the principate and could not
brook even the title of emperor, saying that the name
of empire was all the more onerous because an

was regularly used, as here, to denote the man who was the
first of his family to hold public office.

[3] As chief centurion of a legion, or *primus pilus;* the expression is regularly used in this sense; see *Maxim.,* iv. 4;
Firm., xiv. 2; *Prob.,* iii. 2.

[4] See note to *Ver.,* viii. 4.

[5] *i.e.* C. Cassius Longinus and C. Cassius Parmensis.

5 imperatorem. denique temptasse in pueritia dicitur
extorquere etiam Pio principatum, sed per patrem,
virum sanctum et gravem, adfectionem tyrannidis
latuisse, habitum tamen semper a ducibus suspectum.
6 Vero autem illum parasse insidias, ipsius Veri epistula
7 indicat, quam inserui. ex epistula Veri: "Avidius
Cassius avidus est, quantum et mihi videtur et iam [1]
sub avo meo, patre tuo, innotuit, imperii; quem velim
8 observari iubeas. omnia ei nostra displicent,[2] opes
non mediocres parat, litteras nostras ridet. te phil-
osopham aniculam, me luxuriosum morionem vocat.
9 vide quid agendum sit. ego hominem non odi, sed
vide ne tibi et liberis tuis non bene consulas,[3] cum
talem inter praecinctos habeas qualem milites libenter
II. audiunt, libenter vident." rescriptum Marci de
Avidio Cassio: "Epistulam tuam legi, sollicitam
potius quam[4] imperatoriam et non nostri temporis.
2 nam si ei divinitus debetur imperium, non poterimus
interficere, etiamsi velimus. scis enim proavi tui
dictum: 'successorem suum nullus occidit'. sin
minus, ipse sponte sine nostra crudelitate fatales
3 laqueos inciderit. adde quod non possumus reum
facere, quem et nullus accusat et, ut ipse dicis, milites

[1] *inde,* following *iam* in P, removed by Novak.   [2] *omnia ei nostra displicent* P corr. (*ediplicent* P¹); *omnia enim nostra ei d.* Peter.   [3] *consulat* P.   [4] *quam* omitted by P¹, added by P corr.

[1] It is now generally agreed that the letters and other al-leged documents contained in this *vita* are pure forgeries, and the same is in general true about the other documents of this sort in the *Historia Augusta;* see Intro., p. xx.
[2] Pius. The allusion to Pius as the grandfather of Verus is in itself enough to prove the letter a forgery, since it pre-supposes that Verus was adopted by Marcus, which was not

234

emperor could not be removed from the state except by another emperor. In his youth, they say, he tried to wrest the empire from Pius too, but through his father, a righteous and worthy man, he escaped detection in this attempt to seize the throne, though he continued to be suspected by Pius' generals. Against Verus he organized a genuine conspiracy, as a letter of Verus' own, which I append, makes clear. Extract from the letter of Verus [1]: "Avidius Cassius is avid for the throne, as it seems to me and as was well-known in the reign of my grandfather,[2] your father; I wish you would have him watched. Everything we do displeases him, he is amassing no inconsiderable wealth, and he laughs at our letters. He calls you a philosophical old woman, me a half-witted spendthrift. Consider what should be done. I do not dislike the man, but look to it lest you take too little heed for yourself and for your children when you keep in active service a man whom the soldiers are glad to hear and glad to see." II. Marcus' answer concerning Avidius Cassius: " I have read your letter, which is that of a disquieted man rather than that of a general, and one not worthy of our times. For if the empire is divinely decreed to be his, we cannot slay him even should we so desire. Remember what your great-grandfather [3] used to say, 'No one ever kills his successor'. And if this is not the case, he will of himself fall into the toils of fate without any act of cruelty on our part. Add that we cannot judge a man guilty whom no one has accused, and whom, as you say yourself, the soldiers love. Furthermore,

the case ; see note to *Marc.*, v. 1. The forger is not consistent, for in c. ii. 5 Hadrian is referred to as Verus' grandfather.

[3] Trajan.

4amant. deinde in causis maiestatis haec natura est
ut videantur vim pati etiam quibus probatur. scis
enim ipse quid avus tuus Hadrianus dixerit : 'misera
condicio imperatorum, quibus de adfectata [1] tyrannide
6nisi occisis non potest credi'. eius autem exemplum
ponere malui [2] quam Domitiani, qui hoc primus dixisse
fertur. tyrannorum enim etiam bona dicta non habent
7tantum auctoritatis quantum debent. sibi ergo
habeat suos mores, maxime cum bonus dux sit et
8severus et fortis et rei publicae necessarius. nam
quod dicis, liberis meis cavendum esse morte illius ;
plane liberi mei pereant, si magis amari merebitur
Avidius quam illi, et si rei publicae expediet, Cassium
vivere quam liberos Marci." haec de Cassio Verus,
haec Marcus.

III. Sed nos hominis naturam et mores breviter ex-
plicabimus. neque enim plura de his sciri possunt,
quorum vitam et inlu·trare nullus audet eorum causa
2a quibus oppressi fuerint. addemus autem quemadmodum ad imperium venerit et quemadmodum sit
3occisus et ubi victus. proposui enim, Diocletiane
Auguste, omnes qui imperatorum nomen sive iusta
causa sive iniusta [3] habuerunt, in litteras mittere, ut
omnes purpuratos Augustos cognosceres.

4 Fuit his moribus, ut nonnumquam trux et asper
videretur, aliquando mitis et lenis, saepe religiosus,
alias contemptor sacrorum, avidus vini item abstinens,

---

[1] *adfectata* Petschenig; *adfectu* P ; *adfecta* Peter.   [2] *malui*
omitted by P[1], supplied by P corr.   [3] *siue iusta causa siue
iniusta* Novak ; *siue iniusta* P[1]; *siue iuste siue iniuste* P
corr.; *siue iusta ex causa siue iniusta* Peter with Mommsen.

It is attributed to Domitian in Suet., *Dom.*, xxi.
[2] Cf. *Ael.*, i. 1.

in cases of treason it is inevitable that even those who
have been proved guilty seem to suffer injustice.   For
you know yourself what your grandfather Hadrian
said, ' Unhappy is the lot of emperors, who are never
believed when they accuse anyone of pretending to the
throne, until after they are slain '.   I have preferred,
moreover, to quote this as his, rather than as Domitian's,[1] who is reported to have said it first, for good
sayings when uttered by tyrants have not as much
weight as they deserve.   So let Cassius keep his own
ways, especially as he is an able general and a stern
and brave man, and since the state has need of him.
And as for your statement that I should take heed for
my children by killing him, by all means let my
children perish, if Avidius be more deserving of love
than they and if it profit the state for Cassius to live
rather than the children of Marcus.''   Thus did Verus,
thus did Marcus, write about Cassius.

III.   But let us briefly portray the nature and character of the man ; for not very much can be known
about those men whose lives no one has dared to
render illustrious through fear of those by whom they
were overcome.   We will add, moreover, how he
came to the throne, and how he was killed, and where
he was conquered.   For I have undertaken, Diocletian Augustus, to set down in writing the lives of all
who have held the imperial title [2] whether rightfully
or without right, in order that you may become acquainted with all the emperors that have ever worn
the purple.

Such was his character, then, that sometimes he
seemed stern and savage, sometimes mild and gentle,
often devout and again scornful of sacred things,
addicted to drink and also temperate, a lover of eat-

cibi adpetens et inediae patiens, Veneris cupidus et
5 castitatis amator. nec defuerunt qui illum Catilinam
vocarent, cum et ipse se ita gauderet appellari, addens
futurum se Sergium si dialogistam occidisset, An-
6 toninum hoc nomine significans, qui tantum enituit
in philosophia, ut iturus ad bellum Marcomannicum,
timentibus cunctis ne quid fatale proveniret, rogatus
sit non adulatione sed serio, ut praecepta philosophiae
7 ederet. nec ille timuit, sed per ordinem paraeneseos [1]
8 per triduum disputavit. fuit praeterea disciplinae
militaris Avidius Cassius tenax et qui se Marium dici
vellet.

IV. Quoniam de severitate illius dicere coepimus,
multa exstant crudelitatis potius quam severitatis eius
2 indicia. nam primum milites qui aliquid provincialibus
tulissent per vim, in illis ipsis locis, in quibus peccave-
3 rant, in crucem sustulit. primus etiam id supplicii genus
invenit, ut stipitem grandem poneret pedum octoginta
et centum [2] et a summo usque ad imum damnatos
ligaret et ab imo focum adponeret incensisque aliis
4 alios fumo, cruciatu, timore etiam necaret. idem
denos catenatos in profluentem mergi iubebat vel in
5 mare. idem multis desertoribus manus excidit, aliis
crura incidit ac poplites, dicens maius exemplum esse

---

[1] The words *hoc est praeceptionum*, which follow *paraeneseos*
in P, removed by Cas.   [2] The words *id est materiam*,
following *centum* in P, removed by Cas.

---

[1] Apparently in allusion to Catiline's plan for the murder
of Cicero, although Sallust's description of Catiline seems also
to have been in the writer's mind.
[2] The τὰ εἰς ἑαυτόν in 12 books.

ing yet able to endure hunger, a devotee of Venus and a lover of chastity. Nor were there lacking those who called him a second Catiline,[1] and indeed he rejoiced to hear himself thus called, and added that he would really be a Sergius if he killed the philosophizer, meaning by that name Antoninus. For the emperor was so illustrious in philosophy that when he was about to set out for the Marcomannic war, and everyone was fearful that some ill-luck might befall him, he was asked, not in flattery but in all seriousness, to publish his "Precepts of Philosophy";[2] and he did not fear to do so, but for three days discussed the books of his "Exhortations" one after the other. Moreover, Avidius Cassius was a strict disciplinarian and wished to be called a Marius.[3]

IV. And since we have begun to speak of his strictness, there are many indications of what must be called savagery, rather than strictness, on his part. For, in the first place, soldiers who had forcibly seized anything from the provincials he crucified on the very spot where they had committed the crime. He was the first, moreover, to devise the following means of punishment: after erecting a huge post, 180 feet high, and binding condemned criminals on it from top to bottom, he built a fire at its base, and so burned some of them and killed the others by the smoke, the pain, and even by the fright. Besides this, he had men bound in chains, ten together, and thrown into rivers or even the sea. Besides this, he cut off the hands of many deserters, and broke the legs and hips of others, saying that a criminal alive and

[3] As the type of a stern disciplinarian and successful general.

239

6 viventis [1] miserabiliter criminosi quam occisi. cum exercitum duceret, et inscio ipso manus auxiliaria centurionibus suis auctoribus tria milia Sarmatarum neglegentius agentum in Danuvii ripis occidissent et cum praeda ingenti ad eum redissent sperantibus centurionibus praemium, quod perparva manu tantum hostium segnius agentibus tribunis et ignorantibus occidissent, rapi eos iussit et in crucem tolli servilique supplicio adfici, quod exemplum non exstabat, dicens evenire potuisse ut essent insidiae, ac periret Romani 7 imperii reverentia. et cum ingens seditio in exercitu [2] orta esset, processit nudus campestri solo tectus et ait, "Percutite," inquit, "me, si audetis, et corruptae 8 disciplinae facinus addite". tunc conquiescentibus 9 cunctis meruit timeri, quia ipse [3] non timuit. quae res tantum disciplinae Romanis addidit, tantum terroris barbaris iniecit, ut pacem annorum centum ab Antonino absente peterent; si quidem viderant damnatos Romani ducis iudicio etiam eos qui contra fas vicerant.

V. De hoc multa gravia contra militum licentiam facta inveniuntur apud Aemilium Parthenianum, qui adfectatores tyrannidis iam inde a veteribus historiae 2 tradidit. nam et virgis caesos in foro et in mediis

---

[1] *auiuentis* (a later erased) P; *aduiuentis* Peter [2] with Baehrens. [2] *in exercitum orta* P, Peter. [3] *ipse* om. by Peter.

---

[1] Known only from this citation.

wretched was a more terrible example than one who
had been put to death. Once when he was commanding the army, a band of auxiliaries, at the suggestion of their centurions and without his knowledge,
slaughtered 3,000 Sarmatians, who were camping
somewhat carelessly on the bank of the Danube, and
returned to him with immense plunder. But when
the centurions expected a reward because they had
slain such a host of the enemy with a very small force
while the tribunes were passing their time in indolence
and were even ignorant of the whole affair, he had
them arrested and crucified, and punished them with
the punishment of slaves, for which there was no
precedent; "It might," he said, "have been an
ambush, and the barbarians' awe for the Roman
Empire might have been lost." And when a fierce
mutiny arose in the camp, he issued forth clad only
in a wrestler's loin-cloth and said : "Strike me, if
you dare, and add the crime of murder to breach of
discipline". Then, as all grew quiet, he was held in
well deserved fear, because he had shown no fear
himself. This incident so strengthened discipline
among the Romans and struck such terror into the
barbarians, that they besought the absent Antoninus
for a hundred years' peace, since they had seen even
those who conquered, if they conquered wrongfully,
sentenced to death by the decision of a Roman
general.

V. Many of the stern measures he took to put down
the licence of the soldiers are recorded in the works
of Aemilius Parthenianus,[1] who has related the history
of the pretenders to the throne from ancient times
even to the present. For example, after openly
beating them with the lictors' rods in the forum and

castris securi percussit, qui ita meruerunt, et manus
3 multis amputavit. et praeter laridum ac buccellatum
atque acetum militem in expeditione portare prohibuit et si aliud quippiam repperit luxuriem non levi
4 supplico adfecit. exstat de hoc epistula divi Marci
5 ad praefectum suum talis : " Avidio Cassio legiones
Syriacas dedi diffluentes luxuria et Daphnidis moribus agentes, quas totas excaldantes se repperisse Cae-
6 sonius Vectilianus scripsit. et puto me non errasse,
si quidem et tu notum habeas Cassium, hominem
7 Cassianae severitatis et disciplinae. neque enim
milites regi possunt nisi vetere disciplina. scis enim
versum a bono poeta dictum et omnibus frequenta-
tum :

‘ Moribus antiquis res stat Romana virisque.

8 tu tantum fac adsint legionibus abunde commeatus,
quos, si bene Avidium novi, scio non perituros."
9 praefecti ad Marcum : " Recte consuluisti, mi domine,
10 quod Cassium praefecisti[1] Syriacis legionibus. nihil
enim tam expedit quam homo severior Graecanicis
11 militibus. ille sane omnes excaldationes, omnes
12 flores de capite collo et sinu militi excutiet. annona
militaris omnis parata est, neque quicquam deest sub
bono duce ; non enim multum aut quaeritur aut
VI. impenditur." nec fefellit de se iudicium habitum.

[1] *praefecisti* P corr. ; *praefectis* P[1].

---

[1] Also brought as a reproach against the Syrian army in
Alex., liii. 2.
[2] A line from Ennius' *Annales*, quoted in Cicero, *de Rep.*,
v. ; see Augustinus, *Civ. Dei*, ii. 21.

in the midst of the camp, he beheaded those who deserved it with the axe, and in numerous instances cut off his soldiers' hands. He forbade the soldiers, moreover, to carry anything when on the march save lard and biscuit and vinegar, and if he discovered anything else he punished the breach of discipline with no light hand. There is a letter concerning Cassius that the Deified Marcus wrote to his prefect, running somewhat as follows: "I have put Avidius Cassius in command of the Syrian legions, which are running riot in luxury and conducting themselves with the morals of Daphne; concerning these legions Caesonius Vectilianus has written that he found them all accustomed to bathe in hot water.[1] And I think I have made no mistake, for you too know Cassius, a man of true Cassian strictness and rigour. Indeed, the soldiers cannot be controlled except by the ancient discipline. You know what the good poet says, a line universally quoted:

'The state of Rome is rooted in the men and
    manners of the olden time.'[2]

Do you take care only that provisions are abundantly provided for the legions, for if I have judged Avidius correctly I know that they will not be wasted." The prefect's answer to Marcus runs: "You planned wisely, Sire, when you put Cassius in command of the Syrian legions. Nothing benefits Grecianized soldiers like a man who is somewhat strict. He will certainly do away with all warm baths, and will strike all the flowers from the soldiers' heads and necks and breasts. Food for the soldiers is all provided; and nothing is lacking under an able general, for but little is either asked or expended." VI. And

nam statim et ad signa edici iussit et programma in parietibus fixit, ut, si quis cinctus inveniretur apud 2 Daphnen, discinctus rediret. arma militum septima die semper respexit, vestimenta etiam et calciamenta et ocreas, delicias omnes de castris summovit iussitque eos hiemem sub pellibus agere nisi corrigerent suos 3 mores; et egissent, nisi honestius vixissent. exercitium septimi diei fuit omnium militum, ita ut et 4 sagittas mitterent et armis luderent. dicebat enim miserum esse, cum exercerentur athletae venatores et gladiatores, non exerceri milites; quibus minor esset futurus labor, si consuetus esset.

5 Ergo correcta disciplina et in Armenia et in Arabia 6 et in Aegypto res optime gessit amatusque est ab omnibus orientalibus et speciatim ab Antiochensibus, qui etiam imperio eius consenserunt, ut docet Marius 7 Maximus in vita divi Marci. nam et cum[1] Bucolici milites per Aegyptum gravia multa facerent, ab hoc retunsi sunt, ut item[2] Marius Maximus refert in eo libro quem secundum de vita Marci Antonini edidit.

VII. Hic imperatorem se in oriente appellavit, ut

---

[1] *cum et* P.   [2] *item* P; *idem* Peter.

---

[1] *Discinctus* means "deprived of his sword-belt"—a punishment inflicted upon disobedient soldiers.
[2] An attempt to summarize the important and brilliant campaign of 164-166, in which Cassius drove the Parthians out of Syria, overran Mesopotamia, and finally captured Ctesiphon, the Parthian capital; see *Marc.*, ix. 1; *Ver.*, vii. 1-2; Dio, lxxi. 2.

Cassius did not disappoint the expectation that had
been formed of him, for he immediately had the
proclamation made at assembly, and posted notices
on the walls, that if any one were discovered at
Daphne in his uniform he would return without it.[1]
Regularly once a week he inspected his soldiers'
equipment, even their clothes and shoes and leggings,
and he banished all dissipation from the camp and
issued an order that they would pass the winter in
their tents if they did not mend their ways ; and they
would have done so, had they not conducted themselves more respectably. Once a week there was a
drill of all the soldiers, in which they even shot
arrows and engaged in contests in the use of arms.
For he said that it was shameful that soldiers should
not be trained, while athletes, wild beast fighters and
gladiators were, for the soldiers' future labours, if
familiar to them, would be less onerous.

And so, having stiffened military discipline, he
conducted affairs in Armenia and Arabia and Egypt
with the greatest success.[2] He was well loved by
all the eastern nations, especially by the citizens of
Antioch, who even acquiesced in his rule, as Marius
Maximus relates in his Life of the Deified Marcus.
And when the warriors of the Bucolici did many
grievous things in Egypt, they were checked by
Cassius,[3] as Marius Maximus also relates in the
second book of those he published on the Life of
Marcus.

VII. Finally, while in the East,[4] he proclaimed him- 175

---

[3] See *Marc.*, xxi. 2 and note.
[4] After his victorious campaign against the Parthians he
was appointed governor-general of all the eastern provinces ;
see Dio, lxxi. 3, 1.

quidam dicunt, Faustina volente, quae valetudini Marci
iam diffidebat et timebat, ne infantes filios tueri sola
non posset, atque aliquis exsisteret, qui capta statione
2 regia infantes de medio tolleret. alii autem dicunt,
hanc artem adhibuisse militibus et provincialibus
Cassium contra Marci amorem, ut sibi posset con-
sentiri, quod diceret Marcum diem suum obisse.
3 nam et divum eum appellasse dicitur, ut desiderium
illius leniret.

4   Imperatorio animo cum processisset, eum qui sibi
aptaverat ornamenta regia statim praefectum praetorii fecit ; qui et ipse occisus est Antonino invito ab
exercitu, qui et Maecianum, cui erat commissa
Alexandria quique consenserat[1] spe participatus
Cassio, invito atque ignorante Antonino interemit.
5   Nec tamen Antoninus graviter est iratus rebellione
cognita nec in eius liberos aut adfectus saevit.
6 senatus illum hostem appellavit bonaque eius proscripsit. quae Antoninus in privatum aerarium con-
geri noluit, quare senatu praecipiente in aerarium
7 publicum sunt relata. nec Romae terror defuit, cum

[1] So also *Marc.*, xxiv. 6, and Dio, lxxi. 22, 3 f. Dio adds
the not improbable story that Faustina bade Cassius hold
himself in readiness, in case aught befell Marcus, to marry
her and seize the sovereignty, and that when a false report of
Marcus' death was brought he declared himself emperor.
According to c. ix. 9, the version in the text was given by
Marius Maximus.

[2] *i.e.* on receipt of the report of his death ; see last note.

[3] Cf. *Marc.*, xxv. 4.

[4] The prefect of Egypt, Flavius Calvisius, declared for
Cassius ; see Dio, lxxi. 28, 3. Evidence that Egypt recognized him as emperor is afforded by a papyrus, dated in the

self emperor, some say, at the wish of Faustina,[1] who now despaired of Marcus' health and was afraid that she would be unable to protect her infant children by herself, and that some one would arise and seize the throne and make away with the children. Others, however, say that Cassius employed an artifice with the soldiers and provincials to overcome their love for Marcus so that they would join him, saying that Marcus had met his end. ' And, indeed, he called him "the Deified," [2] it is said, in order to lessen their grief for him.

When his plan of making himself emperor had been put into effect, he forthwith appointed prefect of the guard the man who had invested him with the imperial insignia. This man was later put to death by the army [3] against the wishes of Antoninus. The army also slew Maecianus, in whose charge Alexandria had been placed ; he had joined Cassius [4] in the hope of sharing the sovereignty with him, and he too was slain against the wishes and without the knowledge of Antoninus.

For all that, Antoninus was not seriously angered on learning of this revolt, nor did he vent his rage on Cassius' children or on his kin. The senate, however, pronounced him a public enemy and confiscated his property.[5] But Antoninus was unwilling that this should be forfeited to the privy-purse, and so, at the bidding of the senate, it was delivered to the public treasury. And there was no slight consternation at Rome ; for many said that Avidius Cassius would advance on the city in the absence of

first year of Imperator Caesar Julius Avidius Cassius ; see *Bull. Inst. Egypt.*, vii. (1896), p. 123.
    [5] Cf. *Marc.*, xxiv. 9.

quidam Avidium Cassium dicerent absente Antonino,
qui nisi a voluptariis unice amabatur, Romam esse
venturum atque urbem tyrannice direpturum, maxime
senatorum causa, qui eum hostem iudicaverant bonis
8 proscriptis. et amor Antonini hoc maxime enituit,
quod consensu omnium praeter Antiochenses Avidius
9 interemptus est ; quem quidem occidi non iussit sed
passus est, cum apud cunctos clarum esset, si pote-
VIII. statis suae fuisset, parsurum [1] illi fuisse. caput eius
ad Antoninum cum delatum esset, ille non exsultauit,
non elatus est, sed etiam doluit ereptam sibi esse
occasionem misericordiae, cum diceret se vivum
illum voluisse capere, ut illi exprobraret beneficia
2 sua eumque servaret. denique cum quidam diceret
reprehendendum Antoninum, quod tam mitis esset in
hostem suum eiusque liberos et adfectus atque omnes
quos conscios tyrannidis repperisset, addente illo qui
reprehendebat " Quid si ille vicisset ? " dixisse dicitur
" Non sic deos coluimus nec sic vivimus, ut ille nos
3 vinceret ". enumeravit deinde omnes principes qui
occisi essent habuisse causas quibus mererentur occidi,
nec quemquam facile bonum vel victum a tyranno vel
4 occisum, dicens meruisse Neronem, debuisse Cali-
gulam, Othonem et Vitellium nec imperare voluisse.

[1] *parsurum* P corr. ; *passurum* P[1].

---

[1] Cf. *Marc.*, xxv. 3. According to Dio, lxxi. 27, 2-3,
Cassius was killed by two petty-officers, who then took his
head to Marcus.

[2] Nero committed suicide in order to escape death at the
hands of the guard after Galba had been proclaimed emperor
and he himself had been declared a public enemy by the
senate ; see Suet., *Nero*, xlvii.-xlix. Caligula was assassinated
by two officers of the guard ; see Suet., *Cal.*, lviii. Otho
committed suicide after his defeat by the army of Vitellius

Antoninus, who was singularly loved by all but the profligates, and that he would ravage it like a tyrant, especially because of the senators who had declared him an enemy to the state and confiscated his property. The love felt for Antoninus was most clearly manifested in the fact that it was with the consent of all save the citizens of Antioch that Avidius was slain. Antoninus, indeed, did not so much order his execution as suffer it; for it was clear to all that he would have spared him had it been in his power. VIII. And when his head was brought to Antoninus he did not rejoice or exult,[1] but rather was grieved that he had lost an opportunity for showing mercy; for he said that he had wished to take him alive, so that he might reproach him with the kindness he had shown him in the past, and then spare his life. Finally, when some one said that Antoninus deserved blame because he was so indulgent toward his enemy and his enemy's children and kin, and indeed toward every one whom he had found concerned in the outbreak, and added furthermore, "What if Cassius had been successful?" the Emperor said, it is reported: "We have not worshipped the gods in such a manner, or lived such lives, that he could overcome us". Thereupon he pointed out that in the case of all the emperors who had been slain there had been reasons why they deserved to die, and that no emperor, generally recognized as good, had been conquered or slain by a pretender, adding that Nero had deserved to die and Caligula had forfeited his life, while neither Otho nor Vitellius had really wished to rule.[2] He expressed similar

(Suet., *Otho*, xi.), and Vitellius was murdered by the soldiers of Vespasian (Suet., *Vit.*, xvii).

AVIDIUS CASSIUS

5 etiam[1] de Galba[2] paria sentiebat, cum diceret in
imperatore avaritiam esse acerbissimum malum.
6 denique non Augustum, non Traianum, non Hadrianum, non patrem suum a rebellibus potuisse su-
perari, cum et multi fuerint et ipsis vel invitis vel
7 insciis exstincti. ipse autem Antoninus a senatu petiit
ne graviter in conscios defectionis animadverteretur,
eo ipso tempore quo rogavit ne quis senator temporibus suis capitali supplicio adficeretur, quod illi
8 maximum amorem conciliavit. denique paucissimis
centurionibus punitis deportatos revocari iussit.
IX. Antiochensibus,[3] qui[4] Avidio Cassio consenserant, et
his[5] et aliis civitatibus, quae illum iuverant, ignovit,
cum primo Antiochensibus graviter iratus esset iisque
spectacula sustulisset et multa alia civitatis orna-
2 menta, quae postea reddidit. filios Avidii Cassii
Antoninus Marcus parte media paterni patrimonii
donavit, ita ut filias eius auro argento et gemmis
3 cohonestaret. nam et Alexandriae, filiae Cassii, et
genero Drunciano liberam evagandi ubi vellent
4 potestatem dedit. vixeruntque non quasi tyranni
pignora sed quasi senatorii ordinis in summa securi-
tate, cum illis etiam[6] in lite obici fortunam propriae
vetuisset domus, damnatis aliquibus iniuriarum, qui

---

[1] So Peter with Boxhorn ; *nam* P.   [2] *de Pertinace et
Galba* P.   [3] So P corr ; *antiochensis* P[1].   [4] *qui* P ; *quoque*
Peter with Madvig.   [5] *sed et his* P, Peter[2].   [6] *illi seuam*
P[1] ; *illis* P corr.

---

[1] Galba's refusal to give the expected donative to the troops
so embittered the soldiers that they refused to swear allegiance
to him (Suet., *Galb.*, xvi.) ; his stinginess also caused the
guard to join Otho in the conspiracy by which he was
murdered (*id.*, xvii f.).
[2] Cf. *Marc.*, xxv. 5-6 and note.

sentiments concerning Galba also, saying that in an
emperor avarice was the most grievous of all failings.[1]
And lastly, he said, no rebels had succeeded in over-
coming either Augustus, or Trajan, or Hadrian, or
his own father, and, although there had been many
of them, they had been killed either against the
wishes or without the knowledge of those emperors.
Antoninus himself, moreover, asked the senate to refrain from inflicting severe punishment on those men
who were implicated in the rebellion; he made this
request at the very same time in which he requested
that during his reign no senator be punished with
capital punishment[2]—an act which won him the
greatest affection. Finally, after he had punished a
very few centurions, he gave orders that those who had
been exiled should be recalled.[3] IX. The citizens of
Antioch also had sided with Avidius Cassius, but
these, together with certain other states which had
aided Cassius, he pardoned, though at first he was
deeply angered at the citizens of Antioch and took
away their games and many of the distinctions of the
city, all of which he afterwards restored. To the
sons of Avidius Cassius Antoninus presented half of
their father's property,[4] and his daughters he even
graced with gold and silver and jewels. To Alexandria, Cassius' daughter, and Druncianus, his son-in-
law, he gave unrestricted permission to travel wherever they liked. And they lived not as the children
of a pretender but as members of the senatorial order
and in the greatest security, as was shown by the
orders he gave that not even in a law-suit should they
be taunted with the fortunes of their family, and by
his convicting certain people of personal affront who

[3] Cf. *Marc.*, xxv. 7 f.   [4] Cf. *Marc.*, xxvi. 12.

AVIDIUS CASSIUS

in eos petulantes fuissent. quos quidem amitae suae
marito commendavit.

5 Si quis autem omnem hanc historiam scire de-
siderat, legat Marii Maximi secundum librum de vita
Marci, in quo ille ea dicit quae solus[1] Marcus mortuo
6 iam Vero egit. tunc enim Cassius rebellavit, ut
probat epistula missa ad Faustinam, cuius hoc exem-
7 plum est : "Verus mihi de Avidio verum scripserat,
quod cuperet imperare. audisse enim te arbitror
8 quod Veri statores[2] de eo nuntiarent. veni igitur in
Albanum, ut tractemus omnia dis volentibus, nil
9 timens." hinc autem apparet Faustinam ista nescisse,
cum dicat Marius infamari eam cupiens quod ea
10 conscia Cassius imperium sumpsisset. nam et ipsius
epistula exstat ad virum, qua urget[3] Marcum ut in
11 eum graviter vindicet. exemplum epistulae Faustinae
ad Marcum : "Ipsa in Albanum cras, ut iubes, mox
veniam ; tamen iam hortor, ut, si amas liberos tuos,
12 istos rebelliones acerrime persequaris. male enim
assueverunt duces et milites,[4] qui nisi opprimuntur,
X. oppriment." item alia epistula eiusdem Faustinae
ad Marcum : "Mater mea Faustina patrem tuum
Pium in defectione[5] Celsi hortata[6] est, ut pietatem
2 primum circa suos servaret, sic circa alienos. non
enim pius est imperator, qui non cogitat uxorem et
3 filios. Commodus noster vides in qua aetate sit,
4 Pompeianus gener et senior est et peregrinus. vide

---

[1] *solum* P.   [2] So Peter with Salm.; *herispatores* P.
[3] *urget* P ; *urguet* edd.   [4] *et duces milites* P[1] ; *et duces et
milites* P corr.   [5] *eiusdem in def.* P ; *eiusdem* removed by
Cas.   [6] *sic hortata* P ; *sic* removed by Novak ; *cohortata*
Peter[2].

---

[1] See note to c. i. 7.   [2] See note to q. vii. 1.
[3] Nothing is known of any such revolt.

had been insulting to them. He even put them
under the protection of his uncle by marriage.

If any one wishes, moreover, to know the whole of
this story, let him read the second book of Marius
Maximus on the life of Marcus, in which he relates
everything that Marcus did as sole emperor after the
death of Verus. For it was during this time that
Cassius rebelled, as a letter written to Faustina shows,
from which the following is an extract:[1] "Verus told
me the truth about Avidius, that he desired to rule.
For I presume you heard what Verus' messengers reported about him. Come, then, to our Alban villa,
so that with the help of the gods we may prepare for
everything, and do not be afraid." It would appear
from this that Faustina knew nothing of the affair,
though Marius Maximus, wishing to defame her, says
that it was with her connivance that Cassius attempted
to seize the throne.[2] Indeed, we have also a letter
of hers to her husband in which she urges Marcus
to punish Cassius severely. A copy of Faustina's
letter to Marcus reads: "I shall come to our Alban
villa to-morrow, as you command. Yet I urge you
now, if you love your children, to punish those rebels
with all severity. For soldiers and generals have an
evil habit of crushing others if they are not crushed
themselves." X. Another letter of this same Faustina to Marcus reads similarly: "When Celsus revolted,[3] my mother, Faustina, urged your father, Pius,
to deal righteously first with his own kin, and then with
strangers. For no emperor is righteous who does not
take thought for his wife and children. You can see
how young our son Commodus is; our son-in-law
Pompeianus[4] is an elderly man and a foreigner be-

[4] See *Marc.*, xx. 6.

5 quid agas de Avidio Cassio et de eius consciis. noli parcere hominibus, qui tibi non pepercerunt et nec 6 mihi nec filiis nostris parcerent, si vicissent. ipsa iter tuum mox consequor ; quia Fadilla nostra 7 aegrotabat, in Formianum venire non potui. sed si te Formiis invenire non potuero, adsequar Capuam, quae civitas et meam et filiorum nostrorum aegri- 8 tudinem poterit adiuvare. Soteridam medicum in Formianum ut demittas, rogo. ego autem Pisitheo nihil credo, qui puellae virgini curationem nescit 9 adhibere. signatas [1] mihi litteras Calpurnius dedit ; ad quas rescribam, si tardavero, per Caecilium senem 10 spadonem, hominem, ut scis, fidelem. cui verbo mandabo, quid uxor Avidii Cassii et filii et gener de te iactare dicantur."

XI. Ex his litteris intellegitur Cassio Faustinam consciam non fuisse, quin etiam supplicium eius graviter exegisse, si quidem Antoninum quiescentem et clementiora cogitantem ad vindictae necessitatem 2 impulit. cui [2] Antoninus quid rescripserit, subdita 3 epistula perdocebit : "Tu quidem, mea Faustina, religiose pro marito et pro nostris liberis agis. nam relegi epistulam tuam in Formiano, qua me hortaris, 4 ut in Avidii conscios vindicem. ego vero et eius liberis parcam et genero et uxori, et ad senatum scribam, ne aut proscriptio gravior sit aut poena 5 crudelior. non enim quicquam est, quod imperatorem Romanum melius commendet gentibus quam cle-

---

signitas P, which Ellis thinks perhaps right in sense of "in cipher". [2] cū, i.e. cum. P.

sides. Consider well what you will do about Avidius
Cassius and his accomplices. Do not show forbearance
to men who have shown no forbearance to you and
would show none either to me or to your children,
should they be victorious. I shall follow you on your
way presently; I have not been able to come to the
Formian villa because our dear Fadilla[1] was ill.
However, if I shall fail to find you at Formiae, I will
follow on to Capua, a city which can furnish help to
me and our children in our sickness. Please send the
physician Soteridas to Formiae. I have no confidence
in Pisitheus, who does not know how to treat a young
girl. Calpurnius has brought me a sealed letter; I
shall reply to it, if I linger on here, through Caecilius,
the old eunuch, a man to be trusted, as you know. I
shall also report through him, in a verbal message,
what Cassius' wife and children and son-in-law are
said to be circulating about you."

XI. From these letters it can be seen that Faustina
was not in collusion with Cassius, but, on the contrary,
earnestly demanded his punishment; for, indeed, it
was she who urged on Antoninus the necessity of
vengeance when he was inclined to take no action
and was considering more merciful measures. The
following letter tells what Antoninus wrote to her in
reply: "Truly, my Faustina, you are over-anxious
about your husband and children. For while I was
at Formiae I re-read the letter wherein you urged
me to take vengeance on Avidius' accomplices. I,
however, shall spare his wife and children and son-
in-law, and I will write to the senate forbidding any
immoderate confiscation or cruel punishment. For
there is nothing which endears a Roman emperor to

---

[1] Arria Fadilla, fourth child of Marcus, born about 150.

6 mentia. haec Caesarem deum fecit, haec Augustum consecravit, haec patrem tuum specialiter Pii nomine 7 ornavit. denique si ex mea sententia de bello iudi- 8 catum esset, nec Avidius esset occisus. esto igitur secura ;

> 'di me tuentur, dis pietas mea
> — — cordi est'.

Pompeianum nostrum in annum sequentem consulem dixi." haec Antoninus ad coniugem.

XII. Ad senatum autem qualem orationem miserit, 2 interest scire. ex oratione Marci Antonini : " Habetis igitur, patres conscripti, pro gratulatione victoriae generum meum consulem, Pompeianum dico, cuius aetas olim remuneranda fuerat consulatu, nisi viri fortes intervenissent, quibus reddi debuit 3 quod a re publica debebatur. nunc quod ad defectionem Cassianam pertinet, vos oro atque obsecro, patres conscripti, ut censura vestra deposita meam pietatem clementiamque servetis, immo vestram, neque 4 quemquam [1] senatus occidat. nemo senatorum puniatur, nullius fundatur viri nobilis sanguis, deportati rede- 5 ant, proscripti bona recipiant. utinam possem multos [2] etiam ab inferis excitare! non enim umquam placet in imperatore vindicta sui doloris, quae si iustior 6 fuerit, acrior videtur. quare filiis Avidii Cassii et

---

[1] *quemquam ullum* P ; *ullum* removed by Lessing ; *quemquam unum* Peter.   [2] *multos* P, which Lessing restores; *multatos* Peter.

---

[1] Cf. *Hadr.*, xxiv. 4 ; *Pius*, ii. 4.
[2] Horace, *Odes*, i. 17, 13.
[3] The fact that the second consulship of Pompeianus (see *Marc.*, xx. 6) was in 173, two years prior to Cassius' revolt, shows that this letter is not genuine.

mankind as much as the quality of mercy. This quality caused Caesar to be deified and made Augustus a god, and it was this characteristic, more than any other, that gained your father his honourable name of Pius.[1] Indeed, if the war had been settled in accordance with my desires, Avidius would not have been killed. So do not be anxious ;

'Over me the gods keep guard, the gods hold dear
    my righteousness.'[2]

I have named our son-in-law Pompeianus consul for next year." [3] Thus did Antoninus write to his wife.

XII. It is of interest, moreover, to know what sort of a message he sent to the senate. An extract from the message of Marcus Antoninus : "So then, in return for this manifestation of joy at our victory, Conscript Fathers, receive my son-in-law as consul—Pompeianus, I mean, who has come to an age that were long since rewarded with the consulship, had there not stood in the way certain brave men, to whom it was right to give what was due them from the state. And now, as to Cassius' revolt, I pray and beseech you, Conscript Fathers, lay aside your severity, and preserve the righteousness and mercy that are mine—nay rather I should say, yours—and let the senate put no man to death. Let no senator be punished ; let the blood of no distinguished man be shed ; let those who have been exiled return to their homes ; let those who have been outlawed recover their estates. Would that I could also recall many from the grave ! Vengeance for a personal wrong is never pleasing in an emperor, for the juster the vengeance is, the harsher it seems. Wherefore, you will grant pardon to the sons and son-in-law and wife of Avidius Cassius. For that matter,

genero et uxori veniam dabitis. et quid dico veniam?
7 cum illi nihil fecerint. vivant igitur securi, scientes
sub Marco vivere. vivant in patrimonio parentum
pro parte donato, auro argento vestibus fruantur, sint
divites, sint securi, sint vagi et liberi et per ora omnium ubique populorum circumferant meae, circum-
8 ferant vestrae pietatis exemplum. nec magna haec
est, patres conscripti, clementia, veniam proscriptorum
9 liberis et coniugibus dari. ego vero a vobis peto, ut
conscios senatorii ordinis et equestris a caede, a proscriptione, a timore, ab infamia, ab invidia, et postremo
ab omni vindicetis iniuria detisque hoc meis tem-
10 poribus, ut in causa tyrannidis qui in tumultu cecidit
probetur occisus."

XIII. Hanc eius clementiam senatus his adclama-
2 tionibus prosecutus est : " Antonine pie, di te servent.
Antonine clemens, di te servent. Antonine clemens,[1]
3 di te servent. tu voluisti quod licebat, nos fecimus
quod decebat. Commodo imperium iustum rogamus.
progeniem tuam robora. fac securi sint liberi nostri.
4 bonum imperium nulla vis laedit. Commodo Antonino
tribuniciam potestatem rogamus, praesentiam tuam
5 rogamus. philosophiae tuae, patientiae tuae, doctrinae tuae, nobilitati tuae, innocentiae tuae. vincis
inimicos, hostes exsuperas, di te tuentur," et reli-
qua.
6   Vixerunt igitur posteri Avidii Cassii securi et ad

---

[1] So P; repetition from the preceding has crowded out
some other adj.

---

[1] For similar outcries alleged to have taken place in the
senate see *Com.*, xviii.-xix.; *Alex.*, vi.-xi.
[2] Bestowed in 177; see *Marc.*, xxvii. 5, and note.

why should I say pardon ? They have done nothing.
Let them live, therefore, free from all anxiety, know-
ing that they live under Marcus. Let them live in
possession of their parents' property, granted to each
in due proportion ; let them enjoy gold, silver, and
raiment; let them be rich ; let them be free from
anxiety ; let them, unrestricted and free to travel
wheresoever they wish, carry in themselves before the
eyes of all nations everywhere an example of my forbearance, an example of yours. Nor is it any great act
of mercy, Conscript Fathers, to grant pardon to the
wives and children of outlawed men. I do beseech
you to save these conspirators, men of the senatorial
and equestrian orders, from death, from proscription,
from terror, from disgrace, from hatred, and, in short,
from every harm, and to grant this to my reign, that
whoever, in the cause of the pretender, has fallen in
the strife may, though slain, still be esteemed."

XIII. The senate honoured this act of mercy with
these acclamations : [1] "God save you, righteous Antoninus. God save you, merciful Antoninus. God
save you, merciful Antoninus. You have desired what
was lawful, we have done what was fitting. We ask
lawful power for Commodus. Strengthen your offspring. Make our children free from care. No violence troubles righteous rule. We ask the tribunician
power [2] for Commodus Antoninus. We beseech your
presence. All praise to your philosophy, your
patience, your principles, your magnanimity, your
innocence ! You conquer your foes within, you
prevail over those without, the gods are watching
over you," and so forth.

And so the descendants of Avidius Cassius lived unmolested and were admitted to offices of honour.

7 honores admissi sunt. sed eos Commodus Antoninus
post excessum divi patris sui omnes vivos incendi
iussit, quasi in factione deprehensos.

8   Haec sunt quae de Cassio Avidio comperimus.
9 cuius ipsius mores, ut supra diximus, varii semper fuerunt sed ad censuram crudelitatemque propensiores.
10 qui, si optinuisset imperium, fuisset non clemens et
XIV. bonus,[1] sed utilis et optimus imperator. nam exstat
epistula eius ad generum suum iam imperatoris huius-
2 modi : "Misera res publica, quae istos divitiarum
3 cupidos et divites patitur, misera. Marcus homo sane
optimus, qui dum clemens dici cupit,[2] eos patitur
4 vivere quorum ipse non probat vitam. ubi Lucius
Cassius, cuius nos frustra tenet nomen ? ubi Marcus
ille Cato Censorius ? ubi omnis disciplina maiorum ?
quae olim quidem intercidit, nunc vero nec quaeritur.
5 Marcus Antoninus philosophatur et quaerit de ele-
mentis [3] et de animis et de honesto et iusto nec
6 sentit pro re publica. vides multis opus esse gladiis,
multis elogiis, ut in antiquum statum publica forma
7 reddatur. ego vero istis praesidibus provinciarum—
an ego proconsules, an ego praesides putem, qui ob
hoc sibi a senatu et ab Antonino provincias datas cre-
8 dunt, ut luxurientur, ut divites fiant ? audisti, praefectum praetorii nostri philosophi ante triduum quam

---

[1] So Vielhaber ; *non modo clemens sed bonus* P ; *non modo
c. et b.* Peter.   [2] So P ; Peter by error attributes *clementes*
to P, and reads, following Petschenig, *clementem se.*   [3] *de
clementes* P[1] ; *de clementiis* P corr.

But after his deified father's death Commodus Antoninus ordered them all to be burned alive, as if they had been caught in a rebellion.

So much have we learned concerning Avidius Cassius. His character, as we have said before,[1] was continually changing, though inclined, on the whole, to severity and cruelty. Had he gained the throne, he would have made not a merciful and kind emperor but a beneficent and excellent one. XIV. For we have a letter of his, written to his son-in-law after he had declared himself emperor, that reads somewhat as follows : " Unhappy state, unhappy, which suffers under men who are eager for riches and men who have grown rich ! Marcus is indeed the best of men, but one who wishes to be called merciful and hence suffers to live men whose manner of life he cannot sanction. Where is Lucius Cassius,[2] whose name we bear in vain ? Where is that other Marcus, Cato the Censor ? Where is all the rigour of our fathers ? Long since indeed has it perished, and now it is not even desired. Marcus Antoninus philosophizes and meditates on first principles, and on souls and virtue and justice, and takes no thought for the state. There is need, rather, for many swords, as you see for yourself, and for much practical wisdom, in order that the state may return to its ancient ways. And truly in regard to those governors of provinces—can I deem proconsuls or governors those who believe that their provinces were given them by the senate and Antoninus only in order that they might revel and grow rich ? You have heard that our philo-

[1] c. iii. 4.
[2] Evidently an error for Q. Cassius Longinus ; see note to c. i. 4.

fieret mendicum et pauperem, sed subito divitem
factum. unde, quaeso, nisi de visceribus rei publicae
provincialiumque fortunis ? sint sane divites, sint
locupletes. aerarium publicum refercient ;[1] tantum
di faveant bonis partibus,[2] reddant[3] Cassiani rei publicae principatum." haec epistula eius indicat, quam
severus et quam tristis futurus fuerit imperator.

[1] Thus Petrarch ; *referient* P.   [2] *patribus* P.   [3] *reddant* P ; *reddent* Casaubon, Peter.

sopher's prefect of the guard was a beggar and a
pauper three days before his appointment, and then
suddenly became rich. How, I ask you, save from
the vitals of the state and the purses of the provincials? Well then, let them be rich, let them be
wealthy. In time they will stuff the imperial
treasury [1]; only let the gods favour the better side,
let the men of Cassius restore to the state a lawful
government." This letter of his shows how stern
and how strict an emperor he would have been.

---

[1] *i.e.*, they will be forced to disgorge their ill-gotten gains.

COMMODUS ANTONINUS

AELII LAMPRIDII

I. De Commodi Antonini parentibus in vita Marci
2 Antonini satis est disputatum. ipse autem natus est
apud Lanuvium cum fratre Antonino gemino pridie
kal. Sept. patre patruoque consulibus, ubi et avus
3 maternus dicitur natus. Faustina cum esset Commodo cum fratre praegnans, visa est in somnis
4 serpentes parere, sed ex his unum ferociorem. cum
autem peperisset Commodum atque Antoninum,
Antoninus quadrimus elatus est, quem parem astrorum
5 cursu Commodo mathematici promittebant. mortuo
igitur fratre Commodum Marcus et suis praeceptis
et magnorum atque optimorum virorum erudire co-
6 natus est. habuit litteratorem Graecum Onesicratem,
Latinum Capellam Antistium ; orator ei Ateius Sanctus fuit.

7 Sed tot disciplinarum magistri nihil ei profuerunt.
tantum valet aut ingenii vis aut eorum qui in aula
institutores habentur. nam a prima statim pueritia
turpis, improbus, crudelis, libidinosus, ore quoque pol-

---

¹ *Marc.*, i. 1-4.   ² Cf. *Pius*, i. 8.

COMMODUS ANTONINUS

BY

AELIUS LAMPRIDIUS

I. The ancestry of Commodus Antoninus has been
sufficiently discussed in the life of Marcus Antoninus.[1]
As for Commodus himself, he was born, with his twin
brother Antoninus, at Lanuvium—where his mother's
father was born, it is said [2]—on the day before the
Kalends of September, while his father and uncle 31 Aug.,
were consuls. Faustina, when pregnant with Com- 161
modus and his brother, dreamed that she gave birth
to serpents, one of which, however, was fiercer than
the other. But after she had given birth to Commodus and Antoninus, the latter, for whom the astrologers had cast a horoscope as favourable as that
of Commodus, lived to be only four years old. After
the death of Antoninus, Marcus tried to educate
Commodus by his own teaching and by that of the
greatest and the best of men. In Greek literature
he had Onesicrates as his teacher, in Latin, Antistius
Capella; his instructor in rhetoric was Ateius Sanctus.

However, teachers in all these studies profited him
not in the least—such is the power, either of natural
character, or of the tutors maintained in a palace.
For even from his earliest years he was base and dishonourable, and cruel and lewd, defiled of mouth, more-

265

COMMODUS ANTONINUS

8 lutus et constupratus[1] fuit. iam in his artifex, quae
stationis imperatoriae non erant, ut calices fingeret,
saltaret, cantaret, sibilaret, scurram denique et gladia-
9 torem perfectum ostenderet. auspicium crudelitatis
apud Centumcellas dedit anno aetatis duodecimo.
nam cum tepidius forte lautus esset, balneatorem in
fornacem conici iussit; quando a paedagogo, cui hoc
iussum fuerat, vervecina pellis in fornace consumpta
est, ut fidem poenae de foetore nidoris impleret.

10   Appellatus est autem Caesar puer cum fratre suo
Vero.[2] quarto decimo aetatis anno in collegium
11. sacerdotum[3] adscitus est. cooptatus est inter trossulos[4] principes[5] iuventutis, cum togam sumpsit.
adhuc in praetexta puerili congiarium dedit atque
2 ipse in Basilica Traiani praesedit. indutus autem
toga est Nonarum Iuliarum die, quo in terris Romulus
non apparuit, et eo tempore quo Cassius a Marco
3 descivit. profectus est commendatus militibus cum
patre in Syriam et Aegyptum et cum[6] eo Romam

---

[1] *constuppatus* P.   [2] *suo Vero* Ursinus; *Seuero* P.
[3] *sacerdotis* P.   [4] *trossulos* Lipsius; *tres solos* P.   [5] *princeps* P.   [6] so P corr.; *et cum* om. in P[1].

---

[1] Dio, on the other hand, describes him as not naturally
vicious, but weak and easily influenced ; see lxxii. 1, 1.

[2] On the coast of Etruria, near the southern end ; it is the
modern Cività Vecchia.

[3] Cf. c. xi. 13 ; *Marc.*, xii. 8 and note.

[4] M. Annius Verus, who died in 169; see *Marc.*, xxi. 3.

[5] Cf. c. xii. 1 ; *Marc.*, xvi. 1 and note. His election to the
college of pontifices is commemorated on a coin ; see Cohen,
iii[2], p. 311, no. 599.

[6] Cf. c. xii. 3; *Marc.*, xxii. 12 and note.

[7] See note to *Marc.*, vi. 3. The title *princeps iuventutis*
appears on his coins of this period (Cohen iii[2], p. 311 f.,
nos. 601-618), and in an inscription from Africa (*C.I.L.*, viii.
11928). *Trossuli* was an old name given to the Roman

266

over, and debauched.[1] Even then he was an adept
in certain arts which are not becoming in an emperor
for he could mould goblets and dance and sing and
whistle, and he could play the buffoon and the
gladiator to perfection. In the twelfth year of his
life, at Centumcellae,[2] he gave a forecast of his
cruelty. For when it happened that his bath was
drawn too cool, he ordered the bathkeeper to be cast
into the furnace ; whereupon the slave who had been
ordered to do this burned a sheep-skin in the furnace,
in order to make him believe by the stench of the
vapour that the punishment had been carried out.

While yet a child he was given the name of
Caesar,[3] along with his brother Verus,[4] and in his fourteenth year he was enrolled in the college of priests.[5]
II. When he assumed the toga,[6] he was elected one of
the leaders of the equestrian youths,[7] the trossuli, and
even while still clad in the youth's praetexta he gave
largess [8] and presided in the Hall of Trajan.[9] He
assumed the toga on the Nones of July—the day on
which Romulus vanished from the earth—at the
time when Cassius revolted from Marcus. After he
had been commended to the favour of the soldiers he
set out with his father for Syria [10] and Egypt, and
with him he returned to Rome.[11] Afterward he was

12 Oct.,
166

20 Jan.,
175

7 July,
175

---

cavalry. It was supposed to have been derived from Tros-
sulum, a town captured by the cavalry, but even in the
second century B.C., its meaning was no longer understood;
see Pliny, *Nat. Hist.*, xxiii. 2, 35 f.

[8] Commemorated on coins; see Cohen, iii[2], p. 266 f., nos.
291-294.

[9] See note to *Hadr.*, vii. 6.

[10] In July, 175. See *Marc.*, xxv. 1.

[11] See *Marc.*, xxvii. 3. Commodus' return to Rome was
celebrated by an issue of coins with the legend *Adventus
Caes(aris) ;* see Cohen, iii[2], p. 228, nos. 1-2.

4rediit. post haec venia legis annariae impetrata consul est factus, et cum patre imperator est appellatus
V kal. Dec. die Pollione et Apro consulibus et
5 triumphavit cum patre. nam et hoc patres decre-
verant. profectus est cum patre et ad Germanicum
bellum.

6   Adhibitos custodes vitae suae honestiores ferre non
potuit, pessimos quosque detinuit et summotos usque
7 ad aegritudinem desideravit. quibus per patris mol-
litiem restitutis popinas et ganeas in Palatinis semper
aedibus fecit neque umquam pepercit vel pudori vel
8 sumptui. in domo aleam exercuit. mulierculas
formae scitioris ut prostibula mancipia per speciem [1]
lupanarium et ludibrium pudicitiae contraxit. imi-
9 tatus est propolas circumforanos. equos currules
sibi comparavit. aurigae habitu currus rexit, gladia-
toribus convixit, atque se [2] gessit ut lenonum minister,
ut probris natum magis quam ei loco eum crederes,[3]
ad quem fortuna provexit.

III. Patris ministeria seniora summovit, amicos senes
2 abiecit. filium Salvii Iuliani, qui exercitibus praeerat,

---

[1] *per speciem* Turnebus; *perficium* P[1]; *perficiens* P corr.
[2] *atque se* Editor; *aquam* P, Peter.   [3] *crederet* P.

---

[1] Cf. *Marc.*, xxii. 12 and note.
[2] On the occasion of Marcus' triumph; see c. xii. 4; *Marc.*,
xvi. 2 and note.
[3] See c. xii. 5 and note to *Marc.*, xvii. 3.
[4] See c. xii. 6 and *Marc.*, xxvii. 9.
[5] But not in public, except on moonless nights; see Dio,
lxxii. 17, 1.

granted exemption from the law of the appointed year and made consul,[1] and on the fifth day before the Kalends of December, in the consulship of Pollio and Aper, he was acclaimed Imperator together with his father,[2] and celebrated a triumph with him.[3] For this, too, the senate had decreed. Then he set out with his father for the German war.[4]

177
27 Nov.,
176
23 Dec.,
176
3 Aug.,
178

The more honourable of those appointed to supervise his life he could not endure, but the most evil he retained, and, if any were dismissed, he yearned for them even to the point of falling sick. And when they were reinstated through his father's indulgence, he always maintained eating-houses and low resorts for them in the imperial palace. He never showed regard for either decency or expense. He diced in his own home. He herded together women of unusual beauty, keeping them like purchased prostitutes in a sort of brothel for the violation of their chastity. He imitated the hucksters that strolled about from market to market. He procured chariot-horses for his own use. He drove chariots in the garb of a professional charioteer,[5] lived with gladiators, and conducted himself like a procurer's servant. Indeed, one would have believed him born rather to a life of infamy than to the high place to which Fortune advanced him.

III. His father's older attendants he dismissed,[6] and any friends[7] that were advanced in years he cast aside.

---

[6] e.g. Tarrutenius Paternus, now prefect of the guard (see c. iv. 1), and C. Aufidius Victorinus, governor of Germania Superior under Marcus. He retained his father's friends for a " few years " (Herodian, i. 8, 1), i.e. until about 183.

[7] See note to Hel., xi. 2.

ob[1] impudicitiam frustra temptavit atque exinde
3 Iuliano tetendit insidias. honestissimos quosque aut
per contumeliam aut per honorem indignissimum
4 abiecit. appellatus est a mimis quasi obstupratus
eosdemque ita ut non apparerent subito deportavit.
5 bellum etiam quod pater paene confecerat legibus
hostium addictus remisit ac Romam reversus est.
6 Romam ut rediit, subactore suo Saotero post se in
curro locato ita triumphavit ut eum saepius[2] cervice
reflexa publice oscularetur. etiam in orchestra hoc
7 idem fecit. et cum potaret in lucem helluareturque
viribus Romani imperii, vespera etiam per tabernas ac
8 lupanaria volitavit. misit homines ad provincias
regendas vel criminum socios vel a criminosis com-
9 mendatos. in senatus odium ita venit[3] ut et ipse
crudeliter in tanti ordinis perniciem saeviret fieretque
e contempto crudelis.

IV. Vita Commodi Quadratum et Lucillam compulit
ad eius interfectionem consilia inire, non sine prae-

[1] *ob* P, Petschenig; *ad* Peter.   [2] *serius* P.   [3] *uehit* P[1].

---

[1] P. Salvius Julianus, consul in 175. He was apparently
in command of troops on the Rhine.
[2] See c. iv. 8.
[3] According to Herodian (i. 6) he gave up the war against
the advice of Marcus' friends and advisers, especially his own
brother-in-law, Pompeianus. He did, however, force the
Quadi, Marcomanni, and Buri to accept terms of peace
which were not discreditable to Rome (Dio, lxxii. 2-3) and was
acclaimed *Imperator* for the fourth time.
[4] For the official expression of reception see c. xii. 7.
His return is commemorated by coins of 180 with the legends
Adventus Aug(usti) and *Fort(una) Red(ux)*; see Cohen, iii[2],
p. 228, no. 3, and p. 248, no. 165.
[5] Called in an inscription *triumphus felicissimus Germanicus secundus*; see *C.I.L.*, xiv. 2922 = Dessau, *Ins. Sel.*, 1420.
[6] Cf. *Ver.*, iv. 6.

The son of Salvius Julianus, the commander of the troops,[1] he tried to lead into debauchery, but in vain, and he thereupon plotted against Julianus.[2] He degraded the most honourable either by insulting them directly or giving them offices far below their deserts. He was alluded to by actors as a man of depraved life, and he thereupon banished them so promptly that they did not again appear upon the stage. He abandoned the war which his father had almost finished and submitted to the enemy's terms,[3] and then he returned to Rome.[4] After he had come back to Rome he led the triumphal procession[5] with Saoterus, his partner in depravity, seated in his chariot, and from time to time he would turn around and kiss him openly, repeating this same performance even in the orchestra. And not only was he wont to drink until dawn and squander the resources of the Roman Empire, but in the evening he would ramble through taverns and brothels.[6] He sent out to rule the provinces men who were either his companions in crime or were recommended to him by criminals. He became so detested by the senate that he in his turn was moved with cruel passion for the destruction of that great order,[7] and from having been despised he became bloodthirsty.

IV. Finally the actions of Commodus drove Quadratus and Lucilla,[8] with the support of Tarrutenius

22 Oct., 180

---

[7] Especially after the conspiracy of Quadratus and Lucilla, according to Herodian, i. 8, 7.

[8] On this conspiracy, formed probably toward the end of 182, see Dio, lxxii. 4, 4-5, and Herodian, i. 8, 3-6. Quadratus was probably the grandson of Marcus' sister; see *Marc.*, vii. 4. Lucilla was Commodus' elder sister, the wife of Lucius Verus, and after his death, of Claudius Pompeianus; see *Marc.*, xx. 6.

COMMODUS ANTONINUS

2 fecti praetorio Tarrutenii Paterni consilio. datum autem est negotium peragendae necis Claudio Pompeiano 3 propinquo. qui ingressus ad Commodum destricto gladio, cum faciendi potestatem habuisset, in haec verba prorumpens 'Hunc tibi pugionem senatus mittit' detexit facinus fatuus nec implevit, multis cum 4 eo participantibus causam. post haec interfecti sunt Pompeianus primo et Quadratus, dein Norbana atque Norbanus et Paralius ; et mater eius et Lucilla in exsilium exacta.

5   Tum praefecti praetorio cum vidissent Commodum in tantum odium incidisse obtentu Saoteri, cuius potentiam populus Romanus ferre non poterat, urbane Saoterum eductum a Palatio sacrorum causa et redeuntem in hortos suos per frumentarios occiderunt. 6 id vero gravius quam de se ipso Commodo fuit. 7 Paternum autem et huius caedis auctorem et, quantum videbatur, paratae necis Commodi conscium et interventorem, ne coniuratio latius puniretur, instigante Tigidio per lati clavi honorem a praefecturae ad-8 ministratione summovit. post paucos dies insimulavit eum coniurationis, cum diceret ob hoc promissam Iuliani filio filiam Paterni, ut in Iulianum

---

[1] According to Dio, lxxii. 5, 2, Paternus had no share in the conspiracy.

[2] Apparently Claudius Pompeianus Quintianus, the son of Lucilla's husband, Claudius Pompeianus, by a former marriage. Herodian speaks of him as a youth at this time.

[3] Lucilla was exiled to Capri, where she was put to death ; see c. v. 7.

[4] See note to *Hadr.*, xi. 4.

[5] Tigidius Perennis, appointed co-prefect with Paternus in 182.

[6] He was granted the right to wear the broad purple stripe on his tunic, the exclusive privilege of the senatorial

272

Paternus, the prefect of the guard,¹ to form a plan for
his assassination. The task of slaying him was assigned to Claudius Pompeianus, a kinsman.² But he,
as soon as he had an opportunity to fulfil his mission,
strode up to Commodus with a drawn sword, and,
bursting out with these words, "This dagger the
senate sends thee," betrayed the plot like a fool, and
failed to accomplish the design, in which many others
along with himself were implicated. After this
fiasco, first Pompeianus and Quadratus were executed,
and then Norbana and Norbanus and Paralius; and
the latter's mother and Lucilla were driven into exile.³

Thereupon the prefects of the guard, perceiving
that the aversion in which Commodus was held was
all on account of Saoterus, whose power the Roman
people could not endure, courteously escorted this
man away from the Palace under pretext of a
sacrifice, and then, as he was returning to his villa,
had him assassinated by their private agents.⁴ But this
deed enraged Commodus more than the plot against
himself. Paternus, the instigator of this murder,
who was believed to have been an accomplice in the
plot to assassinate Commodus and had certainly
sought to prevent any far-reaching punishment of
that conspiracy, was now, at the instigation of
Tigidius,⁵ dismissed from the command of the praetorian guard by the expedient of conferring on him
the honour of the broad stripe.⁶ And a few days
thereafter, Commodus accused him of plotting, saying that the daughter of Paternus had been betrothed to the son of Julianus⁷ with the under-

order. For other instances of the elevation of a prefect of
the guard into the senatorial order see note to *Hadr.*, viii. 7.
⁷ See c. iii. 1-2, and for his execution Dio, lxxii. 5, 1.

transferretur imperium.   quare et Paternum et Iulianum et Vitruvium Secundum, Paterni familiaris-
simum, qui epistulas imperatorias curarat, interfecit.
9 domus praeterea Quintiliorum omnis exstincta, quod
Sextus Condiani[1] filius specie mortis ad defectionem
10 diceretur evasisse.   interfecta et Vitrasia Faustina et
11 Velius Rufus et Egnatius Capito consularis.   in exsilium autem acti sunt Aemilius Iuncus et Atilius Severus consules.   et in multos alios varie saevitum est.

V. Post haec Commodus numquam facile in publicum
processit neque quicquam sibi nuntiari passus est nisi
2 quod Perennis ante tractasset.   Perennis autem Commodi persciens invenit quem ad modum ipse potens
3 esset.   nam persuasit Commodo, ut ipse deliciis
vacaret, idem vero Perennis curis incumberet.   quod
4 Commodus laetanter accepit.   hac igitur lege vivens
ipse cum trecentis concubinis, quas ex matronarum
meretricumque dilectu ad formae speciem concivit,[2]
trecentisque aliis puberibus exoletis, quos aeque ex
plebe ac nobilitate vi pretiisque[3] forma disceptatrice
collegerat, in Palatio per convivia et balneas bac-

---

[1] *Condiani* Casaubon ; *condiciani* P.   [2] *conciuit* Egnatius ; *concilii* P.   [3] *ui pretiisque* Madvig, Peter[2] ; *nuptiisque*
P ; *uultusque* Turnebus, Peter[1].

---

[1] The brothers Sex. Quintilius Condianus and Sex. Quintilius Valerius Maximus.   According to Dio, lxxii. 5, 3-4,
their reputation and wealth caused them to be suspected.

[2] More correctly, the son of Quintilius Valerius Maximus
and consul in 180.   He was included in the sentence pronounced against his father and uncle.   On his escape see
Dio, lxxii. 6.

standing that Julianus would be raised to the throne. On this pretext he executed Paternus and Julianus, and also Vitruvius Secundus, a very dear friend of Paternus, who had charge of the imperial correspondence. Besides this, he exterminated the whole house of the Quintilii,[1] because Sextus, the son of Condianus,[2] by pretending death, it was said, had made his escape in order to raise a revolt. Vitrasia Faustina, Velius Rufus,[3] and Egnatius Capito, a man of consular rank, were all slain. Aemilius Iuncus and Atilius Severus, the consuls,[4] were driven into exile. And against many others he vented his rage in various ways.

V. After this Commodus never appeared in public readily, and would never receive messages unless they had previously passed through the hands of Perennis[5]. For Perennis, being well acquainted with Commodus' character, discovered the way to make himself powerful, namely, by persuading Commodus to devote himself to pleasure while he, Perennis, assumed all the burdens of the government—an arrangement which Commodus joyfully accepted. Under this agreement, then, Commodus lived, rioting in the Palace amid banquets and in baths along with 300 concubines, gathered together for their beauty and chosen from both matrons and harlots, and with minions, also 300 in number, whom he had collected by force and by purchase indiscriminately from the common people and the nobles

[3] Consul in 178.

[4] The year of their consulship is unknown. They were not necessarily consuls in 182.

[5] According to Herodian, i. 11, 5, he spent most of the time in his suburban estate.

5 chabatur. inter haec habitu victimarii victimas im-
molavit. in harena rudibus, inter cubicularios gladiatores pugnavit lucentibus aliquando mucronibus.
6 tunc tamen Perennis cuncta sibimet vindicavit. quos
voluit interemit, spoliavit plurimos, omnia iura sub-
7 vertit, praedam omnem in sinum contulit. ipse autem
Commodus Lucillam sororem, cum Capreas misisset,
8 occidit. sororibus dein suis ceteris, ut dicitur, con-
stupratis, consobrina patris complexibus suis iniuncta
uni etiam ex concubinis matris[1] nomen imposuit.
9 uxorem,[2] quam deprehensam in adulterio exegit,
10 exactam relegavit et postea occidit. ipsas con-
11 cubinas suas sub oculis suis stuprari iubebat. nec
inruentium in se iuvenum carebat infamia, omni parte
corporis atque ore in sexum utrumque pollutus.
12   Occisus est eo tempore etiam Claudius quasi a la-
tronibus, cuius filius cum pugione quondam ad Commodum ingressus est, multique alii senatores sine
13 iudicio interempti, feminae quoque divites. et nonnulli per provincias a Perenni ob divitias insimulati
14 spoliati sunt vel etiam interempti. iis autem quibus
deerat ficti criminis adpositio obiciebatur, quod
scribere noluissent[3] Commodum heredem.

[1] *matris* P; *patris* Salmasius, Peter.   [2] *inposuit. uxorem*
Heer; *inposuit uxoris* P, Peter.   [3] *noluissent* Casaubon,
Baehrens; *uoluissent* P, Peter.

---

[1] Dio, on the other hand, declares that his administration
was characterized by integrity and restraint; see lxxii. 10, 1.
Herodian (i. 8) has the same point of view as the biography.
[2] See note to c. vii. 7.

solely on the basis of bodily beauty. Meanwhile, dressed in the garb of an attendant at the sacrifice, he slaughtered the sacrificial victims. He fought in the arena with foils, but sometimes, with his chamberlains acting as gladiators, with sharpened swords. By this time Perennis had secured all the power for himself. He slew whomsoever he wished to slay, plundered a great number, violated every law, and put all the booty into his own pocket.[1] Commodus, for his part, killed his sister Lucilla, after banishing her to Capri. After debauching his other sisters, as it is said, he formed an amour with a cousin of his father,[2] and even gave the name of his mother to one of his concubines. His wife,[3] whom he caught in adultery, he drove from his house, then banished her, and later put her to death. By his orders his concubines were debauched before his own eyes, and he was not free from the disgrace of intimacy with young men, defiling every part of his body in dealings with persons of either sex.

At this time Claudius also, whose son had previously come into Commodus' presence with a dagger, was slain,[4] ostensibly by bandits, and many other senators were put to death, and also certain women of wealth. And not a few provincials, for the sake of their riches, were charged with crimes by Perennis and then plundered or even slain; and some, against whom there was not even the imputation of a fictitious crime, were accused of having been unwilling to name Commodus as their heir.

[3] Crispina ; see note to *Marc.*, xxvii. 8.
[4] See c. iv. 2 and note. The biographer has apparently confused the father with the son, for Claudius Pompeianus was alive in 193 ; see *Pert.*, iv. 10 ; *Did. Jul.*, viii. 3.

COMMODUS ANTONINUS

VI. Eo tempore in Sarmatia res bene gestas per
2 alios duces in filium suum Perennis referebat. hic
tamen Perennis, qui tantum potuit, subito, quod
bello Britannico militibus equestris loci viros prae-
fecerat amotis senatoribus, prodita re per legatos
exercitus hostis appellatus lacerandusque militibus
3 est deditus. in cuius potentiae locum Cleandrum ex
cubiculariis subrogavit.

4   Multa sane post interfectum Perennem eiusque
filium quasi a se non gesta rescidit, velut in integrum
5 restituens. et hanc quidem paenitentiam scelerum
ultra triginta dies tenere non potuit, graviora per
Cleandrum faciens quam fecerat per supradictum
6 Perennem. et in potentia quidem Cleander Perenni
successerat, in praefectura vero Niger, qui sex tantum
7 horis praefectus praetorio fuisse perhibetur. muta-
bantur enim praefecti praetorio per horas ac dies,

---

[1] According to Herodian, i. 9, this son of Perennis, in
command of the Illyrian troops, formed a conspiracy in the
army to overthrow Commodus, and the detection of the plot
led to Perennis' fall and death.

[2] In 184. According to Dio, lxxii. 8, the Britons living
north of the boundary-wall invaded the province and annihilated a detachment of Roman soldiers. They were finally
defeated by Ulpius Marcellus, and Commodus was acclaimed
Imperator for the seventh time and assumed the title
Britannicus; see c. viii. 4 and coins with the legend *Vict(oria)
Brit(annica),* Cohen, iii², p. 349, no. 945.

[3] An innovation which became general in the third century, when senatorial commanders throughout the empire
were gradually replaced by equestrian.

[4] According to Dio, lxxii. 9, it was at the demand of a
delegation of 1500 soldiers of the army of Britain, whom
Perennis had censured for mutinous conduct (cf. c. viii. 4).

VI. About this time the victories in Sarmatia won by other generals were attributed by Perennis to his own son.[1] Yet in spite of his great power, suddenly, because in the war in Britain[2] he had dismissed certain senators and had put men of the equestrian order in command of the soldiers,[3] this same Perennis was declared an enemy to the state, when the matter was reported by the legates in command of the army, and was thereupon delivered up to the soldiers to be torn to pieces.[4] In his place of power Commodus put Cleander,[5] one of his 185. chamberlains.

After Perennis and his son were executed, Commodus rescinded a number of measures on the ground that they had been carried out without his authority, pretending that he was merely re-establishing previous conditions. However, he could not maintain this penitence for his misdeeds longer than thirty days, and he actually committed more atrocious crimes through Cleander than he had done through the aforesaid Perennis. Although Perennis was succeeded in general influence by Cleander, his successor in the prefecture was Niger, who held this position as prefect of the guard, it is said, for just six hours. In fact, prefects of the guard were changed hourly and

The mutiny was finally quelled by Pertinax; see *Pert.*, iii. 5-8.
[5] A Phrygian by birth, brought to Rome as a slave; see Herodian, i. 12, 3. After securing his freedom he rose in the Palace and finally became chamberlain, after bringing about the fall and death of his predecessor, Saoterus; see c. iv. 5 and Dio, lxxii. 12, 2. He also contributed to the fall of Perennis; see Dio, lxxii. 9, 3. He was not made prefect until 186, but exercised great influence in his capacity as chamberlain (see §§ 6 and 12).

COMMODUS ANTONINUS

Commodo peiora omnia, quam fecerat ante, faciente. 8 fuit Marcius Quartus praefectus praetorio diebus quinque. horum successores ad arbitrium Cleandri 9 aut retenti sunt aut occisi. ad cuius nutum etiam libertini in senatum[1] atque in patricios lecti sunt, tuncque primum viginti quinque consules in unum 10 annum, venditaeque omnes provinciae. omnia Cleander pecunia venditabat; revocatos de exsilio 11 dignitatibus ornabat, res iudicatas rescindebat. qui tantum per stultitiam Commodi potuit, ut Burrum, sororis Commodi virum, reprehendentem nuntiantemque Commodo quae fiebant in suspicionem regni adfectati traheret et occideret, multis aliis, qui Burrum 12 defendebant, pariter interemptis. praefectus etiam Aebutianus inter hos est interemptus; in cuius locum ipse Cleander cum aliis duobus, quos ipse delegerat, 13 praefectus est factus. tuncque primum tres praefecti praetorio fuere, inter quos libertinus,[2] qui a pugione appellatus est.

VII. Sed et Cleandro dignus tandem vitae finis impositus. nam cum insidiis illius Arrius Antoninus fictis[3] criminibus in Attali gratiam, quem in pro-

---

[1] *senatu* P.   [2] *libertinus* Jordan; *libertinos* P.   [3] *factis* P.

---

[1] So also Dio, lxxii. 12, 3-5.
[2] L. Antistius Burrus; he seems to have been previously accused on the same charge by Pertinax; see *Pert.*, iii. 7.

daily, Commodus meanwhile committing all kinds of
evil deeds, worse even than he had committed before.
Marcius Quartus was prefect of the guard for five
days. Thereafter, the successors of these men were
either retained in office or executed, according to the
whim of Cleander. At his nod even freedmen were
enrolled in the senate and among the patricians, and
now for the first time there were twenty-five consuls
in a single year. Appointments to the provinces 189
were uniformly sold ; in fact, Cleander sold everything
for money.[1] He loaded with honours men who were
recalled from exile ; he rescinded decisions of the
courts. Indeed, because of Commodus' utter de-
generacy, his power was so great that he brought
Burrus,[2] the husband of Commodus' sister, who was
denouncing and reporting to Commodus all that was
being done, under the suspicion of pretending to the
throne, and had him put to death ; and at the same
time he slew many others who defended Burrus.
Among these Aebutianus was slain, the prefect of
the guard ; in his place Cleander himself was made
prefect, together with two others whom he himself
chose. Then for the first time were there three
prefects of the guard, among whom was a freedman,
called the " Bearer of the Dagger ".[3]

VII. However, a full worthy death was at last meted
out to Cleander also. For when, through his intrigues,
Arrius Antoninus [4] was put to death on false charges
as a favour to Attalus, whom Arrius had condemned

[3] *i.e.* Cleander himself. The dagger was the symbol of
the office of prefect.
[4] Together with Burrus he had been accused by Pertinax
of aspiring to the throne (see *Pert.*, iii. 7), but he seems to
have been a highly respected man and official.

consulatu Asiae damnaverat, esset occisus, nec eam
tum invidiam populo saeviente Commodus ferre
2 potuisset, plebi ad poenam donatus est, cum etiam
Apolaustus aliique liberti aulici pariter interempti
sunt. Cleander inter cetera etiam concubinas eius
3 constupravit, de quibus filios suscepit, qui post eius
interitum cum matribus interempti sunt.

4 In cuius locum Iulianus et Regillus subrogati sunt,
5 quos et ipsos postea poenis adfecit. his occisis interemit Servilium et Dulium Silanos cum suis, mox
Antium Lupum et Petronios Mamertinum et Suram
filiumque Mamertini Antoninum ex sorore sua geni-
6 tum. et post eos sex simul ex consulibus Allium
Fuscum, Caelium Felicem, Lucceium Torquatum,
Larcium Eurupianum, Valerium Bassianum, Pac-
7 tumeium [1] Magnum cum suis, atque in Asia Sulpicium
Crassum pro consule et Iulium Proculum cum suis
Claudiumque Lucanum consularem et consobrinam
patris sui Faustinam Anniam in Achaia et alios in-
8 finitos. destinaverat et alios quattuordecim occidere,
cum sumptus eius vires [2] Romani imperii sustinere
non possent.

---

[1] *Pactumeium* Casaubon; *Pactuleium* P.   [2] *u res* Ursinus; *iuriis* P[1]; *iniuriis* P corr.

---

[1] In 189, on the occasion of a riot due to a lack of grain,
for which the mob held Cleander responsible; see Dio,
lxxii. 13.

[2] See *Ver.*, viii. 10.

[3] He married one of them, Damostratia, according to
Dio, lxxii. 12, 1.

[4] For Julianus' death see Dio, lxxii. 14, 1. He is probably to be identified with L. Julius Vehilius Gratus Julianus,
whose interesting career is recorded in an inscription from
Rome; see Dessau, *Ins. Sel.*, 1327.

[5] Perhaps M. Servilius Silanus, consul in 188.

during his proconsulship in Asia, Commodus could not endure the hatred of the enraged people and gave Cleander over to the populace for punishment.[1] At the same time Apolaustus[2] and several other freedmen of the court were put to death. Among other outrages Cleander had debauched certain of Commodus' concubines,[3] and from them had begotten sons, who, together with their mothers, were put to death after his downfall.

As successors to Cleander Commodus appointed Julianus and Regillus, both of whom he afterwards condemned.[4] After these men had been put to death he slew the two Silani, Servilius[5] and Dulius, together with their kin, then Antius Lupus[6] and the two Petronii, Mamertinus and Sura,[7] and also Mamertinus' son Antoninus, whose mother was his own sister;[8] after these, six former consuls at one time, Allius Fuscus, Caelius Felix, Lucceius Torquatus, Larcius Eurupianus, Valerius Bassianus and Pactumeius Magnus,[9] all with their kin; in Asia Sulpicius Crassus, the proconsul, Julius Proculus, together with their kin, and Claudius Lucanus, a man of consular rank; and in Achaia his father's cousin, Annia Faustina,[10] and innumerable others. He had intended to kill fourteen others also, since the revenues of the Roman empire were insufficient to meet his expenditures.

[6] His grave-inscription is preserved; see *C.I.L.*, vi. 1343.
[7] The brothers M. Petronius Sura Mamertinus and M. Petronius Sura Septimianus were consuls in 182 and 190 respectively.
[8] Perhaps Cornificia.   [9] Consul in 183.
[10] Annia Fundania Faustina, daughter of M. Annius Libo, Marcus' uncle (see *Marc.*, i. 3). She is probably the woman referred to in c. v. 8.

COMMODUS ANTONINUS

VIII. Inter haec Commodus senatu semet inridente,[1] cum adulterum matris consulem designasset,
appellatus est Pius ; cum occidisset Perennem, appellatus est Felix, inter plurimas caedes multorum
2 civium quasi quidam novus Sulla. idem Commodus,
ille Pius, ille Felix, finxisse etiam quandam contra se
3 coniurationem dicitur, ut multos occideret. nec alia
ulla fuit defectio praeter Alexandri, qui postea se et
4 suos interemit, et [2] sororis Lucillae. appellatus est
Commodus etiam Britannicus ab adulatoribus, cum
Britanni etiam imperatorem contra eum deligere
5 voluerint. appellatus est etiam Romanus Hercules,
quod feras Lanuvii [3] in amphitheatro occidisset. erat
enim haec illi consuetudo, ut domi bestias interficeret.
6 fuit praeterea ea dementia, ut urbem Romanam
coloniam Commodianam vocari voluerit. qui [4] furor

---

[1] *senatu semet inridente* Peter[2] ; *senatu semettridente* P[1] ;
senatu ridente Peter[1].   [2] *et* om. in P.   [3] *lanuuium* P.
[4] *cui* P.

---

[1] Probably L. Tutilius Pontianus Gentianus, said to have
been one of Faustina's lovers (see *Marc.* xxix. 1), and *consul
suffectus* in 183, the year in which the name *Pius* was bestowed on Commodus.

[2] The name is borne by Commodus in the Acts of the
Arval Brothers for 7 Jan., 183 ; see *C.I.L.*, vi. 2099, 12. It
also appears on the coins of 183, *e.g.* Cohen, iii[2], p. 229,
no. 13 ; the real reason for its assumption is not known.

[3] This name appears on his coins of 185 ; *e.g.* Cohen, iii[2],
p. 233, no. 49. It had been assumed as a cognomen by the
Dictator Sulla.

[4] Julius Alexander, from Emesa in Syria. According to
Dio, lxxii. 14, 1-3, his execution was ordered because he had
speared a lion while on horseback ; he killed those sent to
execute him and then made his escape, but was overtaken.

[5] See c. iv. 1-4.

[6] An allusion to the mutiny in Britain ; see note to c. vi. 2.

VIII. Meanwhile, because he had appointed to the consulship a former lover of his mother's,[1] the senate 183 mockingly gave Commodus the name Pius;[2] and after he had executed Perennis, he was given the name Felix,[3] as though, amid the multitudinous 185 executions of many citizens, he were a second Sulla. And this same Commodus, who was called Pius, and who was called Felix, is said to have feigned a plot against his own life, in order that he might have an excuse for putting many to death. Yet as a matter of fact, there were no rebellions save that of Alexander,[4] who soon killed himself and his near of kin, and that of Commodus' sister Lucilla.[5] He was called Britannicus by those who desired to flatter him, whereas the Britons even wished to set up an emperor against him.[6] He was called also the Roman Hercules,[7] on the ground that he had killed 192 wild beasts in the amphitheatre at Lanuvium; and, indeed, it was his custom to kill wild beasts on his own estate. He had, besides, an insane desire that the city of Rome should be renamed Colonia Commodiana.[8] This mad idea, it is said, was inspired in

---

[7] See also § 9. *Romanus Hercules* appears among his titles as given by Dio, lxxii. 15, 5, and also in an inscription of Dec., 192; see *C.I.L.*, xiv. 3449 = Dessau, *Ins. Sel.*, 400. He had the lion's skin and club, the attributes of Hercules, carried before him in the streets (Dio, lxxii. 17, 4), and had himself portrayed as Hercules on coins (Cohen, iii², p. 251 f., nos. 180-210), and in statues (c. ix. 2; Dio, lxxii. 15, 6), *e.g.* the famous bust in the Capitoline Museum, Rome.

[8] So also Dio, lxxii. 15, 2. *Col(onia) L(ucia) An(toniniana) Com(modiana)* appears on coins of 190; see Cohen, iii², p. 233, nos. 39-40. He also gave the name Commodianus to the senate (§ 9 and Dio, *ibid.*). the people (c. xv. 5), the Palace (c. xii. 7), the legions (Dio, *ibid.*), the city of Carthage, and the African fleet (c. xvii. 8).

7 dicitur ei inter delenimenta Marciae iniectus. voluit
8 etiam in Circo quadrigas agitare. dalmaticatus in
publico processit atque ita signum quadrigis emit-
9 tendis dedit. et eo quidem tempore quo ad senatum
rettulit de Commodiana facienda Roma, non solum
senatus hoc libenter accepit per inrisionem, quantum intellegitur, sed etiam se ipsum Commodianum
vocavit, Commodum Herculem et deum appellans.

IX. Simulavit se et in Africam iturum, ut sumptum itinerarium exigeret, et exegit eumque in con-
2 vivia et aleam convertit. Motilenum, praefectum
praetorii, per ficus veneno interemit. accepit statuas
in Herculis habitu, eique immolatum est ut deo.
3 multos praeterea paraverat interimere. quod per
parvulum quendam proditum est, qui tabulam e
cubiculo eiecit, in qua occidendorum erant nomina
scripta.

4   Sacra Isidis coluit, ut et caput raderet et Anubim
5 portaret. Bellonae servientes vere exsecare brac-
6 chium praecepit studio crudelitatis. Isiacos vere

---

[1] His mistress, who afterwards conspired against him ; see
c. xvii. 1.
[2] Called *chiridotae Dalmatarum* in *Pert.*, viii. 2. It was a
long-sleeved tunic reaching to the knee. Dio describes it
(lxxii. 17, 2) as made of white silk with gold threads.
[3] See note to c. viii. 5.
[4] An Egyptian deity regarded as the protector of corpses
and tombs and represented with the head of a jackal, or, by
the Greeks and Romans, with that of a dog. His cult was
often combined with that of Isis, and according to Juvenal

him while listening to the blandishments of Marcia.[1]
He had also a desire to drive chariots in the Circus,
and he went out in public clad in the Dalmatian
tunic [2] and thus clothed gave the signal for the
charioteers to start. And in truth, on the occasion
when he laid before the senate his proposal to call
Rome Commodiana, not only did the senate gleefully
pass this resolution, out of mockery, as far as we
know, but also took the name " Commodian " to itself,
at the same time giving Commodus the name Hercules, and calling him a god.

IX. He pretended once that he was going to Africa,
so that he could get funds for the journey, then got
them and spent them on banquets and gaming instead.
He murdered Motilenus, the prefect of the guard, by
means of poisoned figs. He allowed statues of himself to be erected with the accoutrements of Hercules ; [3] and sacrifices were performed to him as to a
god. He had planned to execute many more men
besides, but his plan was betrayed by a certain young
servant, who threw out of his bedroom a tablet on
which were written the names of those who were to
be killed.

He practised the worship of Isis and even went so
far as to shave his head and carry a statue of Anubis.[4]
In his passion for cruelty he actually ordered the
votaries of Bellona to cut off one of their arms,[5] and
as for the devotees of Isis, he forced them to beat

(vi. 534), the chief priest of Isis was often dressed as
Anubis.
   [5] The cult of Bellona, brought to Rome from Asia Minor in
the time of Sulla, was characterised by orgiastic music and
dances, in which the votaries, like Mohammedan dervishes,
slashed their arms and bodies ; for a description see Tibullus,
i. 6, 45 f.

pineis usque ad perniciem pectus tundere cogebat.
cum Anubim portaret, capita Isiacorum graviter ob-
tundebat ore simulacri. clava non solum leones in
veste muliebri et pelle leonina sed etiam homines
multos adflixit. debiles pedibus et eos, qui ambulare non possent, in gigantum modum formavit, ita
ut a genibus [1] de pannis et linteis quasi dracones
tegerentur,[2] eosdemque sagittis confecit. sacra
Mithriaca homicidio vero polluit, cum illic [3] aliquid
ad speciem timoris vel dici vel fingi soleat.

X. Etiam puer et gulosus et impudicus fuit. adulescens omne genus hominum infamavit quod erat
2 secum, et ab omnibus est infamatus. inridentes se
feris obiciebat. eum etiam, qui Tranquilli librum
vitam Caligulae continentem legerat, feris obici iussit,
quia eundem diem natalis habuerat, quem et Caligula.
3 si quis sane [4] se mori velle praedixisset, hunc invitum
praecipitari iubebat.

In iocis quoque perniciosus. nam eum,[5] quem
4 vidisset albescentes inter nigros capillos quasi ver-

---

[1] *gentibus* P.   [2] *tegerentur* Petschenig, Peter [2]; *degerer-*
entur P, Peter [1].   [3] *illihic* P.   [4] *sane* P, Peter ; *ante*
Mommsen.   [5] *eum* Jordan ; *eam* P.

---

[1] *i.e.* dressed as Hercules; see note to c. viii. 5.
[2] According to Dio, lxxii. 20, he actually attached figures
of serpents to their legs. The performance was an imitation
of the mythical combats between the gods and the giants, in
which the latter are usually represented, *e.g.* on the great
altar from Pergamum, as having serpents for legs.

their breasts with pine-cones even to the point of death. While he was carrying about the statue of Anubis, he used to smite the heads of the devotees of Isis with the face of the statue. He struck with his club, while clad in a woman's garment or a lion's skin,[1] not lions only, but many men as well. Certain men who were lame in their feet and others who could not walk, he dressed up as giants, encasing their legs from the knee down in wrappings and bandages to make them look like serpents,[2] and then despatched them with his arrows. He desecrated the rites of Mithra [3] with actual murder, although it was customary in them merely to say or pretend something that would produce an impression of terror.

X. Even as a child he was gluttonous and lewd.[4] While a youth, he disgraced every class of men in his company and was disgraced in turn by them. Whosoever ridiculed him he cast to the wild beasts. And one man, who had merely read the book by Tranquillus [5] containing the life of Caligula, he ordered cast to the wild beasts, because Caligula and he had the same birthday.[6] And if any one, indeed, expressed a desire to die, he had him hurried to death, however really reluctant.

In his humorous moments, too, he was destructive. For example, he put a starling on the head of one

[3] A Persian deity, whose cult was brought to Rome in the time of Pompey, and became very popular about the end of the first century after Christ. In the course of the next two centuries the god, under the name *Sol Invictus Mithras*, was worshipped throughout the Empire, and his cult was probably the most formidable rival of Christianity.

[4] But see note to c. i. 7.

[5] *i.e.* Suetonius; see note to *Hadr.*, xi. 3.

[6] See c. i. 2, and Suetonius, *Caligula*, viii. 1.

miculos habere, sturno adposito, qui se vermes sectari
crederet, capite suppuratum reddebat obtunsione oris.[1]
5 pinguem hominem medio ventre dissicuit, ut eius
6 intestina subito funderentur. monopodios et luscinios
eos, quibus aut singulos tulisset oculos [2] aut singulos
7 pedes fregisset, appellabat. multos praeterea passim
exstinxit alios, quia barbarico habitu occurrerant,
8 alios, quia nobiles et speciosi erant. habuit in deliciis
homines appellatos nominibus verendorum utriusque
9 sexus, quos libentius suis osculis [3] applicabat. habuit
et hominem pene prominente ultra modum animalium,
quem Onon appellabat, sibi carissimum. quem et
ditavit et sacerdotio Herculis rustici praeposuit.
XI. dicitur saepe pretiosissimis cibis humana stercora
miscuisse nec abstinuisse gustum aliis, ut putabat,
2 inrisis. duos gibbos retortos in lance argentea sibi
sinapi perfusos exhibuit eosdemque statim promovit
3 ac ditavit. praefectum praetorii suum Iulianum
togatum praesente officio suo in piscinam detrusit.
quem saltare etiam nudum ante concubinas suas iussit
4 quatientem cymbala deformato vultu. genera [4] legu-
minum coctorum ad convivium propter luxuriae con-
5 tinuationem raro vocavit. lavabat per diem septies

---

[1] obtunsione oris Petschenig, Peter[2]; obtunsioneris P; ob-
tunsionibus Peter[1].   [2] oculos om. in P[1], add. in P corr.
[3] osculis Ursinus; oculis P.   [4] genera . . . uocauit P,
Peter [2]; genere . . . uacauit Salmasius, Peter.[1]

---

[1] i.e. ass.
[2] Apparently a private cult, carried on in one of the emperor's suburban estates.
[3] See c. vii. 4.

man who, as he noticed, had a few white hairs, resembling worms, among the black, and caused his
head to fester through the continual pecking of the
bird's beak—the bird, of course, imagining that it
was pursuing worms.   One corpulent person he cut
open down the middle of his belly, so that his in-
testines gushed forth.   Other men he dubbed one-
eyed or one-footed, after he himself had plucked out
one of their eyes or cut off one of their feet.   In addition to all this, he murdered many others in many
places, some because they came into his presence in
the costume of barbarians, others because they were
noble and handsome.   He kept among his minions
certain men named after the private parts of both
sexes, and on these he liked to bestow kisses.   He also
had in his company a man with a male member larger
than that of most animals, whom he called Onos.[1]
This man he treated with great affection, and he
even made him rich and appointed him to the priesthood of the Rural Hercules.[2]   XI. It is claimed
that he often mixed human excrement with the most
expensive foods, and he did not refrain from tasting
them, mocking the rest of the company, as he thought.
He displayed two misshapen hunchbacks on a silver
platter after smearing them with mustard, and then
straightway advanced and enriched them.   He
pushed into a swimming-pool his praetorian prefect
Julianus,[3] although he was clad in his toga and accompanied by his staff; and he even ordered this
same Julianus to dance naked before his concubines,
clashing cymbals and making grimaces.   The various
kinds of cooked vegetables he rarely admitted to his
banquets, his purpose being to preserve unbroken the
succession of dainties.   He used to bathe seven and

6 atque octies et in ipsis balneis edebat. adibat[1]
deorum templa pollutus[2] stupris et humano sanguine.
7 imitatus est et medicum, ut sanguinem hominibus
emitteret scalpris feralibus.

8   Menses quoque in honorem eius pro Augusto Commodum, pro Septembri Herculem, pro Octobri In-
victum, pro Novembri Exsuperatorium, pro Decembri
Amazonium ex signo ipsius adulatores vocabant.
9 Amazonius autem vocatus est ex amore concubinae
suae Marciae, quam pictam in Amazone diligebat,
propter quam et ipse Amazonico habitu in arenam
Romanam procedere voluit.
10   Gladiatorium etiam certamen subiit et nomina
gladiatorum recepit eo gaudio quasi acciperet trium-
11 phalia. ludum semper[3] ingressus est et, quotiens in-
12 grederetur, publicis monumentis indi iussit. pugnasse
autem dicitur septingenties tricies quinquies.
13   Nominatus inter Caesares quartum iduum Octobrium,
quas Herculeas postea nominavit, Pudente et Polli-
14 one consulibus. appellatus Germanicus idibus Hercu-

---

[1] *adibat* ins. by Klein.   [2] *pollutus* P; *polluit* Peter.
[3] *semper* P, Lenze ; *saepe* Casaubon, Peter.

---

[1] Similar mutilations are recorded by Dio, lxxii. 17, 2.

[2] The complete list of the new names as given to the months
is contained in Dio, lxxii. 15, 3.   They are all Commodus' own
names and titles.   In Dio's enumeration the new names are
applied differently from the list as given here, but the dates
given in c. xi.-xii. accord with Dio, and comparison with
known events shows that his is the correct order.

[3] See note to c. viii. 6.

[4] For a description of a spectacle lasting fourteen days, in
which Commodus fought with wild beasts and gladiators, see
Dio, lxxii. 18-21.

[5] See c. xv. 8.   [6] Cf. c. xv. 4.   [7] But see c. xii. 11.

eight times a day, and was in the habit of eating while in the baths. He would enter the temples of the gods defiled with adulteries and human blood. He even aped a surgeon, going so far as to bleed men to death with scalpels.[1]

Certain months were renamed in his honour by his flatterers ; for August they substituted Commodus, for September Hercules, for October Invictus, for November Exsuperatorius, and for December Amazonius, after his own surname.[2] He had been called Amazonius, moreover, because of his passion for his concubine Marcia,[3] whom he loved to have portrayed as an Amazon, and for whose sake he even wished to enter the arena of Rome dressed as an Amazon.

He engaged in gladiatorial combats,[4] and accepted the names usually given to gladiators[5] with as much pleasure as if he had been granted triumphal decorations. He regularly took part in the spectacles, and as often as he did so, ordered the fact to be inscribed in the public records.[6] It is said that he engaged in gladiatorial bouts seven hundred and thirty-five times.[7]

He received the name of Caesar on the fourth day before the Ides of the month usually called October, which he later named Hercules,[8] in the consulship of Pudens and Pollio.[9] He was called Germanicus[10] on the Ides of "Hercules" in the consulship of Maxi-

12 Oct., 166

15 Oct., 172

[8] On these names of the months see note to c. xi. 8.

[9] For these dates see c. ii. 1-5, and notes.

[10] The surname was doubtless assumed by Commodus at the same time that it was taken by Marcus (see note to *Marc.*, xii. 9). It appears on a coin of Marcus and Commodus of 172 ; see Cohen, iii², p. 133, no. 2.

COMMODUS ANTONINUS

XII. leis Maximo et Orfito consulibus. adsumptus est in omnia collegia sacerdotalia sacerdos XIII kal. Invictas 2 Pisone Iuliano consulibus. profectus in Germaniam 3 XIIII kal. Aelias, ut postea nominavit. iisdem con- 4 sulibus togam virilem accepit. cum patre appellatus imperator V kal. Exsuperatorias Pollione et Apro 5 iterum[1] consulibus. triumphavit X kal. Ian. iisdem 6 consulibus. iterum profectus III nonas Commodias 7 Orfito et Rufo consulibus. datus in perpetuum ab exercitu et senatu in domo Palatina Commodiana con- servandus XI kal. Romanas Praesente iterum consule. 8 tertio meditans de profectione a senatu et populo suo 9 retentus est. vota pro eo facta sunt nonis Piis 10 Fusciano iterum consule. inter haec refertur in litteras pugnasse illum sub patre trecenties sexagies 11 quinquies.[2] item postea tantum palmarum gladia- toriarum confecisse vel victis retiariis vel occisis, ut 12 mille contingeret. ferarum autem diversarum manu sua occidit, ita ut elephantos occideret, multa milia. et haec fecit spectante saepe populo Romano.

XIII. Fuit autem validus ad haec, alias debilis et infirmus, vitio etiam inter inguina prominenti, ita ut

---

[1] so Peter; *iterum et Apro* P.   [2] *quinties* P.

---

[1] The official language describing his enthronement.
[2] See note to c. viii. 6.
[3] Perhaps because of the plague (see *Marc.*, xiii. 3) which seems to have broken out again about this time; see Dio, lxxii. 14, 3; Herodian, i. 12, 1-2.
[4] A gladiator provided with a heavy net in which he tried to entangle his opponent; if successful he then killed him with a dagger.
[5] But see c. xi. 12.   [6] See note to c. xi. 10.

mus and Orfitus. XII. He was received into all the
sacred colleges as a priest on the thirteenth day 20 Jan.
before the Kalends of "Invictus," in the consulship 175
of Piso and Julianus. He set out for Germany on
the fourteenth day before the Kalends of the month 19 May,
which he later named Aelius, and assumed the toga 175
in the same year. Together with his father he was
acclaimed Imperator on the fifth day before the 27 Nov.,
Kalends of "Exsuperatorius," in the year when 176
Pollio and Aper served their second consulships, and
he celebrated a triumph on the tenth day before the 23 Dec.,
Kalends of January in this same year. He set out 176
on his second expedition on the third day before the 3 Aug.,
Nones of "Commodus" in the consulship of Orfitus 178
and Rufus. He was officially presented by the
army and the senate to be maintained in perpetuity
in the Palatine mansion,[1] henceforth called Commodiana,[2] on the eleventh day before the Kalends of 22 Oct.,
"Romanus," in the year that Praesens was consul 180
for the second time. When he laid plans for a third
expedition, he was persuaded by the senate and
people to give it up. Vows[3] were assumed in his
behalf on the Nones of "Pius," when Fuscianus was 5 April,
consul for the second time. Besides these facts, it is 188
related in records that he fought 365 gladiatorial
combats in his father's reign. Afterwards, by van-
quishing or slaying retiarii,[4] he won enough gladiatorial crowns to bring the number up to a thousand.[5]
He also killed with his own hand thousands of wild
beasts of all kinds, even elephants. And he frequently did these things before the eyes of the Roman
people.[6]

XIII. But, though vigorous enough for such exploits, he was otherwise weak and diseased; indeed,

eius tumorem per sericas vestes populus Romanus
2 agnosceret. versus in eo multi scripti sunt, de quibus
3 etiam in opere suo Marius Maximus gloriatur. virium
ad conficiendas feras tantarum fuit, ut elephantum
conto transfigeret [1] et orygis cornu basto transmiserit
et singulis ictibus multa milia ferarum ingentium con-
4 ficeret. impudentiae tantae fuit, ut cum muliebri
veste in amphitheatro vel theatro sedens publice
saepissime biberit.

5   Victi sunt sub eo tamen, cum ille sic viveret, per
legatos Mauri, victi Daci, Pannoniae quoque compositae, in [2] Britannia, in Germania et in Dacia im-
6 perium eius recusantibus provincialibus. quae omnia
7 ista per duces sedata sunt. ipse Commodus in sub-
scribendo tardus et neglegens, ita ut libellis una
forma multis subscriberet, in epistulis autem plurimis
8 ' Vale ' tantum scriberet. agebanturque omnia per
alios, qui etiam condemnationes in sinum vertisse
XIV. dicuntur. per hanc autem neglegentiam, cum et
annonam vastarent ii qui tunc rem publicam gerebant,

---

[1] *transigeret* P.   [2] *in* om. in P.

---

[1] An inscription from Mauretania, set up between 184 and
the death of Commodus, records the construction and repair
of redoubts along the border, and is probably to be connected
with this outbreak; see Dessau, *Ins. Sel.*, 396. This may
also be the revolt alluded to in *Pert.*, iv. 2.
[2] Probably in 182, when Commodus was acclaimed *Imperator* for the fifth time (see Cohen, iii[2], p. 337, nos. 840-
847). A large number of Dacians who had been driven from
their homes were granted land in Roman territory; see Dio,
lxxii. 3, 3.

he had such a conspicuous growth on his groin that
the people of Rome could see the swelling through his
silken robes. Many verses were written alluding to
this deformity; and Marius Maximus prides himself
on preserving these in his biography of Commodus.
Such was his prowess in the slaying of wild beasts,
that he once transfixed an elephant with a pole,
pierced a gazelle's horn with a spear, and on a
thousand occasions dispatched a mighty beast with a
single blow. Such was his complete indifference to
propriety, that time and again he sat in the theatre
or amphitheatre dressed in a woman's garments
and drank quite publicly.

The Moors[1] and the Dacians[2] were conquered
during his reign, and peace was established in the
Pannonias,[3] but all by his legates, since such was the
manner of his life. The provincials in Britain,[4] Dacia,
and Germany[5] attempted to cast off his yoke, but all
these attempts were put down by his generals.
Commodus himself was so lazy and careless in signing
documents that he answered many petitions with the
same formula, while in very many letters he merely
wrote the word "Farewell". All official business was
carried on by others, who, it is said, even used con-
demnations to swell their purses. XIV. And because
he was so careless, moreover, a great famine arose in

[3] An inscription of 185 records the construction of redoubts
along the Danube; see *C.I.L.*, iii. 3385 = Dessau, *Ins. Sel.*,
395.

[4] See c. vi. 2 and note.

[5] Probably in 187-188. It is referred to in an inscription as
expeditio felicissima tertia Germanica; see *C.I.L.*, v. 2155
= Dessau, *Ins. Sel.*, 1574. According to c. xii. 8, Commodus
wished to lead the expedition but the "senate and people"
would not allow it.

COMMODUS ANTONINUS

etiam inopia ingens Romae exorta est, cum fruges
2 non [1] deessent. et eos quidem qui omnia vastabant
3 postea Commodus occidit atque proscripsit. ipse vero
saeculum aureum Commodianum nomine adsimulans
vilitatem proposuit, ex qua maiorem penuriam fecit.
4 Multi sub eo et alienam poenam et salutem suam
5 pecunia redemerunt. vendidit etiam suppliciorum
diversitates et sepulturas et inminutiones malorum et
6 alios pro aliis occidit. vendidit etiam provincias et
administrationes, cum ii per quos venderet partem
7 acciperent, partem vero Commodus. vendidit nonnullis et inimicorum suorum caedes. vendiderunt
8 sub eo etiam eventus litium liberti. praefectos
Paternum et Perennem non diu tulit, ita tamen ut
etiam de iis praefectis quos ipse fecerat triennium
nullus impleret, quorum plurimos interfecit vel veneno
vel gladio. et praefectos urbi eadem facilitate mutavit.
XV. cubicularios suos libenter occidit, cum omnia ex nutu
2 eorum semper fecisset. Eclectus [2] cubicularius cum
videret eum tam facile cubicularios occidere, praevenit
eum et factioni mortis eius interfuit.
3 Spectator gladiatoria sumpsit arma, panno purpureo
4 nudos umeros advelans. habuit praeterea morem, ut

[1] So P (Ballou in "Class. Philol.," iii. p. 273); *et non* in P
acc. to Peter. [2] *Eclectus* Mommsen, Peter; *electus* P.

[1] See note to c. vii. 1.
[2] It was enacted by special decree, according to Dio, lxxii.
15, 6.
[3] See c. iv. 7-8 and vi. 2.
[4] Cf. c. vi. 6-8; vii. 4; ix. 2. Even Cleander was prefect
only from 186 to 189.
[5] He had been a freedman and favourite of Lucius Verus;
see *Ver.*, ix. 6.
[6] See c. xvii. 1.

298

Rome, not because there was any real shortage of
crops, but merely because those who then ruled the state
were plundering the food supply.[1]   As for those who
plundered on every hand, Commodus afterwards put
them to death and confiscated their property ; but
for the time he pretended that a golden age had
come,[2] " Commodian " by name, and ordered a general
reduction of prices, the result of which was an even
greater scarcity.

In his reign many a man secured punishment for
another or immunity for himself by bribery.   Indeed,
in return for money Commodus would grant a change
of punishment, the right of burial, the alleviation of
wrongs, and the substitution of another for one condemned to be put to death.   He sold provinces and
administrative posts, part of the proceeds accruing to
those through whom he made the sale and part to
Commodus himself.   To some he sold even the
lives of their enemies.   Under him the imperial
freedmen sold even the results of law-suits.   He did
not long put up with Paternus and Perennis as prefects ;[3] indeed, not one of the prefects whom he himself had appointed remained in office as long as three
years.[4]   Most of them he killed, some with poison,
some with the sword.   XV. Prefects of the city
he changed with equal readiness.   He executed his
chamberlains with no compunctions whatever, even
though all that he had done had been at their bidding.
One of these chamberlains, however, Eclectus by
name,[5] forestalled him when he saw how ready
Commodus was to put the chamberlains to death, and
took part in a conspiracy to kill him.[6]

At gladiatorial shows he would come to watch and
stay to fight, covering his bare shoulders with a purple

omnia quae turpiter, quae impure, quae crudeliter,
quae gladiatorie, quae lenonie faceret, actis urbis indi
5 iuberet, ut Marii Maximi scripta testantur. Commodianum etiam populum Romanum dixit, quo saepis-
6 sime praesente gladiator pugnavit. sane cum illi
saepe pugnanti ut deo populus favisset, irrisum se
credens populum Romanum a militibus classiariis,
qui vela ducebant, in amphitheatro interimi prae-
7 ceperat. urbem incendi iusserat, utpote coloniam
suam. quod factum esset, nisi Laetus praefectus
8 praetorii Commodum deterruisset. appellatus est
sane inter cetera triumphalia nomina etiam sescenties
vicies Palus Primus Secutorum.

XVI. Prodigia eius imperio et publice et privatim
2 haec facta sunt : crinita stella apparuit. vestigia
deorum in foro visa sunt exeuntia. et ante bellum
desertorum caelum arsit. et repentina caligo ac
tenebra in Circo kalendis Ianuariis oborta ; et ante

---

[1] The *Acta Urbis* or *Acta Diurna* was a publication begun
by Julius Caesar and continued by his successors, which contained official announcements, and general news that the
government desired to convey to the public.

[2] Cf. c. xi. 11.   [3] See c. viii. 6 and note.

[4] See c. xi. 10 and note.

[5] In 192 a fire devastated the district east of the Forum and
a portion of the Palatine ; see Dio, lxxii. 24, and Herodian, i.
14, 2-6. This seems to be the fire here alluded to, but according to Dio, Commodus was in no way responsible for it.
After rebuilding what the fire had destroyed, Commodus assumed the title *Conditor ;* see Cohen, iii[2], p. 251 f., nos. 181-
184.

[6] See c. xvii. 1.

[7] According to Dio, lxxii. 22, 3, this was engraved along with
his other titles on the Colossus (see c. xvii. 10).   The term

cloth. And it was his custom, moreover, to order
the insertion in the city-gazette [1] of everything he
did that was base or foul or cruel, or typical of a
gladiator [2] or a procurer—at least, the writings of
Marius Maximus so testify. He entitled the
Roman people the " People of Commodus," [3] since he
had very often fought as a gladiator in their presence. [4]
And although the people regularly applauded him in
his frequent combats as though he were a god, he became convinced that he was being laughed at, and
gave orders that the Roman people should be slain in
the Amphitheatre by the marines who spread the
awnings. He gave an order, also, for the burning of
the city, [5] as though it were his private colony, and
this order would have been executed had not Laetus, [6]
the prefect of the guard, deterred him. Among
other triumphal titles, he was also given the name
"Captain of the Secutores " [7] six hundred and twenty
times.

XVI. The prodigies that occurred in his reign, both
those which concerned the state and those which
affected Commodus personally, were as follows. A
comet appeared. Footprints of the gods were seen in
the Forum departing from it. Before the war of the
deserters [8] the heavens were ablaze. On the Kalends ^{1 Jan.,}
¹⁹³

primus palus is formed on the analogy of *primus pilus*, the
first centurion of a legion. The *palus* was the wooden pike
used by gladiators in practice. A *secutor* wore a helmet and
greaves and was armed with a long shield and a sword.

[8] An outbreak in Gaul in 186, headed by a soldier named
Maternus, who gathered a band of fellow-soldiers and desper-
adoes and plundered the country. The Roman troops under
Pescennius Niger defeated and scattered them; whereupon,
Maternus himself fled to Italy and attempted to assassinate
Commodus, but was caught and beheaded; see Herodian, i.
10, and *Pesc. Nig.*, iii. 4.

COMMODUS ANTONINUS

3 lucem fuerant etiam incendiariae aves ac dirae. de
Palatio ipse ad Caelium montem in Vectilianas aedes
4 migravit, negans se in Palatio posse dormire. Ianus
geminus sua sponte apertus est, et Anubis simulacrum
5 marmoreum moveri visum est. Herculis signum
aeneum sudavit in Minucia per plures dies. bubo
etiam supra cubiculum eius deprehensa est tam Romae
6 quam Lanuvii. ipse autem prodigium non leve sibi
fecit ; nam cum in gladiatoris occisi vulnus manum
misisset, ad caput sibi detersit, et contra consuetudinem paenulatos iussit spectatores non togatos ad munus convenire, quod funeribus solebat, ipse in pullis
7 vestimentis praesidens. galea eius bis per portam
Libitinensem elata est.

8 Congiarium dedit populo singulis denarios septingenos vicenos quinos. circa alios omnes parcissimus
fuit, quod luxuriae sumptibus aerarium minuerat.[1]

¹ *minueret* P.

---

[1] Regarded in early times as birds of ill-omen ; in the first
century after Christ, however, there was considerable difference
of opinion as to their identification ; see Plin., *Nat. Hist.*, x. 36.

[2] The school for gladiators ; it was in the general neighbourhood of the Colosseum. Commodus planned to spend the
night of 31 Dec., 192 here, before appearing in public on the
next day as a *secutor* ; see Dio, lxxii. 22, 2.

[3] It was an ancient custom that these gates should be open
when Rome was at war.

[4] See note to c. ix. 4.

[5] The two *porticus Minuciae* were situated in the low-lying
district between the Capitoline Hill and the Tiber, close to
the Theatre of Marcellus. They were called respectively
Vetus and *Frumentaria* ; in the latter were distributed the
tickets which entitled the holders to receive grain from the
public granaries.

[6] According to Dio, lxxii. 21, 3, these cloaks were never
worn at the theatre except when an emperor died.

of January a swift coming mist and darkness arose in
the Circus ; and before dawn there had already been
fire-birds [1] and ill-boding portents. Commodus himself moved his residence from the Palace to the
Vectilian Villa [2] on the Caelian hill, saying that he
could not sleep in the Palace. The twin gates of the
temple of Janus [3] opened of their own accord, and a
marble image of Anubis [4] was seen to move. In
the Minucian Portico [5] a bronze statue of Hercules
sweated for several days. An owl, moreover, was
caught above his bed-chamber both at Lanuvium and
at Rome. He was himself responsible for no inconsiderable an omen relating to himself ; for after he had
plunged his hand into the wound of a slain gladiator he
wiped it on his own head, and again, contrary to custom, he ordered the spectators to attend his gladiatorial shows clad not in togas but in cloaks, a practice
usual at funerals,[6] while he himself presided in the
vestments of a mourner. Twice, moreover, his helmet
was borne through the Gate of Libitina.[7]

He gave largess to the people, 725 denarii to each
man.[8] Toward all others he was close-fisted to a
degree, since the expense of his luxurious living had
drained the treasury. He held many races in the
Circus,[9] but rather as the result of a whim than as

[7] The gate of an amphitheatre through which were dragged
the bodies of slain gladiators. Libitina was the goddess who
presided over funerals.

[8] This sum must be greatly exaggerated, unless it is a computation of what each citizen received during the whole of
Commodus' reign. According to Dio, lxxii. 16, 1, he often
gave individual largesses of 140 denarii, and his coins show
nine occasions when largess was given by him, seven of which
date from the time of his reign as sole emperor.

[9] On one occasion he exhibited thirty races in two hours;
see Dio, lxxii. 16, 1.

9 circenses multos addidit ex libidine potius quam religione et ut dominos factionum ditaret.

XVII. His incitati, licet nimis sero, Quintus Aemilius Laetus praefectus et Marcia concubina eius 2 inierunt coniurationem ad occidendum eum. primumque ei venenum dederunt ; quod cum minus operaretur, per athletam, cum quo exerceri solebat, eum strangulaverunt.

3 Fuit forma quidem corporis iusta, vultu insubido, ut ebriosi solent, et sermone incondito, capillo semper fucato et auri ramentis inluminato, adurens comam et barbam timore tonsoris.

4 Corpus eius ut unco traheretur atque in Tiberim mitteretur, senatus et populus postulavit, sed postea iussu Pertinacis in monumentum Hadriani translatum est.

5 Opera eius praeter lavacrum, quod Cleander nomine 6 ipsius fecerat, nulla exstant. sed nomen eius alienis 7 operibus incisum senatus erasit. nec patris autem sui opera perfecit. classem Africanam instituit, quae subsidio esset, si forte Alexandrina frumenta cessassent. 8 ridicule etiam Carthaginem Alexandriam Commodianam togatam appellavit, cum classem quoque Africanam 9 Commodianam Herculeam appellasset. ornamenta

---

[1] See note to *Ver.*, iv. 8.

[2] The story of the murder is given in greater detail by Dio, lxxii. 22, 4, and especially by Herodian, i. 16-17. Eclectus was also one of the conspirators ; see c. xv. 2.

[3] It was customary to fasten a hook to the bodies of condemned criminals and thus drag them to the Tiber. The populace had demanded that this should be done to the body of Tiberius (Suetonius, *Tiberius*, lxv. 1).

[4] Cf. c. xx. 1, and Dio, lxxiii. 2, 1. For his sepulchral inscription see *C.I.L.*, vi. 992 = Dessau, *Ins. Sel.*, 401.

[5] The *Thermae Commodianae ;* their exact site is unknown.

an act of religion, and also in order to enrich the leaders of the factions.[1]

XVII. Because of these things—but all too late— Quintus Aemilius Laetus, prefect of the guard, and Marcia, his concubine, were roused to action and entered into a conspiracy against his life. First they gave him poison; and when this proved ineffective they had him strangled by the athlete with whom he was accustomed to exercise.[2]

Physically he was very well proportioned. His expression was dull, as is usual in drunkards, and his speech uncultivated. His hair was always dyed and made lustrous by the use of gold dust, and he used to singe his hair and beard because he was afraid of barbers.

The people and senate demanded that his body be dragged with the hook and cast into the Tiber;[3] later, however, at the bidding of Pertinax, it was borne to the Mausoleum of Hadrian.[4]

No public works of his are in existence, except the bath which Cleander built in his name.[5] But he inscribed his name on the works of others; this the senate erased.[6] Indeed, he did not even finish the public works of his father. He did organize an African fleet, which would have been useful, in case the grain-supply from Alexandria were delayed.[7] He jestingly named Carthage Alexandria Commodiana Togata, after entitling the African fleet Commodiana Herculea.[8] He made certain additions

---

[6] Cf. c. xx. 5. Many inscriptions found throughout the empire show Commodus' name carefully erased. The same procedure followed the death of Domitian.

[7] The fleet was to convey grain to Rome from the province of Africa.

[8] See note to c. viii. 6.

sane quaedam Colosso addidit, quae postea cuncta
10 sublata sunt. Colossi autem caput dempsit, quod
Neronis esset, ac suum imposuit et titulum more solito
subscripsit, ita ut illum Gladiatorium et Effeminatum
11 non praetermitteret. hunc tamen Severus, imperator
gravis et vir nominis sui, odio, quantum [1] videtur, senatus inter deos rettulit, flamine addito, quem ipse vivus
sibi paraverat, Herculaneo Commodiano.
12   Sorores tres superstites reliquit. ut natalis eius
celebraretur, Severus instituit.

    XVIII. Adclamationes senatus post mortem Com-
2 modi graves fuerunt. ut autem sciretur quod iudicium senatus de Commodo fuerit, ipsas adclamationes
de Mario Maximo indidi et sententiam senatus con-
sulti :
3   " Hosti patriae honores detrahantur. parricidae
honores detrahantur. parricida trahatur. hostis
patriae, parricida, gladiator in spoliario lanietur.
4 hostis deorum, carnifex senatus, hostis deorum, par-
5 ricida senatus ; hostis deorum, hostis senatus. gladiatorem in spoliario. qui senatum occidit, in spoliario
ponatur ; qui senatum occidit, unco trahatur ; qui
innocentes occidit, unco trahatur. hostis, parricida,

1 *quantum* Peter ; *quam* P.

---

[1] On the Colossus see *Hadr.*, xix. 12-13 and note. This
passage is incorrect, since Hadrian had replaced the head of
Nero by that of the Sun. According to Dio, lxxii. 22, 3,
Commodus also added the club and lion's skin characteristic
of Hercules (see c. viii. 5). Dio also gives the inscription
(cf. c. xv. 8).
[2] Commemorated by coins with the legend *Consecratio ;*
306

to the Colossus by way of ornamentation, all of which
were later taken off, and he also removed its head,
which was a likeness of Nero, and replaced it by a
likeness of himself, writing on the pedestal an inscription in his usual style, not omitting the titles Gladia-
torius and Effeminatus.[1] And yet Severus, a stern
emperor and a man whose character was well in keeping with his name, moved by hatred for the senate—
or so it seems—exalted this creature to a place among
the gods [2] and granted him also a flamen, the
" Herculaneus Commodianus," whom Commodus
while still alive had planned to have for himself.

Three sisters [3] survived him. Severus instituted
the observance of his birthday.

XVIII. Loud were the acclamations of the senate
after the death of Commodus. And that the senate's
opinion of him may be known, I have quoted from
Marius Maximus the acclamations themselves,[4] and
the content of the senate's decree :

" From him who was a foe of his fatherland let his
honours be taken away ; let the honours of the
murderer be taken away ; let the murderer be dragged
in the dust. The foe of his fatherland, the murderer,
the gladiator, in the charnel-house let him be
mangled. He is foe to the gods, slayer of the senate,
foe to the gods, murderer of the senate, foe of the
gods, foe of the senate. Cast the gladiator into the
charnel-house. He who slew the senate, let him be
dragged with the hook ; he who slew the guiltless, let

see Cohen, iii², p. 234, no. 61 ; see also p. 359, nos. 1009-1010.
He also appears as Divus Commodus in inscriptions.
    [3] Arria Fadilla, Cornificia, and Vibia Aurelia Sabina.
    [4] Cf. *Av. Cass.*, xiii. 1 and note. The outcries are mentioned
by Dio, lxxiii. 2, 2-4.

COMMODUS ANTONINUS

6 vere vere.[1] qui sanguini suo non pepercit, unco
7 trahatur. qui te occisurus fuit, unco trahatur. nobiscum timuisti, nobiscum periclitatus es. ut salvi
simus, Iuppiter optime maxime, serva nobis Per-
8 tinacem. fidei praetorianorum feliciter. praetoriis
cohortibus feliciter. exercitibus Romanis feliciter.
pietati senatus feliciter.

9 Parricida trahatur. rogamus, Auguste, parricida
10 trahatur. hoc rogamus, parricida trahatur. exaudi
Caesar : delatores ad leonem. exaudi Caesar : Spera-
11 tum ad leonem. victoriae populi Romani feliciter.
fidei militum feliciter. fidei praetorianorum feliciter.
cohortibus praetoriis feliciter.

12 Hostis statuas undique, parricidae statuas undique,
gladiatoris statuas undique. gladiatoris et parricidae
13 statuae detrahantur. necator civium trahatur. parricida civium trahatur. gladiatoris statuae detrahantur.
14 te salvo salvi et securi sumus, vere vere, modo vere,
modo digne, modo vere, modo libere.

15 Nunc securi sumus ; delatoribus metum. ut securi
simus,[2] delatoribus metum. ut [3] salvi simus, delatores
de senatu, delatoribus fustem. te salvo delatores ad
16 leonem. te imperante delatoribus fustem.

---

[1] *uere* Peter; *seuere* P.   [2] *sumus* P.   [3] *ut* ins. by
Salmasius; om. in P.

---

[1] Evidently addressed to Pertinax
[2] Cf. *Pert.*, v. 1.   [3] Apparently an informer.

308

him be dragged with the hook—a foe, a murderer, verily, verily. He who spared not his own blood, let him be dragged with the hook; he who would have slain you,[1] let him be dragged with the hook. You were in terror along with us, you were endangered along with us. That we may be safe, O Jupiter Best and Greatest, save for us Pertinax.[2] Long life to the guardian care of the praetorians! Long life to the praetorian cohorts! Long life to the armies of Rome! Long life to the loyalty of the senate!

Let the murderer be dragged in the dust. We beseech you, O Sire, let the murderer be dragged in the dust. This we beseech you, let the murderer be dragged in the dust. Hearken, Caesar: to the lions with the informers! Hearken Caesar: to the lions with Speratus![3] Long life to the victory of the Roman people! Long life to the soldiers' guardian care! Long life to the guardian care of the praetorians! Long life to the praetorian cohorts!

On all sides are statues of the foe, on all sides are statues of the murderer, on all sides are statues of the gladiator. The statues of the murderer and gladiator, let them be cast down. The slayer of citizens, let him be dragged in the dust. The murderer of citizens, let him be dragged in the dust. Let the statues of the gladiator be overthrown. While you are safe, we too are safe and untroubled, verily, verily, if in very truth, then with honour, if in very truth, then with freedom.

Now at last we are secure; let informers tremble. That we may be secure, let informers tremble. That we may be safe, cast informers out of the senate, the club for informers! While you are safe, to the lions with informers! While you are ruler, the club for informers!

XIX. Parricidae gladiatoris memoria aboleatur, parricidae gladiatoris statuae detrahantur. impuri gladiatoris memoria aboleatur. gladiatorem in spoli-2 ario. exaudi Caesar : carnifex unco trahatur. carnifex senatus more maiorum unco trahatur. saevior Domitiano, impurior Nerone. sic fecit, sic patiatur. memoriae innocentium serventur. honores innocentium restituas, rogamus. parricidae cadaver unco 3 trahatur. gladiatoris cadaver unco trahatur. gladiatoris cadaver in spoliario ponatur. perroga, perroga: 4 omnes censemus unco trahendum. qui omnes occidit, unco trahatur. qui omnem aetatem occidit, unco trahatur. qui utrumque sexum occidit, unco trahatur. 5 qui sanguini suo non pepercit, unco trahatur. qui templa spoliavit, unco trahatur. qui testamenta delevit, unco trahatur. qui vivos spoliavit, unco trahatur. 6 servis serviimus. qui pretia vitae exegit, unco trahatur. qui pretia vitae exegit et fidem non servavit, unco trahatur. qui senatum vendidit, unco trahatur. qui filiis abstulit hereditatem, unco trahatur.

7 Indices de senatu, delatores de senatu, servorum

Let the memory of the murderer and the gladiator be utterly wiped away. Let the statues of the murderer and the gladiator be overthrown. Let the memory of the foul gladiator be utterly wiped away. Cast the gladiator into the charnel-house. Hearken, Caesar: let the slayer be dragged with the hook. In the manner of our fathers let the slayer of the senate be dragged with the hook. More savage than Domitian, more foul than Nero. As he did unto others, let it be done unto him. Let the remembrance of the guiltless be preserved. Restore the honours of the guiltless, we beseech you. Let the body of the murderer be dragged with the hook, let the body of the gladiator be dragged with the hook, let the body of the gladiator be cast into the charnel-house. Call for our vote, call for our vote: with one accord we reply, let him be dragged with the hook. He who slew all men, let him be dragged with the hook. He who slew young and old, let him be dragged with the hook. He who slew man and woman, let him be dragged with the hook. He who spared not his own blood, let him be dragged with the hook. He who plundered temples, let him be dragged with the hook. He who set aside the testaments of the dead, let him be dragged with the hook. He who plundered the living, let him be dragged with the hook. We have been slaves to slaves. He who demanded a price for the life of a man, let him be dragged with the hook. He who demanded a price for a life and kept not his promise, let him be dragged with the hook. He who sold the senate, let him be dragged with the hook. He who took from sons their patrimony, let him be dragged with the hook.

Spies and informers, cast them out of the senate.

subornatores de senatu. et tu nobiscum timuisti;
8 omnia scis et bonos et malos nosti. omnia scis,
omnia emenda; pro te timuimus. o nos felices, te
vere [1] imperante! de parricida refer, refer, perroga.
9 praesentiam tuam rogamus. innocentes sepulti non
sunt. parricidae cadaver trahatur. parricida sepultos
eruit; parricidae cadaver trahatur."

XX. Et cum iussu Pertinacis Livius Laurensis, procurator patrimonii, Fabio Ciloni consuli designato
dedisset, per noctem Commodi cadaver sepultum est.
2, 3 senatus adclamavit: "Quo auctore sepelierunt? parricida sepultus eruatur,[2] trahatur." Cincius Severus
dixit: "Iniuste sepultus est. qua pontifex dico, hoc
4 collegium pontificum dicit. quoniam laeta[3] percensui,
nunc convertar ad necessaria: censeo quas[4] is, qui
nonnisi ad perniciem civium et ad dedecus suum vixit,
ob honorem suum decerni coegit, abolendas statuas,
5 quae undique sunt abolendae, nomenque ex omnibus
privatis publicisque monumentis eradendum menses-
que iis nominibus nuncupandos quibus nuncupabantur,
cum primum illud malum in re publica incubuit."

---

[1] *uere* Editor (cf. *Claud.*, iv. 3); *uiro* P; *uero* Exc. Cusana,
Mommsen; *uiso* Hirschfeld, Peter[2].   [2] *seruatur* P.
[3] *laeta* Peter[1]; *laetam* P; *laeta iam* Baehrens, Peter[2].
[4] *quae* P.

---

[1] Commemorated in an inscription from Rome, *C.I L.*, vi.
2126. He is one of the characters in the *Deipnosophistai* of
Athenaeus.
[2] An office probably created by Claudius. The *patrimonium*
comprised the estates regarded as the property of the emperor
and transmitted from one emperor to another, even when
there was no direct succession. It was distinguished, both
from the *fiscus*, or imperial treasury, and from the *res privata*,
the private property of any individual emperor; the latter

Suborners of slaves, cast them out of the senate.
You, too, were in terror along with us; you know all,
you know both the good and the evil. You know all
that we were forced to purchase; all we have feared
for your sake. Happy are we, now that you are
emperor in truth. Put it to the vote concerning the
murderer, put it to the vote, put the question. We
ask your presence. The guiltless are yet unburied;
let the body of the murderer be dragged in the
dust. The murderer dug up the buried; let the
body of the murderer be dragged in the dust."

XX. The body of Commodus was buried during
the night, after Livius Laurensis,[1] the steward of the
imperial estate,[2] had surrendered it at the bidding of
Pertinax[3] to Fabius Cilo,[4] the consul elect. At this
the senate cried out: "With whose authority have
they buried him? The buried murderer, let him be
dug up, let him be dragged in the dust." Cincius
Severus[5] said: "Wrongfully has he been buried.
And as I speak as pontifex, so speaks the college of
the pontifices. And now, having recounted what is
joyful, I shall proceed to what is needful: I give it
as my opinion that the statues should be overthrown
which this man, who lived but for the destruction of
his fellow-citizens and for his own shame, forced us to
decree in his honour; wherever they are, they should
be cast down. His name, moreover, should be erased
from all public and private records,[6] and the months[7]
should be once more called by the names whereby they
were called when this scourge first fell upon the state."

was placed in charge of a special procurator by Severus; see
Sev., xii. 4.

[3] See c. xvii. 4.   [4] See *Carac.*, iii. 2 and note.
[5] See *Sev.*, xiii. 9.   [6] See c. xvii. 6.   [7] See c. xi. 8.

HELVIUS PERTINAX

IULII CAPITOLINI

I. Publio Helvio Pertinaci pater libertinus Helvius
Successus fuit, qui filio nomen ex continuatione lig-
nariae negotiationis, quod pertinaciter eam rem
2 gereret, imposuisse fatetur. natus est Pertinax in
Appennino in villa matris. equus pullus ea hora qua
natus est in tegulas ascendit atque ibi breviter com-
3 moratus decidit et [1] exspiravit. hac re motus pater
ad Chaldaeum venit. qui cum illi futura ingentia
praedixisset, stirpem [2] se perdidisse dixit.
4   Puer litteris elementariis et calculo imbutus, datus
etiam Graeco grammatico atque inde Sulpicio Apol-
linari, post quem idem Pertinax grammaticen professus
est.
5   Sed cum in ea minus quaestus proficeret, per
Lollianum Avitum, consularem virum, patris pat-
6 ronum, ducendi ordinis dignitatem petiit. dein prae-

---

[1] *et* om. in P.   [2] *stirpem* P; *stipem* Peter.

---

[1] At Alba Pompeia in Liguria, according to Dio, lxxiii. 1.
For the date see c. xv. 6.
[2] The text is almost certainly corrupt.
[3] Frequently cited in the *Noctes Atticae* of Aulus Gellius,
one of his pupils. He is well known as the composer of metri-
cal summaries of the *Aeneid* and of Terence's comedies.
[4] Consul in 144.

PERTINAX

BY

JULIUS CAPITOLINUS

I. Publius Helvius Pertinax was the son of a freed-man, Helvius Successus by name, who confessed that he gave this name to his son because of his own long-standing connection with the timber-trade, for he had conducted that business with pertinacity. Pertinax himself was born in the Apennines[1] on an estate which belonged to his mother. The hour he was born a black horse climbed to the roof, and after remaining there for a short time, fell to the ground and died. Disturbed by this occurrence, his father went to a Chaldean, and he prophesied future greatness for the boy, saying that he himself had lost his child.[2] As a boy, Pertinax was educated in the rudiments of literature and in arithmetic and was also put under the care of a Greek teacher of grammar and, later, of Sulpicius Apollinaris;[3] after receiving instruction from this man, Pertinax himself took up the teaching of grammar.

But when he found little profit in this profession, with the aid of Lollianus Avitus, a former consul[4] and his father's patron, he sought an appointment to a command in the ranks.[5] Soon afterwards, in the

---

[5] As chief centurion ; see note to *Av. Cass.*, i. 1.

fectus cohortis in Syriam profectus Tito Aurelio
imperatore, a praeside Syriae, quod sine diplomatibus
cursum usurpaverat, pedibus ab Antiochia ad lega-
II. tionem suam iter facere coactus est. bello Parthico
industria sua promeritus in Britanniam translatus est
2 ac retentus. post in Moesia rexit alam. deinde
3 alimentis dividendis in Via Aemilia procuravit. inde
classem Germanicam rexit. mater eum usque in
Germaniam prosecuta[1] est ibique obiit. cuius etiam
4 sepulchrum stare nunc dicitur. inde ad ducenum
sestertiorum stipendium translatus in Daciam sus-
pectusque a Marco quorundam artibus[2] remotus est, et
postea per Claudium Pompeianum, generum Marci,
quasi adiutor eius futurus vexillis regendis adscitus
5 est. in quo munere adprobatus lectus est in senatu.
6 postea iterum re bene gesta prodita est factio, quae
illi concinnata fuerat, Marcusque imperator, ut com-

[1] *persecuta* P.   [2] *artibus* Peter; *a partibus* P.

---

[1] *i.e.* Antoninus Pius.

[2] An independent company of infantry, normally number-
ing five hundred and usually commanded by a young man of
the equestrian order as the first stage in his official career.

[3] The war waged under the nominal command of Verus in
162-166 ; see *Marc.*, ix. 1 and *Ver.*, vii.

[4] Probably as tribune of a legion ; see Dio, lxxiii. 3, 1.   Dio
adds that he secured this post through the favour of Claudius
Pompeianus (cf. § 4), his former school-mate.

[5] As *praefectus alae*, or commander of an independent
squadron of cavalry.   This was the third of the military posts
required of members of the equestrian order who were aspirants for a political career.

[6] On the *alimenta* see note to *Hadr.*, vii. 8.   The Via
Aemilia ran from Ariminum (Rimini) on the Adriatic through
Bononia (Bologna) to Placentia (Piacenza) on the Po.

reign of Titus Aurelius,[1] he set out for Syria as prefect of a cohort,[2] and there, because he had used the
imperial post without official letters of recommendation, he was forced by the governor of Syria to
make his way from Antioch to his station on foot.
II. Winning promotion because of the energy he
showed in the Parthian war,[3] he was transferred to
Britain[4] and there retained. Later he led a squadron[5]
in Moesia, and after that he supervised the distribution
of grants to the poor on the Aemilian Way.[6] Next,
he commanded the German fleet.[7] His mother
followed him all the way to Germany, and there she
died, and her tomb is said to be still standing there.
From this command he was transferred to Dacia[8] at
a salary of two hundred thousand sesterces, but
through the machinations of certain persons he came
to be distrusted by Marcus and was removed from
this post ; afterwards, however, through the influence
of Claudius Pompeianus, the son-in-law of Marcus,[9]
he was detailed to the command of detachments on
the plea that he would become Pompeianus' aide.[10]
Meeting with approval in this position, he was enrolled in the senate. Later, when he had won success in war for the second time, the plot which had
been made against him was revealed, and Marcus, in
order to remedy the wrong he had done him, raised

[7] The fleet on the Rhine.
[8] As procurator, with the rank of *ducenarius*. He had the
supervision of the finances of the province.
[9] See *Marc.*, xx. 6. Pompeianus had befriended him previously (see § 1 and note).
[10] Pompeianus was governor of Pannonia Inferior in 167
(see note to *Marc.*, xx. 7), and it was probably at this time
that he appointed Pertinax to this command.

pensaret iniuriam, praetorium eum fecit et primae
legioni regendae imposuit, statimque Raetias et
7 Noricum ab hostibus vindicavit. ex quo eminente
industria studio Marci imperatoris consul est desig-
8 natus. exstat oratio apud Marium Maximum laudes
eius continens et omnia vel quae fecit vel quae per-
9 pessus est. et praeter illam orationem, quam longum
fuit conectere, saepissime Pertinax a Marco et in contione militari et in senatu laudatus est, doluitque
palam Marcus, quod senator esset et [1] praefectus
10 praetorii fieri a se non posset. Cassiano motu composito e Syria ad Danuvii tutelam profectus est atque
11 inde Moesiae utriusque, mox Daciae regimen accepit.
bene gestis his provinciis Syriam meruit.

III. Integre se usque ad Syriae regimen Pertinax
tenuit, post excessum vero Marci pecuniae studuit;
2 quare etiam dictis popularibus lacessitus. curiam
Romanam post quattuor provincias consulares, quia
consulatum absens gesserat, iam dives ingressus est,
3 cum eam senator antea non vidisset. iussus est praeterea statim a Perenni in Liguriam secedere in villam
paternam; nam pater eius tabernam coactiliariam [2] in

---

[1] et om. in P.   [2] coactiliariam Scaliger, Mommsen;
coactiliriam P; coctiliciam Salmasius, Peter.

---

[1] i.e. the rank in the senate of those who had held the
praetorship.
[2] The First Adiutrix, which in the second century was
quartered in Upper Pannonia.
[3] In connection with Marcus' campaign in Pannonia; see
note to Marc., xiv. 6.
[4] He evidently accompanied Marcus thither at the time of
Cassius' revolt; see Marc., xxv. 1.
[5] Cf. c. ix. 4-6; xiii. 4.

him to the rank of praetor [1] and put him in command
of the First Legion.[2]   Whereupon Pertinax straightway rescued Raetia and Noricum from the enemy.[3]
Because of his conspicuous prowess in this campaign
he was appointed, on the recommendation of Marcus,
to the consulship.   Marcus' speech has been preserved ca. 175
in the works of Marius Maximus ; it contains a eulogy
of him and relates, moreover, everything that he did
and suffered.   And besides this speech, which it would
take too much space to incorporate in this work,
Marcus praised Pertinax frequently, both in the assemblies of soldiers and in the senate, and publicly
expressed regret that he was a senator and therefore
could not be made prefect of the guard.   After Cassius'
revolt had been suppressed, Pertinax set out from Syria [4] 175
to protect the bank of the Danube, and presently he
was appointed to govern both the Moesias and, soon
thereafter, Dacia.   And by reason of his success in
these provinces, he won the appointment to Syria.

III. Up to the time of his administration of Syria,
Pertinax preserved his honesty, but after the death
of Marcus he became desirous of wealth, and was in
consequence assailed by popular gibes.[5]   It was
not until after he had governed four consular provinces and had become a rich man that he entered
the Roman senate-chamber, which, during all his
career as senator, he had never before seen, for
during his term as consul he had been absent from
Rome.[6]   Immediately after this, he received orders
from Perennis to retire to his father's farm in 182
Liguria,[7] where his father had kept a cloth-maker's

---

[6] He seems to have been in Syria during the short term for
which he was appointed consul ; see c. ii. 7 and 10.

[7] See note to c. i. 2.

4 Liguria exercuerat. sed posteaquam in Liguriam
venit, multis agris coemptis tabernam paternam
manente forma priore infinitis aedificiis circumdedit.
fuitque illic per triennium et mercatus est per suos
servos.

5 Occiso sane Perenni Commodus Pertinaci satisfecit
eumque petiit litteris,[1] ut ad Britanniam proficiscere-
6 tur. profectusque milites ab omni seditione deter-
ruit, cum illi quemcumque imperatorem vellent habere
7 et ipsum specialiter Pertinacem. tunc Pertinax
malevolentiae notam subiit, quod dictus est insimu-
lasse apud Commodum adfectati imperii Antistium
8 Burrum et Arrium Antoninum. et seditiones quidem
contra se ipse [2] compescuit in Britannia,[3] verum ingens periculum adiit seditione legionis paene occisus,
9 certe inter occisos relictus. quam quidem rem idem
10 Pertinax acerrime vindicavit. denique postea veniam
legationis petiit, dicens sibi ob defensam disciplinam
IV. infestas esse legiones. accepto successore alimentorum ei cura mandata est. dein pro consule Africae
2 factus est. in quo proconsulatu multas seditiones
perpessus dicitur vaticinationibus carminum [4] quae de
templo Caelestis emergunt. post hoc praefectus urbi
3 factus. in qua praefectura post Fuscianum, hominem
severum, Pertinax mitissimus et humanissimus fuit et

---

[1] *litteris* Peter; *litteras* P.   [2] *contra* <*se*> *ipse* Lenze;
contra ipse P; *contra imperatorem* Obrecht, Peter.   [3] *Britanniam* P, Peter.   [4] *carminum* Peter[2]; *earum* P.

---

[1] See *Com.*, vi. 2 and notes.   [2] See *Com.*, vi. 11 and vii. 1.
[3] See *Hadr.*, vii. 8, and c. ii. 2. He was now *praefectus
alimentorum*, charged with the supervision of the *alimenta*
for the whole of Italy, whereas previously he had been responsible for one district.

shop. On coming to Liguria, however, he bought
up a great number of farms, and added countless
buildings to his father's shop, which he still kept in
its original form ; and there he stayed for three years
carrying on the business through his slaves.

After Perennis had been put to death, Commodus 185
made amends to Pertinax, and in a letter asked him
to set out for Britain.[1] After his arrival there he kept
the soldiers from any revolt, for they wished to set
up some other man as emperor, preferably Pertinax
himself. And now Pertinax acquired an evil character
for enviousness, for he was said to have laid before
Commodus the charge that Antistius Burrus and
Arrius Antoninus were aspiring to the throne.[2] And
certainly he did suppress a mutiny against himself in
Britain, but in so doing he came into great danger ;
for in a mutiny of a legion he was almost killed, and
indeed was left among the slain. This mutiny
Pertinax punished very severely. Later on, however,
he petitioned to be excused from his governorship,
saying that the legions were hostile to him because
he had been strict in his discipline. IV. After he had
been relieved of this post, he was put in charge of the
grants to the poor.[3] Next he was made proconsul
of Africa. During this proconsulship, it is said, he
suppressed many rebellions by the aid of prophetic
verses which issued from the temple of Caelestis.[4]
Next he was made prefect of the city, and in this office,
as successor to Fuscianus,[5] a very stern man, Pertinax

[4] The tutelary goddess of Carthage, Tanith, worshipped in
the imperial period under the name of *Caelestis Afrorum Dea*.
Her cult extended through northern Africa to Spain and was
spread by soldiers over the empire. See also *Macr.*, iii. 1.

[5] See *Marc.*, iii. 8.

ipsi Commodo plurimum placuit, quia . . . . illi esset
4 iterum cum Pertinax factus est.   tunc Pertinax inter-
ficiendi Commodi conscientiam delatam sibi ab aliis
non fugit.
5   Commodo autem interempto Laetus praefectus
praetorii et Eclectus[1] cubicularius ad eum venerunt
et[2] eum confirmarunt atque in castra duxerunt.
6 illic Pertinax milites adlocutus est, donativum promisit, ingeri sibi imperium a Laeto et Eclecto[3] dixit.
7 fictum est autem quod morbo esset Commodus exstinctus. quia et milites, ne temptarentur, pertimes-
cebant.   denique a paucis primum est Pertinax
8 imperator appellatus.   factus est autem sexagenario
9 maior imperator pridie kal. Ian.   de castris nocte
cum ad senatum venisset et cellam curiae iussisset
aperiri, neque inveniretur aedituus, in Templo Con-
10 cordiae resedit.   et cum ad eum Claudius Pompeianus,
gener Marci,[4] venisset casumque Commodi[5] lacri-
masset, hortatus Pertinax ut imperium sumeret.
sed ille recusavit, quia iam imperatorem Pertinacem
11 videbat.   statim ergo omnes magistratus cum consule
ad curiam venerunt ingressumque Pertinacem nocte

[1] *electus* P.   [2] *et* Salmasius; *ut* P.   [3] *electo* P.   [4] *germanici* P.   [5] *commodo* P.

---

[1] No successful attempt has been made to fill this lacuna.
[2] See *Com.*, xvii. 1.
[3] Twelve thousand sesterces, or three thousand denarii;
see c. xv. 7, and Dio, lxxiii. 1, 2. According to c. xv. 7, he
paid only half of it, but according to Dio, lxxiii. 5, 4, he paid
all that he had promised.
[4] According to Dio, lxxiii. 1, 3, the soldiers were not en-
thusiastic.

was exceedingly gentle and considerate, and he proved very pleasing to Commodus himself, for he was . . .[1] when Pertinax was made consul for the 192 second time. And while in this position, Pertinax did not avoid complicity in the murder of Commodus, when a share in this plot was offered him by the other conspirators.

After Commodus was slain,[2] Laetus, the prefect of the guard, and Eclectus, the chamberlain, came to Pertinax and reassured him, and then led him to the camp. There he harangued the soldiers, promised a donative,[3] and said that the imperial power had been thrust upon him by Laetus and Eclectus. It was pretended, moreover, that Commodus had died a natural death, chiefly because the soldiers feared that their loyalty was merely being tested. Finally, and at first by only a few, Pertinax was hailed as emperor.[4] He was made emperor on the day before the Kalends 31 Dec., of January, being then more than sixty years old.[5] 192 During the night he came from the camp to the senate, but, when he ordered the opening of the hall of the senate-house and the attendant could not be found, he seated himself in the Temple of Concord.[6] And when Claudius Pompeianus, Marcus' son-in-law, came to him and bemoaned the death of Commodus, Pertinax urged him to take the throne; Claudius, however, seeing that Pertinax was already invested with the imperial power, refused. Without further delay, therefore, all the magistrates, in company with the consul, came to the senate-house, and Pertinax, who had come in by night, was saluted as emperor.

[5] Sixty-six.
[6] At the western end of the Forum at the foot of the Capitoline Hill. The senate often met there.

PERTINAX

V. imperatorem appellaverunt. ipse autem Pertinax post laudes suas a consulibus dictas et post vituperationem Commodi adclamationibus senatus ostensam egit gratias senatui et praecipue Laeto, praefecto praetorii, quo auctore et Commodus interemptus et ipse imperator est factus.

2 Sed cum Laeto gratias egisset Pertinax, Falco consul dixit: "Qualis imperator es futurus, hinc intellegimus, quod Laetum et Marciam,[1] ministros 3 scelerum Commodi, post te videmus". cui Pertinax respondit: "Iuvenis es consul nec parendi scis necessitates. paruerunt[2] inviti Commodo, sed ubi habuerunt facultatem, quid semper voluerint osten-4 derunt". eadem die qua Augustus est appellatus, et Flavia Titiana uxor eius Augusta est appellata, iis horis quibus ille in Capitolium vota solvebat. 5 primus sane omnium ea die qua Augustus est appel-6 latus, etiam patris patriae nomen recepit nec non[3] simul etiam imperium proconsulare nec non[3] ius quartae relationis. quod ominis[4] loco fuit Pertinaci. 7 Ad Palatium ergo Pertinax profectus, quod tunc vacuum erat, quia Commodus in Vectilianis occisus est, petenti signum prima die tribuno dedit "militemus," exprobrans utique segnitiem temporum superiorum. quod quidem etiam ante in omnibus ducatibus

---

[1] *marcianum* P.   [2] *paruerunt* P.   [3] *non* ins. in P corr.; om. in P[1].   [4] *omnis* P[1].

---

[1] See *Com.*, xviii.-xix.

[2] Pertinax refused this name for his wife and that of Caesar for his son; see c. vi. 9 and Dio, lxxiii. 7, 1-2. Dio suggests that it was on account of her bad character; see also c. xiii. 8. However, Titiana is called Augusta in inscriptions and on coins.

[3] See *Hadr.*, vi. 4 and note.   [4] See note to *Marc.*, vi. 6.

V. Pertinax, on his part, after his own praises had been recited by the consuls and Commodus had been execrated in the outcries of the senate,[1] returned thanks to the senate in general, and in particular to Laetus, the prefect of the guard, through whose instrumentality Commodus had been slain and he himself declared emperor.

When Pertinax had returned thanks to Laetus, however, Falco, the consul, said: "We may know what sort of an emperor you will be from this, that we see behind you Laetus and Marcia, the instruments of Commodus' crimes". To him Pertinax replied: "You are young, Consul, and do not know the necessity of obedience. They obeyed Commodus, but against their will, and as soon as they had an opportunity, they showed what had always been their desire." On the same day that he was entitled Augustus, at the very hour at which he was paying his vows on the Capitolium, Flavia Titiana, his wife, was also given the name of Augusta.[2] Of all the emperors he was the first to receive the title of Father of his Country on the day when he was named Augustus.[3] And at the same time he received the proconsular power and the right of making four proposals to the senate[4]—a combination which Pertinax regarded as an omen.

And so Pertinax repaired to the Palace, which was vacant at that time, for Commodus had been slain in the Vectilian Villa.[5] And on the first day of his reign, when the tribune asked for the watchword, he gave "let us be soldiers," as if reproving the former reign for its inactivity. As a matter of fact, he had really used this same watchword before in all his

[5] See *Com.*, xvi. 3.

325

VI. dederat. exprobrationem autem istam milites non tulerunt statimque de imperatore mutando cogitarunt. 2 ea die etiam ad convivium magistratus et proceres senatus rogavit, quam consuetudinem Commodus 3 praetermiserat. sane iam [1] postero kalendarum die cum statuae Commodi deicerentur, gemuerunt milites, simul quia iterum signum idem dederat imperator. 4 timebatur autem militia sub sene imperatore. denique tertium nonarum diem votis ipsis milites Triarium Maternum Lascivium, senatorem nobilem, ducere in castra voluerunt, ut eum rebus Romanis imponerent. 5 sed ille nudus fugit atque ad Pertinacem in Palatium venit et post ex urbe decessit.

6 Timore sane Pertinax coactus omnia quae Commo- 7 dus militibus et veteranis dederat confirmavit. suscipere se etiam imperium a senatu dixit, quod iam sponte 8 inierat. quaestionem maiestatis penitus tulit cum iureiurando, revocavit etiam eos qui deportati fuerant crimine maiestatis, eorum memoria restituta qui occisi 9 fuerant. filium eius senatus Caesarem appellavit. sed Pertinax nec uxoris Augustae appellationem re- 10 cepit et de filio dixit: "cum meruerit". et cum Commodus adlectionibus innumeris praetorias miscuisset, senatus consultum Pertinax fecit iussitque

[1] *iam* Peter ; *cum* P.

---

[1] Cf. *Com.*, xx. 4-5.
[2] Yet according to c. iv. 11 and Dio, lxxiii. 1, 4, he was regularly elected by the senate.
[3] According to Dio, lxxiii. 5, 3, their bodies were disinterred and then laid in their ancestral tombs.
[4] See note to c. v. 4.   [5] See note to c. ii. 6.

commands.   VI. But the soldiers would not tolerate a reproof and straightway began to make plans for changing the emperor.   On this same day also he invited the magistrates and the chief men of the senate to a banquet, a practice which Commodus had discontinued.   But, indeed, on the day after the Kalends of January, when the statues of Commodus were overthrown,[1] the soldiers groaned aloud, for he gave this same watchword for the second time, and besides they dreaded service under an emperor advanced in years.   Finally on the third of the month, just as the vows were being assumed, the soldiers tried to lead Triarius Maternus Lascivius, a senator of distinction, to the camp, in order to invest him with the sovereignty of the Roman Empire.   He, however, fled from them quite naked and came to Pertinax in the Palace and presently departed from the city.

Induced by fear, Pertinax ratified all the concessions which Commodus had made to the soldiers and veterans.   He declared, also, that he had received from the senate the sovereignty which, in fact, he had already assumed on his own responsibility.[2]   He abolished trials for treason absolutely and bound himself thereto by an oath, he recalled those who had been exiled on the charge of treason, and he reestablished the good name of those who had been slain.[3]   The senate granted his son the name of Caesar, but Pertinax not only refused to allow the name Augusta to be conferred on his wife but also, in the case of his son, said : " Only when he earns it ".[4] And since Commodus had obscured the significance of the praetorian rank [5] by countless appointments thereto, Pertinax, after securing the passage of a decree of the senate, issued an order that those who

eos, qui praeturas non gessissent sed adlectione ac-
cepissent, post eos esse qui vere praetores fuissent.
11 sed hinc quoque grande odium sibi multorum com-
VII. movit.   census retractari iussit.   delatores convictos [1]
graviter puniri iussit et tamen mollius quam priores
imperatores, unicuique dignitati, si delationis crimen
2 incurreret, poenam statuens.   legem sane tulit, ut
testamenta priora non prius essent inrita quam alia
perfecta essent, neve ob hoc fiscus aliquando succe-
3 deret.   ipseque professus est nullius se aditurum [2]
hereditatem, quae aut adulatione alicuius delata esset
aut lite perplexa, ut legitimi heredes et necessarii
privarentur.   additque senatus consulto haec verba :
4 "Satius [3] est, patres conscripti, inopem rem publicam
obtinere, quam ad divitiarum cumulum per discrimi-
5 num atque dedecorum vestigia pervenire".   donativa
6 et congiaria, quae Commodus promiserat, solvit.   an-
nonae consultissime providit.   et cum tantam penuriam [4] aerarii haberet, ut praeter decies sestertium
non se invenisse fateretur, coactus est ea exigere
quae Commodus indixerat, contra quam professus
7 fuerat.   denique aggressus eum Lollianus Gentianus
consularis, quod contra promissum faceret, necessitatis
rationem accepit.

---

[1] *conuictos* Faber, Peter ; *uinctos* P.   [2] *adituram* P.
[3] *satius* Gruter ; *statius* P[1] ; *sanctius* P corr.   [4] *pecuniam* P.

---

[1] In cases where there was no will or no natural heir the
property reverted to the imperial treasury.
[2] Cf. c. vi. 6.
[3] This figure is also given by Dio, lxxiii. 5, 4 (250,000
denarii).
[4] Q. Hedius Rufus Lollianus Gentianus was the son of the
patron of Pertinax' father ; see c. i. 5.

had secured the rank of praetor not by actual service, but by appointment, should be ranked below those who had been praetors in reality. But by this act also he brought on himself the bitter enmity of many men. VII. He gave orders for the taking of a new census. He gave orders, too, that men convicted of lodging false accusations should be punished with severity, exercising, nevertheless, greater moderation than former emperors, and at the same time ordaining a separate punishment for each rank in case any of its members should be convicted of this offence. He enacted a law, moreover, that an old will should not become invalid before the new one was formally completed, fearing that some time the privy-purse might in this way succeed to an inheritance.[1] He declared that for his own part he would accept no legacy which came to him either through flattery or by reason of legal entanglements if thereby the rightful heirs and the near of kin should be robbed of their rights, and when the decree of the senate was passed, he added these words: " It is better, O Conscript Fathers, to rule a state that is impoverished, than to attain to a great mass of wealth by paths of peril and dishonour ". He paid the donatives and largesses which Commodus had promised,[2] and provided with the greatest care for the grain-supply. And when the treasury was drained to such a degree that he was unable to put his hands on more than a million sesterces,[3] as he himself admitted, he was forced, in violation of a previous promise, to exact certain revenues which Commodus had remitted. And finally, when Lollianus Gentianus,[4] a man of consular rank, brought him to task for breaking his promise, he excused himself on the ground that it was a case of necessity.

8 Auctionem rerum Commodi habuit, ita ut et pueros et concub:nas vendi iuberet, exceptis iis qui per vim 9 Palatio videbantur inserti. et de iis quos vendi iussit multi´ postea reducti ad ministerium oblectarunt senem, qui[1] quidem per alios principes usque ad 10 senatorium dignitatem pervenerunt. scurras turpissimorum nominum dedecora praeferentes[2] proscripsit 11 ac vendidit. cuius nundinationis pecuniam, quae VIII. ingens fuit, militibus donativo dedit. a libertis etiam ea exegit quibus Commodo vendente ditati fuerant. 2 auctio sane rerum Commodi in his insignior fuit: vestis subtegmine serico aureis filis insigni opere,[3] tunicas paenulasque, lacernas et chiridotas Dalmatarum et cirratas militares purpureasque chlamydes Grae- 3 canicas atque castrenses. et cuculli Bardaici et toga 4 armaque gladiatoria gemmis auroque composita. et machaeras Herculaneas et torques gladiatorias vasaque de luto[4] auro ebore argento citroque composita. 5 atque etiam phallovitrobuli[5] ex materie eadem et vasa Samnitica calfactandae resinae ac pici devel- 6 lendis hominibus ac leviginandis. nec non vehicula arte fabricae nova perplexis divisisque rotarum orbi-

---

[1] *qui* om. in P.   [2] *perferentes* P.   [3] *insigni opere* Casaubon; *insignior per* P.   [4] *de luto* Editor; *eludo* P; *eluto* Peter[1]; *de ludo* Krauss, Peter[2].   [5] *phallouitrobuli* Egnatius, Peter[1]; *phandouitrobuli* P, Peter[2].

---

[1] See *Com.*, v. 4.

[2] *Com.*, x. 8. According to Dio, lxxiii. 6, 2, it was Laetus who offered these for sale.

[3] See c. iv. 6. He also gave a largess of 100 denarii to each; see c. xv. 7; Dio, lxxiii. 5, 4; and the coins with the legend *Liberalitas Aug(usti)*, Cohen, iii[2], p. 392 f., nos. 23-28.

[4] See *Com.*, xiv., 4-7.   [5] *Com.*, viii. 8.

[6] The *bardocucullus*, a heavy coarse cloak with a hood. It seems to have been named from the Bardaei, a tribe in

He held a sale of Commodus' belongings, even ordering the sale of all his youths and concubines, except those who had apparently been brought to the Palace by force.[1] Of those whom he ordered sold, however, many were soon brought back to his service and ministered to the pleasures of the old man, and under other emperors they even attained to the rank of senator. Certain buffoons, also, who bore the shame of unmentionable names,[2] he put up at auction and sold. The moneys gained in this trafficking, which were immense, he used for a donative to the soldiers.[3] VIII. He also demanded from Commodus' freedmen the sums wherewith they had been enriched when Commodus held his sales.[4] In the sale of Commodus' goods the following articles were especially noteworthy : robes of silk foundation with gold embroidery of remarkable workmanship ; tunics, mantles and coats ; tunics made with long sleeves in the manner of the Dalmatians [5] and fringed military cloaks ; purple cloaks made in the Greek fashion, and purple cloaks made for service in the camp. Also Bardaean hooded cloaks,[6] and a gladiator's toga and harness finished in gold and jewels ; also swords, such as those with which Hercules is represented, and the necklaces worn by gladiators, and vessels, some of pottery, some of gold, some of ivory, some of silver, and some of citrus wood. Also cups in the shape of the phallus, made of these same materials ; and Samnite pots for heating the resin and pitch used for depilating men and making their skins smooth. And furthermore, carriages, the very latest masterpieces of the art, made with entwined and carven

Illyricum, but it was also manufactured in Gaul (see Martial, i. 53, 5).

bus [1] et exquisitis sedilibus nunc ad solem declinandum
7 nunc ad spiritus opportunitatem per vertiginem ; et
alia iter metientia horasque monstrantia et cetera
vitiis eius convenientia.
8   Reddidit praeterea dominis eos qui se ex privatis
9 domibus in aulam contulerant. convivium imperatorium ex immenso ad certum revocavit modum.
10 sumptus etiam omnes Commodi recidit.[2]   exemplo
autem imperatoris, cum ille parcius se ageret, ex
11 omnium continentia vilitas nata est.   nam imperatorium sumptum pulsis non necessariis ad soliti dimi-
IX. dium detraxit.   praemia militantibus posuit.   aes
alienum, quod primo imperii tempore contraxerat,
2 solvit.   aerarium in suum statum restituit.   ad opera
publica certum sumptum constituit.   reformandis
viis [3] pecuniam contulit.   stipendia plurimis retro
debita exsolvit.   obeundis postremo cunctis muneri-
3 bus fiscum parem fecit.   alimentaria etiam compendia,
quae novem annorum ex instituto Traiani debebantur,
obdurata verecundia sustulit.
4   Avaritiae suspicione privatus non caruit, cum apud [4]
Vada Sabatia oppressis faenore possessoribus latius
5 suos tenderet [5] fines.   denique ex versu Luciliano
6 agrarius mergus est appellatus.   multi autem eum

---

[1] *urbibus* P.   [2] *recidit* Egnatius ; *reddit* P.   [3] *uiis*
Casaubon ; *suis* P.   [4] *aplit* P.   [5] *tenderet* Casaubon ;
teneret P.

---

[1] Cf. c. xii. 5.
[2] See note to *Hadr.*, vii. 8.   Pertinax had himself held
offices in this branch of the government ; see c. ii. 2 and c.
iv. 1.
[3] Cf. c. iii. 1.   [4] Cf. c. xiii. 4.
[5] The famous satirist of the second century B.C.

wheels and carefully planned seats that could be
turned so as to avoid the sun at one moment, at
another, face the breeze. There were other carriages
that measured the road, and showed the time; and
still others designed for the indulgence of his vices.

Pertinax restored to their masters, moreover, all
slaves who had come from private homes to the
Palace. He reduced the imperial banquets from
something absolutely unlimited to a fixed standard,[1]
and, indeed, cut down all expenses from what they
had been under Commodus. And from the example
set by the emperor, who lived rather simply, there
resulted a general economy and a consequent reduction in the cost of living; for by eliminating the
unessentials he reduced the upkeep of the court to
half the usual amount. IX. He established rewards
for the soldiers, paid the debt which he had contracted at the beginning of his reign, and restored
the treasury to its normal condition. He set aside
a fixed sum for public buildings, furnished funds for
repairing the highways, and paid the arrears in the
salaries of very many men. Finally, he made the
privy-purse capable of sustaining all the demands
made upon it, and with rigorous honesty he even
assumed the responsibility for nine years' arrears of
money for the poor [2] which was owed through a
statute of Trajan's.

Before he was made emperor he was not free from
the suspicion of greed,[3] for he had extended his own
holdings at Vada Sabatia [4] by foreclosing mortgages ;
indeed, in a line quoted from Lucilius [5] he was called
a land-shark.[6] Many men, moreover, have set down

[6] Properly a kind of sea-gull, proverbial as a type of voracious-
ness ; see Pliny, *Nat. Hist.*, xi. 202.

etiam in provinciis, quas consularis gessit, sordide se
egisse in litteras rettulere. nam vacationes et lega-
7 tiones militares dicitur vendidisse. denique cum
parentum minimum esset patrimonium, et nulla
hereditas obvenisset, subito dives est factus.

8   Omnibus sane possessiones suas reddidit quibus
9 Commodus ademerat, sed non sine pretio. senatui
legitimo semper interfuit ac semper aliquid rettulit.
civilem se salutantibus et interpellantibus semper ex-
10 hibuit. eos qui calumniis adpetiti per servos fuerant
damnatis severius [1] delatoribus liberavit, in crucem
sublatis talibus servis ; aliquos etiam mortuos vindicavit.

X. Insidias paravit ei Falco consul, qui [2] questus est
2 in senatu volens imperare. cui [3] quidem credidit senatus [4] cum [5] sibi quidam servus, quasi Fabiae † setique [6]
filius ex Ceionii Commodi familia, Palatinam domum
ridicule [7] vindicasset, cognitusque iussus esset [8] flagellis
3 caesus domino restitui. in cuius vindicta ii qui [9]
oderant Pertinacem occasionem seditionis invenisse
4 dicuntur. Falconi tamen pepercit et a senatu im-

---

[1] *seucrius* Walter ; *seruis* P. Peter.   [2] *Falco consul, qui
questus* Editor ; *Falco conquestus* P ; lacuna ind. by Peter.
[3] *cui* Editor ; *quo* P ; *quoa* Egnatius, Peter[1] ; †*quo* Peter[2].
[4] *senatus* ins. by Editor ; *credidit,* P, Peter.   [5] *cum* sugg.
by Peter ; *dum* P, Peter.   [6] so P ; *fauiae esset filius* Edit.
princeps, Peter[1].   [7] *ridicula* P.   [8] *esset* Baehrens,
Unger, Peter[2] ; *est* P, Peter[1].   [9] *quod* P.

---

[1] According to D'o, lxxiii. 8, 2, the conspiracy was organized
by Laetus and the guard, which objected to the stern discipline
enforced by Pertinax ; Falco was chosen merely as a promis-
ing candidate for the throne.
[2] The text is hopelessly corrupt and the name of the pretender's father has been lost ; on Fabia see *Marc.*, xxix. 10 ;
Ver., x. 3-4.

in writing that in those provinces which he ruled as proconsul he conducted himself in a grasping manner ; for he sold, they said, both exemptions from service and military appointments.   And lastly, although his father's estate was very small, and no legacy was left him, he suddenly became rich.

As a matter of fact, however, he restored to everyone the property of which Commodus had despoiled him, but not without compensation.   He always attended the stated meetings of the senate and always made some proposal.   To those who came to greet him or who accosted him he was always courteous. He absolved a number of men whose slaves had assailed them with false charges, and punished severely those who brought the accusation, crucifying all such slaves ; and he also rehabilitated the memory of some who had died.

X. A plot was attempted against him[1] by Falco the consul, who, being eager to rule, made complaint in the senate.   He, in fact, was believed by the senate, when a certain slave, on the ground that he was the son of Fabia and . . .[2] of the household of Ceionius Commodus, laid a baseless claim to the residence on the Palatine and, on being recognised, was sentenced to be soundly flogged and returned to his master.   In the punishment of this man those who hated Pertinax are said to have found an opportunity for an outbreak.   Nevertheless, Pertinax spared Falco, and furthermore asked the senate to pardon him.[3]   In the end Falco lived out his life in security

[3] He had been declared a public enemy by the senate, but Pertinax asked that his life should be spared, declaring that he wished no senator to be put to death during his reign ; see Dio, lxxiii. 8, 5.

5 punitatem eius petiit. denique Falco in rebus suis
6 securus vixit et herede filio periit. quamvis multi
7 Falconem nescisse dixerint imperium sibi parari. alii
etiam servis, qui rationes interverterant, falsis testi-
moniis adpetitum eum esse dixerunt.

8   Sed Pertinaci factio praeparata est per Laetum
praefectum praetorii et eos quos Pertinacis sancti-
9 monia offenderat. Laetum enim paenituerat quod
imperatorem fecerat Pertinacem, idcirco quia eum
velut stultum intimatorem nonnullarum rerum
10 reprehendebat. grave praeterea militibus visum,
quod in causa Falconis multos milites ad unius servi
XI. testimonium occidi praeceperat. trecenti igitur de
castris armati ad imperatorias aedes[1] cuneo facto
2 milites venere. eadem tamen die immolante Pertinace negatur in hostia cor repertum ; et cum id vellet
procurare, caput extorum non deprehendit. et tunc
3 quidem omnes milites in castris manebant. qui cum
e[2] castris ad obsequium principis convenissent, et
Pertinax eo die processionem, quam[3] ad Athenaeum
paraverat, ut audiret poetam, ob sacrificii praesagium
distulisset, ii qui ad obsequium venerant redire in
4 castra coeperunt. sed subito globus ille in Palatium
pervenit neque aut arceri potuit aut imperatori nun-

---

[1] *aedes* Egnatius ; *caedes* P.   [2] *e castris* Petschenig ; *castris* P ; *de castris* Peter.   [3] *quam* om. in P.

---

[1] The account of the murder of Pertinax, as given in Dio,
lxxiii. 9-10, agrees in the main with this version.

[2] According to Dio, Laetus had them put to death, alleging
that it was by order of Pertinax.

[3] Two hundred, according to Dio.

[4] An auditorium built by Hadrian, where rhetoricians and

and in possession of his property, and at his death his son succeeded to the inheritance. Many men, however, claimed that Falco was unaware that men were planning to make him emperor, and others said that slaves who had falsified his accounts assailed him with trumped-up charges.

However, a conspiracy [1] was organized against Pertinax by Laetus, the prefect of the guard, and sundry others who were displeased by his integrity. Laetus regretted that he had made Pertinax emperor, because Pertinax used to rebuke him as a stupid babbler of various secrets. It seemed to the soldiers, moreover, a very cruel measure, that in the matter of Falco he had had many of their comrades put to death on the testimony of a single slave.[2] XI. And so three hundred soldiers,[3] formed into a wedge, marched under arms from the camp to the imperial residence. On that day, it was said, no heart had been found in the victim when Pertinax performed a sacrifice, and when he tried to avert this evil omen, he was unable to discover the upper portion of the liver. And so on that day the great body of the soldiers remained in the camp. Some, indeed, had come forth from the camp in order to act as escort to the emperor, but Pertinax, because of the unfavourable sacrifice, postponed for that day a projected visit to the Athenæum,[4] where he had planned to hear a poet, and thereupon the escort began to return to the camp. But just at that moment the band of troops mentioned above arrived at the palace, and neither could they be prevented from entering nor could their entrance be announced to the Emperor.

poets recited their works; see *Alex.*, xxxv. 2; *Gord.*, iii. 4; Victor, *de Caesaribus*, 14.

PERTINAX

5 tiari. enimvero tantum odium in Pertinacem omnium
aulicorum fuit, ut ad facinus milites hortarentur
6 supervenerunt Pertinaci, cum ille aulicum famulicium
ordinaret, ingressique porticus Palatii usque ad locum
7 qui appellatur Sicilia et Iovis cenatio. hoc cognito
Pertinax Laetum praefectum praetorii ad eos misit.
sed ille declinatis militibus per porticus egressus
8 adoperto capite domum se contulit. verum cum ad
interiora prorumperent, Pertinax ad eos processit [1]
9 eosque longa et gravi oratione placavit. sed cum
Tausius quidam, unus e Tungris, in iram et in timo-
rem milites loquendo adduxisset, hastam in pectus
10 Pertinacis obiecit. tunc ille precatus Iovem Ultorem
11 toga caput operuit atque a ceteris confossus est. et
Eclectus [2] quidem confossis duobus cum eodem periit ;
12 reliqui autem cubicularii palatini (nam suos statim, ut
imperator factus est, filiis emancipatis dederat) diffu-
13 gerunt. multi sane dicunt, etiam cubiculum milites
inrupisse atque illic circa lectum fugientem Pertinacem
occidisse.

XII. Fuit autem senex venerabilis, inmissa barba,
reflexo capillo, habitudine corporis pinguiore, ventre
prominulo, statura imperatoria, eloquentia mediocri,
et magis blandus quam benignus nec umquam credi-
2 tus simplex. et cum verbis esset affabilis, re erat

[1] *praecessit* P.   [2] *Eclectus* Peter ; *eiectus* P.

---

[1] Consisting mostly of the *liberti Augusti*, or imperial freedmen. They hated Pertinax because he had compelled them
to disgorge their ill-gotten wealth; see c. viii. 1 ; xiii. 9;
Dio, lxxiii. 8, 1.
[2] *i.e.* a son and a daughter ; see c. xiii. 7 and Dio, lxxiii. 7,
3. Dio relates that Pertinax, after becoming emperor, transferred his property to them and bade them take up their
338

In fact, the palace-attendants [1] hated Pertinax with so bitter a hatred that they even urged on the soldiers to do the deed. The troops arrived just as Pertinax was inspecting the court-slaves, and, passing through the portico of the Palace, they advanced as far as the spot called Sicilia and the Banqueting-Hall of Jupiter. As soon as he learned of their approach, Pertinax sent Laetus, the prefect of the guard, to meet them; but he, avoiding the soldiers, passed out through the portico and betook himself home with his face hidden from sight. After they had burst into the inner portion of the Palace, however, Pertinax advanced to meet them and sought to appease them with a long and serious speech. In spite of this, one Tausius, a Tungrian, after haranguing the soldiers into a state of fury and fear, hurled his spear at Pertinax' breast. And he, after a prayer to Jupiter the Avenger, veiled his head with his toga and was stabbed by the rest. Eclectus also, after stabbing two of his assailants, died with him, and the other court-chamberlains (his own chamberlains, as soon as he had been made emperor, Pertinax had given to his emancipated children [2]) fled away in all directions. Many, it is true, say that the soldiers even burst into his bedroom, and there, standing about his bed, slew him as he tried to flee.

XII. He was a stately old man, with a long beard and hair brushed back. His figure was somewhat corpulent, with somewhat prominent abdomen, but his bearing was regal. He was a man of mediocre ability in speaking, and suave rather than kindly, nor was he ever considered ingenuous. Though friendly

residence with their grandfather (see also c. xiii. 4). They were accordingly regarded as freed from the *patria potestas*, and so are described as *emancipati*.

inliberalis [1] ac prope sordidus, ut dimidiatas lactucas
3 et cardus in privata vita conviviis adponerat. et nisi
quid missum esset edulium, quotquot essent amici,
4 novem libras carnis per tres missus ponebat. si autem
plus aliquid missum esset, etiam in alium diem differ-
5 ebat, cum semper ad convivium multos vocaret. imperator etiam, si sine convivis esset, eadem consuetu-
6 dine cenitabat. amicis si quando de prandio suo
mittere voluit, misit offulas binas aut omasi [2] partem,
aliquando lumbos gallinaceos. phasianum numquam
7 privato convivio comedit aut [3] alicui misit. cum sine
amicis cenaret, adhibebat uxorem suam et Valerianum,
qui cum eodem docuerat, ut [4] fabulas litteratas [5] haberet.
8   Sane nullum ex iis quos Commodus rebus gerendis
imposuerat mutavit, exspectans urbis natalem, quod
eum diem rerum principium volebat esse, atque ideo
etiam in balneis ei Commodiani ministri necem parasse
XIII. dicuntur. imperium et omnia imperialia sic horruit,
ut sibi semper ostenderet displicere. denique non
2 alium se, quam fuerat, videri volebat. fuit in curia
honorificentissimus, ita ut senatum faventem adoraret
et quasi praefectus urbi cum omnibus sermonem

[1] *inliberalis* Jordan; *inliberabilis* P.   [2] *pomasi* P.
[3] *cumeditauit* P.   [4] *ut* om. in P.   [5] *litteratus* P.

---

[1] Cf. c. viii. 9-11. So also Dio, lxxiii. 3, 4.
[2] Regarded as great dainties, and used by wise and frugal
emperors only on occasions of especial importance ; see *Alex.*,
xxxvii. 6 and *Tac.*, xi. 5. For the converse see *Hel.*, xxxii. 4.
[3] Cf. c. i. 4.
[4] The Parilia, celebrated on the 21st April ; for the rites
that were performed see Ovid, *Fasti*, iv. 721 f.
[5] Cf. c. xv. 8.
[6] The favourable impression made by Pertinax on the senate

enough in speech, when it came to deeds, he was
ungenerous and almost mean—so mean, in fact, that
before he was made emperor he used to serve at his
banquets lettuce and the edible thistle in half portions.
And unless someone made him a present of food, he
would serve nine pounds of meat in three courses, no
matter how many friends were present; if anyone
presented him with an additional amount, moreover,
he would put off using it until the next day, and
would then invite a great number of guests. Even
after he had become emperor, if he had no guests he
would dine in the same style.[1] And whenever he in
turn wished to send his friends something from his
table, he would send a few scraps or a piece of tripe,
or occasionally the legs of a fowl. But he never ate
pheasants [2] at his own banquets or sent them to others.
And when he dined without guests, he would invite
his wife and Valerianus, who had been a teacher together with him,[3] in order that he might have literary
conversation.

He removed none of those whom Commodus had
put in charge of affairs, preferring to wait until the
anniversary of the founding of the city,[4] which he
wished to make the official beginning of his reign ;
and thus it came about, it is said, that the servants of
Commodus plotted to slay him in his bath.   XIII. The
imperial power and all the appurtenances thereof
he abhorred,[5] and he always made it quite evident
that they were distasteful to him. In short, he did
not wish to seem other than he really was. In the
senate-house he was most punctilious,[6] doing reverence
to the senate when it expressed its good will and con-

is reflected all through the narrative of Dio (himself a senator
at the time), but particularly in lxxiii. 3, 4.

3 participaret. voluit etiam imperium deponere atque
4 ad privatam vitam redire. filios suos in Palatio nutriri
noluit.[1]

Tam parcus autem et tam lucri cupidus fuit, ut
apud Vada Sabatia mercaturas exercuerit imperator
per homines suos, non aliter quam privatus solebat.
5 nec multum tamen amatus est ; si quidem omnes qui
libere fabulas conferebant male Pertinacem loque-
bantur, christologum eum appellantes, qui bene
6 loqueretur et male faceret. nam et cives sui, qui ad
eum confluxerant iam imperatorem et nihil de eo
meruerant, sic eum appellabant. munera quoque
lucri libidine libenter accepit.

7 Reliquit filium et filiam superstites et [2] uxorem,
Flavii Sulpiciani filiam, quem praefectum urbi loco
8 suo fecerat. circa uxoris pudicitiam minus curiosus
fuit, cum palam citharoedum illa diligeret. ipse prae-
9 terea Cornificiam infamissime dicitur dilexisse. libertos
aulicos vehementissime compressit, unde grande quoque odium contraxit.

XIV. Signa interitus haec fuerunt : ipse ante triduum quam occideretur in piscina sibi visus est videre
2 hominem cum gladio infestantem. et ea die qua occisus

¹ *uoluit* P.   ² *///ut* P.

---

¹ See note to c. xi. 12.   ² Cf. c. ix. 4.
³ A rendering of the Greek χρηστολόγος, which, according
to Victor, *Epitome*, 18, 4, w is applied to Pertinax because he
was *blandus magis quam beneficus.*
⁴ See note to c. xi. 12.   ⁵ Flavia Titiana ; see c. v. 4.
⁶ See *Did. Jul.*, ii. 4 f.

versing with all the senators as though still prefect of
the city. He even wished to resign the throne and
retire to private life, and was unwilling to have
his children reared in the Palace.[1]

On the other hand, he was so stingy and eager for
money that even after he became emperor he carried
on a business at Vada Sabatia[2] through agents, just
as he had done as a private citizen. And despite his
efforts, he was not greatly beloved; certainly, all
who talked freely together spoke ill of Pertinax,
calling him the smooth-tongued,[3] that is, a man who
speaks affably and acts meanly. In truth, his
fellow-townsmen, who had flocked to him after his
accession, and had obtained nothing from him, gave
him this name. In his lust for gain, he accepted
presents with eagerness.

He was survived by a son and a daughter,[4] and by
his wife,[5] the daughter of the Flavius Sulpicianus[6]
whom he made prefect of the city in his own place.
He was not in the least concerned about his wife's
fidelity, even though she carried on an amour quite
openly with a man who sang to the lyre. He himself, it is said, caused great scandal by an amour with
Cornificia.[7] The freedmen attached to the court he
kept within bounds with a strong hand, and in this
way also he brought upon himself a bitter hatred.[8]

XIV. The warnings of his death were these: three
days before he was killed he himself, on looking into
a pool, seemed to behold a man attacking him with
a sword. And on the day he was killed, they say,
the pupils of his eyes, as well as the little pictures

[7] Probably the daughter of Marcus; see note to *Com.*, xvii.
12.
[8] See c. xi. 5 and note.

est negabant in oculis eius pupulas cum imaginibus,
3 quas reddunt, spectantibus visas. et cum apud Lares
sacrificaret, carbones vivacissimi exstincti sunt, cum
inflammari soleant. et, ut supra dictum est, cor et
caput in hostiis non est repertum. stellae etiam
iuxta solem per diem clarissimae visae [1] ante diem [2]
4 quam obiret. et ipse omen de Iuliano successore
dedisse dicitur. nam cum ei Didius Iulianus fratris
filium obtulisset, cui despondebat filiam suam, adhortatus est iuvenem ad patrui observationem et [3] adiecit : "Observa collegam et successorem meum".
5 nam ante Iulianus ei et in consulatu collega fuerat et
in proconsulatu successerat.
6 Milites eum et aulici odio habuerunt, populus mortem eius indignissime tulit, quia videbat omnia per
7 eum antiqua posse restitui. caput eius conto fixum
milites qui eum occiderant per urbem in castra per-
8 tulerunt. reliquiae eius recuperato capite in sepul-
9 chro avi uxoris locatae sunt. et Iulianus, successor
illius, corpus eius quanto potuit honore funeratus est,
10 cum id in Palatio repperisset. qui numquam eius
ullam mentionem vel apud populum vel apud senatum publice fecit, sed cum ipse quoque a militibus
desertus iam esset, per senatum et populum Pertinax
XV. in deos relatos est. sub Severo autem imperatore
cum senatus ingens testimonium habuisset Pertinax,

---

[1] *uisae* P ; *uisae sunt* Peter. [2] *diem* Casaubon ; *dies* P.
[3] *et* ins. by Peter ; om. in P.

---

[1] c. xi. 2. [2] Cf. *Did. Jul.*, ii. 3.
[3] In Africa ; see c. iv. 1 and *Did. Jul.*, ii. 3.
[4] Cf. c. x. 10 and xi. 5.
[5] See *Sev.*, vii. 8, and the coins with *Divus Pertinax* and
Consecratio, Cohen, iii², p. 390 f., nos. 6-12. The elaborate

which they reflect, were invisible to those who looked into them. And when he was performing sacrifices to the Lares the living coals died out, though they are wont to flame up. Furthermore, as we related above,[1] the heart and upper portion of the liver could not be found in the victims. And on the day before he died, stars of great brilliancy were seen near the sun in the day-time. He was responsible himself, it is said, for an omen about his successor, Julianus. For when Didius Julianus presented a nephew of his, to whom he was betrothing his daughter, the Emperor exhorted the young man to show deference to his uncle, and added: "Honour my colleague and successor."[2] For Julianus had previously been his colleague in the consulship and had succeeded him ca. 175 in his proconsular command.[3]

The soldiers and court-retainers regarded him with hatred,[4] but the people felt great indignation at his death, since it had seemed that all the ancient customs might be restored through his efforts. His head, fixed on a pole, was carried through the city to the camp by the soldiers who killed him. His remains, including his head, which was recovered, were laid in the tomb of his wife's grandfather. And Julianus, his successor, buried his body with all honour, after he had found it in the Palace. At no time, however, did he make any public mention of Pertinax either before the people or in the presence of the senate, but when he, too, was deserted by the soldiers Pertinax was raised to the rank of the gods by the senate and the people.[5] XV. In the reign of Severus, moreover, after Pertinax had received the full official approval

funeral-ceremonies are described in detail by Dio, an eye-witness; see lxxiv. 4-5.

PERTINAX

funus imaginarium ei et censorium ductum est, et ab
2 ipso Severo funebri laudatione ornatus est. ipse
autem Severus amore boni principis a senatu Perti-
3 nacis nomen accepit. filius Pertinacis patri flamen est
4 factus. Marciani sodales, qui divi Marci sacra cura-
bant, Helviani sunt dicti propter Helvium Pertinacem.
5 circenses et imperii natalis additi, qui a Severo postea
sublati sunt, et genitalicii, qui [1] manent.

6   Natus autem kal. Augustis Vero et Ambibulo [2] consulibus. interfectus est V kal. Apr. Falcone et Claro
consulibus. vixit annis LX mensibus VII diebus
7 XXVI. imperavit mensibus II diebus XXV. congiarium dedit populo denarios centenos. praetorianis promisit duodena milia nummum sed dedit sena. quod
exercitibus promissum est datum non est, quia mors
eum praevenit. horruisse autem illum imperium epis-
8 tula docet, quae vitae illius a Mario Maximo apposita
est. quam ego inserere [3] ob nimiam longitudinem
nolui.

---

[1] *genitalicii qui* Casaubon ; *geniti aliqui* P.   [2] *Bibulo* P.
[3] *inserere* Puteanus ; *inseri* P.

---

[1] See note to *Sev.*, vii. 8.   [2] See *Sev.*, vii. 9 and note.
[3] See note to *Marc.*, xv. 4.
[4] They are listed in the Calendar of Philocalus of 354 A.D. ;
see *C.I.L.*, i², p. 270. On the custom of celebrating an
emperor's birthday by races in the circus see note to *Hadr.*,
viii. 2.

of the senate, an honorary funeral, of the kind that
would be accorded to a censor, was held for him,[1]
and Severus himself honoured him with a funeral
eulogy.   Severus, furthermore, out of respect for so
good a ruler, accepted from the senate the name
Pertinax.[2]   Pertinax' son was made his father's priest,
and the Marcian brotherhood,[3] who performed the
sacrifices to the Deified Marcus, were called Helviani
in honour of Helvius Pertinax.   There were added,
also, circus-games and a celebration to commemorate
the anniversary of his accession, but these were afterwards abolished by Severus.   The birthday-games
decreed for him, however, are still observed.[4]

He was born on the Kalends of August in the
consulship of Verus and Ambibulus, and was killed
on the fifth day before the Kalends of April in the
consulship of Falco and Clarus.   He lived sixty
years,[5] seven months and twenty-six days, and reigned
for two months and twenty-five days.   He gave the
people a largess of one hundred denarii apiece,[6] and
promised twelve thousand sesterces to each soldier of
the guard, though he gave only six thousand.[7]   The
sum promised to the armies he did not give for the
reason that death forestalled him.   A letter which
Marius Maximus included in his life of Pertinax shows
that he shrank from taking the imperial power,[8] but
this letter, on account of its great length, I have not
thought best to insert.

1 Aug.,
126

26 Mar.,
193

---

[5] More correctly, sixty-six.
[7] See note to c. iv. 6.
[6] See note to c. vii. 11.
[8] Cf. c. xiii. 1.

DIDIUS IULIANUS

AELII SPARTIANI

I. Didio Iuliano, qui post Pertinacem imperium
adeptus est, proavus fuit Salvius [1] Iulianus, bis consul,
praefectus urbi et iuris consultus, quod magis eum
2 nobilem fecit, mater Clara Aemilia, pater Petronius
Didius Severus, fratres Didius Proculus et Nummius
Albinus, avunculus Salvius Iulianus. avus paternus
Insubris Mediolanensis, maternus ex Hadrumetina
colonia.

3 Educatus est apud Domitiam Lucillam, matrem
4 Marci imperatoris. inter viginti viros lectus est
suffragio matris Marci. quaestor ante annum quam
5 legitima aetas sinebat designatus est. aedilitatem
suffragio Marci consecutus est. praetor eiusdem
6 suffragio fuit. post praeturam legioni praefuit in

[1] *albius* P.

---

[1] See *Hadr.*, xviii. 1 and note. It is improbable that Didius
was related to Salvius Julianus, for his family came from
Milan, and since an inscription which connected Salvius with
this city has been shown to be a forgery, there is no reason for
supposing that he was a native of Milan. At any rate,
Salvius, who was born toward the end of the first century,
was not the great-grandfather of Didius, who was born not
later than 137 (see c. ix. 3 and note).
[2] See *Marc.*, i. 3.

DIDIUS JULIANUS

BY

AELIUS SPARTIANUS

I. Didius Julianus, who gained possession of the
empire after Pertinax, was the great-grandson of
Salvius Julianus,[1] a man who was twice consul, prefect of the city, and an authority in jurisprudence—
which, more than anything else, had made him
famous. His mother was Aemilia Clara, his father
Petronius Didius Severus, his brothers Didius Proculus and Nummius Albinus ; another Salvius Julianus
was his uncle. His father's father was an Insubrian
from Milan, his mother's came from the colony of
Hadrumetum.

He himself was reared at the home of Domitia
Lucilla,[2] the mother of the Emperor Marcus, and
through the support of this lady he was elected to
the Board of Twenty.[3] He was appointed quaestor
a year before he reached the legal age,[4] and through
the support of Marcus he attained to the office of
aedile. Again with the support of Marcus he became
praetor.[5] After his praetorship he commanded the

[3] According to an inscription found at Rome (*C.I.L.*, vi.
1401 = Dessau, *Ins. Sel.*, 412) he was *decemvir litibus iudi-*
candis, on which see note to *Hadr.*, ii. 2.
[4] See note to *Pius*, vi. 10.
[5] A rescript addressed to him by Marcus is mentioned in
Digesta, xxviii. 1, 20, 9.

DIDIUS JULIANUS

7 Germania vicensimae secundae Primigeniae. inde
Belgicam sancte ac diu rexit. ibi Chaucis, Germaniae
populis qui Albim fluvium adcolebant, erumpentibus
8 restitit tumultuariis auxiliis provincialium. ob quae
consulatum meruit testimonio imperatoris. Chattos
9 etiam debellavit. inde Dalmatiam regendam accepit
eamque a confinibus hostibus vindicavit. post Ger-
II. maniam inferiorem rexit. post hoc curam alimentorum in Italiam meruit. tunc factus est reus per
quendam Severum Clarissimum militem coniurationis
cum Salvio contra Commodum, sed a Commodo, quia
multos iam senatores occiderat et quidem nobiles ac
potentes in causis maiestatis, ne tristius gravaretur,
2 Didius liberatus est accusatore damnato. absolutus
iterum ad regendam provinciam missus est. Bithyniam deinde rexit, sed non ea fama qua ceteras.

3 Fuit consul cum Pertinace et in proconsulatu
Africae eidem [1] successit et semper ab eo collega est
et successor appellatus. maxime eo die cum filiam
suam Iulianus despondens adfini suo ad Pertinacem
venisset idque intimasset, dixit : ". . . . que debita
reverentia, quia collega et successor meus est."
4 statim enim mors Pertinacis secuta est. quo inter-

[1] *idem* P.

---

[1] The inscription does not mention this command, but records that he was assistant (*legatus*) to the proconsuls both of
Achaia and Africa.

[2] This and the four other provincial governorships are all
enumerated in the inscription.

[3] See note to *Pert.*, iv. 1. The mention of this office seems
to be out of the chronological order, for he was consul about
175 (see below), and the alleged conspiracy of P. Salvius
Julianus against Commodus was not until 182 (see *Com.*, iv.
8).

Twenty-second Legion,[1] the Primigenia, in Germany, and following that he ruled Belgium [2] long and well. Here, with auxiliaries hastily levied from the provinces, he held out against the Chauci (a people of Germany who dwelt on the river Elbe) as they attempted to burst through the border ; and for these services, on the recommendation of the emperor, he was deemed worthy of the consulship. He also gained a crushing victory over the Chatti. Next he took charge of Dalmatia and cleared it of the hostile tribes on its borders. II. Then he governed Lower Germany ; and after that he was deemed worthy of superintending the distribution of grants of money to the poor in Italy.[3] In this position he was accused by one Severus Clarissimus, a soldier, of being an associate of Salvius [4] in his conspiracy against Commodus. But Commodus had already put many senators and many distinguished and powerful men to death on the charge of treason, and so he was afraid of acting too harshly and therefore pardoned Didius and executed his accuser. Thus acquitted, Didius was sent again to govern a province. Then he governed Bithynia, but not as creditably as the other provinces.

His consulship he served with Pertinax; in the proconsulship of Africa,[5] moreover, he succeeded him. ca. 175 Pertinax always spoke of him as his colleague and successor ; on that day, in particular, when Julianus, after betrothing his daughter to a kinsman of his own, came to Pertinax and informed him of the fact, Pertinax said : " . . . and due respect, for he is my colleague and successor ".[6] The death of Pertinax ensued immediately afterwards. After his death,

---

[4] *i.e.* P. Salvius Julianus.
[5] Cf. *Pert.*, iv. 1.   [6] Cf. *Pert.*, xiv. 4.

fecto cum Sulpicianus imperator in castris appellari
vellet, et Iulianus cum genero ad senatum venisset,
quem indictum acceperat, cumque clausas valvas in-
5 venisset atque illic duos tribunos repperisset, Publium [1]
Florianum et Vectium [2] Aprum, coeperunt cohortari
tribuni, ut locum arriperet. quibus cum [3] diceret iam
alium imperatorem appellatum, retinentes eum ad
6 praetoria castra duxerunt. sed posteaquam in castra
ventum est, cum [4] Sulpiciano praefecto urbi, socero
Pertinacis, contionante sibique imperium vindicante
Iulianum e muro ingentia pollicentem nullus ad-
mitteret, primum Iulianus monuit praetorianos, ne
eum facerent imperatorem, qui Pertinacem vindicaret; deinde scripsit in tabulis se Commodi memo-
7 riam restituturum. atque ita est admissus et [5] imperator appellatus, rogantibus praetorianis ne
Sulpiciano aliquid noceret, quod imperator esse
voluisset.

III. Tunc Iulianus Flavium Genialem et Tullium
Crispinum suffragio praetorianorum praefectos praetorii
fecit stipatusque est caterva imperatoria per Mauren-
2 tium, qui et ante Sulpiciano coniunxerat. sane cum
vicena quina milia militibus promisisset, tricena dedit.

---

[1] *publicum* P.　　　[2] *uectium* P.; *Vettium* Jordan, Peter.
[3] *cum* om. in P[1].　　[4] *cum* om. in P[1].　　[5] *est admissus et*
Peter; *et admissus est* P.

---

[1] Cf. *Pert.*, xiii. 7.
[2] The scene at the camp is described in greater detail by
Dio (lxxiii. 11), especially the famous auction of the empire
by the soldiers, in which Sulpicianus and Didius bid against

when Sulpicianus[1] was making plans to be hailed
emperor in the camp, Julianus, together with his
son-in-law, came to the senate, which, he heard,
had been summoned, but found the doors closed.
At the same time he discovered there two tribunes, Publius Florianus and Vectius Aper, who
immediately began urging him to seize the throne;
and though he pointed out to them that another
man was already proclaimed emperor, they held
him fast and conducted him to the praetorian
camp.[2] When they arrived at the camp, however,
Sulpicianus, the prefect of the city and the father-in-
law of Pertinax, was holding an assembly and claiming
the empire himself, and no one would let Julianus
inside, despite the huge promises he made from outside the wall.   Julianus then first warned the soldiers
not to proclaim anyone emperor who would avenge
Pertinax, and next wrote on placards that he would
restore the good name[3] of Commodus; so he was admitted and proclaimed emperor, the soldiers at the
same time requesting that he would not in any way
injure Sulpicianus for aiming at the throne.

III. Immediately thereafter, on the recommendation of the praetorians themselves, Julianus appointed
Flavius Genialis and Tullius Crispinus prefects of
the guard, and through the efforts of Maurentius,
who had previously declared for Sulpicianus, he was
attended by the imperial body-guard.   Although he
had promised five and twenty thousand sesterces to

---

each other. Dio's account, however, must be used with
caution, for his whole narrative shows a decided animus
against Didius.

[3] *i.e.* restore it to the public records and monuments; see
Com., xvii. 6; xx. 5.

3 dein [1] habita contione militari vespera in senatum
venit totumque se senatui permisit factoque senatus
consulto imperator est appellatus, et tribuniciam
potestatem ius proconsulare in patricias familias re-
4 latus emeruit. uxor etiam Manlia Scantilla et filia
5 eius Didia Clara Augustae sunt appellatae. inde se
ad Palatium recepit, uxore ac filia illuc vocatis
trepidis invitisque [2] transeuntibus, quasi iam imminens
6 exitium praesagirent. praefectum urbi Cornelium
Repentinum, generum suum, fecit in locum Sulpiciani.
7   Erat interea in odio populi Didius Iulianus ob hoc,
quod creditum fuerat emendationem temporum Commodi Pertinacis auctoritate reparandam, habebaturque
8 ita, quasi Iuliani consilio esset interemptus. et iam
hi primum qui Iulianum odisse coeperant dissemina-
runt prima statim die Pertinacis cena despecta
luxuriosum parasse convivium ostreis et altilibus et
piscibus adornatum. quod falsum fuisse constat.
9 nam Iulianus tantae parsimoniae fuisse perhibetur,

---

[1] *dein* Peter; *in* P[1].   [2] *inuitisque* Peter[1]; *inuitis eo* P;
† *inuitis eo* Peter[3].

---

[1] Marcus and Verus had given twenty thousand (*Marc.*, vii.
9), Pertinax twelve thousand (*Pert.*, xv. 7). According to
Herodian (ii. 7, 1) Didius did not pay what he had promised,
because the money was not available.

[2] His appearance before the senate is more fully described
by Dio, who was present; see lxxiii. 12. Dio's account is
much less favourable to Didius than the account given here,
which seems to aim at representing him as the choice of the
senate.

[3] The emperors of the Julio-Claudian house had been patricians, and hence it was considered necessary for the emperor
to have this rank. Accordingly, when a plebeian was elected

each soldier, he gave thirty.[1]   Then, after holding an
assembly of the soldiers, he came in the evening to
the senate,[2] and entrusted himself to it without conditions ; thereupon, by decree of the senate he was
acclaimed emperor and, after being raised to a place
among the patrician families,[3] he received the tribunician power and the rights of a proconsul.[4]   His
wife Manlia Scantilla, moreover, and his daughter,
Didia Clara, were given the name Augusta ;[5] and
thereupon he betook himself to the Palace and
thither summoned his wife and daughter, who came,
though with considerable trepidation and reluctance
as if they already foresaw impending doom.[6]   Cornelius Repentinus, his son-in-law, he made prefect of
the city in place of Sulpicianus.

The people, meanwhile, detested Julianus because
it had been their belief that the abuses of Commodus' régime were to be reformed by the influence
of Pertinax, and he was considered to have been
killed with Julianus' connivance.   And now, those
who had begun to hate Julianus were the first
to spread it abroad that on the very first day of
his reign, to show his contempt for Pertinax' board,
he had served an extravagant banquet embellished
with such dainties as oysters and fatted birds and fish.
This story, it is generally agreed, was false.[7]   For
according to report, Julianus was so frugal as to make

(as was the case from Vespasian onward, with the sole exception of Nerva), the senate raised him to the patriciate.
  [4] See note to *Pius*, iv. 7.
  [5] *Augusta* appears on the coins of both ; see Cohen, iii², p.
401 f.
  [6] According to Herodian (ii. 6, 7) it was the two women
who persuaded Didius to bid for the throne.
  [7] Dio, however, asserts it as a fact ; see lxxiii. 13. 1.

ut per triduum porcellum, per triduum leporem
divideret, si quis ei[1] forte misisset, saepe autem
nulla exsistente religione holeribus leguminibusque
10 contentus sine carne cenaverit. deinde neque cenavit
priusquam sepultus esset Pertinax, et tristissimus
cibum ob eius necem sumpsit et primam noctem
vigiliis continuavit, de tanta necessitate sollicitus.

IV. Ubi vero primum inluxit, senatum et equestrem
ordinem in Palatium venientem admisit atque unumquemque, ut erat aetas, vel fratrem[2] vel filium vel
2 parentem adfatus blandissime est. sed populus in
Rostris atque ante curiam ingentibus eum conviciis
lacessebat, sperans deponi ab eo posse imperium quod
3 milites[3] dederant. lapidationem quoque fecere. de-
scendenti cum militibus et senatu in curiam diras
imprecati sunt, rem divinam facienti ne litaret[4]
4 optarunt. lapides etiam in eum iecerunt, cum Iuli-
5 anus manu eos semper placare cuperet. ingressus
autem curiam, placide et prudenter verba fecit. egit
gratias, quod esset adscitus, quod et ipse et uxor et
filia eius Augustorum nomen acceperunt. patris
patriae quoque nomen recepit, argenteam statuam
6 respuit. e senatu in Capitolium pergenti populus
obstitit, sed ferro et vulneribus et pollicitationibus

---

[1] *et* P.   [2] *fratrem* Peter[2]; *patrem* P.   [3] *mites* P[1].
[4] *ne litaret* Edit. princeps ; *elitaret* P.

---

[1] On the other hand, Herodian (ii. 7, 1) emphasizes his
luxury and extravagance.
[2] A similar description of what happened in front of the

a suckling pig or a hare last for three days, if anyone
by chance presented him with one ; and often, moreover, even when there was no religious reason therefor, he was content to dine on cabbages and beans
without meat.[1] Furthermore, he gave no banquet
until after Pertinax was buried, and, because of his
death, took what food he did in a very depressed
state of mind, and passed the first night in continual
wakefulness, disquieted by such a fate.

IV. But when the day dawned, he admitted the
senators and knights who came to the Palace, and
greeted each very cordially, either as brother, or son,
or father, according to his age. The populace, however, at the Rostra and in front of the senate-house,[2]
assailed him with violent revilings, hoping that he
might resign the sovereignty which the soldiers had
given him ; and they even launched a shower of
stones. As he came down to the senate-house with
the soldiers and senate, they heaped curses upon him,
and when he performed the sacrifices, wished that he
might not obtain favourable omens ; they even hurled
stones at him, though Julianus, with uplifted hand,
continually sought to calm them. When he entered
the senate-house, he spoke calmly and discreetly, and
returned thanks because he had been chosen, and because he, his wife, and his daughter, had been given
the titles of Augustus and Augusta. He accepted
also the name of Father of his Country, but refused
a silver statue. Then, as he proceeded from the
senate-house to the Capitol, the populace placed
themselves in his way, but by the sword, by wounds,
and by promises of gold-pieces, the number of which

senate-house and in the Circus is given in Dio, lxxiii. 13,
3-5.

aureorum, quos [1] digitis ostendebat ipse Iulianus ut
7 fidem faceret, summotus atque depulsus est. inde
ad circense spectaculum itum est. sed occupatis
. indifferenter omnium subselliis populus geminavit
convicia in Iulianum ; Pescennium Nigrum, qui iam
imperare dicebatur, ad urbis praesidium vocavit.
8 haec omnia Iulianus placide tulit totoque imperii sui
tempore mitissimus fuit. populus autem in milites
vehementissime invehebatur, qui ob pecuniam Pertinacem occidissent. multa igitur quae Commodus
statuerat, Pertinax tulerat, ad conciliandum favorem
9 populi restituit. de ipso Pertinace neque male neque
bene quicquam egit, quod gravissimum plurimis visum
10 est. constitit autem propter metum militum de
honore Pertinacis tacitum esse.[2]

V. Et Iulianus quidem neque Britannicos exercitus
neque Illyricos timebat, Nigrum vero misso primipilario occidi praeceperat, timens praecipue Syriacos
2 exercitus. ergo Pescennius Niger in Syria, Septimius
Severus in Illyrico [3] cum exercitibus quibus praeside-
3 bant a Iuliano descivere. sed cum ei nuntiatum esset
Severum descivisse, quem suspectum non habuerat,
perturbatus est et [4] ad senatum venit impetravitque [5]
4 ut hostis Severus renuntiaretur ; militibus etiam qui

---

[1] *quod* P.   [2] *est* P.   [3] *niger in illyrico s. seuerus in*
syria P.   [4] *et* om. in P.   [5] *impetrauitque* P (Dessau) ;
imperauitque Peter.

---

[1] The populace took the seats that were reserved for senators
and knights.

[2] Cf. *Pesc. Nig.*, iii. 1.

[3] Except to give his body honourable burial; see c. iii. 10
and *Pert.*, xiv. 9.

[4] Under the command of Clodius Albinus.

[5] Cf. *Pesc. Nig.*, ii. 4.

he himself, in order to inspire trust, kept showing to them on his fingers, they were dispersed
and beaten back. Thereupon, all went to the games
at the Circus ; but here, after everyone had seized
seats indiscriminately,[1] the populace redoubled their
insults against Julianus and called for Pescennius
Niger (who was said to have already declared himself
emperor) to protect the city.[2] All this Julianus took
with perfect equanimity ; indeed all through the time
he was on the throne he was exceedingly tolerant.
The populace, however, kept inveighing with the utmost violence against the soldiers, who had slain
Pertinax, so they said, for money. And so, in order
to win favour with the people, Julianus restored many
measures which Commodus had enacted and Pertinax
had repealed. Concerning Pertinax himself he took
no steps either good or evil,[3] a fact which to very
many seemed a serious matter. It is generally agreed,
however, that it was his fear of the soldiers that
caused him to keep silent about the honours due
Pertinax.

V. As a matter of fact, however, Julianus had no fear
of either the British [4] or the Illyrian army ; but being
chiefly afraid of the Syrian army, he despatched a
centurion of the first rank with orders to murder
Niger.[5] Consequently Pescennius Niger in Syria [6]
and Septimius Severus in Illyricum,[7] together with
the armies which they commanded, revolted from
Julianus. But when he received the news of the
revolt of Severus, whom he had not suspected, then
he was greatly troubled and came to the senate and
prevailed upon them to declare Severus a public
enemy. As for the soldiers who had followed Severus,

[6] See *Pesc. Nig.*, ii. 1. [7] See *Sev.*, v. 1.

DIDIUS JULIANUS

Severum secuti fuerant dies praestitutus, ultra quam,
si cum Severo fuissent, hostium numero haberentur.
5 missi sunt praeterea legati a senatu consulares ad
milites, qui suaderent ut Severus repudiaretur, et is
6 esset imperator quem senatus elegerat.   inter ceteros
legatus est Vespronius Candidus, vetus consularis,
olim militibus invisus ob durum et sordidum im-
7 perium.   missus est successor Severo Valerius Catullinus, quasi posset ei succedi, qui militem iam sibi
8 tenebat.   missus praeterea Aquilius centurio, notus
9 caedibus senatoriis, qui Severum occideret.   ipse
autem Iulianus praetorianos in campum deduci iubet,
muniri turres, sed milites desides et urbana luxuria
dissolutos invitissimos ad exercitium militare produxit,
ita ut vicarios operis, quod unicuique praescribebatur,
mercede conducerent.

VI. Et Severus quidem ad urbem infesto agmine
veniebat, sed Didius Iulianus nihil cum exercitu
praetoriano proficiebat, quem cotidie populus et magis
2 oderat et ridebat.   et Iulianus sperans Laetum fau-
torem Severi, cum per eum Commodi manus evasisset
ingratus tanto beneficio iussit eum occidi.   iussit
etiam Marciam una [1] interfici.

---

[1] *Marciam una* Mommsen; *marci mannum* P.

---

[1] He had been governor of Dacia under Commodus; see
C.I.L., iii. 1092.
[2] Cf. *Pesc. Nig.*, ii. 5.   [3] Cf. *Sev.*, v. 8; *Pesc. Nig.*, ii. 6.
[4] A picture of the confusion in Rome is given in Dio, lxxiii. 16.
[5] According to Dio (lxxiii. 16, 5) he executed Laetus,
Marcia and the athlete Narcissus in order in punish those
guilty of the murder of Commodus.

a day was appointed for them after which they would be considered as public enemies if they were still with Severus. Besides this, legates of consular rank were sent by the senate to the soldiers to persuade them that they should reject Severus and let him be emperor whom the senate had chosen. Among others of the legates was Vespronius Candidus,[1] an old man of consular rank, now for a long time repugnant to the soldiers because of his harsh and penurious rule. Valerius Catullinus was sent as Severus' successor,[2] as if, in sooth, it were possible to appoint a successor to a man who already had an army devoted to himself. And in addition to these others, the centurion Aquilius, notorious as the assassin of senators, was sent for the purpose of murdering Severus.[3] But as for Julianus himself, he gave orders that the praetorians should be led outside the city, and that the fortifications should be manned;[4] but it was a slothful force that he led out, and one demoralized by the fleshpots of the city and intensely averse to active service, so much so, indeed, that they actually hired substitutes for the duties severally enjoined upon them.

VI. All the while, Severus was approaching the city with a hostile army; but in spite of that, Didius Julianus accomplished nothing with his praetorian troops, and the populace hated and laughed at him more and more every day. And although he had escaped from Commodus' clutches by the aid of Laetus, nevertheless, unmindful of this great favour, Julianus ordered Laetus to be put to death in the expectation that he would side with Severus.[5] He gave orders likewise that Marcia should be put to death at the same time.

3 Sed dum haec egit Iulianus, Severus classem
Ravennatem occupat, legati senatus, qui Iuliano
promiserant operam suam, ad Severum transierunt.
4 Tullius Crispinus, praefectus praetorio, contra Severum
missus ut classem produceret, repulsus Romam rediit.
5 haec cum Iulianus videret, senatum rogavit ut
virgines Vestales et ceteri sacerdotes cum senatu
obviam exercitui Severi prodirent et praetentis infulis
rogarent, inanem rem [1] contra barbaros milites parans.
6 haec tamen agenti Iuliano Plautius [2] Quintillus consularis augur contradixit, adserens non debere imperare
7 eum qui armis adversario non posset resistere. cui
multi senatores consenserunt. quare iratus Didius
milites e castris petiit, qui senatum ad obsequium
8 cogerent aut obtruncarent. sed id consilium dis-
plicuit. neque enim decebat, ut, cum senatus hostem
Severum Iuliani causa iudicasset, eundem Iulianum
9 pateretur infestum.   quare meliore consilio ad senatum venit petiitque, ut fieret senatus consultum de
participatione imperii. quod statim factum est.

VII. Tunc omen quod sibi Iulianus, cum imperium
2 acciperet, fecerat omnibus venit in mentem. nam
cum consul designatus de eo sententiam dicens ita pro-

---

[1] *rem* ins. by Peter ; om. in P.   [2] *Plautius* Peter ; *phaus-
tius* P.

---

[1] The station of the Adriatic fleet ; the headquarters of the
fleet that guarded the western coast were at Misenum, on the
Bay of Naples.
[2] Cf. *Sev.*, v. 6.
[3] His troops deserted to Severus ; see c. viii. 4 and Dio,
lxxiii. 17, 1.

While Julianus was engaged in these activities, however, Severus seized the fleet stationed at Ravenna ;[1] whereupon the envoys of the senate who had promised their services to Julianus passed over to Severus.[2] Tullius Crispinus, the prefect of the guard, who had been sent to oppose Severus and lead out the fleet, failed in his attempt[3] and therefore returned to Rome. When Julianus learned of these events, he came to the senate with a proposal that the Vestal Virgins and the priests, along with the senate itself, should go out to meet Severus' troops and entreat them with fillets held in outstretched hands[4]—a futile step, surely, to take against soldiers of barbarian blood. In this proposal, however, Plautius Quintillus, an augur and man of consular rank,[5] opposed him, declaring that he who could not withstand an opponent by force of arms had no right to rule ; in this objection many senators agreed with him. Infuriated at this, Didius Julianus called for soldiers from the camp in order either to force the senators to obedience or to slaughter them. But this plan found no favour. For it was scarcely fitting that the senate, after declaring Severus a public enemy for Julianus' sake, should find an enemy in this same Julianus. And so Julianus came to the senate with a better plan, and asked it to pass a decree effecting a division of empire.[6] And this was forthwith done.

VII. At that time an omen, for which Julianus himself had been responsible when he accepted the imperial power, came to everyone's mind. For when the consul-elect, in voting on Julianus, delivered

---

[4] The conventional attitude of suppliants.
[5] He was consul in 177.   [6] Cf. *Sev.*, v. 7.

nuntiasset: "Didium Iulianum imperatorem appel-
landum esse censeo," Iulianus suggessit "Adde et
Severum," quod cognon_entum avi [1] et proavi sibi
3 Iulianus adsciverat. sunt tamen qui dicant nullum
fuisse Iuliani consilium de obtruncando senatu, cum
tanta in eum senatus consuluisset.[2]

4 Post senatus consultum statim Didius Iulianus
5 unum ex praefectis, Tullium Crispinum, misit. ipse
autem tertium fecit praefectum Veturium Macrinum,
ad quem Severus litteras miserat, ut esset praefectus.
6 sed pacem simulatam esse mandatamque [3] caedem
Severi Tullio Crispino, praefecto praetorii, et populus
7 locutus est et Severus suspicatus. denique hostem
se Iuliano Severus esse maluit quam participem con-
8 sensu militum. Severus autem statim et ad plurimos
Romam scripsit et occulto misit edicta, quae proposita
9 sunt. fuit praeterea in Iuliano haec amentia, ut per
magos pleraque faceret, quibus putaret [4] vel odium
10 populi deleniri vel militum arma compesci. nam et
quasdam non convenientes Romanis sacris hostias im-
molaverunt et carmina profana incantaverunt, et ea
quae ad speculum dicunt [5] fieri, in quo pueri prae-
ligatis oculis incantato vertice respicere dicuntur,
11 Iulianus fecit. tuncque puer vidisse dicitur et adven-
tum Severi et Iuliani decessionem.

---

[1] *habui* P.   [2] *consuluisset* P; *contulisset* Peter.   [3] *mandatamque* Ursinus; *tantamque* P.   [4] *putaret* Egnatius;
uitaret P.   [5] *ducunt* P.

---

[1] This name appears in the inscription cited above (see note
to c. i. 4) and on some of his coins; see Cohen iii², p. 398 f.,
nos., 1, 3, 7, etc.
[2] *i.e.* to Severus, offering him a share of the empire.
[3] See note to *Hadr.*, ix. 5.

himself of the following: "I vote that Didius Julianus be declared emperor," Julianus prompted "Say also Severus," the name of his grandfather and great-grandfather, which he had added to his own.[1] However, there are some who say that Julianus never planned to slaughter the senate, because it had passed so many decrees in his favour.

After the senate had passed this decree, Didius Julianus forthwith despatched[2] one of the prefects, Tullius Crispinus, and he also created a third prefect[3] in the person of Veturius Macrinus, whom Severus had already notified by letter that he was to be prefect. Nevertheless, the people avowed and Severus suspected that this peace was merely a strategem and that Tullius Crispinus, the prefect of the guard, was commissioned to murder Severus. Finally, in accordance with the general wish of his soldiers, Severus declared that he would rather be Julianus' enemy than colleague ; he at once, moreover, wrote to a great number of men at Rome, and secretly sent proclamations, which were posted up. Julianus, furthermore, was mad enough to perform a number of rites with the aid of magicians, such as were calculated either to lessen the hate of the people or to restrain the arms of the soldiers. For the magicians sacrificed certain victims that are foreign to the Roman ritual[4] and chanted unholy songs, while Julianus performed rites, which took place, so we are told, before a mirror, into which boys are said to gaze, after bandages have been bound over their eyes and charms muttered over their heads. And in this performance one lad, it is said, saw the arrival of Severus and the retirement of Julianus.

[4] According to Dio, lxxiii. 16, 5, he sacrificed a number of children.

VIII. Et Crispinus quidem, cum occurrisset praecur-
soribus Severi, Iulio Laeto auctore a Severo interemp-
2 tus est. deiecta sunt etiam consulta senatus. Iulianus
convocato senatu quaesitisque sententiis, quid facto
3 opus esset, certi nihil comperit a senatu. sed postea
sponte sua gladiatores Capuae iussit armari per Lollianum Titianum, et Claudium Pompeianum e Tarraci-
nensi ad participatum evocavit, quod et gener imperatoris fuisset et diu militibus praefuisset. sed hoc ille
recusavit, senem se et debilem luminibus respondens.
4, 5 transierant et ex Umbria milites ad Severum. et
praemiserat quidem litteras Severus, quibus iubebat
interfectores Pertinacis servari.
6   Brevi autem desertus est ab omnibus Iulianus et
remansit in Palatio cum uno de praefectis suis Geniali
7 et genero Repentino. actum est denique ut Iuliano
senatus auctoritate abrogaretur imperium. et abroga-
tum est, appellatusque statim Severus imperator, cum
fingeretur quod veneno se[1] absumpsisset Iulianus.
8 missi tamen a senatu, quorum cura per militem
gregarium in Palatio idem Iulianus occisus est fidem
9 Caesaris implorans, hoc est Severi. filiam suam
potitus imperio dato patrimonio emancipaverat.

[1] *se* P; om. by Peter.

---

[1] See c. vii. 4.
[2] He was very old and in poor health. During the reign of
Pertinax he remained at Rome and attended meetings of the
senate, but when Pertinax was killed, he withdrew to his
country estate; see Dio, lxxiii. 3.
[3] See c. vi. 4 and note.
[4] Acting on this order the soldiers of the guard seized the
murderers and informed the consul of the fact; see Dio, lxxiii.
17, 3.
[5] Cf. c. iii. 6.

VIII. And as for Crispinus,[1] he met with Severus' advance-guard and was put to death by Severus on the advice of Julius Laetus. The decrees of the senate, moreover, were torn down, and when Julianus called a meeting of the senate and asked their opinions as to what should be done, he could get nothing definite out of them. Presently, however, on his own responsibility he ordered Lollianus Titianus to arm the gladiators at Capua, and called Claudius Pompeianus from his estate at Tarracina[2] to share the empire with him, because he had been an emperor's son-in-law and had long been in command of troops. Claudius, however, refused on the ground that he was now old and his eye-sight was weak. The soldiers in Umbria had meanwhile deserted to Severus,[3] and Severus had sent on letters in advance in which he ordered the murderers of Pertinax to be kept under guard.[4]

In a short time Julianus was deserted by all and left alone in the Palace with one of his prefects, Genialis, and with Repentinus, his son-in-law.[5] Finally, it was proposed that the imperial power be taken away from Julianus by order of the senate.[6] This was done, and Severus was forthwith acclaimed emperor, while it was given out that Julianus had taken poison. Nevertheless, the senate despatched a delegation and through their efforts Julianus was slain in the Palace by a common soldier, while beseeching the protection of Caesar, that is to say, Severus. He had emancipated[7] his daughter when he got control of the empire and had presented her with her patrimony, but this, together with the name

---

[6] A description of this meeting is given in Dio, lxxiii. 17, 4. See note to *Pert.*, xi. 12.

quod ei cum Augustae nomine statim sublatum est.
10 corpus eius a Severo uxori Manliae Scantillae ac filiae
ad sepulturam est redditum et in proavi monumenta
translatum miliario quinto Via Labicana.

IX. Obiecta sane sunt Iuliano haec : quod gulosus
fuisset, quod aleator, quod armis gladiatoriis exercitus esset, eaque omnia senex fecerit, cum antea
numquam adulescens his esset vitiis infamatus. obiecta est etiam superbia, cum ille etiam in imperio
2 fuisset humillimus. fuit autem contra humanissimus
ad convivia, benignissimus ad subcriptiones, modera-
tissimus ad libertatem.

3   Vixit annis quinquaginta sex mensibus quattuor.
imperavit mensibus duobus diebus quinque. reprehensum in eo praecipue, quod eos, quos regere
auctoritate sua debuerat, regendae rei publicae sibi
praesules ipse fecisset.

---

[1] This road ran S.E. from the city, joining the *Via Latina*
at Toleria. It took its name from the town of Labici, on the
northern slope of the Alban hills.
[2] See c. iii. 9 and note.
[3] Sixty years, according to Dio, lxxiii. 17, 5 ; this figure is

Augusta, was at once taken away from her.   His
body was, by order of Severus, delivered for burial
to his wife, Manlia Scantilla, and to his daughter,
and it was laid in the tomb of his great-grandfather
by the fifth mile-stone on the Labican Way.[1]

IX. These charges were brought against Julianus:
that he had been a glutton and a gambler; that he
had exercised with gladiatorial arms; and that he had
done all these things, moreover, when advanced in
years, and after escaping the stain of these vices in
his youth. The charge of pride was also brought
against him, although he had really been very unassum-
ing as emperor.[2] He was, moreover, very affable at
banquets, very courteous in the matter of petitions,
and very reasonable in the matter of granting liberty.

He lived fifty-six years[3] and four months. He
ruled two months and five days.[4] This particularly
was held to his discredit: that men whom he ought
to have kept under his own governance he appointed
as his officials for governing the state.

---

usually regarded as more correct than that given in the biography; accordingly, he was born in 133.

[4] Sixty-six days, according to Dio, *l.c.*   Accordingly, he
was killed on 1st June, 193.

SEVERUS

AELII SPARTIANI

I. Interfecto Didio Iuliano Severus Africa oriundus
2 imperium obtinuit. cui civitas Lepti, pater Geta,
maiores equites Romani ante civitatem omnibus
datam; mater Fulvia Pia, patrui magni [1] Aper et
Severus consulares, avus paternus Macer, maternus [2]
3 Fulvius Pius fuere. ipse natus est Erucio Claro bis et
4 Severo consulibus, VI idus Apriles. in prima pueritia,
priusquam Latinis Graecisque litteris imbueretur,
quibus eruditissimus fuit, nullum alium inter pueros
ludum nisi ad iudices exercuit, cum [3] ipse praelatis
fascibus ac securibus ordine puerorum circumstante [4]
5 sederet ac iudicaret. octavo decimo anno publice
declamavit. [5] postea studiorum causa Romam venit,

---

[1] *magni Aper* Madvig, Peter²; *magnaper* P; *Marcus Aper*
Peter¹.   [2] So Casaubon; *maternus Macer paternus* P, Peter.
[3] *eum* P¹.   [4] *circumstantes* P¹.   [5] *adclamauit* P.

---

[1] His full name was P. Septimius Geta, according to an
inscription found at Cirta in Africa; see *C.I.L.*, viii. 19493.

[2] Citizenship was granted to all the free inhabitants of the
Empire, except the Dediticii and the Latini Tuniani, by an
edict of Caracalla, Severus' son, in 212.

[3] Aper was consul in some year under Pius; Severus is
perhaps to be identified with the Severus who was consul in
155.

SEVERUS

BY

AELIUS SPARTIANUS

I. On the murder of Didius Julianus, Severus, a native of Africa, took possession of the empire. His native city was Leptis, his father was Geta ; [1] his ancestors were Roman knights before citizenship was made universal.[2] Fulvia Pia was his mother, Aper and Severus, both of consular rank,[3] his great-uncles. His father's father was Macer, his mother's father Fulvius Pius. He himself was born six days before the Ides of April,[4] in the first consulship of Severus and the second of Erucius Clarus. While still a child, even before he had been drilled in the Latin and Greek literatures (with which he was very well acquainted), he would engage in no game with the other children except playing judge, and on such occasions he would have the rods and axes borne before him, and, surrounded by the throng of children, he would take his seat and thus give judgments. In his eighteenth year he delivered an oration in public. Soon after, in order to continue his studies, he came to Rome ; and with the support of his kins-

8 Apr.,
146

---

[4] His birthday was the 11th April, according to Dio, lxxvi. 17, 4, and this date is confirmed by the Calendar of Philocalus (see *C.I.L.*, i², p. 262) and by inscriptions set up on this day ; see *C.I.L.*, xi. 1322 ; xiv. 168 and 169.

latum clavum a divo Marco petiit et accepit, favente
sibi Septimio Severo adfini suo, bis iam consulari.

6 Cum Romam venisset, hospitem nanctus qui
Hadriani vitam imperatoriam eadem hora legeret,
7 quod sibi omen futurae felicitatis arripuit. habuit
et aliud omen imperii : cum rogatus ad cenam imperatoriam palliatus venisset, qui togatus venire
debuerat, togam praesidiariam ipsius imperatoris ac-
8 cepit. eadem nocte somniavit lupae se uberibus ut
9 Remum inhaerere vel Romulum. sedit et in sella
imperatoria temere a ministro posita, ignarus quod
10 non liceret. dormienti etiam in stabulo serpens
caput cinxit et sine noxa expergefactis et adclamanti-
bus familiaribus, abiit.[1]

II. Iuventam plenam furorum, nonnumquam et cri-
2 minum habuit. adulterii causam dixit absolutusque
est a Iuliano proconsule, cui et in proconsulatu successit et in consulatu collega fuit et in imperio item
3 successit. quaesturam diligenter egit omisso tribunatu[2] militari. post quaesturam sorte Baeticam accepit atque inde Africam petiit, ut mortuo patre rem
4 domesticam componeret. sed dum in Africa est,

---

[1] *habuit* P.   [2] *omisso tribunatu* Hirschfeld, Golisch,
Peter[2] ; *omnis sortibus natu* P.

---

[1] See note to *Com.*, iv. 7.   [2] See *Hadr.*, xxii. 2.
[3] It is impossible to know who is meant here. The biographer is certainly wrong in identifying him with Didius
Julianus, who was proconsul of Africa after Pertinax and
shortly before his own elevation to the throne; see *Did. Jul.*,
ii. 3.

man Septimius Severus, who had already been consul twice, he sought and secured from the Deified
Marcus the broad stripe.[1]

Soon after he had come to Rome he fell in with
a stranger who at that very moment was reading the
life of the Emperor Hadrian, and he snatched at this
incident as an omen of future prosperity. He had
still another omen of empire: for once, when he
was invited to an imperial banquet and came wearing
a cloak, when he should have worn his toga,[2] he was
lent an official toga of the emperor's own. And that
same night he dreamed that he tugged at the udders
of a wolf, like Remus and Romulus. He sat down,
furthermore, in the emperor's chair, which a servant
had carelessly left accessible, being quite unaware
that this was not allowed. And once, while he was
sleeping in a tavern, a snake coiled about his head,
and when his friends awoke from their sleep and
shouted at it, it departed without doing him any harm.

II. His early manhood was filled with follies and
not free from crime. He was charged with adultery,
but pleaded his own case and was acquitted by the
proconsul Julianus,[3] the man who was his immediate
predecessor in the proconsulship, his colleague in the
consulship, and likewise his predecessor on the
throne. Omitting the office of tribune of the soldiers,
he became quaestor and performed his duties with
diligence. At the expiration of his quaestorship he
was allotted the province of Baetica,[4] and from here
he crossed over to Africa in order to settle his

[4] He was quaestor in Rome and was then allotted to serve as
quaestor (properly proquaestor) of the senatorial province of
Hispania Baetica. Such double quaestorships appear frequently in inscriptions.

pro Baetica Sardinia ei attributa est, quod Baeticam
5 Mauri populabantur. acta igitur quaestura Sardini-
6 ensi legationem proconsulis Africae accepit. in qua
legatione cum eum quidam municipum suorum Lepti-
tanus [1] praecedentibus fascibus ut antiquum contu-
bernalem ipse plebeius amplexus esset, fustibus eum
sub eiusmodi elogio [2] praeconis cecidit : " Legatum
populi Romani homo plebeius temere amplecti noli ".
7 ex quo factum ut in vehiculo etiam legati sederent,
8 qui ante pedibus ambulabant. tunc in quadam
civitate Africana, cum sollicitus mathematicum consuluisset, positaque hora ingentia vidisset astrologus,
dixit ei : " Tuam non alienam pone genituram ".
9 cumque Severus iurasset suam esse, omnia ei dixit
quae postea facta sunt.

III. Tribunatum plebis Marco imperatore decern-
ente promeruit eumque severissime exsertissimeque
2 egit. uxorem tunc Marciam duxit, de qua tacuit in
historia vitae privatae. cui postea in imperio statuas
3 conlocavit. praetor designatus a Marco est non in

---

[1] bracketed by Peter[2].　　[2] *eiusmodi elogio* Hirschfeld;
elogio eiusdem P, Peter.

---

[1] See *Marc.*, xxi. 1. The year was about 172, since Severus
was quaestor probably about the normal age of twenty-five ;
see note to *Pius.*, vi. 10. The invasion of the Moors seems to
have made it necessary to administer Baetica as an imperial
province, and Sardinia was accordingly temporarily assigned
to the senate as a substitute.

[2] Her name was Paccia Marciana, according to an inscription from Africa ; see *C.I.L.*, viii. 19494 = Dessau, *Ins. Sel.*,
440.

[3] *i.e.* his autobiography, written after the death of Albinus,

374

domestic affairs, for his father had meanwhile died.
But while he was in Africa, Sardinia was assigned him
in place of Baetica, because the latter was being
ravaged by the Moors.[1]   He therefore served his
quaestorship in Sardinia, and afterwards was appointed
aide to the proconsul of Africa.   While he was in this
office, a certain fellow-townsman of his, a plebeian,
embraced him as an old comrade, though the fasces
were being carried before him ; whereupon he had
the fellow beaten with clubs and then ordered a proclamation to be made by the herald to this effect :
"Let no plebeian embrace without due cause a legate
of the Roman people".   On account of this incident,
legates, who had previously gone on foot, thereafter
rode in carriages.   About this time, also, being
worried about the future, he had recourse to an
astrologer in a certain city of Africa.   The astrologer,
when he had cast the horoscope, saw high destinies in
store for him, but added : "Tell me your own
nativity and not that of another man".   And when
Severus swore an oath that it was really his, the
astrologer revealed to him all the things that did
later come to pass.

III. He was promoted to be tribune of the plebs by
order of the Emperor Marcus, and he performed his
duties with austerity and vigour.   It was then that
he married Marcia,[2] but of her he made no mention
in the history of his life as a private man.[3]   Afterwards, however, while emperor, he erected statues in
her honour.   In the thirty-second year of his life 178
Marcus appointed him praetor, although he was not

apparently with the purpose of accusing his rivals and clear-
ing himself of charges of cruelty ; see c. xviii. 6; *Cl. Alb.*,
vii. 1 ; Dio, lxxv. 7, 3.

candida sed in competitorum grege anno aetatis
4 xxxii. tunc ad Hispaniam missus somniavit primo
sibi dici, ut templum Tarraconense Augusti, quod
5 iam labebatur,[1] restitueret. dein ex altissimi montis
vertice orbem terrarum Romamque despexit, con-
cinentibus provinciis lyra voce vel tibiâ. ludos absens
6 edidit. legioni iiii Scythicae dein praepositus est
7 circa Massiliam. post hoc Athenas petiit studiorum
sacrorumque causa et operum ac vetustatum. ubi
cum iniurias quasdam ab Atheniensibus pertulisset,
inimicus his factus minuendo eorum privilegia iam
8 imperator se ultus est. dein Lugdunensem provin-
9 ciam legatus accepit. cum amissa uxore aliam vellet
ducere, genituras sponsarum requirebat, ipse quoque
matheseos peritissimus, et cum audisset esse in Syria
quandam quae id geniturae haberet ut regi iungere-
tur, eandem uxorem petiit, Iuliam scilicet, et accepit
interventu amicorum. ex qua statim pater factus
IV. est. a Gallis ob severitatem et honorificentiam et
abstinentiam tantum quantum nemo dilectus est.

[1] *leuabatur* P.

---

[1] A certain number of each board of magistrates were not
chosen by the senate but nominated directly by the emperor.
These appointees were called technically *candidati Caesaris*,
and the phrase *in candida* (*toga*) seems to be only a variation
of this expression.

[2] See *Hadr.*, xii. 3 and note.

[3] In the time of the empire the conduct of the public games
was one of the most important functions of the praetor.

[4] There is some error here, for this legion was never
quartered at Marseilles, and from the middle of the first
century on it was stationed in Syria.

one of the Emperor's candidates but only one of the
ordinary crowd of competitors.[1]   He was thereupon
sent to Spain, and here he had a dream, first that he
was told to repair the temple of Augustus at Tarraco,[2]
which at that time was falling into ruin, and then
that from the top of a very high mountain he beheld
Rome and all the world, while the provinces sang
together to the accompaniment of the lyre and
flute.   Though absent from the city, he gave games.[3]
Presently he was put in command of the Fourth
Legion, the Scythica, stationed near Massilia,[4] and
after that he proceeded to Athens—partly in order
to continue his studies and perform certain sacred
rites, and partly on account of the public buildings
and ancient monuments there.   Here he suffered
certain wrongs at the hands of the Athenians ; and
on that account he became their foe, and afterwards,
as emperor, took vengeance on them by curtailing
their rights.   After this he was appointed to the
province of Lugdunensis as legate.   He had meanwhile lost his wife, and now, wishing to take another,
he made inquiries about the horoscopes of marriage-
able women, being himself no mean astrologer ; and
when he learned that there was a woman in Syria
whose horoscope predicted that she would wed a king
(I mean Julia,[5] of course), he sought her for his wife,
and through the mediation of his friends secured her.
By her, presently, he became a father.[6]   IV. And
because he was strict, honourable and self-restrained,
he was beloved by the Gauls as was no one else.

[5] Julia Domna, the elder daughter of Julius Bassianus,
high-priest of the god Elagabalus at Emesa in Syria.
[6] His elder son Bassianus (Caracalla) was born at Lyons on
the 4th April, 186.

SEVERUS

Dein Pannonias proconsulari imperio rexit. post hoc Siciliam proconsularem sorte meruit. suscepitque 3 Romae alterum filium. in Sicilia, quasi de imperio vel vates vel Chaldaeos consuluisset, reus factus, sed [1] a praefectis praetorii, quibus audiendus datus fuerat, iam Commodo in odio veniente, absolutus est calum- 4 niatore in crucem acto. consulatum cum Apuleio Rufino primum egit, Commodo se inter plurimos designante. post consulatum anno ferme fuit otio- sus ; dein Laeto suffragante exercitui Germanico [2] 5 praeponitur. proficiscens ad Germanicos exercitus hortos spatiosos comparavit, cum antea aedes brevis- simas Romae habuisset et unum fundum in Venetia. 6 et iam [3] in his hortis cum humi iacens epularetur cum filiis parca cena, pomaque adposita maior filius, qui tunc quinquennis erat, conlusoribus puerulis manu largiore divideret, paterque illum reprehendens dixis- set, " Parcius divide, non enim regias opes possides," quinquennis puer respondit, " Sed possidebo " inquit. 7 in Germaniam profectus ita se in ea legatione egit, ut famam nobilitatam [4] iam ante cumularet.

[1] *sed* Peter; *et* P.   [2] *Germanico* Baehrens, Peter[2]; *Germano* P, Peter[1].   [3] *in Venetia* Salmasius; *et iam* Editor; *inuenit etiam* P; *in uicinia* Peter.   [4] *nobilitatem* P.

---

[1] This item is out of its proper order. He was not appointed to Pannonia until after his consulship ; see § 4.
[2] Geta, born in 189, the year, as it seems, of Severus' consulship ; see *Get.*, iii. 1.
[3] Under the régime of Cleander ; see *Com.*, vi. 7 f. ; vii. 1.

Next he ruled the Pannonias[1] with proconsular powers, and after this he drew in the allotment the proconsular province of Sicily. At Rome, meanwhile, he was presented with a second son.[2] While he was in Sicily he was indicted for consulting about the imperial dignity with seers and astrologers, but, because Commodus was now beginning to be detested,[3] he was acquitted by the prefects of the guard to whom he had been handed over for trial, while his accuser was crucified. He now served his first consulship, having Apuleius Rufinus[4] for his colleague—an office to which Commodus appointed him from among a large number of aspirants. After the consulship he spent about a year free from public duties; then, on the recommendation of Laetus, he was put in charge of the army in Germany.[5] Just as he was setting out for Germany, he acquired elaborate gardens, although he had previously kept only an unpretentious dwelling in the city and a single farm in Venetia. And now, when he was reclining on the ground in these gardens, partaking of a frugal supper with his children, his elder son, who was then five years old, divided the fruit, when it was served, with rather a bounteous hand among his young playmates. And when his father reproved him, saying: " Be more sparing; for you have not the riches of a king," the five-year-old child replied : " No, but I shall have ". On coming to Germany, Severus conducted himself in this office in such a manner as to increase a reputation which was already illustrious.

[4] His name is given as Vitellius in *Get.*, iii. 1.

[5] An error for Pannonia (cf. § 2), for he was acclaimed emperor at Carnuntum (see c. v. 1); see also Dio, lxiii. 14, 3 and Herodian, ii. 9, 2.

V. Et hactenus rem militarem privatus egit. dehinc a Germanicis legionibus, ubi auditum est Commodum occisum, Iulianum autem cum odio cunctorum imperare, multis hortantibus repugnans imperator est 2appellatus apud Carnuntum idibus Augustis. qui etiam sestertia, quot [1] nemo umquam principum, 3militibus dedit. dein firmatis quas post tergum relinquebat provinciis Romam iter [2] contendit, cedentibus sibi cunctis, quacumque iter fecit, cum iam Illyriciani exercitus et Gallicani [3] cogentibus ducibus 4in eius verba iurassent. excipiebatur enim ab omni-5bus quasi ultor Pertinacis. per idem tempus auctore Iuliano Septimius Severus a senatu hostis est appellatus, legatis ad exercitum senatus verbis missis, qui iuberent ut ab eo milites senatu praecipiente dis-6cederent. et Severus quidem cum audisset senatus consentientis auctoritate missos legatos, primo pertimuit, postea id egit corruptis legatis, ut apud exercitum pro se loquerentur transirentque in eius 7partes. his compertis Iulianus senatus consultum [4] 8fieri fecit de participando imperio cum Severo. incertum vere id an dolo fecerit, cum iam ante misis-set [5]notos ducum interfectores quosdam, qui Severum

---

[1] *quot* Rühl; *quod* P, Peter.   [2]*iter* Peter; *item* P.
[3]*gallicanis* P.   [4] *consulatum* P[1].   [5] *misissent* P.

---

[1] Cf. *Did. Jul.*, iv. 2 f.
[2] An error, for Didius Julianus was killed on the 1st June (see note to *Did. Jul.*, ix. 3), and Severus was then not far from Rome. The date was probably the Ides of April.
[3] *i.e.* each legionary.
[4] Used inexactly to denote the armies of the Danube and the Rhine. His coins of 193 show the names of fifteen different legions belonging to these armies (see Cohen iv[2], p. 31 f., nos. 255-278). To these is to be added the Tenth

V. So far did he pursue his military career as a subject. Now, when it was learned that Commodus had been slain and that Julianus was holding the throne amid general hatred,[1] at the behest of many, but against his own will, he was hailed emperor by the German legions; this took place at Carnuntum on the Ides of August.[2] A thousand sesterces—a sum which no prince had ever given before—were presented to each soldier.[3] And then, after garrisoning the provinces which he was leaving in his rear, he hastened his march on Rome. Wherever his path lay, all yielded to him, and the legions in Illyricum and Gaul [4] had already, under compulsion from their generals, espoused his cause, for he was universally regarded as the avenger of Pertinax. Meanwhile, at Julianus' instigation, the senate declared him a public enemy,[5] and legates were sent to his army with a message from the senate ordering his soldiers in the name of the senate to desert him.[6] And in truth, when Severus heard that legates had been sent by unanimous order of the senate, he was at first terrified; afterwards, however, he managed to bribe the legates to address the army in his favour and then to desert to his side themselves.[7] When Julianus learned of this, he caused the senate to pass a decree that Severus and he should share the throne.[8] Whether this was done in good faith or treacherously is not clear; for already, ere this, Julianus had sent certain fellows, notorious assassins of generals, to murder Severus,[9] and indeed he had sent men

13 Aug.,
193

Legion, the Gemina, stationed in Pannonia Superior, of which, as it happens, no coin has been preserved.

[5] Cf. *Did. Jul.*, v. 3.   [6] Cf. *Did. Jul.*, v. 5.
[7] Cf. *Did. Jul.*, vi. 3.   [8] Cf. *Did. Jul.*, vi. 9.
[9] Cf. *Did. Jul.*, v. 8; *Pesc. Nig.*, ii. 6.

occiderent, ita ut ad Pescennium Nigrum interficien-
dum miserat, qui et ipse imperium contra eum
9 susceperat auctoribus Syriacis exercitibus. verum
Severus evitatis eorum manibus quos ad se interficien-
dum Iulianus miserat, missis ad praetorianos litteris
signum vel deserendi vel occidendi Iuliani dedit
10 statimque auditus est. nam et Iulianus occisus est
11 in Palatio, et Severus Romam invitatus. ita, quod
nulli umquam contigit, nutu tantum Severus victor
est factus armatusque Romam contendit.

VI. Occiso Iuliano cum Severus in castris et tentoriis
quasi per hosticum veniens adhuc maneret, centum
senatores legatos ad eum senatus misit ad gratulan-
2 dum rogandumque. qui ei occurrerunt Interamnae
armatumque circumstantibus armatis salutarunt, ex-
3 cussi ne quid ferri haberent. et postera die occur-
4 rente omni famulicio aulico, septingenos [1] vicenos
aureos legatis dedit eosdemque praemisit, facta
potestate si qui vellent remanere ac secum Romam
5 redire. fecit etiam statim praefectum praetorii
Flavium Iuvenalem, quem etiam Iulianus tertium
praefectum sibi adsumpserat.

---

[1] *septingenos* Hirschfeld; *septuagenos* P, Peter.

---

[1] Cf. *Did. Jul.*, v. 1; *Pesc. Nig.*, ii. 4.
[2] Cf. *Pesc. Nig.* ii. 1.　　　[3] Cf. *Did. Jul.*, viii. 5 f.
[4] Hirschfeld points out that through the use of base metal
the denarius had so depreciated that 25,000 den. (100,000
sesterces) was now equal to only 720 aurei instead of 1000.
Accordingly, the sum that was presented to each of the

to murder Pescennius Niger as well,[1] who, at the
instigation of the armies in Syria,[2] had also declared
himself emperor in opposition to Julianus. However, Severus escaped the clutches of the men whom
Julianus had sent to kill him and despatched a letter
to the guard instructing them either to desert
Julianus or to kill him; and his order was immediately obeyed.[3] For not only was Julianus slain
in the Palace, but Severus was invited to Rome.
And so, by the mere nod of his head, Severus became
the victor—a thing that had befallen no man ever
before—and still under arms hastened towards Rome.

VI. After the murder of Julianus Severus still remained encamped and in his tents as though he were
advancing through a hostile territory; the senate,
therefore, sent a delegation of a hundred senators to
bear him congratulations and sue for pardon. 'And
when these met him at Interamna, they were searched
for concealed weapons and only then suffered to greet
him as he stood armed and in the midst of armed
men. But on the following day, after all the palace
attendants had arrived, he presented each member of
the delegation with seven hundred and twenty pieces
of gold,[4] and sent them on ahead, granting to such as
desired, however, the privilege of remaining and returning to Rome with himself. Without further delay, he appointed as prefect of the guard that Flavius
Juvenalis whom Julianus had chosen for his third
prefect.[5]

legates was the equivalent of 100,000 sesterces reckoned according to the later standard. See von Domaszewski in *Rhein.
Mus.*, liv. (1899), p. 312.
    [5] Probably on the death of Tullius Crispinus; see *Did. Jul.*,
viii. 1.

6 Interim Romae ingens trepidatio militum civium-
que, quod armatus contra eos Severus veniret, qui
7 se hostem iudicassent. his accessit quod comperit
Pescennium Nigrum a Syriacis legionibus imperatorem
8 appellatum. cuius edicta et litteras ad populum vel
senatum intercepit per eos qui missi fuerant, ne vel
9 proponerentur populo vel legerentur in curia. eodem
tempore etiam de Clodio Albino sibi substituendo
cogitavit, cui Caesareanum decretum auctore Com-
10 modo iam [1] videbatur imperium. sed eos ipsos per-
timescens de [2] quibus recte iudicabat,[3] Heraclitum ad
obtinendas Britannias, Plautianum ad occupandos
11 Nigri liberos misit. cum Romam Severus venisset,
praetorianos cum subarmalibus inermes sibi iussit
occurrere. eosdem sic ad tribunal vocavit armatis
undique circumdatis.

VII. Ingressus deinde Romam armatus cum armatis
militibus Capitolium ascendit. inde in [4] Palatium
eodem habitu perrexit, praelatis signis quae praeto-
2 rianis ademerat supinis non erectis. tota deinde urbe

---

[1] *auctore Commodo iam nomen* Oberdick; *nomen* om. by
Editor; *aut Commodianum* P.   [2] so Peter[1]; *pertimescende*
P; *pertimescendo* P corr., Peter[2].   [3] *iudicabat* P, Peter[1];
inuidebat Peter[2].   [4] om. in P.

---

[1] Cf. *Cl. Alb.*, ii. 1; vi. 4-5; xiii. 4. This is doubtless a
fiction.

[2] Or Bithynia, according to *Pesc. Nig.*, v. 2, but the reading
Britannias is probably the correct one. About this time
Severus, in order to attach Albinus to his cause, offered him
the name Caesar (see note to *Cl. Alb.*, i. 2), and Heraclitus
may have been sent for this purpose.

[3] Cf. *Pesc. Nig.*, v. 2. On C. Fulvius Plautianus see c. xiv.
5 f.

[4] He then reproached them for their treachery to Pertinax,

Meanwhile at Rome a mighty panic seized both soldiers and civilians, for they realized that Severus was advancing under arms and against those who had declared him a public enemy. The excitement was further increased when Severus learned that Pescennius Niger had been hailed emperor by the legions in Syria. However, the proclamations and letters that Pescennius sent to the people and senate were, with the connivance of the messengers who had been sent with them, intercepted by Severus, for he wished to prevent their being published among the people or read in the senate-house. At the same time, too, he considered abdicating in favour of Clodius Albinus, to whom, it appeared, the power of a Caesar [1] had already been decreed at the instance of Commodus. But instead, he sent Heraclitus to secure Britain [2] and Plautianus to seize Niger's children,[3] in fear of these men and having formed a correct opinion about them. And when he arrived at Rome, he ordered the guard to meet him clad only in their undergarments and without arms; then, with armed men posted all about him, he summoned them, thus apparelled, to the tribunal.[4]

VII. Severus, armed himself and attended by armed men, entered the city and went up to the Capitol ; [5] thence he proceeded, still fully armed, to the Palace, having the standards, which he had taken from the praetorians, borne before him not raised erect but trailing on the ground. And then throughout the whole

disarmed and disbanded them, and banished them from the city ; see Dio, lxxiv. 1, 1 and Herodian, ii. 13, 4 f. This took place just outside the walls.

[5] A vivid description of his triumphal entry is given in Dio, lxxiv. 1, 3-5.

milites in templis, in porticibus, in aedibus Palatinis,
3 quasi in stabulis manserunt, fuitque ingressus Severi
odiosus atque terribilis, cum milites inempta diripe-
4 rent, vastationem urbi minantes. alia die armatis
stipatus non solum militibus sed etiam amicis in
senatum venit. in curia reddidit rationem suscepti
imperii causatusque est, quod ad se occidendum
5 Iulianus notos ducum caedibus misisset. fieri etiam
senatus consultum coegit, ne liceret imperatori in-
6 consulto senatu occidere senatorem. sed cum in
senatu esset, milites per seditionem dena milia
poposcerunt a senatu, exemplo eorum qui Augustum
Octavianum Romam deduxerant tantumque accepe-
7 rant. et cum eos voluisset comprimere Severus nec
potuisset, tamen mitigatos addita liberalitate dimisit.
8 funus deinde censorium Pertinacis imagini duxit
eumque inter divos sacravit, addito flamine et soda-
9 libus Helvianis, qui Marciani fuerant. se quoque

---

[1] Cf. c. v. 8 ; *Did. Jul.*, v. 8 ; *Pesc. Nig.*, ii. 5.
[2] So also Dio, lxxiv. 2, 1 and Herodian, ii. 14, 3-4. Dio ob-
serves that Severus violated this decree almost at once.
[3] See Dio, xlvi. 46.
[4] He gave to each one thousand sesterces ; see Dio, *ibid.*
[5] This funeral is described in detail in Dio, lxxiv. 4-5.
[6] A survival of the republican period, when the senate frequently honoured a dead ex-magistrate by decreeing that he
might be buried in his robe of office. Of these robes the
purple toga of the censor was considered the highest, and a
funus censorium was, accordingly, the most honourable type
of public funeral. It was later accorded by vote of the senate
to emperors, *e.g.* to Augustus (Tacitus, *Annals.*, xii. 69) and to
Claudius (*id.*, xiii. 2).
[7] See note to *Marc.*, xv. 4 ; see also *Pert.*, xv. 3-4.

city, in temples, in porticoes, and in the dwellings on
the Palatine, the soldiers took up their quarters as
though in barracks; and Severus' entry inspired both
hate and fear, for the soldiers seized goods they did
not pay for and threatened to lay the city waste.   On
the next day, accompanied not only by armed soldiers
but also by a body of armed friends, Severus appeared
before the senate, and there, in the senate-house,
gave his reasons for assuming the imperial power,
alleging in defence thereof that men notorious for
assassinating generals had been sent by Julianus to
murder him.[1]   He secured also the passage of a
senatorial decree to the effect that the emperor should
not be permitted to put any senator to death without
first consulting the senate.[2]   But while he was still
in the senate-house, his soldiers, with threats of
mutiny, demanded of the senate ten thousand sesterces each, citing the precedent of those who had
conducted Augustus Octavian to Rome and received a
similar sum.[3]   And although Severus himself desired
to repress them, he found himself unable; eventually,
however, by giving them a bounty he managed to appease them and then sent them away.[4]   Thereupon
he held for an effigy of Pertinax[5] a funeral such as is
given a censor,[6] elevated him to a place among the
deified emperors and gave him, besides, a flamen
and a Helvian Brotherhood, composed of the priests
who had previously constituted the Marcian Brotherhood.[7]   Moreover, he himself was, at his own command, given the name Pertinax;[8] although later he

[8] According to Herodian, ii. 10, 1, he assumed this name before he left Pannonia.   It appears in his inscriptions and on
his coins, especially those issued during the first part of his
reign.

Pertinacem vocari iussit, quamvis postea id nomen aboleri voluerit quasi[1] omen.

VIII. Amicorum dehinc aes alienum[2] dissolvit. filias suas dotatas maritis Probo et Aetio dedit. et cum Probo genero suo praefecturam urbi obtulisset, ille recusavit dixitque minus sibi videri praefectum 2 esse quam principis generum. utrumque autem gen-3 erum statim consulem fecit, utrumque ditavit. alia die ad senatum venit et amicos Iuliani incusatos pro-4 scriptioni ac neci dedit. causas plurimas audivit. accusatos a provincialibus iudices probatis rebus 5 graviter punivit. rei frumentariae, quam minimam reppererat, ita consuluit, ut excedens vita septem annorum canonem populo Romano relinqueret.

6 Ad orientis statum confirmandum profectus est, 7 nihil adhuc de Nigro palam dicens. ad Africam tamen legiones misit, ne per Libyam atque Aegyptum Niger Africam occuparet ac populo Romano penuria 8 rei frumentariae perurgueret. Domitium Dextrum in locum Bassi praefectum[3] urbi reliquit atque intra triginta dies quam Romam venerat est profectus. 9 egressus ab urbe ad Saxa Rubra seditionem ingentem ob locum castrorum metandorum ab exercitu passus 10 est. occurrit ei et statim Geta frater suus, quem

[1] *quae* P.   [2] *alienos* P.   [3] *praefectum* Mommsen; *praefecti* P.

---

[1] Cf. *Pesc. Nig.*, v. 4 f.

[2] Before setting out he gave largess; see the coins of 193 with the legend *Liberalitas Aug(usti)*; Cohen, iv², p. 32 f., nos. 279-287.

[3] On the Via Flaminia, about ten miles north of Rome.

[4] P. Septimius Geta. His province was probably Dacia, of which he was governor in 195; see *C.I.L.*, iii. 905.

wished it withdrawn, for fear that it would prove an omen.

VIII. Next he freed his friends from debt. He then settled dowries on his daughters and gave them in marriage to Probus and Aetius. As for his son-in-law Probus, when he offered to make him prefect of the city, Probus declined, averring that it meant less to him to be prefect of the city than son-in-law to the emperor. However, he immediately appointed each of them consul and made each rich. Soon there- ? 193 after he appeared before the senate, and bringing in accusations against the friends of Julianus, caused them to be outlawed and put to death. He heard a vast number of lawsuits, and magistrates who had been accused by the provincials he punished severely whenever the accusations against them were proved; and finding the grain-supply at a very low ebb, he managed it so well that on departing this life he left the Roman people a surplus to the amount of seven years' tribute.

And now he set out to remedy the situation in the July, 193 East, still making no public mention of Niger. None the less, however, he sent troops to Africa, for fear that Niger might advance through Libya and Egypt and seize this province, and thereby distress the Roman people with a scarcity of grain.[1] Then, leaving Domitius Dexter as prefect of the city in place of Bassus, within thirty days of his coming to Rome he set out again;[2] and he had proceeded from the city no farther than Saxa Rubra[3] when he had to face a great mutiny in his army, which arose on account of the place selected for pitching camp. Then his brother Geta[4] came at once to meet him, but merely received orders to rule the province already

389

provinciam sibi creditam regere praecepit[1] aliud
11 sperantem. Nigri liberos ad se adductos in eo habuit
12 honore quo suos. miserat sane legionem, quae
Graeciam Thraciamque praeciperet, ne eas Pescennius
13 occuparet. sed iam Byzantium Niger tenebat. Per-
inthum etiam Niger volens occupare plurimos de
exercitu interfecit atque ideo hostis cum Aemiliano
14 est appellatus. cumque Severum ad participatum
15 vocaret, contemptus est. promisit sane Nigro tutum
exsilium, si vellet, Aemiliano autem non ignovit.
16 Aemilianus dehinc victus in Hellesponto a Severi
ducibus Cyzicum primum confugit atque inde in
aliam civitatem, in qua eorum iussu occisus est.
17 fusae sunt item copiae ab iisdem ducibus etiam Nigri.
IX. his auditis ad senatum Severus quasi confectis rebus
litteras misit. dein conflixit cum Nigro eumque apud
Cyzicum interemit caputque eius pilo circumtulit.
2 filios Nigri post hoc, quos suorum liberorum cultu
habuerat, in exsilium cum matre misit.
3 Litteras ad senatum de victoria dedit. neque

[1] *accepit* P.

---

[1] See c. vi. 10 and ix. 2.
[2] Asellius Aemilianus, the proconsul of Asia and commander
of Niger's army.
[3] See *Pesc. Nig.*, v. 6-7.
[4] This was after the defeat at Perinthus (§ 16); see *Pesc.
Nig.*, v. 8.
[5] Probably at Perinthus on the Propontis.
[6] Near Nicaea in Bithynia; see Dio, lxxiv. 6, 5 f.
[7] This is an error, repeated in *Pesc. Nig.*, v. 8. Niger was
finally defeated near Issus in Cilicia; see Dio, lxxiv. 7 and
Herodian, iii. 4, 2 f. The date has recently been determined

in his charge, though Geta had other hopes. Niger's children, who were brought to him, he treated with the same care that he showed his own.[1] Previous to this, he had sent a legion to occupy Greece and Thrace, and thereby prevent Niger from seizing them. But Niger already held Byzantium, and now wishing to seize Perinthus too, he slew a great number of this force and accordingly, together with Aemilianus,[2] was declared an enemy to the state.[3] He next proposed joint rule with Severus; this was rejected with scorn. As a matter of fact, Severus did promise him an unmolested exile if he wished it,[4] but refused to pardon Aemilianus. Soon thereafter Aemilianus was defeated by Severus' generals at the Hellespont[5] and fled first to Cyzicus and from there to another city, and here he was put to death by order of Severus' generals. Niger's own forces, moreover, were routed by the same generals.[6]
IX. On receipt of this news Severus despatched letters to the senate as if the whole affair were finished. And not long afterwards he met with Niger near Cyzicus,[7] slew him, and paraded his head on a pike. Niger's children, whom he had maintained in the same state as his own,[8] he sent into exile after this event, together with their mother.

He sent a letter to the senate announcing the victory,[9] but he inflicted no punishment upon any of

as the close of 193. Niger fled but was overtaken by some of Severus' soldiers between Antioch and the Euphrates and beheaded; see Dio, lxxiv. 8, 3.

[8] See c. viii. 11. They were afterwards put to death; see c. x. 1 and *Pesc. Nig.*, vi. 1-2.

[9] He was acclaimed *Imperator* for the third time; see the coins of 194 with the legends *Mars Pacator* and *Paci Augusti*, Cohen, iv^2, p. 35, no. 308, and p. 40, no. 359.

quemquam senatorum qui Nigri partium fuerant
4 praeter unum supplicio adfecit. Antiochensibus ira-
tior fuit, quod et administrantem se in oriente[1]
5 riserant et Nigrum etiam victu[2] iuverant. denique
multa his ademit. Neapolitanis etiam Palaestinensi-
bus ius civitatis tulit, quod pro Nigro diu in armis
6 fuerunt. in multos saeve[3] animadvertit, praeter or-
7 dinem senatorium, qui Nigrum fuerant secuti. multas etiam civitates eiusdem partis iniuriis adfecit et
8 damnis. eos senatores occidit qui cum Nigro mili-
taverant ducum vel tribunorum nomine.

9 Deinde circa Arabiam plura gessit, Parthis etiam
in dicionem redactis nec non etiam Adiabenis, qui
10 quidem omnes cum Pescennio senserant. atque ob
hoc reversus triumpho delato appellatus est Arabicus
11 Adiabenicus Parthicus. sed triumphum respuit, ne
videretur de civili triumphare victoria. excusavit et
Parthicum nomen, ne Parthos lacesseret.

X. Redeunti sane Romam post bellum civile Nigri

---

[1] *orientem* P, Peter. [2] *uictum* Peter[2] with P. [3] *saeue*
Peter; *se* P.

---

[1] See c. vii. 5. This statement is confirmed by Dio; see
lxxiv. 8, 4.
[2] Niger's head appears on a coin of Colonia Aelia Capitolina
(Jerusalem); see Cohen, iii[3], p. 413, no. 82.
[3] Notably Byzantium, which his army captured after a long
siege; see Dio, lxxiv. 14, 3.
[4] The campaign actually took place in northern Mesopotamia, in the neighbourhood of Nisibis, which had been
invaded by the surrounding tribes. Most of the fighting
seems to have been done under the command of the legates,
Laetus, Anulinus, and Probus, who crossed the Tigris and invaded Adiabene; see Dio, lxxv. 1-3.
[5] In the inscriptions and on the coins of this period he is

the senators who had sided with Niger,[1] with the exception of one man. Towards the citizens of Antioch he was more resentful, because they had laughed at him in his administration of the East and also had aided Niger with supplies. Eventually he deprived them of many privileges. The citizens of Neapolis in Palestine, because they had long been in arms on Niger's side,[2] he deprived of all their civic rights, and to many individuals, other than members of the senatorial order, who had followed Niger he meted out cruel punishments. Many communities,[3] too, which had been on Niger's side, were punished with fines and degradation ; and such senators as had seen active service on Niger's side with the title of general or tribune were put to death.

Next, he engaged in further operations in the region about Arabia [4] and brought the Parthians back to allegiance and also the Adiabeni—all of whom had sided with Pescennius. For this exploit, after he returned home, he was given a triumph and the names Arabicus, Adiabenicus, and Parthicus.[5] He refused the triumph, however, lest he seem to triumph for a victory over Romans ; and he declined the name Parthicus lest he hurt the Parthians' feelings.

X. And then, just as he was returning to Rome after the civil war caused by Niger, he received news 196

called *Arabicus Adiabenicus*, or *Parthicus Arabicus Parthicus Adiabenicus*; see Dessau, *Ins. Sel.*, 417 f., and Cohen, iv², p. 8, nos. 48-52, and p. 40 f., nos. 363-368. The statement in § 11, accordingly, is not accurate. However, the cognomen *Parthicus* is not used without these qualifying words until after his campaign of 198 (see c. xvi. 2). These names were taken in 194, when he was acclaimed *Imperator* for the fourth time.

aliud bellum civile Clodii Albini nuntiatum est, qui
rebellavit in Gallia. quare postea occisi sunt filii
2 Nigri [1] cum matre. Albinum igitur statim hostem
iudicavit et eos qui ad illum mollius vel scripserunt
3 vel rescripserunt. et cum iret contra Albinum, in
itinere apud Viminacium filium suum maiorem Bassianum adposito Aurelii Antonini nomine Caesarem
appellavit, ut fratrem suum Getam ab spe imperii,
4 quam ille conceperat, summoveret. et nomen quidem Antonini idcirco filio adposuit, quod somniaverat
5 Antoninum sibi successurum. unde Getam etiam
quidam Antoninum putant dictum, ut et ipse suc-
6 cederet in imperio. aliqui putant idcirco illum Antoninum appellatum, quod Severus ipse in Marci
familiam transire voluerit.

7 Et primo quidem ab Albinianis Severi duces victi
sunt. tunc sollicitus cum consuleret, a Pannoniacis
auguribus comperit se victorem futurum, adversarium

[1] *filii Nigri* om. in P.

---

[1] See c. vi. 9 ; *Cl. Alb.*, viii. 4 f.
[2] More correctly, Britain, of which he was governor. He
had previously received from Severus the title of Caesar (see
note to *Cl. Alb.*, i. 2), and he now assumed that of Augustus.
[3] See c. ix. 2 and note.
[4] On his march from Byzantium through Moesia to Gaul.
As Hirschfeld has pointed out, there is no reason to suppose
that Severus went to Rome at this time ; see *Kl. Schriften*
(Berlin, 1913), p. 432.
[5] From this time on, in inscriptions and on coins he always
bears the name M. Aurelius Antoninus.
[6] See note to *Ael.*, i. 2. In this instance, the purpose of
the step was to nullify Albinus' claim to the name and to the
succession (see note to § 1).
[7] *i.e.* Severus' younger son.

of another civil war, caused by Clodius Albinus,[1] who had revolted in Gaul.[2] It was because of this revolt that Niger's children and their mother were later put to death.[3] As for Albinus, Severus at once declared him a public foe, and likewise those who, in their letters to him or replies to his letters, had expressed themselves as favourably inclined to him. As he was advancing against Albinus, moreover, and had reached Viminacium[4] on his march, he gave his elder son Bassianus the name Aurelius Antoninus[5] and the title of Caesar,[6] in order to destroy whatever hopes of succeeding to the throne his brother Geta had conceived. His reason for giving his son the name Antoninus was that he had dreamed that an Antoninus would succeed him. It was because of this dream, some believe, that Geta[7] also was called Antoninus,[8] in order that he too might succeed to the throne. Others, however, think that Bassianus was given the name Antoninus because Severus himself wished to pass over into the family of Marcus.[9]

At first, Severus' generals[10] were worsted by those of Albinus;[11] but when, in his anxiety, he consulted augurs in Pannonia, he learned that he would be

[8] The statement that Geta was given the name Antoninus is frequently made in these biographies; see c. xvi. 4; xix. 2; *Get.*, i. 1 f.; v. 3. It is questioned, on the other hand, in *Diad.*, vi. 9, and as this name does not appear in the inscriptions or on the coins of Geta, the statement is probably incorrect.

[9] So also Dio, lxxv. 7, 4, and lxxvi. 9. 4. In his inscriptions from this time on he appears as *Divi Marci Antonini Pii Germ. Sarm. filius*, etc. He also assumed the name Pius about this time.

[10] See also *Cl. Alb.*, ix. 1-4.

[11] In particular, Lupus, who was badly defeated by Albinus about this time; see Dio, lxxv. 6, 2.

vero nec in potestatem venturum neque evasurum sed
8 iuxta aquam esse periturum.[1] multi statim amici
Albini deserentes venere, multi duces capti sunt, in
XI. quos Severus animadvertit. multis interim varie
gestis in Gallia primo apud Tinurtium contra Albinum
2 felicissime pugnavit Severus. cum quidem ingens
periculum equi casu adiit,[2] ita ut mortuus ictu plumbeae
crederetur, ita ut alius iam paene imperator ab exer-
3 citu deligeretur. eo tempore lectis actis quae de
Clodio Celsino laudando, qui Hadrumetinus et adfinis
Albini erat, facta sunt, iratus senatui Severus, quasi
hoc Albino senatus praestitisset, Commodum inter
divos referendum esse censuit, quasi hoc genere se de
4 senatu posset ulcisci. primusque inter milites divum
Commodum pronuntiavit idque ad senatum scripsit
5 addita oratione victoriae. senatorum deinde qui in
bello erant interempti cadavera dissipari iussit.
6 deinde Albini corpore adlato paene seminecis caput
abscidi iussit Romamque deferri idque litteris pro-
7 secutus est. victus est Albinus die XI kal. Martias.

---

[1] *sed . . . . periturum* rejected by Peter[2] as repetition from
Pesc. Nig., ix. 5.   [2] *cadit* P.

---

[1] Probably the modern Tournus on the Saône about twenty
miles north of Mâcon. A description of the engagement is
given in Dio, lxxv. 6-7. According to his version, Albinus
killed himself after the defeat; but see §§ 6-9 and *Cl. Alb.*,
ix. 3.

[2] *i.e.* Julius Laetus ; see Herodian, iii. 7, 4 ; cf. c. xv. 6.

[3] His brother, according to *Cl. Alb.*, ix. 6; xii. 9, but this
is probably an error.

[4] See *Com.*, xvii. 11.

[5] According to Dio, lxxv. 7, the announcement of Commodus' deification did cause the senate great consternation.
Severus' real purpose, however, was probably to carry out

the victor, and that his opponent would neither fall
into his hands nor yet escape, but would die close by
the water.   Many of Albinus' friends soon deserted
and came over to Severus; and many of his generals
were captured, all of whom Severus punished.   XI.
Meanwhile, after many operations had been carried
on in Gaul with varying success, Severus had his
first successful encounter with Albinus at Tinurtium.[1]
Through the fall of his horse, however, he was at one
time in the utmost peril; and it was even believed
that he had been slain by a blow with a ball of lead,
and the army almost elected another emperor.[2]   It
was at this time that Severus, on reading the resolu-
tions passed by the senate in praise of Clodius
Celsinus, who was a native of Hadrumetum and
Albinus' kinsman,[3] became highly incensed at the
senate, as though it had recognized Albinus by this
act, and issued a decree that Commodus should be
placed among the deified,[4] as though he could take
vengeance on the senate by this sort of thing.[5]   He
proclaimed the deification of Commodus to the
soldiers first, and then announced it to the senate in
a letter, to which he added a discourse on his own
victory.   Next, he gave orders that the bodies of the
senators who had been slain in the battle should be
mutilated.   And then, when Albinus' body was
brought before him, he had him beheaded while still
half alive,[6] gave orders that his head should be taken
to Rome, and followed up the order with a letter.
Albinus was defeated on the eleventh day before the   19 Feb.,
Kalends of March.   197

further his policy of attaching himself to the house of the
Antonines; see c. x. 6.
   [6] See note to § 1.

397

Reliquum autem cadaver eius ante domum pro-
8 priam exponi ac diu videri [1] iussit. equum praeterea
ipse residens supra cadaver Albini egit expavescen-
temque admonuit et effrenatum ut audacter protereret.
9 addunt alii quod idem cadaver in Rhodanum abici
praecepit, simul etiam uxoris liberorumque eius.

XII. Interfectis innumeris Albini partium viris, inter
quos multi principes civitatis, multae feminae inlustres
fuerunt, omnium bona publicata sunt aerariumque
auxerunt; tum et Hispanorum et Gallorum proceres
2 multi occisi sunt. denique militibus tantum stipen-
3 diorum quantum nemo principum dedit. filiis etiam
suis ex hac proscriptione tantum reliquit quantum
nullus imperatorum, cum magnam partem auri per
Gallias, per Hispanias, per Italiam, imperatoriam [2]
4 fecisset. tuncque primum privatarum rerum pro-
5 curatio constituta est. multi sane post Albinum fidem
6 ei servantes bello a Severo superati sunt. eodem
tempore etiam legio Arabica defecisse ad Albinum
nuntiata est.

7 Ultus igitur graviter Albinianam defectionem interfectis plurimis, genere quoque eius exstincto, iratus
8 Romam et populo et senatoribus venit. Commodum
in senatu et contione laudavit, deum appellavit,
infamibus displicuisse dixit, ut appareret eum aper-

---

[1] *diu uideri* Salmasius; *diuidere* P.   [2] *imperatoriam* von
Domaszewski; *imperator iam* P, Peter.

---

[1] These executions took place in Gaul (Herodian, iii. 8, 2);
they are to be distinguished from the later executions at
Rome; see c. xiii.

The rest of Albinus' body was, by Severus' order, laid out in front of his own home, and kept there for a long time exposed to view. Furthermore, Severus himself rode on horseback over the body, and when the horse shied, he spoke to it and loosed the reins, that it might trample boldly. Some add that he ordered Albinus' body to be cast into the Rhone, and also the bodies of his wife and children.

XII. Countless persons who had sided with Albinus were put to death,[1] among them numerous leading men and many distinguished women, and all their goods were confiscated and went to swell the public treasury. Many nobles of the Gauls and Spains were also put to death at this time. Finally, he gave his soldiers sums of money such as no emperor had ever given before. Yet as a result of these confiscations, he left his sons a fortune greater than any other emperor had left to his heirs, for he had made a large part of the gold in the Gauls, Spains, and Italy imperial property. At this time the office of steward for private affairs[2] was first established. After Albinus' death many who remained loyal to him were defeated by Severus in battle. At this same time, moreover, he received word that the legion in Arabia had gone over to Albinus.[3]

And so, after having taken harsh vengeance for Albinus' revolt by putting many men to death and exterminating Albinus' family, he came to Rome filled with wrath at the people and senate. He delivered a eulogy of Commodus before the senate and before an assembly of the people and declared him a god; he averred, moreover, that Commodus had been un-

[2] See note to *Com.*, xx. 1.
[3] The Third Legion, the Cyrenaica.

9 tissime furere. post hoc de sua clementia disseruit,
cum crudelissimus fuerit et senatores infra scriptos
XIII. occiderit. occidit autem sine causae dictione hos
nobiles: Mummium Secundinum, Asellium Claudi-
2 anum, Claudium Rufum, Vitalium Victorem, Papium
Faustum, Aelium Celsum, Iulium Rufum, Lollium
Professum, Aurunculeium Cornelianum, Antonium[1]
Balbum, Postumium Severum, Sergium Lustralem,
3 Fabium Paulinum, Nonium Gracchum, Masticium
Fabianum, Casperium Agrippinum, Ceionium Albinum,
4 Claudium Sulpicianum, Memmium Rufinum, Casperium Aemilianum, Cocceium Verum, Erucium Cla-
5 rum, Aelium[2] Stilonem, Clodium Rufinum, Egnatu-
6 leium Honoratum, Petronium Iuniorem, Pescennios
Festum et Veratianum et Aurelianum et Materianum
et Iulianum et Albinum, Cerellios Macrinum et Faust-
7 inianum et Iulianum, Herennium Nepotem, Sulpicium
Canum, Valerium Catullinum, Novium Rufum, Claudi-
8 um Arabianum, Marcium[3] Asellionem. horum igitur
tantorum ac tam inlustrium virorum, nam multi in his
consulares, multi praetorii, omnes certe summi viri
9 fuere, interfector ab Afris ut deus habetur.   Cincium
Severum calumniatus est quod se veneno adpetisset,
XIV. atque ita interfecit. Narcissum dein, Commodi
strangulatorem, leonibus obiecit. multos praeterea

---

[1] *Antonium* Hirschfeld, acc. by Peter,[2] *Praef.*, p. xlii. ;
Antoninum P, Peter.   [2] *Aelium* Hirschfeld, acc. by Peter,[2]
Praef., p. xlii.; *L.* P, Peter.   [3] *Marcium* Hirschfeld, acc.
by Peter[2], *Praef.*, p. xlii.; *Marcum* P, Peter.

---

[1] A few telling sentences from the speech are recorded in
Dio, lxxv. 8. Dio also relates that he praised the severity
and cruelty of Marius and Sulla ; these names were afterwards
applied to him ; see *Pesc. Nig.*, vi. 4.

popular only among the degraded.[1] Indeed, it was evident that Severus was openly furious. After this he spoke about the mercy he had shown, whereas he was really exceedingly blood-thirsty and executed the senators enumerated below.[2] XIII. He put to death without even a trial the following noblemen : Mummius Secundinus, Asellius Claudianus, Claudius Rufus, Vitalius Victor, Papius Faustus, Aelius Celsus, Julius Rufus, Lollius Professus, Aurunculeius Cornelianus, Antonius Balbus, Postumius Severus, Sergius Lustralis, Fabius Paulinus, Nonius Gracchus, Masticius Fabianus, Casperius Agrippinus, Ceionius Albinus, Claudius Sulpicianus, Memmius Rufinus, Casperius Aemilianus, Cocceius Verus, Erucius Clarus, Aelius Stilo, Clodius Rufinus, Egnatuleius Honoratus, Petronius Junior, the six Pescennii, Festus, Veratianus, Aurelianus, Materianus, Julianus, and Albinus ; the three Cerellii, Macrinus, Faustinianus, and Julianus ; Herennius Nepos, Sulpicius Canus, Valerius Catullinus, Novius Rufus, Claudius Arabianus, and Marcius Asellio. And yet he who murdered all these distinguished men, many of whom had been consuls and many praetors, while all were of high estate, is regarded by the Africans as a god. He falsely accused Cincius Severus of attempting his life by poison, and thereupon put him to death ; next, he cast to the lions Narcissus, the man who had strangled Commodus.[3] XIV. And besides, he put to death many men from

---

[2] According to Dio, *ibid.*, he executed twenty-nine and pardoned thirty five. The following list of forty-one probably includes some of the partisans of Niger, whom Severus had previously refrained from putting to death ; see c. ix. 3.

[3] Cf. *Com.*, xvii. 2. But according to Dio, Narcissus was put to death by Didius Julianus ; see note to *Did. Jul.*, vi. 2.

obscuri loci homines interemit praeter eos quos vis
proelii absumpsit.

2   Post haec, cum se vellet commendare hominibus,
vehicularium munus a privatis ad fiscum traduxit.
3 Caesarem dein Bassianum Antoninum a senatu ap-
4 pellari fecit, decretis imperatoriis insignibus.   ru-
more deinde belli Parthici excitus [1] patri matri avo et
5 uxori priori per se statuas conlocavit.   Plautianum
ex amicissimo cognita eius vita ita odio habuit, ut et
hostem publicum appellaret et depositis statuis eius
per orbem terrae gravi eum insigniret iniuria, iratus
praecipue, quod inter propinquorum et adfinium
Severi simulacra suam statuam ille posuisset.
6 Palaestinis poenam remisit quam ob causam Nigri
7 meruerant.   postea iterum cum Plautiano in gratiam
rediit et veluti ovans urbem ingressus Capitolium [2]
petiit, quamvis et ipsum procedenti tempore occiderit.

---

[1] *excitus* Editor; *exciti* Petschenig; *extiti* P; *extincti*
Peter [1]; *rumor . . . extitit* Peter.[2]   [2] *cum eo Capitolium*
Peter; *cum eo* om. in P.

---

[1] See note to *Hadr.*, vii. 5.
[2] Bassianus had already received the name Caesar (see c.
x. 3) ; it was now confirmed by the senate.   He was also at
this time made a member of some of the priestly colleges to
which the emperor belonged (see note to *Marc.*, vi. 3), and he
was apparently recognized officially as his father's successor,
for from now on he bore the title of *Imperator Destinatus;*
see Dessau, *Ins. Sel.*, 442, 446, 447.
[3] See c. xv. f.   [4] See c. iii. 2 and note.
[5] C. Fulvius Plautianus, prefect of the guard.   For an account of his great power and his influence over Severus see
Dio, lxxv. 14-15.   He received the *ornamenta consularia*
(see note to *Hadr.*, viii. 7), and was consul in 203.

the more humble walks of life, not to speak of those
whom the fury of battle had consumed.

After this, wishing to ingratiate himself with the
people, he took the postal service [1] out of private
hands and transferred its cost to the privy-purse.
Then he caused the senate to give Bassianus Antoninus the title of Caesar and grant him the imperial
insignia.[2] Next, when called away by the rumour of 201
a Parthian war,[3] he set up at his own expense statues
in honour of his father, mother, grandfather and first
wife.[4] He had been very friendly with Plautianus; [5]
but, on learning his true character, he conceived such
an aversion to him as even to declare him a public ca. 203-4
enemy, overthrow his statues,[6] and make him famous
throughout the entire world for the severity of his
punishment, the chief reason for his anger being that
Plautianus had set up his own statue among the
statues of Severus' kinsmen and connections. He re-
voked the punishment which had been imposed upon
the people of Palestine [7] on Niger's account. Later,
he again entered into friendly relations with Plautianus, and after entering the city in his company like
one who celebrates an ovation,[8] he went up to the
Capitol, although in the course of time he killed him.
He bestowed the toga virilis on his younger son,

[6] This incident is described quite differently in Dio, lxxv.
16, 2; apparently, an order to melt some of the bronze
statues of Plautianus gave rise to the belief that he had been
disgraced.
[7] See c. ix. 5.
[8] A minor triumph, in which the general rode through the
city instead of driving a chariot. It was celebrated in case
the war had not been formally declared, or the vanquished
was not a recognized *hostis*, or the victory had been bloodless;
see Gellius, v. 6, 21.

8 Getae minori filio togam virilem dedit, maiori Plau-
9 tiani filiam uxorem iunxit. ii qui hostem publicum
Plautianum dixerant deportati sunt. ita omnium
10 rerum semper quasi naturali lege mutatio est. filios
dein consules designavit. Getam fratrem extulit.
11 profectus dehinc ad bellum Parthicum est, edito
12 gladiatorio munere et congiario populo dato. multos
inter haec causis vel veris vel simulatis occidit,
13 damnabantur autem plerique, cur iocati essent, alii,
cur tacuissent, alii, cur pleraque figurata[1] dixissent.
ut "ecce imperator vere nominis sui, vere Pertinax,
vere Severus".

XV. Erat sane in sermone vulgari Parthicum bellum adfectare Septimium Severum, gloriae cupiditate
2 non aliqua necessitate deductum. traiecto denique
exercitu a Brundisio continuato itinere venit in
3 Syriam Parthosque summovit. sed postea in Syriam
rediit, ita ut se pararet ac bellum Parthis inferret.
4 inter haec Pescennianas reliquias Plautiano auctore
persequebatur, ita ut nonnullos etiam ex amicis suis
5 quasi vitae suae insidiatores appeteret. multos etiam,
quasi Chaldaeos aut vates de sua salute consuluissent,

---

[1] *figurata* P ; *figurate* Peter.

---

[1] Fulvia Plautilla. The marriage took place in 202 ; she received the title of Augusta, which appears in inscriptions and on her coins (Cohen, iv², pp. 243 and 247 f.). When her father was assassinated in the Palace (see Dio, lxxvi. 4) in 205, she was banished ; later on she was put to death.

[2] Apparently after Geta's death—by a public funeral and a statue in the Forum; see Dio, lxxvi. 2, 4.

[3] The Parthians had entered Mesopotamia and were at-

Geta, and he united his elder son in marriage with
Plautianus' daughter.[1] Those who had declared
Plautianus a public enemy were now driven into
exile. Thus, as if by a law of nature, do all things
ever shift and change. Soon thereafter he appointed
his sons to the consulship; also he greatly honoured 205
his brother Geta.[2] Then, after giving a gladiatorial
show and bestowing largess upon the people, he set
out for the Parthian war. Many men meanwhile
were put to death, some on true and some on trumped-
up charges. Several were condemned because they
had spoken in jest, others because they had not
spoken at all, others again because they had cried
out many things with double meaning, such as
" Behold an emperor worthy of his name—Perti-
nacious in very truth, in very truth Severe ".

XV. It was commonly rumoured, to be sure, that in
planning a war on the Parthians, Septimius Severus
was influenced rather by a desire for glory than by
any real necessity.[3] Finally, he transported his army
from Brundisium, reached Syria without breaking
his voyage, and forced the Parthians to retreat.[4]
After that, however, he returned to Syria in order to
make preparations to carry on an offensive war against
the Parthians. In the meantime, on the advice of
Plautianus, he hunted down the last survivors of
Pescennius' revolt, and he even went so far as to
bring charges against several of his own friends on
the ground that they were plotting to kill him. He
put numerous others to death on the charge of having
asked Chaldeans or soothsayers how long he was

tacking Nisibis, the seat of Severus' operations in his former
campaign; see note to c. ix. 9.
    [4] *i.e.* from Nisibis.

interemit, praecipue suspectans[1] unumquemque
idoneum imperio, cum ipse parvulos adhuc filios
haberet idque dici ab his vel crederet vel audiret,
6 qui sibi augurabantur imperium. denique cum occisi
essent nonnulli, Severus se excusabat et post eorum
mortem negabat fieri iussisse quod factum est. quod
7 de Laeto praecipue Marius Maximus dicit. cum soror
sua Leptitana ad eum venisset vix Latine loquens, ac
de illa multum imperator erubesceret, dato filio eius
lato clavo atque ipsi multis muneribus redire mulier-
em in patriam praecepit, et quidem cum filio, qui
brevi[2] vita defunctus est.

XVI. Aestate igitur iam exeunte Parthiam ingressus Ctesiphontem pulso rege pervenit et cepit hiemali
prope tempore, quod in illis regionibus melius per
hiemem bella tractantur, cum herbarum[3] radicibus
milites viverent atque inde morbos aegritudinesque
2 contraherent. quare cum obsistentibus Parthis,
fluente quoque per insuetudinem cibi alvo militum,
longius ire non posset, tamen perstitit et oppidum
cepit et regem fugavit et plurimos interemit et
3 Parthicum nomen meruit. ob hoc[4] etiam filium eius

[1] *suspectans* Casaubon, Peter[2]; *suspectos* P; *suspectus*
Salmasius, Peter[1]. [2] *quibus seui* P. [3] *herbarum* Eg-
natius, Peter[1]; *culparum* P; † *culparum* Peter[2]; *caeparum*
Kellerbauer. [4] *ob hoc* Ed. princeps, Peter[1]; *ob* P; *ideo*
Peter[2].

---

[1] His legate in his former campaign and the defender of
Nisibis against the Parthians; see notes to c. xv. 1-2. He
was put to death during the siege of Hatra, which followed
the capture of Ctesiphon; see Dio, lxxv. 10, 3.
[2] See note to *Com.*, iv. 7.

destined to live; and he was especially suspicious of anyone who seemed qualified for the imperial power, for his sons were still very young, and he believed or had heard that this fact was being observed by those who were seeking omens regarding their own prospects of the throne. Eventually, however, when several had been put to death, Severus disclaimed all responsibility, and after their death denied that he had given orders to do what had been done. Marius Maximus says that this was particularly true in the case of Laetus.[1] His sister from Leptis once came to see him, and, since she could scarcely speak Latin, made the emperor blush for her hotly. And so, after giving the broad stripe [2] to her son and many presents to the woman herself, he sent her home again, and also her son, who died a short time afterwards.

XVI. When the summer was well-nigh over, Severus invaded Parthia, defeated the king, and came 198 to Ctesiphon; and about the beginning of the winter season he took the city. For indeed in those regions it is better to wage war during the winter, although the soldiers live on the roots of the plants and so contract various ills and diseases. For this reason then, although he could make no further progress, since the Parthian army was blocking the way and his men were suffering from diarrhœa because of the unfamiliar food, he nevertheless held his ground, took the city, put the king to flight, slew a great multitude, and gained the name Parthicus.[3] For this feat, likewise, the soldiers declared his son,

[3] Parthicus Maximus; this cognomen appears in his inscriptions and on his coins from 198 onward. On his previous cognomina see note to c. ix. 10.

Bassianum Antoninum, qui Caesar appellatus iam
fuerat, annum XIII agentem participem imperii
4 dixerunt milites. Getam quoque, minorem filium,
Caesarem dixerunt, eundem Antoninum, ut plerique
5 in litteras tradunt, appellantes. harum appellationum
causa donativum militibus largissimum dedit, concessa omni praeda oppidi Parthici, quod milites
6 quaerebant. inde in Syriam rediit victor, et Parthicum[1]
deferentibus sibi patribus triumphum idcirco recusavit,
quod consistere in curru adfectus articulari morbo
7 non posset. filio sane concessit, ut triumpharet ; cui
senatus Iudaicum triumphum decreverat, idciro quod
et in Syria res bene gestae fuerant a Severo.
8 Dein cum Antiochiam transisset, data virili toga
filio maiori secum eum consulem designavit, et statim
9 in Syria consulatum inierunt. post hoc dato stipendio
XVII. cumulatiore militibus Alexandriam petiit. in itinere
Palaestinis plurima iura fundavit. Iudaeos fieri sub
gravi poena vetuit. idem etiam de Christianis sanxit.
2 deinde Alexandrinis ius buleutarum dedit, qui sine
publico consilio ita ut sub regibus ante vivebant, uno

[1] *parthicus* P.

---

[1] He was acclaimed Augustus by the soldiers and received
the tribunician power from Severus. The date was prior to
the 3rd May, 198, since he is called Augustus in an African
inscription of that date ; see *C.I.L.*, viii. 2465 = Dessau, *Ins.
Sel.* 2485.

[2] Cf. c. x. 3 and xiv. 3.

[3] He is called *Nobilissimus Caesar* in inscriptions from 198
onward.

[4] See note to c. x. 5.

[5] Ctesiphon. The sack of the city is also mentioned in
Dio, lxxv. 9, 4.

[6] But not until after two unsuccessful sieges of Hatra in
Mesopotamia ; see Dio, lxxv. 10-12.

Bassianus Antoninus, co-emperor;[1] he had already been named Caesar[2] and was now in his thirteenth year. And to Geta, his younger son, they gave the name Caesar,[3] and called him in addition Antoninus,[4] as several men relate in their writings. To celebrate the bestowal of these names Severus gave the soldiers an enormous donative, none other, in truth, than liberty to plunder the Parthian capital,[5] a privilege for which they had been clamouring. He then returned victorious to Syria.[6] But when the senators offered him a triumph for the Parthian campaign, he declined it because he was so afflicted with gout that he was unable to stand upright in his chariot. Notwithstanding this, he gave permission that his son should celebrate a triumph; for the senate had decreed to him a triumph over Judaea because of the successes achieved by Severus in Syria.[7]

Next, when he had reached Antioch, he bestowed the toga virilis upon his elder son and appointed him consul as colleague to himself; and without further delay, while still in Syria, the two entered upon their consulship. XVII. After this, having 202. first raised his soldiers' pay, he turned his steps toward Alexandria, and while on his way thither he conferred numerous rights upon the communities of Palestine.[8] He forbade conversion to Judaism under heavy penalties and enacted a similar law in regard to the Christians. He then gave the Alexandrians the privilege of a local senate, for they were still without any public council, just as they had been under their own kings,[9] and were obliged to be content with

---

[7] As Caracalla was only twelve years old it is hardly likely that he won a victory in person.
[8] Cf. c. xiv. 6.   [9] The Ptolemaic dynasty.

SEVERUS

3 iudice contenti, quem¹ Caesar dedisset. multa prae-
4 terea his iura mutavit. iucundam sibi peregrinationem
hanc propter religionem dei Serapidis et propter
rerum antiquarnm cognitionem et propter novitatem
animalium vel locorum² fuisse Severus ipse postea
semper ostendit. nam et Memphim et Memnonen
et pyramides et labyrinthum diligenter inspexit.

5 Et quoniam longum est minora persequi, huius
magnifica illa: quod victo et occiso Iuliano prae-
torianas cohortes exauctoravit, Pertinacem contra
voluntatem militum in deos rettulit, Salvii³ Iuliani
6 decreta iussit aboleri; quod non obtinuit. denique
cognomentum Pertinacis non tam ex sua voluntate
7 quam ex⁴ morum parsimonia videtur habuisse. nam
et infinita multorum caede crudelior habitus et, cum
quidam ex hostibus eidem se suppliciter obtulisset
atque dixisset⁵ illi "quid facturus esses?"⁶, non

¹om. in P¹, added in P corr.   ²*bello eorum* P.   ³*saluti*
P.   ⁴*quam ex* P; *atque* Peter.   ⁵*obtulisset atque dixisset*
Peter²; *obtulissetque dixisst* t P; *obtulisset dixissetque* Peter.¹
⁶*illi quid facturus esses* Mommsen; *ille quod facturus esset*
P; *ille . . . quod facturus esset* Peter.

---

¹The *iuridicus Alexandriae*. Augustus had refused to
allow Alexandria to have a local senate; see Dio, li. 17, 2.
²The famous "singing Memnon" at Thebes, a colossal
statute of Amenophis III.
³In the Fayûm in Middle Egypt. A description of it is
given by Herodotus, iii. 148.
⁴This section of the biography (xvii. 5—xix. 4) bears a close
resemblance, often in the actual wording, to Victor, *de
Caesaribus*, xx., and in some passages it seems to be a mere
abbreviation of Victor's narrative; see Intro., p. xxii.
⁵See note to c. vi. 11.   ⁶Cf. c. vii. 8; *Pert.*, xiv. 10.
⁷In both this passage and the corresponding sentence in
Victor (*Caes.*, xx. 1) there seems to be a confusion between

410

the single governor appointed by Caesar.[1] Besides
this, he changed many of their laws. In after years
Severus himself continually avowed that he had
found this journey very enjoyable, because he had
taken part in the worship of the god Serapis, had
learned something of antiquity, and had seen unfamiliar animals and strange places. For he visited
Memphis, Memnon,[2] the Pyramids, and the Laby-
rinth,[3] and examined them all with great care.

But since it is tedious to mention in detail the
less important matters, only the most noteworthy of
his deeds are here related.[4] He discharged the
cohorts of the guard[5] after Julianus was defeated
and slain; he deified Pertinax against the wishes of
the army;[6] and he gave orders that the decisions of
Salvius Julianus should be annulled,[7] though this he
did not succeed in accomplishing. Lastly, he was
given the surname Pertinax, not so much by his
own wish,[8] it seems, as because of his frugal ways.[9]
In fact, he was considered somewhat cruel, both on
account of his innumerable executions[10] and because,
when one of his enemies came before him on a certain
occasion to crave forgiveness and said "What would
you have done?",[11] Severus was not softened by so

Salvius Julianus and his *Edictum Perpetuum* (see note to
Hadr., xviii. 1), on the one hand, and Didius Julianus and his
Acta, on the other. The *Acta* were doubtless rescinded, but
the *Edictum* remained in force.

[8] But see c. vii. 9 and note. He assumed the name in
order to strengthen his own position.

[9] Cf. c. xix. 7-8. Pertinax was famous for his frugality;
see *Pert.*, viii. 9-11; xii. 2-6.

[10] See c. xii-xiii.

[11] The story is preserved in complete form in Victor, *Caes.*,
xx. 11.

411

emollitus[1] tam prudente dicto interfici eum iussit.
8 fuit praeterea delendarum cupidus factionum. prope
XVIII. a nullo congressu digressus[2] nisi victor. Persarum
regem Abgarum subegit. Arabas in dicionem accepit.
2 Adiabenos in tributarios coegit. Britanniam, quod
maximum eius imperii decus est, muro per trans-
versam insulam ducto utrimque[3] ad finem Oceani
munivit. unde etiam Britannici nomen accepit.
3 Tripolim, unde oriundus erat, contusis bellicosissimis
gentibus securissimam reddidit, ac populo Romano
diurnum[4] oleum gratuitum et fecundissimum in
aeternum donavit.
4 Idem cum implacabilis delictis fuit, tum ad
erigendos industrios quosque iudicii singularis.
5 philosophiae ac dicendi studiis satis deditus, doctrinae
6 quoque nimis cupidus. latronum ubique hostis.
vitam suam privatam publicamque ipse composuit ad
7 fidem, solum tamen vitium crudelitatis excusans. de
hoc senatus ita iudicavit, illum aut nasci non debuisse

---

[1] so Peter[2]; *est emollitus* P, Peter.[1]   [2] inserted by Casaubon.   [3] *utrumque* P.   [4] *diurnum* Casaubon; *diuturnam* P.

---

[1] The ambiguity of this sentence is due to excessive com-
pression of the original as preserved in Victor, *Caes.*, xx. 13-
14. The transition from the suppression of conspiracies to
success in foreign wars is entirely omitted.
[2] Abgar IX., King of Osroene, who joined Severus on his
Parthian campaign, gave his sons as hostages and assumed
the name Septimius; see Herodian, iii. 9, 2. According to
Herodian, this happened in connection with Severus' second
campaign, in 198, but it has been maintained that the incident should be connected with the first campaign, in 195.
[3] Cf. c. ix. 9 and note.
[4] This does not refer to the construction of a new wall, but
to the restoration probably of the wall of Hadrian (see *Hadr.*,
xi. 2; *Pius*, v. 4).

sensible a speech, but ordered him to be put to death. He was determined to crush out conspiracies. He seldom departed from a battle except as victor.[1] XVIII. He defeated Abgarus, the king of the Persians.[2] He extended his sway over the Arabs. He forced the Adiabeni to give tribute.[3] He built a wall[4] across the island of Britain from sea to sea, and thus made the province secure—the crowning glory of his reign; in recognition thereof he was given the name Britannicus.[5] He freed Tripolis, 210 the region of his birth, from fear of attack by crushing sundry warlike tribes. And he bestowed upon the Roman people, without cost, a most generous daily allowance of oil in perpetuity.[6]

He was implacable toward the guilty; at the same time he showed singular judgment in advancing the efficient. He took a fair interest in philosophy and oratory, and showed a great eagerness for learning in general. He was relentless everywhere toward brigands.[7] He wrote a trustworthy account of his own life, both before and after he became emperor,[8] in which the only charge that he tried to explain away was that of cruelty. In regard to this charge, the senate declared that Severus either should never have

[5] Britannicus Maximus; it appears in his inscriptions of 210. The cognomen *Britannicus* is found on his coins of 211, bearing the legend *Victoriae Britannicae*; see Cohen, iv², p. 75 f., no. 722 f.

[6] Cf. c. xxiii. 2; *Alex.*, xxii. 2. Previous to this time oil, like grain, had been sold by the government at low prices, but from now on until after the time of Constantine it was given to the populace.

[7] Especially one famous brigand named Bulla Felix, who with a band of six hundred men terrorized Italy for two years; see Dio, lxxvi. 10.

[8] See note to c. iii. 2.

aut mori, quod et nimis crudelis et nimis utilis rei
8 publicae videretur. domi tamen minus cautus, qui
uxorem Iuliam famosam adulteriis tenuit, ream [1] etiam
9 coniurationis. idem, cum pedibus aeger bellum
moraretur, idque milites anxie ferrent eiusque filium
Bassianum, qui una erat, Augustum fecissent, tolli se
atque in tribunal ferri iussit, adesse deinde omnes
10 tribunos centuriones duces et cohortes quibus auctoribus id acciderat, sisti deinde filium, qui Augusti
nomen acceperat. cumque animadverti in omnes auctores facti praeter filium iuberet rogareturque [2] omnibus ante tribunal prostratis, caput manu contingens ait :
11 "Tandem sentitis caput imperare, non pedes ". huius
dictum est, cum eum ex humili per litterarum et
militiae officia ad imperium plurimis gradibus fortuna
duxisset : " Omnia," inquit, "fui et nihil expedit."

XIX. Periit Eboraci in Britannia, subactis gentibus
quae Britanniae videbantur infestae, anno imperii
2 xviii, morbo gravissimo exstinctus iam senex. re-

---

[1] *ream* Salmasius; *eam* P.   [2] *rogareturque* Peter [1];
rogareturquem P ; *rogareturque* <*uenia*>*m* Klein, Peter[2],
but see use of *rogatus* in *Pesc. Nig.*, x. 5.

---

[1] There is no suggestion in Dio that she was guilty of either
adultery or conspiracy. Both charges are probably due to the
machinations of Plautianus, who tried to poison Severus'
mind against her ; see Dio, lxxv. 15, 6 ; lxxviii. 24, 1. The
statement of an incestuous relationship between her and
Caracalla found in the *Historia Augusta* (c. xxi. 7 and *Carac.*,
x. 1-4) and in other writings of a late date (*e.g.* Victor, *Caes.*,
xxi.) represents a definite historical tradition composed by a
traducer of Julia.

been born at all or never should have died, because
on the one hand, he had proved too cruel, and on the
other, too useful to the state. For all that, he was
less careful in his home-life, for he retained his wife
Julia even though she was notorious for her adulteries
and also guilty of plotting against him.[1] On one
occasion,[2] when he so suffered from gout as to delay
a campaign, his soldiers in their dismay conferred on
his son Bassianus, who was with him at the time,
the title of Augustus. Severus, however, had himself lifted up and carried to the tribunal, summoned
all the tribunes, centurions, generals, and cohorts
responsible for this occurrence, and after commanding
his son, who had received the name Augustus, to
stand up, gave orders that all the authors of this deed,
save only his son, should be punished. When they
threw themselves before the tribunal and begged for
pardon, Severus touched his head with his hand and
said, "Now at last you know that the head does the
ruling, and not the feet". And even after fortune
had led him step by step through the pursuits of
study and of warfare even to the throne, he used to
say: "Everything have I been, and nothing have I
gained".

XIX. In the eighteenth year of his reign, now an
old man and overcome by a most grievous disease,
he died at Eboracum in Britain, after subduing
various tribes that seemed a possible menace to the

4 Feb.,
211

[2]The following incident is related in almost exactly the
same words in Victor, *Caes.*, xx. 25-26. It probably occurred
during the war in Britain, where, according to Dio, lxxvi. 14,
Caracalla made various plots against his father. The title of
Augustus had been conferred on Caracalla some years previously in Mesopotamia; see note to c. xvi. 3.

liquit filios duos, Antoninum Bassianum et Getam, cui
et ipsi in honorem Marci Antonini nomen imposuit.
3 inlatus [1] sepulchro Marci Antonini, quem ex omnibus
imperatoribus tantum coluit, ut et Commodum in
divos referret et Antonini nomen omnibus deinceps
4 quasi Augusti adscribendum putaret. ipse a senatu
agentibus liberis, qui [2] ei funus amplissimum exhib-
uerant, inter divos est relatus.

5 Opera publica praecipua eius exstant Septizonium
et Thermae Severianae. eiusdemque etiam Septimianae [3] in Transtiberina regione ad portam nominis
sui, quarum forma intercidens statim usum publicum
invidit.

6 Iudicium de eo post mortem magnum omnium
fuit, maxime quod diu nec a filiis eius boni aliquid rei
publicae venit, et postea invadentibus multis rem
publicam res Romana praedonibus direptui fuit.

[1] *inlegatus* P. [2] *liberisque* P. [3] *Septimianae* Zangemeister; *eius denique etiam ianae* P; *eiusdemque etiam ianuae*
Peter; *aliae* Hirschfeld, acc. by Peter[2], *Praef.*, p. xlii.

---

[1] Especially the Caledonii and the Maeatae, the former of
whom lived north of the " wall which divides the island into
two parts," the latter south of it; see Dio, lxxvi. 12, 1.
[2] See note to c. x. 5.
[3] *i.e.* the Tomb of Hadrian (see note to *Hadr.*, xix. 11), in
which Marcus and the other members of the house of the
Antonines were buried.
[4] See c. xi. 3.
[5] Commemorated on coins with the legends *Divo Severo
Pio* and *Consecratio;* see Cohen, iv[2], p. 12 f., nos. 80-91.
[6] This was a three-storied portico at the south-eastern
corner of the Palatine Hill. Its purpose was to give an orna-

province.[1] He left two sons, Antoninus Bassianus and Geta, also named by him Antoninus[2] in honour of Marcus. Severus was laid in the tomb of Marcus Antoninus,[3] whom of all the emperors he revered so greatly that he even deified Commodus[4] and held that all emperors should thenceforth assume the name Antoninus as they did that of Augustus. At the demand of his sons, who gave him a most splendid funeral, he was added to the deified.[5]

The principal public works of his now in existence are the Septizonium[6] and the Baths of Severus.[7] He also built the Septimian Baths in the district across the Tiber near the gate named after him,[8] but the aqueduct fell down immediately after its completion and the people were unable to make any use of them.

After his death the opinion that all men held of him was high indeed; for, in the long period that followed, no good came to the state from his sons, and after them, when many invaders came pouring in upon the state, the Roman Empire became a thing for free-booters to plunder.

mental front to the Palace at the place where it faced the Appian Way; see c. xxiv. 3.

[7] According to an ancient description of Rome dating from the time of Constantine (the *Notitia Regionum*), these baths were in the First Region, the southernmost part of the city. All trace of them, however, has disappeared, and they may have been absorbed in the *Thermae Antoninianae*, *i.e.*, Baths of Caracalla; see *Carac.*, ix. 4 f.

[8] The Porta Septimiana, where the modern Via della Lungara passes through the Wall of Aurelian, probably corresponds with the site of this gate. The *Thermae Septimianae* (if Zangemeister's reading be correct) must have been in this neighbourhood. The name seems to be preserved in the expression *il Settignano*, which was formerly applied to the southern end of the Via della Lungara.

7 Hic tam exiguis vestibus usus est ut vix et [1] tunica
eius aliquid purpurae haberet, cum hirta chlamyde
8 umeros velaret.[2] cibi parcissimus, leguminis patrii
avidus, vini aliquando cupidus, carnis frequenter
9 ignarus. ipse decorus, ingens, promissa barba, cano
capite et crispo, vultu reverendus, canorus voce, sed
10 Afrum quiddam usque ad senectutem sonans. ac
multum post mortem amatus vel invidia deposita vel
crudelitatis metu.

XX. Legisse me apud Aelium [3] Maurum Phlegontis
Hadriani libertum memini Septimium Severum in-
moderatissime, cum moreretur, laetatum, quod duos
Antoninos pari imperio rei publicae relinqueret,
exemplo Pii, qui Verum et Marcum Antoninos per
2 adoptionem filios rei publicae reliquit, hoc melius
quod ille filios per adoptionem, hic per se genitos
rectores Romanae rei publicae daret; Antoninum
scilicet Bassianum quidem ex priore matrimonio
3 susceperat et Getam de Iulia genuerat. sed illum
multum spes fefellit; nam unum parricidium, alterum sui mores rei publicae inviderunt. sanctumque
4 illud nomen in nullo fere diu bene mansit. et re-
putanti mihi, Diocletiane Auguste, neminem prope [4]

---

[1] *uix et* Salmasius; *uixit* P.   [2] *ualeret* P.   [3] *Helius*
P, Peter.   [4] *neminem prope* Edit. princeps, Peter[1]; *neminem facere prope* P, Peter[2]; *neminem fere [prope]* Salmasius.

---

[1] Cf. c. xvii. 6.   Dio also comments on the simplicity of
Severus' mode of life ; see lxxvi. 17.
[2] See *Hadr.*, xvi. i.
[3] Geta received the title of Augustus in 209; see his coins
of 209, Cohen, iv², p. 266 f., nos. 129-131.
[4] This statement is made in other rhetorical portions of
the *Historia Augusta* (*Carac.*, x. 1; *Geta*, vii. 3) and in

His clothing was of the plainest; indeed, even his tunic had scarcely any purple on it, while he covered his shoulders with a shaggy cloak. He was very sparing in his diet,[1] was fond of his native beans, liked wine at times, and often went without meat. In person he was large and handsome. His beard was long; his hair was gray and curly, his face was such as to inspire respect. His voice was clear, but retained an African accent even to his old age. After his death he was much beloved, for then all envy of his power or fear of his cruelty had vanished.

XX. I can remember reading in Aelius Maurus, the freedman of that Phlegon [2] who was Hadrian's freedman, that Septimius Severus rejoiced exceedingly at the time of his death, because he was leaving two Antonini to rule the state with equal powers,[3] herein following the example of Pius, who left to the state Verus and Marcus Antoninus, his two sons by adoption; and that he rejoiced all the more, because, while Pius had left only adopted sons, he was leaving sons of his own blood to rule the Roman state, namely Antoninus Bassianus, whom he had begotten from his first marriage,[4] and Geta, whom Julia had borne him. In these high hopes, however, he was grievously deceived; for the state was denied the one by murder,[5] the other [6] by his own character. And in scarcely any case did that revered name [7] long or creditably survive. Indeed, when I reflect on the matter, Diocletian Augustus, it is quite clear to me

historians of the later period (*e.g.*, Victor, *Caes.*, xxi., 3). It is not only untrue, but it contradicts the statement of *Sev.*, iii. 9 and iv. 2.

[5] Geta, murdered in 212; see note to c. xxi. 7.
[6] Bassianus.   [7] *i.e.*, Antoninus.

magnorum virorum optimum et utilem filium reliquisse
5 satis claret.   denique aut sine liberis veris [1] interierunt
aut tales habuerunt plerique, ut melius fuerit de
XXI. rebus humanis sine posteritate discedere.   et ut
ordiamur a Romulo, hic nihil liberorum reliquit, nihil Numa Pompilius, quod utile posset esse rei
publicae. quid Camillus ? num sui similes liberos
habuit ? quid Scipio ? quid Catones qui magni
2 fuerunt ? iam vero quid de Homero, Demosthene,
Vergilio, Crispo, Terentio,[2] Plauto ceterisque aliis
loquar ? quid de Caesare ? quid de Tullio, cui soli
3 melius fuerat liberos non habere ? quid de Augusto,
qui nec adoptivum bonum filium habuit, cum illi
eligendi potestas fuisset ex omnibus ? falsus est etiam
ipse Traianus in suo municipe ac nepote deligendo.
4 sed ut omittamus adoptivos, ne nobis Antonini Pius
et Marcus, numina rei publicae, occurrant, veniamus
5 ad genitos. quid Marco felicius fuisset, si Commodum
6 non reliquisset heredem ? quid Severo Septimio,
si Bassianum nec genuisset ? qui statim insimulatum
fratrem insidiarum contra se cogitatarum parricidali
7 etiam figmento interemit ; qui novercam suam—et
quid novercam ? matrem quin immo, in cuius sinu
8 Getam filium eius occiderat, uxorem duxit ; qui

---

[1] *ueris* Salmasius; *uiri* P.   [2] So Peter; *et Terentio* P.

---

[1] Scipio Africanus, the younger, who seems to have left
no children.
[2] C. Sallustius Crispus, the historian.
[3] Cicero's son had none of his father's ability ; he had,
moreover, a bad reputation for drunkenness.
[4] Hadrian. This sentiment represents the tradition hostile
to Hadrian which grew up after his death as a result of the
enmity felt for him by some of the senators.

that practically no great man has left the world a son of real excellence or value. In short, most of them either died without issue of their own, or had such children that it would have been better for humanity had they departed without offspring. XXI. As for Romulus, to begin with him, he left no children who might have proved useful to the state, nor did Numa Pompilius. What of Camillus? Did he have children like himself? What of Scipio?[1] What of the Catos, who were so distinguished? Indeed, for that matter, what shall I say of Homer, Demosthenes, Vergil, Crispus,[2] Terence, Plautus, and such as they? What of Caesar? What of Tully?—for whom, particularly, it had been better had he had no son.[3] What of Augustus, who could not get a worthy son even by adoption, though he had the whole world to choose from? Even Trajan was deceived when he chose for his heir his fellow-townsman and nephew.[4] But let us except sons by adoption, lest our thoughts turn to those two guardian spirits of the state, Pius and Marcus Antoninus, and let us proceed to sons by birth. What could have been more fortunate for Marcus than not to have left Commodus as his heir? What more fortunate for Septimius Severus than not to have even begotten Bassianus?—a man who speedily charged his brother with contriving plots against him—a murderous falsehood—and put him to death; who took his own stepmother to wife[5]—stepmother did I say?—nay rather the mother on whose bosom he had slain Geta, her son;[6] who slew, because

[5] See note to c. xviii. 8.
[6] See *Carac.*, ii. 4, and, for a detailed description of the murder, Dio, lxxvii. 2.

Papinianum, iuris asylum et doctrinae legalis[1] thesaurum, quod parricidium excusare noluisset, occidit, et praefectum quidem, ne homini per se et per scientiam suam magno deesset et dignitas. denique, ut alia omittam, ex huius moribus factum puto, ut[2] Severus tristior vir ad omnia, immo etiam crudelior pius et dignus deorum altaribus duceretur. qui quidem divinam[3] Sallustii orationem, qua Micipsa filios ad pacem hortatur, ingravatus morbo misisse filio dicitur maiori. idque frustra[4] . . . et hominem tantum valitudine. vixit denique in odio populi diu Antoninus, nomenque illud sanctum diu minus amatum est, quamvis et vestimenta populo dederit, unde Caracallus est dictus, et thermas magnificentissimas fecerit. exstat sane Romae Severi porticus gesta eius exprimens a filio, quantum plurimi docent, structa.

XXII. Signa mortis eius haec fuerunt : ipse somniavit quattuor aquilis et gemmato curru praevolante nescio qua ingenti humana specie ad caelum esse raptum ; cumque raperetur, octoginta et novem numeros explicuisse, ultra quot annos ne unum quidem annum vixit, nam ad imperium senex venit. cumque positus

---

[1] *regalis* P.   [2] om. in P.   [3] *diu immo* P.   [4] *frusta* P ; lacuna est. by Casaubon.

---

[1] See *Carac.*, iv. 1 and viii.   [2] Sallust, *Jugurtha*, x.
[3] See *Carac.*, ix. 7.   [4] See *Carac.*, ix. 4 f.

he refused to absolve him of his brother's murder,[1] Papinian, a sanctuary of law and treasure-house of jurisprudence, who had been raised to the office of prefect that a man who had become illustrious through his own efforts and his learning might not lack official rank. In short, not to mention other things, I believe that it was because of this man's character that Severus, a gloomier man in every way, nay even a crueller one, was considered righteous and worthy of the worship of a god. Once indeed, it is said, Severus, when laid low by sickness, sent to his elder son that divine speech in Sallust in which Micipsa urges his sons to the ways of peace.[2] In vain, however. . . . For a long time, finally, the people hated Antoninus, and that venerable name was long less beloved, even though he gave the people clothing (whence he got his name Caracallus[3]) and built the most splendid baths.[4] There is a colonnade of Severus at Rome,[5] I might mention, depicting his exploits, which was built by his son, or so most men say.

XXII. The death of Severus was foreshadowed by the following events: he himself dreamed that he was snatched up to the heavens in a jewelled car drawn by four eagles, whilst some vast shape, I know not what, but resembling a man, flew on before. And while he was being snatched up, he counted out the numbers eighty and nine,[6] and beyond this number of years he did not live so much as one, for he was an old man when he came to the throne. And then, after he

[5] Also mentioned in *Carac.*, ix. 6. Its site is unknown.
[6] This same number of the years of his life is given in *Pesc. Nig.*, v. 1, but it is in direct contradiction with the positive statement in c. i. 3 that he was born in 146. According to Dio's computation, he was born in 145; see lxxvi. 17, 4.

esset in circulo ingenti aereo, diu solus et destitutus
stetit, cum vereretur autem, ne praeceps rueret, a
Iove se vocatum vidit atque inter Antoninos locatum.
3 die circensium cum tres Victoriolae more solito essent
locatae gypseae cum palmis, media, quae ipsius
nomine adscriptum orbem tenebat, vento icta de
podio stans decidit et humi constitit ; at quae Getae
nomine inscripta erat, corruit et omnis conminuta
est ; illa vero quae Bassiani titulum praeferebat,
4 amissa palma venti turbine vix constitit. post murum
apud Luguvallum visum [1] in Britannia cum ad proxi-
mam mansionem rediret non solum victor sed etiam
in aeternum pace fundata, volvens [2] animo quid
ominis sibi occurreret, Aethiops quidam e numero
militari, clarae inter scurras famae et celebratorum
semper iocorum, cum corona e cupressu facta eidem
5 occurrit. quem cum ille iratus removeri ab oculis
praecepisset, et coloris eius tactus omine [3] et coronae,
dixisse ille dicitur ioci causa : "Totum fuisti,[4] totum
6 vicisti, iam deus esto victor". et in civitatem veniens
cum rem divinam vellet facere, primum ad Bellonae
templum ductus est errore haruspicis rustici, deinde

---

[1] So Peter[2]; *maurum apud uallum missum* P, Peter[1].
[2] *uolens* P[1].   [3] *hominis* P[1].   [4] *fuisti* P, Peter[1]; *fudisti*
Hirschfeld, Peter[2].

---

[1] The *podium* was a platform close to the arena, occupied
by members of the imperial family.
[2] Now Carlisle.   [3] Cf. c. xviii. 11.

had been placed in a huge circle in the air, for a long
time he stood alone and desolate, until finally, when
he began to fear that he might fall headlong, he saw
himself summoned by Jupiter and placed among the
Antonines. Again, on the day of the circus-games,
when three plaster figures of Victory were set up in
the customary way, with palms in their hands, the
one in the middle, which held a sphere inscribed
with his name, struck by a gust of wind, fell down
from the balcony [1] in an upright position and remained on the ground in this posture ; while the one
on which Geta's name was inscribed was dashed down
and completely shattered, and the one which bore
Bassianus' name lost its palm and barely managed
to keep its place, such was the whirling of the
wind. On another occasion, when he was returning to his nearest quarters from an inspection of the
wall at Luguvallum [2] in Britain, at a time when he had
not only proved victorious but had concluded a per-
petual peace, just as he was wondering what omen
would present itself, an Ethiopïan soldier, who was
famous among buffoons and always a notable jester,
met him with a garland of cypress-boughs. And when
Severus in a rage ordered that the man be removed
from his sight, troubled as he was by the man's
ominous colour and the ominous nature of the garland, the Ethiopian by way of jest cried, it is said,
"You have been all things,[3] you have conquered all
things, now, O conqueror, be a god ". And when on
reaching the town he wished to perform a sacrifice,
in the first place, through a misunderstanding on the
part of the rustic soothsayer, he was taken to the
Temple of Bellona, and, in the second place, the
victims provided him were black. And then, when

425

7 hostiae furvae sunt adplicitae. quod cum esset aspernatus atque ad Palatium se reciperet, neglegentia ministrorum nigrae hostiae et usque ad limen domus Palatinae imperatorem secutae sunt.

XXIII. Sunt per plurimas civitates opera eius insignia. magnum vero illud in vita [1] eius, quod Romae omnes aedes publicas, quae vitio temporum labebantur, instauravit nusquam prope suo nomine adscripto, 2 servatis tamen ubique titulis conditorum. moriens septem annorum canonem, ita ut cotidiana septuaginta quinque milia modium expendi possent, reliquit ; olei vero tantum, ut per quinquennium non solum urbis [2] usibus, sed et totius Italiae, quae oleo eget, sufficeret. 3 Ultima verba eius dicuntur haec fuisse : " Turbatam rem publicam ubique accepi, pacatam etiam Britannis relinquo, senex et pedibus aeger firmum imperium Antoninis meis relinquens, si boni erunt, 4 imbecillum, si mali ". iussit deinde signum tribuno dari "laboremus," quia Pertinax, quando in imperium 5 adscitus est, signum dederat "militemus". Fortunam deinde regiam, quae comitari principes et in cubiculis poni solebat, geminare statuerat, ut sacratissimum 6 simulacrum utrique relinqueret filiorum ; sed cum videret se perurgueri sub hora mortis, iussisse fertur

---

[1] *uita* Salmasius; *ciuitate* P.   [2] *urbis* add. by Egnatius, om. in P.

---

[1] *i.e.*, the imperial residence in the provincial town.
[2] Cf. c. viii. 5.   [3] See c. xviii. 3.
[4] See *Pert.*, v. 7.   [5] See *Pius*, xii. 5.

he abandoned the sacrifice in disgust and betook himself to the Palace,[1] through some carelessness on the part of the attendants the black victims followed him up to its very doors.

XXIII. In many communities there are public buildings erected by him which are famous, but particularly noteworthy among the achievements of his life was the restoration of all the public sanctuaries in Rome, which were then falling to ruin through the passage of time. And seldom did he inscribe his own name on these restorations or fail to preserve the names of those who built them. At his death he left a surplus of grain to the amount of seven years' tribute,[2] or enough to distribute seventy-five thousand pecks a day, and so much oil,[3] indeed, that for five years there was plenty for the uses, not only of the city, but also for as much of Italy as was in need of it.

His last words, it is said, were these: "The state, when I received it, was harassed on every side; I leave it at peace, even in Britain; old now and with crippled feet, I bequeath to my two Antonini an empire which is strong, if they prove good, feeble, if they prove bad". After this, he issued orders to give the tribune the watchword "Let us toil," because Pertinax, when he assumed the imperial power, had given the word "Let us be soldiers".[4] He then ordered a duplicate made of the royal statue of Fortune which was customarily carried about with the emperors and placed in their bedrooms,[5] in order that he might leave this most holy statue to each of his sons; but later, when he realized that the hour of death was upon him, he gave instructions, they say, that the original should be placed in the bed-chambers

427

ut alternis diebus apud filios imperatores in cubiculis
7 Fortuna poneretur. quod Bassianus prius contempsit
quam faceret parricidium.

XXIV. Corpus eius a Britannia Romam usque cum
2 magna provincialium reverentia susceptum est ; quamvis aliqui urnulam auream tantum fuisse dicant Severi
reliquias continentem eandemque Antoninorum sepulchro inlatam, cum Septimius illic ubi vita functus est
esset incensus.

3 Cum Septizonium[1] faceret, nihil aliud cogitavit,
quam ut ex Africa venientibus suum opus occurreret.
4 nisi absente eo per[2] praefectum urbis medium simulacrum eius esset locatum, aditum Palatinis aedibus,
id est regium atrium, ab ea parte facere voluisse per-
5 hibetur. quod etiam post Alexander cum vellet
facere, ab haruspicibus dicitur esse prohibitus, cum
hoc sciscitans non litasset.

---

[1] *septizodium* P, Peter[2].   [2] *absente opere* P.

---

[1] It was made of porphyry. according to Dio, lxxvi. 15, 4, of
alabaster, according to Herodian, iii. 15, 7.

of each of his sons, the co-emperors, on alternate days. As for this direction, Bassianus ignored it and then murdered his brother.

XXIV. His body was borne from Britain to Rome, and was everywhere received by the provincials with profound reverence. Some men say, however, that only a golden urn [1] containing Severus' ashes was so conveyed, and that this was laid in the tomb of the Antonines,[2] while Septimius himself was cremated where he died.

When he built the Septizonium [3] he had no other thought than that his building should strike the eyes of those who came to Rome from Africa. It is said that he wished to make an entrance on this side of the Palatine mansion—the royal dwelling, that is —and he would have done so had not the prefect of the city planted his statue in the centre of it while he was away. Afterwards Alexander [4] wished to carry out this plan, but he, it is said, was prevented by the soothsayers, for on making inquiry he obtained unfavourable omens.

[2] See c. xix. 3 and note.   [3] See c. xix. 5 and note.
[4] *i.e.*, Severus Alexander, the emperor.

PESCENNIUS NIGER

AELII SPARTIANI

I. Rarum atque difficile est ut, quos [1] tyrannos aliorum victoria fecerit, bene mittantur in litteras, atque ideo vix omnia de his plene in monumentis atque an-
2 nalibus habentur. primum enim, quae magna sunt in eorum honorem ab scriptoribus depravantur, deinde alia supprimuntur, postremo non magna diligentia in eorum genere ac vita requiritur, cum satis sit audaciam eorum et bellum, in quo victi fuerint, ac poenam proferre.

3 Pescennius ergo Niger, ut alii tradunt, modicis parentibus, ut alii, nobilibus fuisse dicitur, patre Annio Fusco, matre Lampridia, avo curatore Aquini, ex quo [2] familia originem ducebat; quod quidem dubium
4 etiam nunc habetur. hic eruditus mediocriter litteris,[3] moribus ferox, divitiis inmodicus, vita parcus,
5 libidinis effrenatae ad omne genus cupiditatum. or-

[1] *quod* P.   [2] *quo* Closs; *qua* P, Peter.
[3] *Litteris* Peter from Σ; om. in P.

[1] See note to *Marc.*, xi. 2.

PESCENNIUS NIGER

BY

AELIUS SPARTIANUS

I. It is an unusual task and a difficult one to set down fairly in writing the lives of men who, through other men's victories, remained mere pretenders, and for this reason not all the facts concerning such men are preserved in our records and histories in full. For, in the first place, notable events that redound to their honour are distorted by historians; other events, in the second place, are suppressed; and, in the third place, no great care is bestowed upon inquiries into their ancestry and life, since it seems sufficient to recount their presumption, the battle in which they were overcome, and the punishment they suffered.

Pescennius Niger, then, was born of humble parentage, according to some, of noble, according to others. His father was Annius Fuscus, his mother Lampridia. His grandfather was the supervisor of Aquinum,[1] the town to which the family sought to trace its origin, though the fact is even now considered doubtful. As for Pescennius himself, he was passably well versed in literature, savage in disposition, immoderately wealthy, thrifty in his habits, and unbridled in indulgence in every manner of

431

dines diu duxit multisque ducatibus pervenit, ut
exercitus Syriacos iussu Commodi regeret, suffragio
maxime athletae qui Commodum strangulavit, ut
omnia tunc fiebant.

II. Is postquam comperit occisum Commodum,
Iulianum imperatorem appellatum eundemque iussu
Severi et senatus occisum, Albinum etiam in Gallia
sumpsisse nomen et ius [1] imperatoris, ab exercitibus
Syriacis, quos regebat, appellatus est imperator, ut
quidam dicunt, magis in Iuliani odium quam in aemula-
2 tionem Severi. huic ob detestationem Iuliani primis
imperii diebus ita Romae fautum est, a senatoribus
dumtaxat, qui et Severum oderant, ut inter lapida-
tiones exsecrationesque omnium illi feliciter optaretur,
" illum principem superi et illum Augustum " popu-
3 lus adclamaret. Iulianum autem oderant populares,
quod Pertinacem milites occidissent et illum imperatorem adversa populi voluntate appellassent. denique
4 ingentes ob hoc seditiones fuerunt. ad occidendum
autem Nigrum primipilarem Iulianus miserat, stulte
ad eum qui haberet exercitus et [2] se tueri [3] posset ;
proinde quasi qualis libet imperator a primipilario

---

[1] *et ius* Salmasius, Lenze ; *eius* P ; *eius* del. by Peter.
[2] om. in P.   [3] *seueri* P.

---

[1] But see c. vi. 6, where the contrary is stated emphatically.
[2] As chief centurion ; see note to *Avid. Cass.*, i. 1.
[3] The posts are referred to in the letter in c. iv. 4, as military tribuneships, and although this letter, like the others in
the *Historia Augusta*, is fictitious, its statement in this instance is nearer the truth than that of the present sentence.
[4] See *Com.*, xvii. 2.
[5] As a matter of fact, this happened after Niger's revolt ;
see *Sev.*, x. 1 and notes.

passion.[1] For a long time he commanded in the
ranks,[2] and finally, after holding many generalships,[3]
he reached the point where Commodus named him
to command the armies in Syria, chiefly on the
recommendation of the athlete who afterward
strangled Commodus ; [4] for so, at that time, were all
appointments made.

II. And now, after he learned that Commodus had
been murdered, that Julianus had been declared
emperor, and then, by order of Severus and the senate,
put to death, and that Albinus, furthermore, had assumed in Gaul ·the name and power of emperor,[5]
Pescennius was hailed imperator by the armies he
commanded in Syria ;—though more out of aversion
to Julianus, some say, than in rivalry of Severus.
Even before this, during the first days of Julianus'
reign, because of the dislike felt for the Emperor,
Pescennius was so favoured at Rome, that even the
senators, who hated Severus also, prayed for his success, while with showers of stones and general
execrations [6] the commons shouted " May the gods
preserve him as Emperor, and him as Augustus ".
For the mob hated Julianus because the soldiers had
slain Pertinax and declared Julianus emperor contrary to their wishes ; and there was violent rioting
on this account. Julianus, for his part, had sent a
senior centurion to assassinate Niger[7]—a piece of
folly, since the attempt was made against one who
led an army and could protect himself, and as though,
forsooth, any sort of emperor could be slain by a re-
tired centurion ! With equal madness he sent out a

[6] See *Did. Jul.*, iv. 3 f.
[7] Cf. *Did. Jul.*, v. 1 ; *Sev.*, v. 8.

5 posset occidi. eadem autem dementia etiam Severo
6 iam principi Iulianus successorem miserat. denique
etiam Aquilium centurionem notum caedibus ducum
miserat, quasi imperator tantus a centurione posset
7 occidi. par denique insania fuit, quod cum Severo
ex interdicto de imperio egisse fertur, ut iure videretur principatum praevenisse.

III. Et de Pescennio Nigro iudicium populi ex eo
apparuit, quod, cum ludos circenses Iulianus Romae
daret, et indiscrete subsellia [1] Circi Maximi repleta
essent, ingentique iniuria populi [2] adfectus esset, per
omnes uno consensu Pescennius Niger ad tutelam
urbis est expetitus, odio, ut diximus, Iuliani et amore
2 occisi Pertinacis; cum quidem Iulianus dixisse fertur
neque sibi neque Pescennio longum imperium deberi,
sed Severo, qui magis esset odio habendus a senatoribus, militibus, provincialibus, popularibus. quod
probavit rei eventus.

3 Et Pescennius quidem Severo eo tempore quo
Lugdunensem provinciam regebat amicissimus fuit;
4 nam ipse missus erat ad comprehendendos desertores,
5 qui innumeri Gallias tunc vexabant. in quo officio
quod se honeste gessit, iucundissimus fuit Severo, ita
ut de eo ad Commodum Septimius referret, adserens
6 necessarium rei publicae virum. et revera in re

---

[1] *se subsellia* P.   [2] *populi* Kellerbauer; *populus* P, Peter.

[1] Cf. *Did. Jul.*, v. 7-8; *Sev.*, v. 8.
[2] Cf. *Did. Jul.*, iv. 7.   [3] Cf. c. ii. 2.
[4] Cf. *Sev.*, iii. 8.   [5] See *Com.*, xvi. 2 and note.

successor for Severus when Severus had already become emperor; and lastly he sent the centurion Aquilius,[1] notorious as an assassin of generals, as if such an emperor could be slain by a centurion! It was similarly an act of insanity that he, according to report, dealt with Severus by issuing a proclamation forbidding him to seize the imperial power, so that he might seem to have established a prior claim to the empire by process of law!

III. What the people thought of Pescennius Niger is evident from the following: when Julianus gave circus-games at Rome, the people filled the seats of the Circus Maximus without distinction of rank, assailed him with much abuse, and then with one accord called for Pescennius Niger to protect the city[2]— partly out of hatred for Julianus, as we have said,[3] and partly out of love for the slain Pertinax. On this occasion Julianus is reported to have said that neither he himself nor Pescennius was destined to rule for long, but rather Severus, though he it was who was more worthy of hatred from the senators, the soldiers, the provincials and the city-mob. And this proved to be the case.

Now Pescennius was on very friendly terms with Severus at the time that the latter was governor of the province of Lugdunensis.[4] For he was sent to apprehend a body of deserters who were then ravaging Gaul in great numbers,[5] and because he conducted himself in this task with credit, he gained the esteem of Severus, so much so, in fact, that the latter wrote to Commodus about him, and averred that he was a man indispensable to the state. And he was, indeed, a strict man in all things military. No soldier under his command ever forced a provincial

militari vehemens fuit. numquam sub eo miles pro-
7 vinciali lignum, oleum, operam extorsit. ipse a
milite nihil accepit. cum tribunatus ageret, nihil ac-
8 cipi passus est. nam et imperator iam [1] tribunos
duos, quos constitit stellaturas accepisse, lapidibus
obrui ab auxiliaribus iussit.

9 Exstat epistula Severi, qua scribit ad Ragonium
Celsum Gallias regentem: "Miserum est ut imitari
eius disciplinam militarem non possimus [2] quem per
10 bellum vicimus. milites tui vagantur, tribuni medio
die lavant, pro tricliniis popinas habent, pro cubiculis
meritoria; saltant, bibunt,[3] cantant, et mensuras con-
viviorum hoc vocant cum sine mensura potarunt.[4]
11 haec, si ulla vena [5] paternae disciplinae viveret,
fierent? emenda igitur primum tribunos, deinde
militem. quem, quamdiu timuerit, tamdiu tenebis.[6]
12 sed scias idque de Nigro, militem timere non posse,
IV. nisi integri fuerint tribuni et duces militum." haec
de Pescennio Severus Augustus.

De hoc [7] adhuc milite Marcus Antoninus ad Cornelium Balbum: "Pescennium mihi laudas, agnosco;
nam et decessor tuus eum manu strenuum, vita

---

[1] *imperator iam* P corr., Peter; *imperatorium* P[1].   [2] *possumus* P.   [3] *uiuent* P.   [4] *hoc uocant cum s. m. potarunt* Editor; *uocant cum hoc s. m. potare* P; *uocant illi hoc s. m. potare* Peter.   [5] *uana* P.   [6] *timuerit . . . tenebis* Petschenig, cf. Hohl, *Klio*, xiii., p. 143; *timueris . . . timebis* P; <*non*> *timueris t. timeberis* Peter.   [7] *de hoc* om. in P.

---

[1] These were prohibited at this time (see also *Alex.*, xv. 5),
436

to give him fuel, oil, or service. He himself never accepted any presents from a soldier, and when he served as tribune he would not allow any to be accepted. Even as emperor, when two tribunes were proved to have made deductions from the soldiers' rations,[1] he ordered the auxiliaries to stone them.

There is extant a letter written by Severus to Ragonius Celsus, who was then governor of Gaul [2]: "It is a pity that we cannot imitate the military discipline of this man whom we have overcome in war. For your soldiers go straggling on all sides ; the tribunes bathe in the middle of the day; they have cook-shops for mess-halls and, instead of barracks, brothels ; they dance, they drink, they sing, and they regard as the proper limit to a banquet unlimited drinking. How, pray, if any traces of our ancestral discipline still remained, could these things be ? So then, first reform the tribunes, and then the rank and file. For as long as these fear you, so long will you hold them in check. But learn from Niger this also, that the soldiers cannot be made to fear you unless the tribunes and generals are irreproachable." IV. Thus did Severus Augustus write about Pescennius.

While Pescennius was still in the ranks, Marcus Antoninus wrote thus to Cornelius Balbus about him : "You sound the praises of Pescennius to me, and I recognize the man ; for your predecessor also declared that he was vigorous in action, dignified in demeanour,

but at a later period they were recognized by law; see *Cod. Just.*, xii. 38, 12.
[2] On the authenticity of such letters as the following see note to *Avid. Cass.*, i. 6.

2 gravem, et iam tum plus quam militem dixit. itaque
misi litteras recitandas ad signa, quibus eum trecentis
Armeniis et centum Sarmatis et mille nostris praeesse
3 iussi. tuum est ostendere hominem non ambitione,
quod nostris non convenit moribus, sed virtute venisse
ad eum locum quem avus meus Hadrianus, quem
Traianus proavus non nisi exploratissimis dabat."
4 De hoc eodem Commodus : " Pescennium fortem
virum novi et ei tribunatus iam duos dedi ; ducatum
mox dabo, ubi per senectutem Aelius Corduenus rem
5 publicam recusaverit". haec de eo iudicia omnium
fuerunt. sed et [1] Severus ipse saepe dixit ignotu-
rum se Pescennio, nisi perseveraret.
6 A Commodo denique Pescennius consul declaratus
Severo praepositus est, et quidem irato, quod primi-
pilaribus commendantibus consulatum Niger merere-
7 tur. in vita sua Severus dicit se, priusquam filii sui
id aetatis haberent ut imperare possent, aegrotantem
id in animo habuisse, ut, si quid forte sibi accidisset,
Niger Pescennius eodem et Clodius Albinus succe-
derent, qui ambo Severo gravissimi hostes exstiterunt.
8 unde apparet, quod etiam Severi de Pescennio iudicium
V. fuerit. si Severo credimus, fuit gloriae cupidus
Niger, vita fictus, moribus turpis, aetatis provectae,
cum in imperium invasit. ex quo cupiditates eius

[1] *se seuerus* P.

---

[1] See c. i. 5 and note.   [2] Cf. c. v. 8 ; *Sev.*, viii. 15.
[3] Prior to 189, in which year Severus seems to have been
consul ; see *Sev.*, iv. 4.
[4] See note to *Sev.*, iii. 2.

and even then more than a common soldier. Accordingly, I have sent letters to be read at review in which I have ordered him placed in command of three hundred Armenians, one hundred Sarmatians, and a thousand of our own troops. It is your place to show that the man has attained, not by intrigue, which is displeasing to our principles, but by merit, to a post which my grandfather Hadrian and my great-grandfather Trajan gave to none but the most thoroughly tried."

Again, Commodus said of this same man : " I know Pescennius for a brave man, and I have already made him tribune twice.[1] Presently, when advancing years shall make Aelius Corduenus retire from public life, I will make him a general." Such were the opinions that all men had of him. And in truth Severus himself frequently declared that he would have pardoned him had he not persisted.[2]

Finally, Commodus appointed him consul,[3] and advanced him thereby over Severus, greatly indeed to the latter's wrath, since he thought that Niger had gained the consulship on the recommendation of the senior centurions. Yet in his autobiography [4] Severus says that on one occasion, when he had fallen sick and his sons had not yet reached an age when they could rule, he intended, if anything by any chance should happen to him, to appoint Pescennius Niger and Clodius Albinus as his heirs to the throne, even these two men who in time became his bitterest enemies. From this it is evident what Severus thought of Pescennius. V. But if we may believe Severus, Niger was greedy for glory, hypocritical in his mode of life, base in morals, and well advanced in years when he attempted to seize the empire—for which

439

incusat, proinde quasi Severus minor ad imperium
venerit, qui annos suos contrahit, cum decem et octo
annis imperavit et octogensimo nono periit.

2   Sane Severus Heraclitum ad obtinendam Bithyniam
misit, Fulvium autem ad occupandos adultos Nigri
3 filios. nec tamen in senatum quicquam de Nigro
Severus dixit, cum iam audisset de eius imperio, ipse
autem   proficisceretur   ad   componendum   orientis
4 statum. tantum [1] sane illud fecit proficiscens, ut
legiones ad Africam mitteret, ne eam Pescennius occuparet et fame populum Romanum perurgueret.
5 videbatur [2] autem id facere posse per Libyam
Aegyptumque vicinas Africae, difficili licet itinere ac
6 navigatione. et Pescennius quidem veniente ad
orientem Severo Graeciam, Thracias, Macedoniam,
interfectis multis inlustribus viris tenebat, ad partici-
7 patum imperii Severum vocans. a quo, causa eorum
quos occiderat, cum Aemiliano hostis est appellatus.
dein a ducibus Severi per Aemilianum pugnans victus
8 est. et cum illi tutum exsilium promitteret, si ab
armis recederet, persistens iterum pugnavit et victus
est atque apud Cyzicum circa paludem fugiens
sauciatus, et sic ad Severum adductus atque statim

---

[1] *tantum sane illud* P ; *Tantum sane ille* Damsté ; *statum
tantum. sane illud* Peter[1] ; *statum nutantem. sane illud*
Petschenig, Peter[2].   [2] *uidebatur* Peter ; *et uidebatur* P.

---

[1] See *Sev.*, xxii. 1 and note.
[2] See *Sev.*, vi. 10 and notes.   [3] Cf. *Sev.*, viii. 7.
[4] On Niger's revolt see *Sev.*, viii. 12 f. and notes.
[5] Near Nicaea in Bithynia ; see note to *Sev.*, viii. 17.

reason Severus inveighs against his ambition, just
as if he himself came to the throne young! For
though he understated the number of his years,
after ruling eighteen years he died at the age of
eighty-nine.[1]

Now Severus dispatched Heraclitus to secure
Bithynia and Fulvius to seize Niger's adult children.[2]
Nevertheless, although he had already heard that
Niger had seized the empire, and although he himself was on the point of setting out to remedy the
situation in the East, he made no mention of Niger
in the senate. In fact, on setting out, he did only July, 193
this—namely, send troops to Africa, fearing that
Niger would seize it and thereby distress the Roman
people with a famine.[3] For such a plan was possible of accomplishment, it seemed, by way of Libya
and Egypt, the provinces adjacent to Africa, for all
that it was no easy journey either by land or
sea. As for Pescennius,[4] he slew a multitude of
distinguished men and got control of Greece,
Thrace, and Macedonia, while Severus was still on
his way to the East. He then proposed to Severus
that they two share the throne between them;
whereupon Severus, because of the men whom Niger
had slain, declared him and Aemilianus enemies to
the state. Soon after, Niger gave battle under the
leadership of Aemilianus and suffered defeat from
Severus' generals. Even then, Severus promised him
safety in exile if he would lay down his arms.
Niger, however, persisted and gave battle a second
time, but was defeated[5]; and in his flight while near
the lake at Cyzicus he was wounded and was thus
brought before Severus, and presently he was dead.
VI. His head was paraded on a pike and then sent

441

PESCENNIUS NIGER

VI. mortuus. huius caput circumlatum pilo Romam
missum, filii occisi, necata uxor, patrimonium publi-
2 catum, familia omnis exstincta. sed haec omnia,
postquam de Albini rebellione cognitum est, facta
sunt ; nam prius et filios Nigri et matrem in exsilium
3 miserat. sed exarsit secundo civili bello, immo iam
4 tertio, et factus est durior; tunc cum innumeros senatores interemit Severus et ab aliis Sullae Punici, ab
aliis Marii nomen accepit.
5 Fuit statura prolixa, forma decorus, capillo in verti-
cem ad gratiam reflexo, vocis canorae, ita ut in
campo loquens per mille passus audiretur, nisi ventus
adversaretur, oris verecundi et semper rubidi, cervice
adeo nigra, ut, quem ad modum multi dicunt, ab ea
6 Nigri nomen acceperit, cetera corporis parte candidus
et magis pinguis, vini avidus, cibi parcus, rei veneriae
7 nisi ad creandos liberos prorsus ignarus. denique
etiam sacra quaedam in Gallia, quae semper[1] castissimis
decernunt consensu publico celebranda, suscepit.
8 hunc in Commodianis hortis in porticu curva pictum
de musivo[2] inter Commodi amicissimos videmus sacra
9 Isidis ferentem ; quibus Commodus adeo deditus fuit,
ut et caput raderet et Anubin portaret et omnis
pausas[3] expleret.

---

[1] *quae semper* Editor ; *qua se* P ; † *qua se* Peter.   [2] *musio*
P, Peter.   [3] *pausas* Gruter ; *paucas* P.

---

[1] See *Sev.*, x. 1.   [2] The revolt of Albinus.
[3] See *Sev.*, xiii.
[4] An allusion to the proscriptions of Marius and Sulla.
According to Dio, lxxv. 8, 1, Severus in a speech to the senate
praised their severity. He is called " Punic" because he
came from Africa.

442

to Rome. His children were put to death, his wife was murdered, his estates were confiscated, and his entire household utterly blotted out. All this, however, was done after news of the revolt of Albinus was received,[1] for before that Niger's children and their mother had merely been sent into exile. But Severus was exasperated by the second civil war, or rather the third,[2] and became implacable; and it was then that he put countless senators to death[3] and got himself called by some the Punic Sulla, by others the Punic Marius.[4]

In stature Niger was tall, in appearance attractive; and his hair grew back in a graceful way toward the crown of his head. His voice was so penetrating that when he spoke in the open he could be heard a thousand paces away, if the wind were not against him. His countenance was dignified and always somewhat ruddy; his neck was so black that many men say that he was called Niger on this account. The rest of his body, however, was very white and he was inclined to be fat. He was fond of wine, sparing in his use of food, and as for intercourse with women, he abstained from it wholly save for the purpose of begetting children.[5] Indeed, certain religious rites in Gaul, which they always by common consent vote to the most chaste to celebrate, Niger himself performed. On the rounded colonnade in the garden of Commodus he is to be seen pictured in the mosaic among Commodus' most intimate friends and performing the rites of Isis.[6] To these rites Commodus was so devoted as even to shave his head, carry the image of Anubis, and make every one of the ritualistic pauses in the procession.

[5] But see c. i. 4.   [6] See *Com.*, ix. 3 f.

10 Fuit ergo miles optimus, tribunus singularis, dux
praecipuus, legatus severissimus, consul insignis, vir
domi forisque conspicuus, imperator infelix; usui
denique rei publicae sub Severo, homine tetrico, esse
VII. potuisset, si cum eo esse voluisset. sed deceptus est
consiliis scaevis [1] Aureliani, qui filias suas eius filiis
despondens persistere eum fecit in imperio.

2 Hic tantae fuit auctoritatis, ut ad Marcum primum
deinde ad Commodum scriberet, cum videret provincias facili administrationum mutatione subverti,
primum ut nulli ante quinquennium succederetur provinciae praesidi vel legato vel proconsuli, quod prius
deponerent potestatem quam scirent administrare.
3 deinde ne novi ad regendam rem publicam accederent
praeter militares administrationes intimavit, ut assessores in quibus provinciis adsedissent, in his
4 administrarent. quod postea Severus et deinceps
multi tenuerunt, ut probant Pauli et Ulpiani praefecturae, qui Papiniano in consilio fuerunt ac postea,
cum unus ad memoriam, alter ad libellos paruisset,

[1] *scaeuis* Salmasius; *sceui* P.

---

[1] On the distinction see note to *Hadr.*, iii. 9.
[2] The *assessores* (also called *consiliarii*), the governor's
especial assistants in all matters pertaining to the administration of justice, sat by him at trials (hence the name) and
gave him advice in legal matters. On this office see *Digesta*,
i. 22.
[3] In his capacity as prefect of the guard. These three men
were the famous jurists constantly cited in the *Digesta*.
[4] These two officials, together with three others, the secretary of the emperor (*ab epistulis*, see *Hadr.*, xi. 3), the secretary
for the imperial trials (*a cognitionibus*), and the emperor's

As a soldier, then, he was excellent; as a tribune, without peer; as a general, eminent; as a governor, stern; as a consul, distinguished; as a man, one to be noted both at home and abroad; but as an emperor, unlucky. Under Severus, who was a forbidding sort of man, he might have been of use to the state had he been willing to cast in his lot with him. VII. But this could not be, for he was deceived by the sinister counsels of Aurelianus, who espoused his daughters to Niger's sons and made him persist in his attempt at empire.

He was a man of such influence that when he saw the provinces being demoralized by frequent changes of administration, he ventured to write to Marcus, and later to Commodus, making two recommendations: first, that no provincial governor, legate or proconsul,[1] should be superseded within a term of five years, because otherwise they laid down their power before they learned how to rule; and second, that save for posts held by soldiers, no man without previous experience should be appointed to take part in the government of the empire, the purpose of this being that assistants[2] should be promoted to the administration of those provinces only in which they had served as assistants. Afterwards this very principle was maintained by Severus and many of his successors, as the prefectures of Paulus and Ulpian prove—for these men were assistants to Papinian,[3] and afterwards, when the one had served as secretary of memoranda and the other as secretary of petitions,[4] both were next appointed

literary adviser (*a studiis*) were important and influential members of the imperial cabinet. Originally, these posts were held by freedmen of the emperor, but after Hadrian's reform of the civil service they were assigned to Equites; see *Hadr.*, xxii. 8.

5 statim praefecti facti sunt. huius etiam illud fuit, ut
nemo adsideret in sua provincia, nemo administraret
6 nisi Romae Romanus, hoc est oriundus urbe. addidit
praeterea consiliariis salaria, ne eos gravarent quibus
adsidebant, dicens iudicem nec dare debere nec acci-
7 pere. hic erga milites tanta fuit censura, ut, cum
apud Aegyptum ab eo limitanei vinum peterent,
responderit "Nilum habetis et vinum quaeritis?";
si quidem tanta illius fluminis dulcitudo, ut accolae
8 vina non quaerant. idem tumultuantibus iis qui
a Saracenis victi fuerant et dicentibus, "Vinum non
accepimus, pugnare non possumus," "Erubescite,"
9 inquit, "illi qui vos vincunt aquam bibunt". idem
Palaestinis rogantibus ut eorum censitio levaretur
idcirco quod esset gravata respondit: "Vos terras
vestras levari censitione vultis; ego vero etiam aerem
vestrum censere vellem".

VIII. Denique Delphici Apollinis vates in motu [1] rei
publicae maximo, cum nuntiaretur tres esse imperatores, Severum Septimium, Pescennium Nigrum,
Clodium Albinum, consultus quem expediret rei publicae imperare, versum Graecum huiusmodi fudisse
dicitur:

"Optimus est Fuscus, bonus Afer, pessimus Albus."

[1] *immo* P.

---

[1] *i.e.*, the *assessores*. Salaries had already been granted to
them by Antoninus Pius; see *Digesta*, l. 13, 4. If the present
passage and *Alex.*, xlvi. 1 are correct, however, it would seem
that the grant had not been carried out in full.

446

prefects of the guard. It was also a recommendation of his that no one should serve as assistant in the province of his birth, and that no one should govern a province who was not a Roman of Rome, that is, a man born in the city itself. He also recommended salaries for the members of the governor's council,[1] in order to prevent their being a burden to those to whom they were advisers, adding that judges ought neither to give nor receive. With his soldiers he was severity itself; once, for example, when the frontier troops in Egypt asked him for wine, he replied: "Do you ask for wine when you have the Nile?" In fact, the waters of the Nile are so sweet that the inhabitants of the country do not ask for wine. And similarly, when the troops made a great uproar after they had been defeated by the Saracens, and cried out, "We get no wine, we cannot fight!", "Then blush," said he, "for the men who defeat you drink water." Likewise, when the people of Palestine besought him to lessen their tribute, saying that it bore heavily on them, he replied: "So you wish me to lighten the tax on your lands; verily, if I had my way, I would tax your air".

VIII. Now when the confusion in the state was at its height, inasmuch as it was made known that there were three several emperors, Septimius Severus, Pescennius Niger, and Clodius Albinus, the priest of the Delphic Apollo was asked which of them as emperor would prove of most profit to the state, whereupon, it is said, he gave voice to a Greek verse as follows:

"Best is the Dark One, the African good, but the worst is the White One."

2 ex quo intellectum Fuscum Nigrum appellatum vatici-
natione, Severum Afrum, Album vero Albinum dic-
3 tum. nec defuit alia curiositas, qua requisitum est
qui esset obtenturus rem publicam. ad quod ille respondit alium versum talem:

"Fundetur sanguis Albi Nigrique animantis,
    imperium mundi Poena reget urbe profectus."

4 item, cum quaesitum esset quis illi [1] successurus esset,
respondisse itidem Graeco versu dicitur:

"Cui dederint superi nomen habere Pii."

5 quod omnino intellectum non est nisi cum Bassianus
Antonini, quod verum signum Pii fuit, nomen accepit.
6 item cum quaereretur quamdiu imperaturus esset,
respondisse Graece dicitur:

"Bis denis Italum conscendit navibus aequor,
    si tamen una ratis transiliet pelagus."

ex quo intellectum Severum viginti annos expletu-
rum.

IX. Haec sunt, Diocletiane maxime Augustorum,
quae de Pescennio didicimus ex pluribus libris. non
enim facile, ut in principio libri diximus, quisquam

[1] *illis* P.

---

[1] See *Sev.*, x. 3.   [2] An adaptation of *Aeneid*, i. 381.

And in this response it was clearly understood that Niger was meant by the Dark One, Severus by the African, and Albinus by the White One. Thereupon the curiosity of the questioners was aroused, and they asked who would really win the empire. To this the priest replied with further verses somewhat as follows:

"Both of the Black and the White shall the life-blood be shed all untimely;
Empire over the world shall be held by the native of Carthage."

And then when the priest was asked who should succeed this man, he gave answer, it is said, with another Greek verse:

"He whom the dwellers above have called by the surname of Pius."

But this was altogether unintelligible until Bassianus took the name Antoninus,[1] which was Pius' true surname. And when finally they asked how long he should rule, the priest is said to have replied in Greek as follows:

"Surely with twice ten ships he will cleave the Italian waters,[2]
Only let one of his barques bound o'er the plain of the sea."

From this they perceived that Severus would round out twenty years.

IX. This, Diocletian, greatest of emperors, is what we have learned concerning Pescennius, gathering it from many books. For when a man consigns to books the lives of men who were not rulers in the

vitas eorum mittit in libros, qui aut principes in re
publica non fuerunt aut a senatu appellati non sunt
imperatores, aut occisi citius ad famam venire ne-
2 quiverunt. inde quod latet Vindex, quod Piso
nescitur, quod omnes illi qui aut tantum adoptati
sunt aut a militibus imperatores appellati, ut sub
Domitiano Antonius, aut cito interempti vitam cum
3 imperii usurpatione posuerunt. sequitur nunc ut de
Clodio Albino dicam, qui quasi socius huius habetur,
quod et pariter contra Severum rebellarunt et ab
eodem victi atque occisi sunt. de quo ipso neque
4 satis clara exstant, quia eadem fortuna illius fuit
quae Pescennii, etiamsi vita satis dispar.
5   Ac ne quid ex iis quae ad Pescennium pertinent
praeterisse videamur, licet aliis libris cognosci possint,
de hoc Septimio Severo vates dixerunt quod neque
vivus neque mortuus in potestatem Severi venturus
6 esset, sed iuxta aquas illi pereundum esset. quod
quidam[1] dicunt ipsum Severum de mathesi, qua
callebat, dixisse. nec abfuit[2] responsis veritas, cum
ille inventus sit iuxta paludem semivivus.

X. Hic tantae fuit severitatis, ut, cum milites
quosdam in cauco argenteo expeditionis tempore

[1] Cf. c. i. 1.
[2] C. Julius Vindex, the governor of Gallia Lugdunensis, who
led a revolt against Nero in 68 and was defeated by the army
from Germany; see Suetonius, *Nero*, xl. f.
[3] C. Calpurnius Piso, the nominal head of a wide-spread
conspiracy formed against Nero in 65; see Tacitus, *Annals*,
xv. 48-59.

state, or of those, again, who were not declared
emperors by the senate, or, lastly, of those who were
so quickly killed that they could not attain to fame,
his task is difficult, as we said at the beginning of
this work.[1] It is for this reason that Vindex[2] is
obscure and Piso[3] unknown, as well as all those
others also who were merely adopted, or were hailed
as emperors by the soldiers (as was Antonius[4] in
Domitian's time), or were speedily slain and gave up
their lives and their attempt at empire together. It
now remains for me to speak of Clodius Albinus,[5]
who is considered this man's ally, in a way, since
they rebelled against Severus similarly, and were
similarly overcome by him and put to death. But
we have no clear information concerning him either,
since he and Pescennius were the same in fate, however much they differed in their lives.

And lest we seem to omit any of the tales which
are told of Pescennius, for all that they can be read
in other books, the soothsayers told Severus concerning Pescennius that neither living nor yet dead
would he fall into Severus' hands but would perish
near the water. Some say that Severus himself
made this statement, learning it from astrology, in
which he was very skilled. Nor was the augury
devoid of truth, for Pescennius was found half dead
near a lake.[6]

X. Pescennius was a man of unusual rigour; when
he learned, for instance, that various soldiers were
drinking from silver cups while on a campaign, he

---

[4] L. Antonius Saturninus, governor of Upper Germany,
who with two legions attempted a revolt in 88, but was soon
defeated and put to death; see Suetonius, *Domitian*, vi.
[5] See *Sev.*, x-xi; *Cl. Alb.*, ix.   [6] Cf. c. v. 8.

bibere vidisset, iusserit omne argentum summoveri
de usu expeditionali, addito eo ut ligneis vasis ute-
rentur. quod quidem illi odium militare concitavit.
2 dicebat enim posse fieri, ut sarcinae militares in potestatem hostium venirent, nec se barbarae nationes
argento nostro gloriosiores facerent, cum alia minus
3 apta hosticam viderentur ad gloriam. idem iussit
vinum in expeditione neminem bibere, sed aceto
4 universos esse contentos. idem pistores sequi ex-
peditionem prohibuit, bucellato iubens milites et
5 omnes contentos esse. idem ob unius gallinacei
direptionem decem commanipulones, qui raptum ab
uno comederant, securi percuti iussit; et fecisset, nisi
ab omni exercitu prope usque ad metum seditionis
6 esset rogatus. et cum pepercisset, iussit ut denorum
gallinaceorum pretia provinciali redderent decem,
qui simul furto convixerant, addito eo ut tota in expeditione in commanipulatione nemo focum faceret,
ne umquam recens coctum cibum sumerent, sed
pane ac frigida vescerentur, adpositis speculatori-
7 bus, qui id curarent. idem iussit, ne zona milites ad
bellum ituri [1] aureos vel argenteos nummos portarent,
sed publice commendarent, recepturi post proelia

[1] *item* P.

---

[1] Cf. *Hadr.*, x. 2.

gave orders that all silver whatever should be
banished from the camp in war-time, and added that
the soldiers should use wooden cups—a command
that gained him their resentment. For it was not
impossible, he said, that the soldiers' individual
baggage might fall into the hands of the enemy, and
foreign tribes should not be given cause for glorying
in our silver, when there were other articles that
would contribute less to a foeman's glory. He gave
orders, likewise, that in time of campaign the soldiers
should not drink wine but should all content themselves with vinegar.[1] He also forbade pastry-
cooks to follow expeditions, ordering both soldiers
and all others to content themselves with biscuit.
For the theft of a single cock, furthermore, he gave
an order that the ten comrades who had shared the
bird which one of them had stolen, should all be beheaded; and he would have carried out the sentence,
had not the entire army importuned him to such a
degree that there was reason to fear a mutiny. And
when he had spared them, he ordered that each of
the ten who had feasted on the stolen bird should
pay the provincial who owned it the price of ten
cocks. At this same time he ordered that no one
during the whole period of the campaign should
build a hearth in his company-quarters, and that
they should never eat freshly-cooked food, but should
live on bread and cold water. And he set spies to
see that this was done. He gave orders, likewise,
that the soldiers should not carry gold or silver coin
in their money-belts when about to go into action,
but should deposit them with a designated official.
After the battle, he assured them, they would get
back what they had deposited, or the official who had

quod dederant, addens liberis eorum et uxoribus
heredibus certe reddendum, cui[1] venisset, ne ad
hostes aliquid praedae perveniret, si quid forte ad-
8 versi fortuna fecisset.   sed haec omnia, ut se habuerat
Commodi temporum dissolutio, adversa eidem fuere.
9 denique etiamsi nemo fuit, qui suis temporibus dux
severior videretur, ad perniciem[2] illi magis vivo[3] quam
mortuo, ubi et invidia et odium deposita erant, talia
exempla valuerunt.

XI. Idem in omni expeditione ante omnes militarem cibum sumpsit ante papilionem, nec sibi umquam
vel contra solem vel contra imbres quaesivit tecti
2 suffragium, si miles non habuit.   tantum denique
belli tempore, ratione militibus demonstrata, sibi et
servis suis vel contubernalibus putavit[4] quantum a
militibus ferebatur, cum servos suos annona oneraret,
ne illi securi ambularent et onusti milites, idque ab
3 exercitu cum suspirio videretur.   idem in contione
iuravit se, quamdiu in expeditionibus fuisset essetque[5]
adhuc futurus, non aliter egisse[6] acturumque esse
quam militem, Marium ante oculos habentem et
4 duces tales.   nec alias fabulas umquam habuit nisi
5 de[7] Hannibale ceterisque talibus.   denique cum imperatori facto quidam panegyricum recitare vellet,
dixit ei: "Scribe laudes Marii vel Hannibalis vel
cuiusvis[8] ducis optimi vita functi, et dic quid
6 ille fecerit, ut eum nos imitemur.   nam viventes

---

[1] *cui* Salmasius; *qui* P.   [2] *ad perniciem* Edit. Princeps;
perniciem P, Peter.   [3] *magis uiuo quam mortuo* Editor;
magis ista quam mortuo P; lacuna before *mortuo* Peter.
[4] *putauit* Hirschfeld, Peter[2]; *portauit* P, Peter[1].   [5] *esse
quae* P.   [6] *egisse* Salmasius; *esse* P.   [7] om. in P.
[8] <*uel*> *cuiusuis* Baehrens, Peter[2]; *cuius* P; <*uel*> *alius*
Peter[1].

received it would pay it to their heirs—that is, their wives and children—without fail. Thus, he reasoned, no plunder would pass to the enemy, should fortune bring some disaster. All these stern measures, however, worked to his disadvantage in times so slack as those of Commodus. For even if there was no one who seemed to his own times a sterner general, these measures availed to damage him rather during his life than after his death, when both envy and malice were laid by.

XI. On all his campaigns he took his meals in front of his tent and in the presence of all his men, and he ate the soldiers' own fare, too ; nor did he ever seek shelter against sun or against rain if a soldier was without it. In time of war he assigned to himself and to his slaves or aides as heavy burdens as were borne by the soldiers themselves, expounding to the soldiers the reason therefor ; for in order that his slaves might not be without burdens on the march while the soldiers carried packs and this seem a grievous thing to the army, he loaded them with rations. He took an oath, besides, in the presence of an assembly, that as long as he had conducted campaigns and as long as he expected to conduct them, he had not in the past and would not in the future act otherwise than as a simple soldier—having before his eyes Marius and such commanders as he. He never told anecdotes about anyone save Hannibal and others such as he. Indeed, when some one wished to recite him a panegyric at the time that he was declared emperor, he said to him : " Write praises of Marius, or Hannibal, or of any pre-eminent general now dead, and tell what he did, that we may imitate him. For the praise of the living is mere mockery,

455

laudare inrisio est, maxime imperatores, a quibus
speratur, qui timentur, qui praestare publice possunt,
qui possunt necare, qui proscribere.'' se autem
vivum placere velle, mortuum etiam laudari.

XII. Amavit de principibus Augustum, Vespasian-
um, Titum, Traianum, Pium, Marcum, reliquos faeneos
vel venenatos vocans ; maxime tamen in historiis
Marium et Camillum et Quinctium et [1] Marcium
2 Coriolanum dilexit. interrogatus autem quid de
Scipionibus sentiret, dixisse fertur felices illos fuisse
magis quam fortes ; idque probare domesticam vitam
et iuventutem, quae in utroque minus speciosa domi
3 fuisset. apud omnes constat quod, si rerum potitus
fuisset, omnia correcturus fuerit, quae Severus vel
non potuit emendare vel noluit, et quidem sine
crudelitate, immo etiam cum lenitate, sed militari,
non remissa et inepta atque ridicula.

4   Domus eius hodie Romae visitur in Campo Iovis,
quae appellatur Pescenniana.[2] in qua simulacrum eius
in trichoro consistit, positum [3] ex Thebaico marmore,
quod ille ad similitudinem sui factum a grege [4]
5 Thebaeorum acceperat. exstat etiam epigramma
Graecum, quod Latine hanc habet sententiam :

[1] *Quinctium et Marcium* Jordan; *quintum marcium* P.
[2] *pescenniani* P.   [3] *consistit, positum* Peter ; *constituit statim*
post annum P.   [4] *grege* Lumbroso ; *rege* P, Peter.

---

[1] M. Furius Camillus, who as dictator captured Veii in 396
B.C. and later defeated the Volscians.
[2] L. Quinctius Cincinnatus, dictator in 458 B.C., when he
defeated the Aequi.
[3] Leader of the Romans against the Volscians, whom, after

and most of all the praise of emperors, in whose power it lies to kindle hope or fear, to give advancement in public life, to condemn to death, and to declare a man an outlaw." He added that he wished to give satisfaction in his life-time, and after his death to be praised as well.

XII. His favourites among his predecessors were Augustus, Vespasian, Titus, Trajan, Pius, and Marcus; the others, he averred, were either puppets or monsters. Among the characters of history he admired most of all Marius, Camillus,[1] Quinctius,[2] and Marcius Coriolanus.[3] And once, when asked his opinion concerning the Scipios, he replied, it is said, that they were rather fortunate than forceful, as was shown by their home-lives and by their youth, which, in the case of both, had not been conspicuous at home. All men are agreed that he proposed, had he gained the throne, to correct all the evils which Severus, later, either could not or would not correct; and this he would have accomplished without any cruelty, or rather even with mercy, but yet the mercy of a soldier, not weak or absurd and a subject for mockery.

His house, still called by the name of Pescennius, may still be seen in the Field of Jupiter.[4] Within, in a certain room with three compartments there stands his statue, carved in Theban marble,[5] depicting his likeness, and given him by the common people of Thebes. There is preserved, besides, an epigram in Greek which, rendered into Latin, runs as follows:

he was exiled from Rome in 491 B.C., he joined and led against Rome.

[4] The site of this is unknown.

[5] Black basalt, called by the ancients *basanites*, was brought to Rome from upper Egypt; see Pliny, *Nat. Hist.*, xxxvi. 58.

PESCENNIUS NIGER

6 "Terror Aegyptiaci Niger astat militis ingens,
  Thebaidos socius, aurea saecla volens.
  hunc reges, hunc gentes amant, hunc aurea Roma,
  hic Antoninis carus et [1] imperio.
  Nigrum nomen habet, nigrum [2] formavimus ipsi,
  ut consentiret forma, metalle, tibi."

7 quos quidem versus Severus eradi noluit, cum hoc
ei et praefecti suggererent et officiorum magistri,
8 addens : "Si talis fuit, sciant omnes qualem vicerimus ; si talis non fuit, putent omnes nos talem
vicisse ; immo sic sit, quia fuit talis."

---

[1] om. in P.   [2] *nigram* P.

" Glorious Niger stands here, the dread of the soldiers
     of Egypt,
Faithful ally of Thebes, willing a golden age.
Loved by the kings and the nations of earth, and by
     Rome the all golden,
Dear to the Antonines, aye, dear to the Empire too.
Black is the surname he bears, and black is the statue
     we've fashioned,
Thus do surname and hue, hero and marble, agree."

As for these verses, Severus refused to erase them
when this was proposed by his prefects and masters
of ceremonies, and said, besides : " If indeed he was
such a man, let all men learn how great was the man
we vanquished ; if such he was not, let all men deem
that such was the man we vanquished ; no, leave it
as it is, for such he really was ".

CLODII ALBINI

IULII CAPITOLINI

I. Uno eodemque prope tempore post Pertinacem, qui auctore [1] Albino interemptus est, Iulianus a senatu Romae, Septimius Severus ab exercitu in Illyrico,[2] Pescennius Niger in Oriente, Clodius Albinus in Gallia imperatores appellati. et Clodium [3] quidem Herodianus dicit Severi [4] Caesarem fuisse. sed cum alter alterum indignaretur imperare, nec Galli ferre possent aut Germaniciani [5] exercitus quod et ipsi suum specialem principem haberent, undique cuncta turbata sunt.

Fuit autem Clodius Albinus familia nobili, Hadrumetinus tamen ex Africa. quare sortem illam, qua [6] Severum laudatum in Pescennii vita diximus, ad

[1] *auctor* P.　　[2] *Illyrico* Erasmus; *syria* P.　　[3] *clodius* P.　　[4] *seuerum* P.　　[5] *Germaniciani* Salmasius; *germaniani* P.　　[6] *quae* P.

---

[1] Repeated in c. xiv. 2 and 6, and found in other late writers. There is no suggestion of it in Dio or Herodian and it seems to be wholly untrue.

[2] Albinus was not acclaimed emperor until 196, after Niger's revolt was crushed; see *Sev.*, x. 1.

[3] See *Sev.*, x. 7—xi. 2.

CLODIUS ALBINUS

BY

JULIUS CAPITOLINUS

I. After the death of Pertinax, who was slain at Albinus' advice,[1] various men were hailed emperor at about one and the same time[2]—by the senate Julianus at Rome, and by the armies, Septimius Severus in Illyricum, Pescennius Niger in the East, and Clodius Albinus in Gaul.[3] According to Herodian, Clodius had been named Caesar by Severus.[4] But as time went on, each chafed at the other's rule, and the armies of Gaul and Germany demanded an emperor of their own naming, and so all parts of the empire were thrown into an uproar.

Now Clodius Albinus came of a noble family,[5] but he was a native of Hadrumetum in Africa. Because of this, he applied to himself the oracle in praise of Severus, which we quoted in the Life of Pescennius,

---

[4] See Herodian, ii. 15, 3; Dio, lxxiii. 15, 1. These writers indicate that this was merely a trick on Severus' part, the purpose of which was to prevent Albinus from attacking him during his campaign against Niger. According to c. iii. 4-5 and x. 3, on the other hand, Severus really intended to make Albinus his successor. The name Caesar appears in Albinus' inscriptions (see Dessau, *Ins. Sel.*, 414 and 415) and on his coins (see Cohen, iii², p. 416 f.).

[5] According to Herodian, ii. 15, 1, the family was of senatorial rank.

se trahebat, nolens intellegi "Pessimus Albus," [1]
quod eodem versu continebatur quo et Severi laus et
5 adprobatio Nigri Pescennii. sed priusquam vel de
vita eius vel de morte dissero, etiam hoc dicendum
est quod eum nobilem fecit.

II. Nam ad hunc eundem quondam Commodus
tum cum [2] successorem Albino daret, litteras dederat,
quibus iusserat ut Caesar esset. exemplum indidi:
2 "Imperator Commodus Clodio Albino. alias ad
te publice de successione atque honore tuo misi, sed
hanc familiarem et domesticam, omnem, ut vides,
manu mea scriptam, qua tibi do facultatem, ut, si
necessitas fuerit, ad milites prodeas et tibi Caesarea-
3 num nomen adsumas. audio enim et Septimium
Severum et Nonium Murcum male de me apud
milites loqui, ut sibi parent stationis Augustae pro-
4 curationem. habebis praeterea, cum id feceris,
dandi stipendii usque ad tres aureos liberam potestatem, quia et super hoc ad procuratores meos litteras
misi, quas ipse signatas excipies signo Amazonio et,
cum opus fuerit, rationalibus dabis, ne te non audiant,
5 cum de aerario volueris imperare. sane ut tibi insigne
aliquod [3] imperialis maiestatis adiciam,[4] habebis
utendi coccini pallii facultatem in praesenti [5] et ad me,

[1] *Albus* Jordan; *albinus* P.   [2] *tum cum* Peter; *cum eum*
P.   [3] *aliquid* P[1].   [4] *adiciam* Peter; *accedam* P.   [5] *in
praesenti* Damsté; *me praesentem* P; *impraesentiarum* P[2].

---

[1] *Pesc. Nig.*, viii. 1.
[2] On this and the other letters in this biography see note to
Avid. Cass., i. 6.
[3] See *Sev.*, vi. 9 and note.

for he did not wish it to be interpreted as " the worst is the White One," which is contained in the same line in which Severus is praised and Pescennius Niger commended.[1]   But before I discourse on his life and his death I should relate the manner in which he became ennobled.

II. There is a certain letter [2] which Commodus sent Albinus once, on naming his successor in office, in which he bade him assume the name of Caesar ; [3] of this letter I append a copy :

" The Emperor Commodus to Clodius Albinus greeting.   I wrote you once officially about the succession to the throne and your own elevation to honour, but I am now sending you this private and confidential message, all written with my own hand, as you will see, in which I empower you, should emergency arise, to present yourself to the soldiers and assume the name of Caesar.   For I hear that both Septimius Severus and Nonius Murcus are speaking ill of me to their troops, hoping thereby to get the appointment to the post of Augustus.   You shall have full power besides, when you thus present yourself, to give the soldiers a largess of three aurei apiece.   You will get a letter which I am sending to my procurators to this effect, sealed with my signet of an Amazon,[4] which you will deliver to my stewards when the need arises, that they may not refuse your demands on the treasury. And that you may receive some definite symbol of an emperor's majesty, I authorize you to wear both at the present time and at my court the scarlet cloak.[5]

[4] Commodus had his concubine Marcia portrayed as an Amazon ; see *Com.*, xi. 9.

[5] The *paludamentum*, worn in the republican period by the commanding general.   In the imperial era its use was restricted to members of the emperor's family.

et cum mecum fueris, habiturus et purpuram sed sine auro, quia ita et proavus meus Verus, qui puer vita functus est, ab Hadriano, qui eum adoptavit, accepit."

III. His litteris acceptis omnino [1] facere id quod iubebat noluit, videns [2] odiosum [3] Commodum propter mores suos, quibus rem publicam perdiderat et se dedecoraverat, quandocumque feriendum, et timens [4] ne ipse pariter occideretur.

2 Exstat denique illius contio qua,[5] cum accepit imperium, et quidem Severi, ut quidam, voluntate 3 firmatum, huius rei memoriam facit. cuius hoc exemplum est : "Invitum me, commilitones, ductum ad imperium etiam illud probat, quod Commodum donantem me Caesareano nomine contempsi ; sed et vestrae voluntati [6] et Severi Augusti parendum est, quia credo sub homine optimo et viro forti posse bene rem publicam regi ".

4 Nec negari potest,[7] quod [8] etiam Marius Maximus dicit, hunc animum Severo primum fuisse, ut, si quid ei contingeret, Pescennium Nigrum et Clodium 5 Albinum sibi substitueret. sed postea et filiis iam

---

[1] *a nonio* P.   [2] *uidens* Salmasius; *umen* P.   [3] *odiosum* Peter from Σ; om. in P.   [4] *timens* Salmasius; *eum timens* P.   [5] *quam* P.   [6] *uoluntatis* P¹.   [7] *potes* P¹.   [8] *quos* P¹.

---

[1] A development of the *paludamentum* and regarded as the specific costume of the emperor. It was dyed with the liquor of a peculiar variety of shellfish (see Pliny, *Nat. Hist.*, ix. 130), whereas the scarlet *paludamentum* was dyed with cochineal.

Later, when you are with me, you shall have the imperial purple,[1] though without the embroidery in gold.[2] For my great-grandfather Verus,[3] who died in boyhood, received this from Hadrian, who adopted him."

III. Albinus received this letter, but he utterly refused to do what the Emperor bade. For he saw that Commodus was hated because of his evil ways, which were bringing destruction upon the state and dishonour upon himself, and that he would sometime or other be slain, and he feared that he might perish with him.

There is still in existence the speech he made when he accepted the imperial power—some say, indeed, by Severus' wish and authorization—in which he makes allusion to this refusal. Of this speech I append a copy: "It is against my will, my comrades, that I am exalted to empire, and a proof of it is this, that when Commodus once gave me the name of Caesar, I scorned it. Now, however, I must yield to your desire and to that of Severus Augustus, for I believe that under an upright man and a brave one the state can be well ruled."

It is an undeniable fact, moreover, and Marius Maximus also relates it, that Severus at first intended to name Pescennius Niger and Clodius Albinus as his successors, in case aught befell him.[4] Later, as it happened, in the interest of his growing sons, and through envy of the affection in which Albinus was

---

[2] The triumphal toga was purple, embroidered with gold. It was worn by the emperors on occasions of special importance.

[3] L. Aelius Caesar. He was, of course, not an ancestor of Commodus, for he was the father of Lucius Verus.

[4] See c. i. 2 and note.

maiusculis studens et Albini amori invidens sententiam mutasse atque illorum utrumque [1] bello oppres-
6 sisse, maxime precibus uxoris adductus.[2] denique
Severus eum et consulem designavit, quod utique
nisi de optimo viro non fecisset, homo in legendis
magistratibus diligens.

IV. Sed ut ad eum redeam, fuit, ut dixi, Albinus
Hadrumetinus oriundo, sed nobilis apud suos et
originem a Romanis familiis trahens, Postumiorum
2 scilicet et Albinorum et Ceioniorum. quae familia
hodie quoque, Constantine maxime, nobilissima est
et per te aucta et augenda, quae per Gallienum et
3 Gordianos plurimum crevit. hic tamen natus lare
modico, patrimonio pertenui, parentibus sanctis,
patre Ceionio Postumo, matre Aurelia Messalina,
4 primus suis parentibus fuit. cum exceptus utero,
quod contra consuetudinem puerorum, qui, cum
nascuntur, solent [3] rubere,[4] esset [5] candidissimus,
5 Albinus est dictus. quod verum [6] esse patris epistula
ad [7] Aelium Bassianum tunc proconsulem Africae data
designat, adfinem, quantum videtur, eorum ipsorum.
6 epistula Ceionii Postumi ad Aelium Bassianum :
" Filius mihi natus est VII kal. Decembres, ita candi-

---

[1] *illos utrosque* P corr.   [2] *abductus* P corr.   [3] *qui, cum
nascuntur, solent* Lessing; *qui nascuntur et solent* P, Peter.
[4] *rubore* P.   [5] *esse* P.   [6] *ueri* P[1].   [7] om. in P[1].

---

[1] c. i. 3.
[2] This array of names seems to have the purpose of using
Albinus as a means of connecting the Ceionii Albini, a famous
family of the fourth century, with the Postumii Albini, famous
in the republican era and especially in the second century
before Christ. The same purpose seems to appear in the
name assigned to Albinus' father (§ 3), which is composed of
the names of two *gentes* of famous Albini, regardless of the

held, and most of all because of his wife's entreaties, he changed his purpose and crushed both of them in war. But he did name Albinus consul, and this he never would have done had not Albinus been a worthy man, since he was ever most careful in his choice of magistrates.

IV. To return to Albinus, however, he was a native of Hadrumetum, as I have said before,[1] but he was both of noble rank there and traced his descent from noble families at Rome, namely the Postumii, the Albini, and the Ceionii.[2] The last of these families is among the noblest to-day, for you, most puissant Constantine, have exalted it and shall exalt it further, though it gained its greatest prestige by the favour of Gallienus and the Gordians. He was born at Hadrumetum in a modest home, in slender circumstances,[3] and of righteous parents, Ceionius Postumus and Aurelia Messalina, and he was their first-born son. When taken from his mother's womb, unlike the common run of infants, who are red at birth, he was very white in hue, and for this reason he was named Albinus. The truth of this is proved by a letter which his father wrote to Aelius Bassianus, then proconsul of Africa and, as it seems, a kinsman of the family. The letter of Ceionius Postumus to Aelius Bassianus: "A son was born to me on the seventh day before the Kalends of December,

difference in usage between Postumius as the name of a *gens* and Postumus as the *cognomen* of a family. This attempt to find famous ancestors for the Ceionii Albini has been used as an argument for the theory that portions, at least, of the *Historia Augusta* were not written before the end of the fourth century.

[3] According to Herodian, ii. 15, 1, he was brought up in wealth and luxury.

dus statim toto corpore, ut linteamen, quo[1] exceptus
7 est, vinceret.   quare susceptum eum Albinorum familiae, quae mihi tecum communis est, dedi Albini
nomine imposito.   fac ut rem publicam et te et nos,
ut facis, diligas."

V. Hic ergo omnem pueritiam in Africa transegit,
eruditus litteris Graecis ac Latinis [2] mediocriter, quod
2 esset animi iam tum[3] militaris et superbi.   nam [4] fertur in scholis saepissime cantasse inter puerulos

"Arma amens capio, nec sat rationis in armis,"

repetens

"Arma amens capio."

3   Huic multa imperii signa, cum esset natus, facta
dicuntur.   nam et bos albus purpureis ad plenum
4 colorem cornibus natus est.[5]   quae tamen in templo
Apollinis Cumani ab eodem posita iam tribuno diu
fuisse dicuntur, quod, cum illi [6] sortem de fato [7] suo
tolleret, his versibus eidem dicitur esse responsum :

"Hic rem Romanam magno turbante tumultu
sistet eques,[8] sternet Poenos Gallumque rebellem."

5 et in Gallia quidem eum multas gentes domuisse constat.   ipse autem suspicabatur de Severo sibi praedictum "sternet Poenos," quod Septimius Afer esset.

[1] quod P.   [2] ac latinis graecis P[1].   [3] tum Peter; inte
P; inde Salmasius.   [4] superbi. nam Peter; superbiam P.
[5] quod mirandum fuit cum cornibus added in P; rej. by
Peter.   [6] illi Peter[2]; illis P.   [7] facto P.   [8] tumultus
steteque P[1].

[1] Vergil, Aeneid, ii. 314.   [2] Vergil, Aeneid, vi. 857-858.
[3] Cf. c. vi. 3.

and so white was his body at birth that it was whiter
than the linen clothes in which we wrapped him.
I acknowledged him, therefore, as one of the family
of the Albini, who are common kin to you and me,
and bestowed upon him the name Albinus. And
now remember, I pray you, our country, yourself and
me."

V. All his boyhood, then, Albinus spent in Africa,
where he got a fair education in Greek and Latin
letters. And even at that time he showed signs of
a haughty and warlike spirit, for at school, it is said,
he used often to recite to the children :

" Madly I seized my arms, though in arms there
lay little reason ".[1]

And he repeated again and again the words, " Madly
I seized my arms ".

It is said that his rule was predicted by a number
of omens that occurred at the time of his birth. For
instance, a snow-white bull was born, whose horns were
of a deep purple hue. And he is said to have placed
these, when tribune of the soldiers, in the temple of
Apollo at Cumae, and when he made inquiry of
the oracle there concerning his fate, he received a
response, it is said, in the following lines :

" He shall establish the power of Rome though
tumult beset her,
Riding his horse he shall smite both Poeni and
Galli rebellious." [2]

And, indeed, it is well known that he conquered many
tribes in Gaul.[3] He himself always believed, moreover, that the prediction " he shall smite the Poeni "
referred to him and Severus, because Severus was

6 fuit et aliud signum futuri imperii. nam cum Caesar-
eana familia hoc speciale habuerit, ut parvuli domus
eius in testudineis alveis [1] lavarentur, nato infantulo
testudo ingens patri eius munere piscatoris adlata
7 est; quod ille homo litteratus omen accipiens et
testudinem libenter accepit et eam curari iussit atque
infantulo ad excaldationes pueriles dicari, nobilitan-
8 dum etiam hinc sperans. cum rarum esset, aquilas
in his locis videri, in quibus natus est Albinus, septima
eius die [2] hora convivii, quod celebritati pueri deputa-
batur, cum ei [3] fierent nomina, septem aquilae parvulae
de nidis adlatae sunt et quasi ad iocum circa cunas
pueri constitutae. nec [4] hoc omen pater abnuit et [5] iussit
9 aquilas ali et diligenter curari. accessit omen, quod,
cum pueri eius familiae russulis fasciolis inligarentur,
quod forte lotae atque udae essent russulae fasciolae,
quas mater praegnans paraverat, purpurea matris
inligatus [6] est fascea; unde illi ioco nutricis etiam
10 Porphyrii nomen inditum est. haec atque alia signa
imperii futuri fuere. quae qui volet nosse, Aelium
Cordum legat, qui frivola super huius modi ominibus
cuncta persequitur.

---

[1] *testudine albeis* P.   [2] *diei* P.   [3] *eis* P.   [4] *ne* P;
Peter.   [5] *et* ins. by Frankfurter.   [6] *inlitus* P[1].

---

[1] See Intro., p. xviii.

a native of Africa. There was another indication of his future rule besides these. A peculiar custom was observed in the family of the Caesars, namely, that the infants of this house should be bathed in tubs of tortoise-shell. Now when Albinus was a newly born infant, a fisherman brought as a gift to his father a tortoise of enormous size, and he, being well versed in letters, regarded the gift as an omen and accepted the tortoise gladly. He then gave an order that they should prepare the shell and set it apart for the child for use in the hot baths that are given to infants, hoping that this gift portended noble rank for his son. And again, although eagles appear but rarely in the region in which Albinus was born, on the seventh day after his birth, at the very hour of a banquet in honour of the bestowal of his name, seven young eagles were brought in from a nest and placed as though in jest about the cradle of the child. Nor did his father scorn this omen either, but commanded that the eagles be fed and guarded with care. Still another omen occurred. It was customary in his family that the bandages in which the children are wrapped should be of a reddish colour. In his case, however, it chanced that the bandages which had been prepared by his mother during her pregnancy had been washed and were not yet dry, and he was therefore wrapped in a bandage of his mother's, and this, as it happened, was of a purple hue. For this reason his nurse, jestingly, gave him the name Porphyrius. These were the omens that betokened his future rule. There were others besides these, but he who desires to learn what they are may read them in Aelius Cordus,[1] for he relates all trivial details concerning omens of this sort.

CLODIUS ALBINUS

VI. Adulescens igitur statim se ad militiam contulit atque Antoninis per Lollium Serenum et Baebium Maecianum et Ceionium Postumianum suos adfines 2 innotuit. egit tribunus equites Dalmatas ; egit et legionem [1] quartanorum et primanorum ; Bithynicos exercitus eo tempore quo [2] Avidius rebellabat fideliter 3 tenuit. dein per Commodum ad Galliam translatus, in qua fusis gentibus [3] Transrhenanis celebre nomen 4 suum et apud Romanos et apud barbaros fecit. quibus rebus accensus Commodus Caesareanum ei nomen obtulit et dandi stipendii facultatem et pallii coccini 5 utendi. quibus omnibus ille prudenter abstinuit, dicens Commodum quaerere qui aut cum eo perirent 6 aut quos cum causa ipse posset occidere. quaesturae gratia illi facta est. qua concessa aedilis non amplius quam decem diebus fuit, quod ad exercitum festino 7 mitteretur. dein praeturam egit sub Commodo famosis- simam. nam eiusdem ludis Commodus et in foro et in 8 theatro pugnas exhibuisse perhibetur. consul a Severo declaratus est eo tempore quo illum sibi paraverat cum [4] Pescennio subrogare.

VII. Ad imperium venit natu [5] iam grandior et maior Pescennio Nigro, ut Severus ipse in vita sua loquitur

---

[1] *legione* P.   [2] *quod* P.   [3] *gentibus* Peter; *fugentibus* P. [4] *cum Pescennio* Jordan; *Pescennio* P; *<et> Pescennium* Peter[1]; *[Pescennio]* Peter[2].   [5] *natura* P.

---

[1] The Legio I. Italica in Moesia Inferior and the Legio IV. Flavia in Moesia Superior.
[2] Probably as governor of Germania Inferior.
[3] See *Sev.*, vi. 9 and note.

VI. As soon as he came of age he entered military service, and by the aid of Lollius Serenus, Baebius Maecianus and Ceionius Postumianus, all his kinsmen, he gained the notice of the Antonines. In the capacity of a tribune he commanded a troop of Dalmatian horse ; he also commanded soldiers of the First and the Fourth legions.[1] At the time of Avidius' revolt he loyally held the Bithynian army 157 to its allegiance. Next, Commodus transferred him to Gaul ;[2] and here he routed the tribes from over the Rhine and made his name illustrious among both Romans and barbarians. This aroused Commodus' interest, and he offered Albinus the name of Caesar[3] and the privilege, too, of giving the soldiers a present and wearing the scarlet cloak.[4] But all these offers Albinus wisely refused, for Commodus, he said, was only looking for a man who would perish with him,[5] or whom he could reasonably put to death. The duty of holding the quaestorship was in his case remitted. This requirement waived, he became aedile, but after a term of only ten days he was despatched in haste to the army.[6] Next, he served his praetorship under Commodus, and a very famous one it was. For at his games Commodus, it is said, gave gladiatorial combats in both the Forum and the 194 theatre. And finally Severus made him consul at the time when he purposed to make him and Pescennius his successors.

VII. When he at last attained to the empire he was well advanced in years, for he was older, as Severus himself relates in his autobiography,[7] than Pescennius Niger. But Severus, after his victory

---

[4] See note to c. ii. 5.   [5] Cf. c. iii. 1.
[6] See § 2.   [7] See note to *Sev.*, iii. 2.

CLODIUS ALBINUS

2 sed victo Pescennio, cum et filiis suis·imperium servare
cuperet et ingentem senatus amorem circa Clodium
Albinum videret, quod esset vir antiquae familiae,
litteras ad eum per quosdam summi amoris ac summae
adfectionis misit, quibus hortabatur, ut, quoniam
occisus esset Pescennius Niger, ipse cum eo fideliter
3 rem publicam regeret.   quarum exemplum hoc esse
Cordus ostendit: "Imperator Severus Augustus
Clodio Albino Caesari, fratri amantissimo et desider-
4 antissimo, salutem.   victo Pescennio litteras Romam
dedimus, quas senatus tui amantissimus libenter
accepit. te quaeso, ut eo animo rem publicam regas
quo delectus es frater animi mei, frater imperii.
5 Bassianus et Geta te salutant. Iulia nostra et te et
sororem salutat. infantulo tuo Pescennio Princo
6 munera digna suo loco tuoque mittemus. tu velim
exercitus rei publicae ac nobis retentes, mi unanime,
mi carissime, mi amantissime."

VIII. Et has quidem litteras missis stipatoribus fide-
lissimis dedit, quibus praecepit, ut epistulam publice
darent, postea vero dicerent se velle pleraque occulte
suggerere, quae ad res bellicas pertinerent et ad
secreta castrorum atque aulicam fidem; ubi vero in
secretum venissent quasi mandata dicturi, quinque
validissimi eum interimerent gladiolis infra vestem
2 latentibus. nec illorum quidem fides defuit.[1] nam
cum ad Albinum venissent et epistulam dedissent,

---

[1] *fidefuit* P[1].

---

[1] See also Herodian, iii. 5, 2.
[2] This same story of the attempted assassination and the
frustration of the plot is told in Herodian, iii. 5, 3-8.

over Pescennius, desiring to keep the throne for his sons, and observing that Clodius Albinus, inasmuch as he came of an ancient family, was greatly beloved by the senate,[1] sent him certain men with a letter couched in terms of the greatest love and affection, in which he urged that, now that Pescennius Niger was slain, they should loyally rule the state together. The following, so Cordus declares, is a copy of this letter: "The Emperor Severus Augustus to Clodius Albinus Caesar, our most loving and loyal brother, greeting. After defeating Pescennius we despatched a letter to Rome, which the senate, ever devoted to you, received with rejoicing. Now I entreat you that in the same spirit in which you were chosen as the brother of my heart you will rule the empire as my brother on the throne. Bassianus and Geta send you greetings, and our Julia, too, greets both you and your sister. To your little son Pescennius Princus we will send a present, worthy both of his station and your own. I would like you to hold the troops in their allegiance to the empire and to ourselves, my most loyal, most dear, and loving friend."

VIII. This was the letter that he gave to the trusted attendants that were sent to Albinus. He told them to deliver the letter in public; but, later, they were to say that they wished to confer with him privately on many matters pertaining to the war, the secrets of the camp, and the trustworthiness of the court, and when they had come to the secret meeting for the purpose of telling their errand, five sturdy fellows were to slay him with daggers hidden in their garments.[2] And they showed no lack of fidelity. For they came to Albinus and delivered Severus' letter, and then, when he read it, they said

475

CLODIUS ALBINUS

qua lecta cum dicerent quaedam secretius sug-
gerenda et locum semotum ab omnibus arbitris
postularent, et cum omnino neminem paterentur ad
porticum longissimam cum Albino progredi ea specie
ne mandata proderentur, Albinus intellexit insidias.
3 denique indulgens suspicionibus eos tormentis dedit.
qui diu primo pernegarunt sed postea victi necessitate
confessi sunt ea quae Severus iisdem praeceperat.
4   Tunc iam proditis rebus et apertis insidiis, ea quae
suspicabatur Albinus clara esse intellegens exercitu
ingenti collecto contra Severum atque eius duces
IX. venit. et primo quidem conflictu habito contra duces
Severi potior fuit, post autem Severus ipse, cum id
egisset apud senatum, ut hostis iudicaretur Albinus,
contra eum profectus acerrime fortissimeque pugnavit
2 in Gallia non sine varietate fortunae. denique cum
sollicitus augures consuleret, responsum illi est, ut
dicit Marius Maximus, venturum quidem in potestate
eius Albinum, sed non vivum nec mortuum. quod
3 et factum est. nam cum ultimo proelio commissum
esset, innumeris suorum caesis, plurimis fugatis, multis
etiam deditis, Albinus fugit et, ut multi dicunt, se
ipse percussit, ut alii, servo suo percussus semivivus
4 ad Severum deductus est. unde confirmatum est
augurium quod fuerat ante praedictum. multi praeterea dicunt, a militibus, qui eius [1] nece [2] a Severo
gratiam requirebant.

---

[1] *qui eius* Casaubon; *cuius* P, Peter.   [2] *necem* P[1].

---

[1] It was at this time, in 196, that he was acclaimed
Augustus; see c. i. 1.
[2] See *Sev.*, x. 7—xi. 2.   [3] Cf. *Sev.*, xi. 6.

476

that they had some matters to tell him more privately,
and asked for a place far removed from all who could
overhear. But when they refused to suffer anyone to
go with Albinus to this distant portico, on the ground
that their secret mission must not be made known,
Albinus scented a plot and eventually yielded to his
suspicions and delivered them over to torture. And
though at first they stoutly denied their guilt, in
the end they yielded to extreme measures and disclosed the commands that Severus had laid upon
them.

Thus all was revealed and the plot laid bare, and
Albinus, now seeing that what he had merely suspected before was true, assembled a mighty force and
advanced to meet Severus and his generals.[1] IX. In
the first engagement, indeed, which was fought with
Severus' leaders,[2] he proved superior. Later Severus
himself, after causing the senate to declare Albinus
a public enemy, set out against him and fought in
Gaul, bitterly and courageously but not without vicis-
situdes of fortune. At last, being somewhat per-
turbed, Severus consulted an augur, and received
from him the response, according to Marius Maximus,
that Albinus would in truth fall into his power, but
neither alive nor dead. And so it happened. For
after a decisive engagement, where countless of his
soldiers fell, and very many fled, and many, too, surrendered, Albinus also fled away and, according to some,
stabbed himself, according to others, was stabbed by
a slave. At any rate, he was brought to Severus only
half alive.[3] So the prophecy made before the battle
was fulfilled. Many, moreover, declare that he was
slain by soldiers who asked Severus for a bounty for
his death.

5 Fuit Albino unus, ut aliqui dicunt, filius, ut[1] Maximus dicit, duo. quibus primum veniam dedit, postea vero eos cum matre percussit et in profluentem 6 abici iussit. caput eius excisum pilo circumtulit Romamque misit, litteris ad senatum datis quibus insultavit, quod Albinum tantopere dilexissent ut eius adfines et fratrem praecipue ingenti honore 7 cumularent. iacuisse ante praetorium Severi Albini corpus per dies plurimos dicitur usque ad fetorem, laniatumque a canibus in profluentem abiectum est.

X. De moribus eius varia dicuntur. et Severus quidem ipse haec de eodem loquitur, ut eum dicat turpem malitiosum improbum inhonestum cupidum luxuri-2 osum. sed haec belli tempore vel post bellum, 3 quando ei iam velut de hoste credi non poterat, cum et ipse ad eum quasi ad amicissimum frequentes miserit litteras, et multi de Albino bene senserint,[2] et Severus ipse Caesarem suum eundem appellari voluerit et, cum de successore cogitaret, hunc primum habuerit ante oculos.

4 Exstant praeterea Marci epistulae de hoc eodem, quae testimonium et virtutum eius ferant et morum. 5 quarum unam inserere ad praefectos datam super eius nomine absurdum non fuit:

6 " Marcus Aurelius Antoninus praefectis[3] suis salutem. Albino ex familia Ceioniorum, Afro quidem

---

[1] *ut* ins. by Peter; om. in P.   [2] *senserunt* P corr.
[3] *praefectus* P[1].

---

[1] The Rhone; see *Sev.*, xi. 9; cf. also § 7.
[2] See c. xii. 1.   [3] See *Sev.*, xi. 3 and note.

According to certain writers, he had one son, but according to Maximus, two. At first Severus granted these pardon, but later he killed them, together with their mother, and had them cast into running water.[1] Albinus' head was cut off and paraded on a pike, and finally sent to Rome. With it Severus sent a letter to the senate, in which he reviled it bitterly for its great love for Albinus,[2] inasmuch as his kinsmen, and notably his brother,[3] had been heaped with illustrious honours. Albinus' body lay for days, it is said, before Severus' headquarters, until it stank and was mangled by dogs, and then it was thrown into running water.

X. With regard to his character there is great divergence of statement. Severus, for his part, charged him with being depraved and perfidious, unprincipled and dishonourable, covetous and extravagant.[4] But all this he wrote either during the war or after it, at a time when he merits less credence, since he was speaking of a foe. Yet Severus himself sent him many letters, as though to an intimate friend. Many persons, moreover, thought well of Albinus, and even Severus wished to give him the name of Caesar,[5] and when he made plans for a successor, he had Albinus foremost in mind.

There are extant, besides, some letters of Marcus concerning Albinus, which bear witness to his virtues and character. One of these, addressed to his prefects and dealing with Albinus, it were not out of place to include : " Marcus Aurelius Antoninus to his prefects, greeting. Albinus, one of the family of the Ceionii,[6] son-in-law of Plautillus, and a native of

[4] See *Sev.*, iii. 2 and note.   [5] Cf. c. i. 2.
[6] See note to c. iv. 1.

479

homini sed non multa [1] ex Afris habenti, Plautilli
7 genero, duas cohortes alares regendas dedi. est homo
exercitatus, vita tristis, gravis moribus. puto eum rebus castrensibus profuturum, certe offuturum non
8 esse [2] satis novi. huic salarium duplex decrevi, vestem
militarem simplicem sed loci sui, stipendium quadru-
plum. hunc vos adhortamini, ut se rei publicae ostentet,[3] habiturus praemium quod merebitur."
9 Est et alia epistula, qua idem Marcus Avidii Cassii
temporibus de hoc eodem scripsit, cuius exemplum
10 hoc est : " Laudanda est Albini constantia, qui graviter deficientes exercitus tenuit, cum ad Avidium
Cassium confugerent. et nisi hic fuisset, omnes
11 fecissent. habemus igitur virum dignum consulatu,
quem sufficiam in locum Cassii Papirii, qui mihi exani-
12 mis prope iam nuntiatus est. quod interim a te
publicari nolo, ne aut ad ipsum Papirium aut ad eius
adfectus perveniat, nosque videamur in locum viventis
XI. consulem subrogasse." et istae igitur epistulae constantem [4] virum Albinum fuisse [5] indicant, et illud
praecipue, quod ad eas civitates instaurandas quas
Niger adtriverat pecuniam misit, quo facilius sibi
earum accolas conciliaret.
2 Gulosum eum Cordus, qui talia persequitur in suis
voluminibus, fuisse dicit, et ita quidem ut pomorum
tantum hauserit [6] quantum ratio [7] humana non patitur.

---

[1] *multa* Jordan; *multo* P. [2] *esse non* P. [3] *ostentet et*
P[1]. [4] *constantem* Peter; *constat eum* P. [5] *fuissent* P.
[6] *auxerit* P. [7] *oratio* P[1].

---

[1] See c. vi. 2. [2] Cf. c. vi. 2.

Africa, but with little of the African about him, I have placed in command of two squadrons of horse.[1]   He is a man of experience, strict in his mode of life, respected for his character.   He will prove of value, I think, in the service of the camp, and I am certain he will prove no detriment.   I have ordered him double ration-money, a plain uniform but one befitting his station, and fourfold pay.   Do you urge him to make himself known to the state, for he will get the reward that he merits."

There is also another letter, which Marcus wrote about Albinus in the time of Avidius Cassius, a copy 175 of which reads as follows : " Albinus is to be commended for his loyalty.   For he held the soldiers in check when they were wavering in their allegiance and were making ready to join Avidius Cassius,[2] and had it not been for him, they would have done this. We have in him, therefore, a man who deserves the consulship, and I shall name him to succeed Cassius Papirius, who, I am told, is now at the point of death. But this, meanwhile, I would not have you publish, lest somehow it come to Papirius or to his kin, and we seem to appoint a successor to a consul who is still alive."   XI. These letters, then, prove the loyalty of Albinus,[3] as does this fact besides, that he sent a sum of money wherewith to restore the cities that Niger had ravaged.   He did this, also, to win their inhabitants more easily to his cause.

Now Cordus, who recounts such details at length in his books, declares that Albinus was a glutton—so much so, in fact, that he would devour more fruit than the mind of man can believe.   For Cordus says that

[3] Dio speaks of him as a brave soldier and a skilful general ; see lxxv. 6, 2.

3 nam et quingentas ficus passarias, quas Graeci calli-
struthias vocant, ieiunum comedisse dicit et centum
persica Campana et melones Ostienses decem et
uvarum Labicanarum pondo viginti et ficedulas cen-
4 tum et ostrea quadringenta. vini sane parcum fuisse
dicit ; quod Severus negat, qui eum adserit ebrium
5 etiam in bello fuisse. cum suis ei[1] numquam
convenit vel propter vinolentiam, ut dicit Severus, vel
6 propter morum acrimoniam. uxori odiosissimus fuit,
servis iniustus, atrox circa militem. nam saepe etiam
ordinarios centuriones, ubi causae qualitas non postu-
labat,[2] in crucem sustulit. verberavit certe virgis sae-
7 pissime neque umquam delictis pepercit. in vestitu
nitidissimus fuit, in convivio sordidissimus et soli
studens copiae, mulierarius inter primos amatores,
aversae Veneris semper ignarus et talium persecutor,
agri colendi peritissimus, ita ut etiam Georgica scrip-
8 serit. Milesias nonnulli eiusdem esse dicunt, quarum
fama non ignobilis habetur, quamvis mediocriter
scriptae sint.

XII. A senatu tantum amatus est quantum nemo
principum, in odium speciatim Severi, quem vehemen-

---

[1] *ei* Mommsen; *et* P.   [2] *postulabit* P[1].

---

[1] See *Sev.*, iii. 2 and note.
[2] The term *centuriones ordinarii* was applied to centurions
actually in command of centuries, as opposed to those detailed
for service on the staff of a governor, those in the praetorian
guard, and those in command of independent bodies of troops.
[3] Probably in verse, in imitation of Vergil.
[4] A name applied to collections of stories of an erotic character. It was taken from the earliest of these collections,

when hungry he devoured five hundred dried figs
(called by the Greeks *callistruthiae*), one hundred Campanian peaches, ten Ostian melons, twenty pounds'
weight of Labican grapes, one hundred figpeckers, and
four hundred oysters. In his use of wine, however,
Cordus says he was sparing, but Severus denies
this,[1] claiming that even in time of war he was
drunken. As a rule, he was on bad terms with his
household, either because of his drunkenness, as
Severus says, or because of his quarrelsome disposition. Toward his wife he was unbearable, toward
his servants unjust, and in dealings with his soldiers
brutal. For he would often crucify legionary centurions,[2] even when the character of the offence did
not demand it, and he certainly used to beat them
with rods and never spared. His clothing was elegant, but his banquets tasteless, for he had an eye
only to quantity. As a lover of women he was noted
even among the foremost philanderers, but of unnatural lusts he was innocent, and he always punished
these vices. In the cultivation of land he was
thoroughly versed, and he even composed Georgics.[3]
Some say, too, that he wrote Milesian tales,[4] which
are not unknown to fame though written in but a
mediocre style.

XII. He was beloved by the senators[5] as no one
of the emperors before him. This was chiefly due,
however, to their hatred of Severus, who was greatly

called Μιλησιακά, written by Aristeides about the end of the
second century before Christ and translated into Latin by
Cornelius Sisenna. Several stories of this type are included
in Apuleius' *Metamorphoses*.
[5] Cf. c. ix. 6; xiii. 3; Herodian, iii. 5, 2. According to Dio,
most of the senators refrained from any active partisanship;
see lxxv. 4, 2.

CLODIUS ALBINUS

2 ter ob crudelitatem oderant senatores. denique victo
eo plurimi senatores a Severo interfecti sunt, qui eius
3 partium vel vere fuerant vel esse videbantur. denique
cum apud Lugdunum eundem interfecisset, statim
litteras requiri iussit, ut inveniret vel ad quos ipse
scripsisset, vel qui ad eum rescripsissent, omnesque
illos quorum epistulas repperit hostes iudicari a senatu
4 fecit ; nec his pepercit, sed et ipsos interemit et bona
eorum proposuit atque in aerarium publicum rettulit.
5 Exstat epistula Severi, quae ostendit animum suum,
6 missa ad senatum, cuius hoc exemplum est : "Nihil
mihi gravius potest evenire, patres conscripti, quam
ut vestrum iudicium Albinus haberet potius quam
7 Severus. ego frumenta rei publicae detuli, ego
multa bella pro re publica gessi, ego populo Romano
tantum olei detuli quantum rerum natura vix habuit. ego interfecto Pescennio Nigro vos a malis
8 tyrannicis liberavi. magnam sane mihi reddidistis
vicem, magnam gratiam ; unum ex Afris et quidem
Hadrumetinis, fingentem quod de Ceioniorum stem-
mate sanguinem duceret, usque adeo extulistis, ut
eum principem habere velletis me principe, salvis
9 liberis meis. defuitne quaeso tanto senatu quem
amare deberetis, qui vos amaret ? huius fratrem
honoribus extulistis, ab hoc consulatus, ab hoc praeturas, ab hoc speratis [1] cuiusvis magistratus insignia.

[1] *speratis* P, Peter[1] ; *sperastis* Peter[2].

[1] See *Sev.*, xiii.　　[2] See c. ix. 3 and *Sev.*, xi. 1 and 6.
[3] Herodian also says that Severus used Albinus' papers as
evidence against senators ; see iii. 8, 6.
[4] Cf. *Sev.*, viii. 5.　　[5] Cf. *Sev.*, xviii. 3.
[6] See note to c. iv. 1.　　[7] Cf. c. ix. 6.

detested by the senate because of his cruelty. For after he defeated Albinus, Severus put a great number of senators to death, both those who were really of Albinus' party and those who were thought to be.[1] Indeed, when Albinus was slain near Lugdunum,[2] Severus gave orders to search through his letters to find out to whom he had written and who had written to him; [3] and everyone whose letters he found, by his orders the senate denounced as a public enemy. And of these he pardoned none, but killed them all, placing their goods on sale and depositing the proceeds in the public treasury.

There is still in existence a letter from Severus, addressed to the senate, which shows very clearly his state of mind; whereof this is a copy: "Nothing that can happen, O Conscript Fathers, could give me greater sorrow than that you should endorse Albinus in preference to Severus. It was I who gave the city grain,[4] I who waged many wars for the state, I who gave oil to the people of Rome,[5] so much that the world could hardly contain it, and I who slew Pescennius Niger and freed you from the ills of a tyrant. A fine requital, truly, you have made me, a fine expression of thanks! A man from Africa, a native of Hadrumetum, who pretends to derive descent from the blood of the Ceionii,[6] you have raised to a lofty place; you have even wished to make him your ruler, though I am your ruler and my children are still alive. Was there no other man in all this senate whom you might love, who might love you? You raised even his brother to honours; [7] and you expect to receive at his hands, one a consulship, another a praetorship, and another the insignia of any office whatever. You have failed, moreover,

485

10 non eam gratiam mihi redditis quam maiores vestri
contra Pisonianam factionem, quam item pro Traiano,
quam nuper contra Avidium Cassium praestiterunt ;
fictum illum et ad omnia mendaciorum genera paratum, qui nobilitatem quoque mentitus est, mihi prae-
11 posuistis. quin etiam audiendus in senatu fuit
Statilius Corfulenus, qui honores Albino et eius fratri decernendos ducebat, cui hoc superfuit, ut de me
12 illi [1] decerneret homo nobilis et triumphum. maior
fuit dolor, quod illum pro litterato laudandum plerique
duxistis, cum ille neniis quibusdam anilibus occupatus
inter Milesias Punicas Apulei sui et ludicra litteraria
13 consenesceret." hinc apparet quanta severitate
factionem vel Pescennianam vel Clodianam vindi-
14 caverit. quae quidem omnia in vita eius posita sunt.
quae qui diligentius scire velit, legat Marium Maximum de Latinis scriptoribus, de Graecis scriptoribus
Herodianum, qui ad fidem pleraque dixerunt.

XIII. Fuit statura procerus, capillo renodi et crispo,
fronte lata et [2] candore mirabili, ita [3] ut plerique putent
quod ex eo nomen acceperit, voce muliebri et prope
ad eunuchorum sonum, motu facili, iracundia gravi,
furore tristissimo, in luxurie varius, nam [4] saepe ad-
2 petens vini, frequenter abstinens. armorum sciens
prorsus, ut non male sui temporis Catilina diceretur.

---

[1] *illi* Damsté ; *ille* P, Peter.   [2] *et* P, Peter[1] ; om. by
Peter[2].   [3] *ita* Petschenig, Peter[2] ; *et* P ; om. by Peter[1].
[4] *uarius nam* Peter[1] ; *uarium nam* P ; *uarii amans* Petschenig,
Peter[2].

---

[1] See *Pesc. Nig.*, ix. 2 and note.

to show me the spirit of gratitude which your fore-
fathers showed in the face of Piso's plot,[1] which they
showed Trajan, and showed but lately in opposing
Avidius Cassius. This fellow, false and ready for lies
of every kind, who has even fabricated a noble lineage,
you have now preferred to me. Why, even in the
senate we must hear Statilius Corfulenus proposing
to vote honours to Albinus and his brother, and all
that was lacking was that the noble fellow should also
vote him a triumph over me. It is even a greater source
of chagrin, that some of you thought he should be
praised for his knowledge of letters, when in fact he
is busied with old wives' songs, and grows senile am'd
the Milesian stories from Carthage that his friend
Apuleius wrote and such other learned nonsense."
From all this it is clear how severely he attacked the
followers of Pescennius and Albinus. Indeed, all
these things are set down in his autobiography,[2] and
those who desire to know them in detail should read
Marius Maximus among the Latin writers, and
Herodian among the Greek, for they have related
many things and with an eye to truth.

XIII. He was tall of stature, with unkempt curly
hair and a broad expanse of brow. His skin was
wonderfully white; many indeed think it was
from this that he got his name.[3] He had a womanish
voice, almost as shrill as a eunuch's. He was easily
roused, his anger was terrible, his rage relentless.
In his pleasures he was changeable, for he sometimes
craved wine and sometimes abstained. He had
a thorough knowledge of arms[4] and was not ineptly
called the Catiline of his age.

[2] See *Sev.*, iii. 2 and note.
[3] Cf. c. iv. 4.　　　　[4] See c. xi. 1 and note.

CLODIUS ALBINUS

3 Non ab re esse credimus causas ostendere quibus
4 amorem senatus Clodius Albinus meruerit. cum
Britannicos exercitus regeret iussu Commodi atque
illum interemptum adhuc falso comperisset, cum sibi
ab ipso Commodo Caesareanum nomen esset delatum,
5 processit ad milites et hac contione usus est : "Si
senatus populi Romani suum illud vetus haberet
imperium, nec in unius potestate res tanta con-
sisteret, non ad Vitellios neque ad Nerones neque ad
Domitianos publica fata venissent. in imperio consulari nostrae illae gentes Ceioniorum Albinorum
Postumiorum, de quibus patres vestri, qui et ipsi ab
6 avis suis audierant, multa didicerunt.[1]   et certe
Africam Romano imperio senatus adiunxit, Galliam
senatus subegit et [2] Hispanias, orientalibus populis
senatus dedit leges, Parthos temptavit senatus ;
subegisset, nisi tam avarum [3] principem Romano
7 exercitui fortuna rei publicae tunc dixisset.[4]   Britannias Caesar subegit, certe senator, nondum tamen
dictator. hic ipse Commodus quanto melior fuisset, si
8 timuisset senatum ? et usque ad Neronem quidem
senatus auctoritas valuit, qui sordidum et impurum
principem damnare non timuit, cum sententiae in

---

[1] *didicerunt* P, Peter[1] ; *tradiderunt* followed by lacuna
Peter[2].   [2] *et* om. in P, added by Peter[1] ; *senatus subegit* ir.
before *Hispanias* by Peter[2].   [3] *stauarum* P.   [4] *dixisse* P.

---

[1] See c. xii. 1 and note.   [2] See note to c. iv. 1.

CLODIUS ALBINUS XIII. 3-8

We do not believe it wholly irrelevant to recount
the causes which won Clodius Albinus the love of the
senate.[1] After Commodus had bestowed upon him
the name of Caesar, and while by the Emperor's
orders he was in command of the troops in Britain,
false tidings were brought that Commodus had been
slain. Then he came forth before the soldiers and
delivered the following speech: "If the senate of
the Roman people but had its ancient power, and if
this vast empire were not under the sway of a single
man, it would never have come to pass that the
destiny of the state should fall into the hands of
a Vitellius, a Nero, or a Domitian. Under the rule
of consuls there were those mighty families of ours,
the Ceionii, the Albini, and the Postumii,[2] of whom
your fathers heard from their grandsires and from
whom they learned many things. It was surely the
senate, moreover, that added Africa to the dominions
of Rome, the senate that conquered Gaul and the
Spains, the senate that gave laws to the tribes of the
East, and the senate that dared to attack the
Parthians—and would have conquered them, too, had
not the fortune of Rome just then assigned our army
so covetous a leader.[3] Britain, to be sure, was
conquered by Caesar, but he was still a senator and
not yet dictator. Now as for Commodus himself,
how much better an emperor would he have been
had he stood in awe of the senate! Even as late as
the time of Nero, the power of the senate prevailed,
and the senators did not fear to deliver speeches
against a base and filthy prince and condemn him,[4]

[3] Probably Crassus is meant, who was defeated by the
Parthians in 53 B.C.
[4] See Suetonius, *Nero*, xlix. 2.

489

eum dictae sint, qui vitae necisque potestatem atque
9 imperium tunc tenebat.[1] quare, commilitones, ego
Caesareanum nomen, quod mi Commodus detulit, nolo.
10 di faxint ut ne alii quidem velint. senatus imperet,
provincias dividat, senatus nos consules faciat. et
quid[2] dico senatus? vos ipsi et patres vestri; eritis
enim ipsi senatores."

XIV. Haec contio vivo adhuc Commodo Romam delata est. quae Commodum in Albinum exasperavit,
statimque successorem misit Iunium Severum, unum ex
2 contubernalibus suis. senatui autem tantum placuit,
ut miris adclamationibus absentem eum ornaret et
vivo Commodo et deinceps interempto, ita ut nonnulli etiam Pertinaci auctores fuerint, ut eum sibi
socium adscisceret, et[3] apud Iulianum de occidendo[4]
3 Pertinace ipsius plurimum auctoritas valuerit. ut
autem hoc verum intellegatur, epistulam Commodi
ad praefectos praetorii suos datam inserui, qua de
occidendo Albino[5] significavit suam mentem:
4 "Aurelius Commodus suis[6] praefectis salutem.
audisse vos credo, primum fictum esse quod ego
meorum consilio interfectus essem, deinde contionem
Clodii Albini apud milites meos habitam, qua[7] se
multum senatui commendat, idque, quantum videmus,
5 non frustra. nam qui principem unum in re publica

---

[1] *tenebant* P. [2] *quod* P. [3] *et* ins. by Petschenig; om.
in P, Peter. [4] *occidendi* P. [5] *iuliano* P. [6] *suis*
Casaubon, Peter[1]; *seuerus* P; [*Seuerus*] Peter[2]. [7] *qua*
Jordan; *quod* P.

even though he still retained both power of life and death and the empire too. Wherefore, my comrades, the name of Caesar, which Commodus now confers on me, I do not wish to accept. May the gods grant that no one else may wish it! Let the senate have rule, let the senate distribute the provinces and appoint us consuls. But why do I say the senate? It is you, I mean, and your fathers; you yourselves shall be the senators."

XIV. This harangue was reported at Rome while Commodus was still alive and roused him greatly against Albinus. He forthwith despatched one of his aides, Junius Severus, to replace him.[1] The senate, however, was so much pleased that it honoured Albinus, though absent, with marvellous acclamations, both while Commodus still lived and, later, after his murder. Some even counselled Pertinax to ally himself with Albinus, and as for Julianus, Albinus' influence had the greatest weight in his plan for murdering Pertinax.[2] In proof, moreover, that my statements are true, I will quote a letter written by Commodus to the prefects of the guard, in which he makes clear his intention of killing Albinus; "Aurelius Commodus to his prefects, greeting. You have heard, I believe, in the first place, the false statement that I had been slain by a conspiracy of my household; in the second, that Clodius Albinus has delivered an harangue to my soldiers in which he commends himself to the senate at great length—and not for nothing, it seems to me. For whoever asserts that the state ought not

---

[1] This is entirely fictitious, for all the evidence shows clearly that Albinus was governor of Britain when Commodus was killed.

[2] See note on c. i. 1.

negat esse debere quique adserit a senatu oportere totam rem publicam regi, is per senatum sibi petit imperium. cavete igitur diligentissime; iam enim hominem scitis vobis militibus populoque vitandum."

6 Has litteras cum Pertinax invenisset, in Albini odium publicare studuit.[1] quare Albinus occidendi Pertinacis Iuliano auctor fuit.

[1] *publicasse tu id* P.

to be under the sway of one man, and that the senate should rule the empire, he is merely seeking to get the empire himself through the senate. Keep a diligent watch then; for now you know the man whom you and the troops and the people must avoid."

When Pertinax found this letter he desired to make it public in order to stir up hatred against Albinus; and for this reason Albinus advised Julianus to bring about Pertinax's death.